D1526350

AFTER THE HOLOCAUST:
Polish-Jewish Conflict in the Wake of World War II

Marek Jan Chodakiewicz

EAST EUROPEAN MONOGRAPHS, BOULDER
DISTRIBUTED BY COLUMBIA UNIVERSITY PRESS, NEW YORK
2003

East European Monographs, No. DCXIII

To Zofia and Zdzisław Zakrzewski

Copyright 2003 by Marek Jan Chodakiewicz

ISBN: 0-88033-511-4

Library of Congress Control Number: 2003102003

Printed in the United States of America

Table of Contents

ABBREVIATIONS

AK	Armia Krajowa; Home Army
AL	Armia Ludowa; People's Army
AS	Akcja Specjalna; Special Action
AKO	Armia Krajowa Obywatelska; Citizen Home Army
BCh	Bataliony Chłopskie; Peasant Batallions
CKS	Centralna Komisja Specjalna; Central Special Commission
CKŻP	Centralny Komitet Żydów Polskich; Central Committee of Polish Jews
CŻKH	Centralna Żydowska Komisja Historyczna; Central Jewish Historical Commission
DR	Office of the Government Delegate
DSZ	Delegation of the Armed Forces
GG	*Generalgouvernement*; Government General
GL	Gwardia Ludowa; People's Guard
IW	Informacja Wojskowa; Military Intelligence
KAN	Konspiracyjna Armia Narodowa; Clandestine National Army
KBW	Korpus Bezpieczeństwa Publicznego; Internal Security Corps
KRN	Krajowa Rada Narodowa; Home National Council
KS	Komisje Specjalne; Special Commissions
KWP	Konspiracyjne Wojsko Polskie; Conspiratorial Polish Army
LWP	"ludowe" Wojsko Polskie; Polish "people's" Army
MBP	Ministerstwo Bezpieczeństwa Publicznego; Ministry of Public Security
MO	Milicja Obywatelska; Citizens Militia
NIE	Niepodległość; the Independence
NKGB	Narodnyi Komissariat Gosudarstvennoi Bezopastnostii; National Committee for State Security
NKVD	Narodnyi Komissariat Vnutrenykh Diel; National Committee for Internal Affairs

NOW	Narodowa Organizacja Wojskowa; National Military Organization
NPPS	Niezależna Polska Partia Socjalistyczna; Independent Polish Socialist Party
NSZ	Narodowe Siły Zbrojne; National Armed Forces
NZW	Narodowe Zjednoczenie Wojskowe; National Military Union
ORMO	Ochotnicza Rezerwa Milicji Obywatelskiej; Volunteer Reserve of the Citizens Militia
PAS	Pogotowie Akcji Specjalnej; Emergency Special Action
PPR	Polska Partia Robotnicza; Polish (Communist) Workers Party
PPS	Polska Partia Socjalistyczna; Polish Socialist Party
PPS-WRN	Polska Partia Socjalistyczna "Wolność, Równość, Niezawisłość; Polish Socialist Party "Freedom, Equality, Independence"
PSL	Polskie Stronnictwo Ludowe; Polish Peasant Party
ROAK	Ruch Oporu Armii Krajowej; Resistance Movement of the Home Army
SD	Stronnictwo Demokratyczne; Democratic Party
SL	Stronnictwo Ludowe; Peasant Party
Smersh	Smert' shpionom; Death to spies, Soviet counterintelligence
SN	Stronnictwo Narodowe; National Party
SP	Stronnictwo Pracy; Christian democratic Labor Party
UBP	Urząd Bezpieczeństwa Publicznego; Public Security Office
UPA	Ukraińska Powstańcza Armia; Ukrainian Insurgent Army
WiN	Zrzeszenie "Wolność i Niezawisłość"; Association for Freedom and Independence
ZPP	Związek Patriotów Polskich; Union of Polish Patriots
ŻIH	Żydowski Instytut Historyczny; Jewish Historical Institute
ŻZR	Żydowskie Zrzeszenia Religijne; Jewish Confessional Association

FOREWORD

Polish-Jewish relations have been subject to increasingly heated discussions. The temperature of these discussions in the United States is much higher than in Poland where Poles with and without Jewish roots have managed to find better ways to communicate and come to terms with their common history. The ongoing debate on Polish-Jewish relations in America, which is charged with emotional accusations and counteraccusations, leaves little room for a well-balanced view and makes it extremely risky for anyone to stick his or her neck out without fear of being attacked. Even well-informed and moderate authors risk being hit from both sides.

Marek J. Chodakiewicz, a young American scholar with Polish roots, has studied Polish-Jewish relations for many years. His *Sources of Conflict* is related to his Ph.D. thesis recently defended at Columbia University in New York. Chodakiewicz's monograph is not a polemical work. It is a solid and meticulously researched historical study that is based on extremely rich documentation.

When judging the behavior of Poles and Jews in the critical years 1944–47, it is essential to understand that at this time Poland was shedding one invader (the Germans) only to be enslaved by another (the Soviets). The dramatic efforts of the Polish "independendists," using the term coined by Chodakiewicz, to salvage Poland's freedom, including the desperate uprising in Warsaw in August 1944, which was aimed militarily at the Nazis and politically at the Soviets, were in vain. Against the will of the majority of Poles, a country that was the first to resist Hitler in 1939 was turned into a Soviet satellite in 1945. According to Jan Ciechanowski, the Polish Ambassador to the United States, this was a "defeat in victory." For the Polish-Jewish survivors of the Holocaust the post-war disaster of Poland was of secondary, if little, importance. Their main point of reference was the annihilation of their families and community and their own salvation from the Holocaust. Since they were saved by the Red Army, they were grateful to the Soviets and to Stalin. This greatly aroused suspicions and exacerbated mutual relations between Polish Jews and Christians. It also became a source of emotional and the all-too-frequently exaggerated, accusations of Polish anti-Semitism and "Jewish Communism" that gained new strength after 1944.

The Soviets and their Communist proxies who took control of the country gave the Jewish survivors a false sense of security. That is why most of them, and not only the Jewish Communist minority, backed

Poland's new regime. On the other hand, the Communists denied Jews the restoration of their property rights as being inconsistent with the nationalization policies implemented by the regime. The ranks of the Communist party were filled with opportunists and the dregs of the society, who were frequently keen anti-Semites. At the same time the Communists trumpeted to the world their role as the only protectors of the Jewish survivors against the Polish "reactionaries," a term the Communists used to refer to all Polish patriots. It is really amazing to see how much of the recent charges of Polish anti-Semitism and collaboration with the Nazis reflect the Communist propaganda of the years 1944–47. The Polish freedom fighters, or "independentists," consisted of a broad spectrum of people. The term "independentists" may sound clumsy, but it is brief and defines aptly the majority of politically active Poles of that era. They were in a sense political nationalists whose goal was a free Polish state and the rule of law. The independentist were Socialists, Populists, Christian Democrats, and National Democrats, who constituted a multiparty foundation for the Polish government in exile and its plenipotentiary organization (*Delegatura*) at home. Of these, only the National Democrats could be called political anti-Semites, but with no record of actual collaboration with the Nazis in this respect. In 1944–47 the "independentists" were disappointed, frustrated, and struggling for survival against the Communist tide. If they saw Jews in the new state apparatus, it was no wonder they did not like them. Frequently, but more inappropriately, they projected their generalized emotions onto the entire Jewish community. All this was going on when Polish postwar society was deprived of most of its intellectual elite because of the Nazi and Soviet massacres and deportations, post-war political emigration (exile), expropriation, physical and mental exhaustion, and demoralization brought on by six years of total warfare, terror, and chaos. Life was cheap and the level of crime was growing. This also included the institutionalized, Communist-driven crime.

Chodakiewicz does not deny manifestations of Polish antisemitim, before, during, and after the Second World War. Neither does he overestimate the Jewish sympathies for Communism. Just like a thorough historian should, he places these phenomena within the broader and highly complex context of that time and puts them in their proper proportions. He penetrates numerous cases of Poles killing Jews and Jews causing the death of Poles after 1944. He treats these cases with scholarly accuracy, deliberation, impartiality, and judiciousness. As a result of his analyses he arrives at an estimate of between 400 to 700 Jews killed by Poles in the years 1944–47, a number much lower than earlier estimates. Surprisingly, he finds evidence for an even greater number of Poles who lost their lives directly or indirectly at the hands of Jews during the Soviet takeover of Poland. More importantly, Chodakiewicz leaves no doubt that there was no continuation of the Holocaust in Poland after 1944. Chodakiewicz cites various sources – Polish, Jewish, and Soviet – trying first to understand the circumstances and to weigh arguments. One of the chapters refers to a little known phenomenon, namely cases of Jews helping Poles after the war. As a result Chodakiewicz goes a long way toward overcoming simplifications, clichés, and prejudice. Of course, readers of this book may have their own specific opinion on the subject. But let us for a moment put away *a priori* stereotypes, let us forget about "Polish anti-Semitism" and "Jewish Communism" as archetypes that purport to explain everything that happened. Let us follow Chodakiewicz in his attempt to explore the real nature of the complex and painful relationship between Poles and Jews, Communists and non-Communists alike, in those turbulent and cruel times.

Wojciech Roszkowski, Ph.D.
Kościuszko Professor of Polish Studies
Miller Center of Public Affairs
University of Virginia, Charlottesville

INTRODUCTION

There has been a tendency to assume that, in one way or another, Jews who died in Poland after the arrival of the Soviet army in the summer of 1944 were victims of ubiquitous Polish anti-Semitism. In reality, violence against Jews stemmed from a variety of Polish responses to at least three distinct phenomena: the actions of Jewish Communists, who fought to establish a revolutionary Marxist-Leninist regime in Poland; the deeds of Jewish avengers, who endeavored to exact extrajudicial justice on Poles who allegedly harmed Jews during the Nazi occupation; and the efforts of the bulk of the members of the Jewish community, who attempted to reclaim their property confiscated by the Nazis and subsequently taken over by the Poles. In the Polish eyes, the apparent convergence of these phenomena reinforced the stereotype of *żydokomuna*, Jewish-Communist conspiracy. On the Jewish side, the various Polish reactions fused into a uniform phenomenon of violence which allegedly stemmed from omnipresent Polish anti-Semitism. This Jewish assessment concerned the Polish independentist (anti-Communist) insurgents in particular. However, anti-Jewish violence perpetrated by the insurgents resulted mostly from anti-Communism, or, more precisely, from perceptions of Jews as a threat in the context of local conditions of the anti-Soviet rising in Poland between 1944 and 1947.

The rising of the Polish independentists broke out during the Nazi retreat in 1944. The independentist insurgents, who represented all Polish political groups but the Communists, aimed to liberate Poland from the German yoke and prevent a Soviet takeover. Later, many of the independentists fought against the Soviets and their Polish Communist proxies, who were installed in power by Stalin. The Jewish community was caught up in this struggle, often as passive bystanders but sometimes also as active participants on the side of the proxy regime.

The subject of Jewish-Polish relations in the aftermath of the Second World War has been an area of scholarly neglect; comprehensive research has been lacking in particular. Because the existing historiography of the post-1944 period equates anti-Jewish violence with racism, it is imperative to begin our inquiry with a discussion of the problems concerning sources and interpretations. We shall now consider what factors have influenced our perspective and how by examining: Communist propaganda, individual testimonies, corroborative documentary evidence, and the circumstances of anti-Jewish violence.

From the beginning, the Communists endeavored to depict themselves as the sole protectors of the Jews, while imputing to their opponents a genocidal brand of anti-Semitism. In this Manichean world the Communists were "democrats" and their opponents "fascists." This brand of propaganda was employed for two reasons. First, it justified to the West that the Communist police terror in Poland was necessary to defeat fascism. Second, propaganda was used for domestic consumption to link the anti-Communist political opposition and underground to the German Nazis, who were universally hated in Poland. In other words, according to this propaganda ploy, Stalinist terror in Poland was simply a mop-up operation to conclude the struggles of the Second World War. The main targets of the Communists were the overt political opposition, the Polish Peasant Party (PSL), and, especially, underground groups originating from the anti-German resistance, the Home Army (AK) and the National Armed Forces (NSZ).

Communist propaganda of this kind surfaced openly following the Soviet entry into central Poland in 1944. It targeted both the domestic and the Western public via radio broadcasts and press releases. For instance, the Yiddish language broadcasts from Communist-controlled Lublin castigated "the murderers from the Polish reactionary camp, who assisted Hitlerite bandits and participated actively in murdering the Jewish population and Jewish partisans [and who] remained in touch with the [Polish] London government and followed its instructions. The pro-London underground keeps murdering Jews even now."[1] Soon, the propaganda campaign became highly organized and coordinated. On April 21, 1945, in its first official memorandum, the Ministry of Information and Propaganda of the Communist regime in Warsaw gave the following order to its employees, including government journalists:

> We must depict the activities of the AK as hideously as they really are; we must endeavor to isolate politically the bandit [and] fascist elements of the AK and NSZ as people whose political blindness and idiocy as well as hatred toward democracy [i.e. Communism] *have turned them into Hitler's agents...* The [propaganda] campaign against the AK must be conducted very violently albeit without hysteria [emphasis added].[2]

In congruence with this propaganda offensive, at the end of April 1945, the *Soviet News* agency released excerpts of an interview with a Polish Communist general, and an NKVD agent, Artur Łyżwiński, aka Michał Rola-Żymierski.[3] According to the Soviet source, characterising the "Home Army," Gen. Rola-Żymierski [sic] stated that it had ceased to be a military organization and had become a political organization... "The mass of the soldiers of the 'Home Army,' as well as the mass of the Polish people, fully support the Provisional Polish [Communist] Government. One of the component parts of the 'Home Army,' the Fascist organisation 'National Armed Forces,' went underground, began to collaborate with the Germans and engaged in pogroms and anti-semitic activity. In the Sandomierz area these former members of the 'Home Army,' who went underground, stage pogroms, raid townships, [and] murder Jews. This proves that this organization is Fascist and morally corrupt."

General Rola-Żymierski cited examples of the collaboration of the "Home Army" with the Germans... [and stated that] "We [i.e. the Communists] strive... to eliminate manifestations of the Fascist spirit among the elements who formerly belonged to the 'Home Army.'"[4]

In a very revealing study of Communist propaganda, historian Krystyna Kersten shows that the targets of such official vituperations changed with the policy shifts of the proxy regime. First, between July 1944 and July 1945 the Communist party failed to distinguish between the AK and the NSZ, branding all of the insurgents as "fascists," "reactionaries," and "bandits." However, after entering into a sham coalition with the émigré Populists (PSL), the Communists scaled down their rhetoric against the AK. The NSZ was the sole bogeyman until the spring of 1946, when the propaganda began to lump the NSZ, the WiN (Freedom and Independence, AK's successor), and the PSL together. Thus, the allegedly philosemitic "camp of democracy," led by the Communists, battled the anti-Semitic "camp of reaction," which consisted of the PSL, the WiN, and the NSZ. The former was "patriotic," while the latter "treasonous." In this world view the killing of Jews was, of course, "following in the footsteps of Hitler," without any regard to the circumstances under which Jews had died.[5]

This simplistic propaganda ploy managed to influence its target audience in Poland and to fool much of Western public opinion, including such prominent Americans as Joseph Tenenbaum, president of the World Federation of Polish Jews. Unfortunately, the Jewish leadership in Poland joined in the Communist propaganda campaign, hailing Poland's "democratic" government and obediently excoriating "reactionaries" like

August Cardinal Hlond, General Władysław Anders, and General Tadeusz Komorowski (*nom de guerre* "Bór"), as well as, of course, the insurgents.[6] It is not surprising then that, describing the period between 1944 and 1947, Jewish witnesses blamed the "NSZ," the "AK," or simply the "Poles" for the killing of Jews for anti-Semitic reasons. According to a fairly typical opinion, "I had heard someone talk about armed bands of Polish nationalists who were organizing pogroms against Jewish survivors. These people were no better than the Nazis."[7] In an extreme case, a Jewish witness from Rzeszów accused the NSZ of killing a nine-year old Christian girl and dumping her body near Jewish quarters to provoke a pogrom in June 1945.[8] The survivors of violence almost universally ignored the fact that the murders could have been perpetrated by Polish criminals, Communist police, Soviet marauders, or deserters of various armies. Almost invariably "Polish anti-Semitism" was given as the reason for these terrible deeds. Other factors, such as common crime, avarice, anti-Communism, or conflict within the Jewish community itself, were hardly considered.[9]

Nonetheless the stories of the survivors were later repeated earnestly in the West. Likewise, the Communists received a sympathetic hearing when they blamed the "AK," "reactionaries," "the nobility," "boy scouts," "the Polish government-in-exile," and "General Władysław Anders" of the Free Polish Army in the West, for perpetrating pogroms in Poland after the war.[10] As a consequence, many scholars displayed a penchant for condemning the independentists, in particular the allegedly ubiquitous "NSZ," for the violence usually without bothering to substantiate their claims.

This knee-jerk tendency to blame the National Armed Forces for killing of Jews figures prominently among Jewish historians and found its way into many reference works. The authoritative *Encyclopaedia Judaica* states that "there were murderous attacks upon Jews on Polish roads, railroads, buses, and in the towns and cities. The murders were committed by members of Polish reactionary organizations, such as the NSZ. *In cruelty and inhumanity, their crimes often equaled those committed by the Nazis* [emphasis added]."[11] According to another influential source, after the Soviet occupation of Poland in 1944, "various NSZ groups took up an underground struggle against the new regime; they also continued the killing of Jewish survivors of the Holocaust."[12] The authors of another important work claim that the "NSZ terrorized and killed Jewish survivors after the war" but fail to footnote their claim persuasively.[13] Similar sentiments are expressed without any footnotes by an American translator of a Jewish memoir.[14] An eminent historian even claims that "the fascist NSZ declared in a leaflet on March 25, 1945 that it was a sign of patriotism to kill Jews." Alas he provides no original source for this shocking claim.[15] In a work dealing with the post-war period, a Jewish journalist also blames the NSZ, and in particular its Holy Cross Brigade, for killing Jews, although the Brigade had retreated from Poland already in January 1945 before the invading Red Army moved in.[16] None of the aforementioned authors ever carried out any in-depth research on the independentist underground after 1944, in particular on the NSZ. They relied mostly on the Communist propaganda and unverified individual testimonies.

Even those very few scholars who took official propaganda with a pinch of salt[17] nonetheless believed that the chief factor behind anti-Jewish violence was an all-pervasive Polish anti-Semitism, a racist pathology without any rational basis. For instance, according to Leon Shapiro,

> Circles connected with the Polish Government-in-exile have been charged with instigating anti-Jewish riots as a device in their struggle against the existing regime. It must be pointed out, however, that among the Polish emigrants in London there are representatives of groups whose Socialist record and pro-Jewish activities over decades cast doubt on such accusations. Though persons rallying around General Wladyslaw [Władysław] Anders and the old reactionary anti-Semitic parties may have participated in some way or other in the spreading of anti-Jewish propaganda, the fact remains that independently of their efforts the political conditions existing in Poland have created a climate favoring violence and rioting.
>
> It cannot be denied that large groups of the Polish people are still infected with a profoundly irrational hostility toward Jews. This attitude, whatever its causes, reveals century-old prejudice surviving unabated the tragic experience of war and occupation. Polish anti-Semitism is by no means confined to land-owners, peasants or bourgeois; it has taken firm root among workers and professionals as well.[18]

The problems of studying the period after the Communist takeover in 1944 were compounded by the general lack of freedom, including a lack of independent academic research and the inaccessibility of many archival sources in Poland. In fact, for years historians in the West had nothing else to rely on but Communist propaganda (later regurgitated by party hacks as Marxist-Leninist historical scholarship) and individual testimonies. Often, though sweeping in their condemnation, the testimonies were imprecise, inconclusive, and misleading.[19] Erstwhile directives of a senior Jewish scholar, himself a survivor of the Nazis, concerning the study of this tragedy, can be equally applied to the current state of the inquiry into Jewish-Polish relations in the aftermath of the Holocaust:

> The difficulties in studying the great Jewish catastrophe are manifold. There is the vast geographical area of the disaster and the enormity of personal suffering and of social and emotional upheavals brought about by the events of the catastrophe. The political and social reverberations of the catastrophe cannot yet be fully encompassed. Lacking too are the methodological foundations for the study of *Jewish* sociology in general and the cataclysm in particular. Last but not least there is what may perhaps be termed, the hyperhistorical complex of the survivors. Never before was an event so deeply sensed by its participants as being part of an epoch-shaping history in the making, never before was a personal experience felt to be so historically relevant. The result of this hyperhistorical complex has been that the brief post-war years have seen a flood of 'historical materials' — rather 'contrived' than 'collected' — so that to-day one of the most delicate aspects of research is the evaluation of the so-called 'research material.'
>
> The hyperhistorical complex may be described as *judeocentric, lococentric and egocentric*. It concentrates historical relevance on Jewish problems of local events under the aspect of personal experience. This is the reason why most of the memoirs and reports are full of preposterous verbosity, graphomanic exaggeration, dramatic effects, overestimated self-inflation, dilettante philosophizing, would-be lyricism, unchecked rumors, bias, partisan attacks and apologies. The question thus arises whether participants of such a world-shaking epoch can at all be its historians and whether the time has already come when valid historic judgment, free of partisanship, vindictiveness and ulterior motives, is possible [emphasis in the original].[20]

Alas, the process of verifying Jewish accounts and of devising methodological tools to disentangle the intricacies of Polish-Jewish relations was not assisted by Polish historians because after 1956 the issue of anti-Jewish violence was gradually neglected in Poland. In particular, in the wake of the "anti-Zionist" campaign of 1968, Communist historians began significantly to downplay the number of Jewish victims, listing "less than a score [*kilkanaście*] of files of persons of Jewish nationality murdered by the fascist fighting groups of the underground." Nonetheless, these same scholars continued to maintain, albeit substituting euphemisms for invectives, that Jews and others were "murdered by the underground because of the nationality issues [i.e. for reasons of ethnic hatred]."[21]

Only after 1989 could an open debate really commence. In the West, concentrating mostly on mob violence, Joanna Michlic-Coren continued the tradition of arguing that pathological and irrational Polish anti-Semitism, as manifested by "the myth of the Jew as 'The Threatening Other,'" resulted in anti-Jewish violence. On the other hand, Peter Stachura stressed the presence of many prominent Jewish Communists in the proxy regime in Poland as the chief source of conflict.[22] However, several Polish regional historians, including Janusz Kwiek, Zbigniew Romaniuk, Albert Stankowski, and Bożena Szaynok, have suggested that at least some of the killings of Jews (and Poles) were perpetrated by common bandits.[23] A scholar affiliated with the Jewish Historical Institute in Warsaw stated flatly that "in most cases robbery accompanied murder."[24] Other Polish scholars have considered also the broader background of the Polish anti-Soviet insurrection. Finally, the historian David Engel most plausibly postulated a multitude of factors behind the anti-Jewish violence. He has averred that

> it will not do to represent anti-Jewish violence simply as a continuation of ancient hatreds that the Nazi Holocaust either intensified or, at the very least, failed to uproot, without reference to the political context in which it occurred. The bands that were most heavily responsible for killing Jews would not have existed except for the circumstances of the Communist takeover; otherwise, those who carried out the attacks would not have been in a position to do so. Moreover, the civil war [i.e. the insurrection] enabled people who simply coveted Jewish property, without any attached political motives, to justify aggression against Jews in the guise of resistance to a new foreign occupation...
>
> In the final analysis, therefore, it appears that those contemporary observers who, in private discussions at least, pointed to a multiplicity of factors as responsible for armed attacks upon Jews in postwar Poland, while assigning primacy of place to no one factor in particular, displayed a keener understanding of the situation than later writers, who have

insisted upon representing the violence as either contextually or conceptually driven.[25]

Before Engel, rarely, if ever, did Western scholars attempt to verify the veracity of individual Jewish testimonies by checking them against other accounts. Almost all the killings were automatically subsumed under the rubric of "Polish anti-Semitism" or the "reactionary" underground. Alas, many of the events are by no means sufficiently explained. Moreover, although many Polish archives are accessible now, their contents need to be scrutinized very carefully lest scholars give credence to documents falsified by the secret police for political reasons. Two examples of recently declassified documents which most likely were doctored by the Communists follow.

The format of the first, which purports to be a report of the NSZ of February 1945, appears to be different from other orders of this organization. Either it is a clumsy falsification or the author of the report failed to follow the usual standards (cryptonyms, layout). The document was handwritten by a different person than the one who signed it. Also, although the alleged author of the report signed himself as "the commander of the NSZ Special Action [*Akcja Specjalna — AS*] unit," the cryptonym used elsewhere in the document identifies the group in question as "a forest unit" (Oleś. B.2 XVI — *oddział leśny* of the B 2 [region?] of the Lublin Area) of the NSZ, which denoted a regular partisan detachment rather than a special task force. Moreover, the name "Special Action" was used during the Nazi occupation. Under the Soviet occupation, it was superseded with the appellation "Emergency Special Action" (*Pogotowie Akcji Specjalnej — PAS*). Further research is needed to determine the origin of the document which states, in part, that "death sentences [were carried out] on... four Jews, eight women of Ukrainian origin, and seventeen men also of Ukrainian origin, who either harmed Poles or were working to harm them. They were liquidated partly during operations against transports and partly during a special execution."[26]

In another instance, a purported "diary" of an NSZ insurgent is in fact a page typed up by the secret police. This document seems to have been paraphrased and edited, most likely for propaganda purposes or investigative reasons. The person who doctored the diary listed a non-existing village and invented an anti-Jewish motive for an alleged shooting of a Red Army member in the Parish of Kosin, the county of Kraśnik of the Province of Lublin. In the entry for May 13, 1945, the "editor" wrote in lieu of the author: "We are in the forest next to the village of Borów by the Vistula River... Our boys drove to the neighboring village of Hentyn [sic], where they bumped into soviets [sic]. They killed one of them, because he was a jew [sic]." Why would the insurgents need an additional, anti-Jewish excuse to shoot a Soviet? They did it routinely without regard to ethnic or religious background. Moreover, despite access to detailed military maps, I have not been able to locate "Hentyn" near Borów, or anywhere else in the county of Kraśnik. This "copy" (odpis) of a diary should be treated with utmost suspicion if not rejected outright until it can be verified against the original diary, which has not yet been found, or against local Soviet reports, which are still not available.[27]

Last but not least, aside from the problems of methodology and sources, the study of Jewish-Polish relations has been influenced by a general trend to concentrate on Nazi atrocities while neglecting Soviet crimes. On the one hand, the enormity of the Holocaust and the subsequent scholarly focus on this phenomenon seem to have narrowed the context of the scientific inquiry by overlooking, or at least downplaying, the events which were perhaps ultimately of greater importance to non-Jews, notably the Soviet terror after the retreat of the Nazis in 1944. On the other hand, the Holocaust became a teleological font of all subsequent occurrences concerning Jewish-Polish relations. Hence, a perception set in of a continuation between the Nazi effort to exterminate the Jews and the experience of Polish Jewry in post-war Poland. Consequently, Polish reactions against Jews came to be viewed through the prism of the Nazi genocide. All acts of anti-Jewish violence were equated with earlier Nazi crimes since the factor of the Soviet terror as a major reason conditioning Polish attitudes toward Jews was left unresearched. Moreover, this approach largely precluded entertaining the possibility that at least some Jews were victims of the Communists as well.

To summarize, the popular perception and scholarly assessment of the immediate post-war period in Poland have been marred by the crippling legacy of Communist propaganda, the unreliability of some witnesses, the untrustworthiness of some documents, and excessive scholarly concentration on anti-Semitism as the key factor behind anti-Jewish violence. To rectify such handicaps, it is necessary to reconceptualize the general events between 1944 and 1947 in a non-Stalinist framework, to verify individual witness testimonies against other accounts and documents, and to consider other factors behind anti-Jewish violence besides anti-Semitism.

This work describes the events in Poland between 1944 and 1947, surveys its anti-Communist insurgency, examines its Jewish community, tests the roots of anti-Jewish perceptions among the Polish insurgents, and

analyzes the nature of the conflict. Chapter One provides the background
to the conflict, focusing on the Second World War and its aftermath in
Poland and, in particular, on the Nazi and Communist revolutions.
Chapter Two introduces the Polish independentists and their struggle.
Chapter Three describes the Jewish community and its predicament in
post-war Poland, while exploring the Jewish involvement with the
Communists. Chapter Four discusses the independentist propaganda, and
in particular its depiction of Jews. Chapter Five describes Jewish attitudes
toward the Polish population, especially the independentists, after the
entry of the Red Army into Poland, based upon Jewish accounts. Chapter
Six analyzes Jewish actions after 1944 as they were reported by the anti-
Communist insurgents. Chapter Seven delves into the insurgent armed
activities as they pertained to Jews. Chapter Eight examines critically the
genre of oral history as reflected in Jewish accounts. Chapter Nine
investigates the assistance rendered by Jews to Polish independentists
who were persecuted by the Communists. Chapter Ten tackles the
question of statistics in regard to Jewish and Polish casualties under the
Soviet occupation. Finally, the Conclusion summarizes the results of our
research and presents a new theory of Polish-Jewish relations between
1944 and 1947.

This work was originally written as a paper for the annual conference
of the Association for the Study of Nationalities, entitled "Rethinking
Identities: State, Nation, and Culture," held at the Harriman Institute,
Columbia University, New York, between April 15 and 17, 1999, and, in
particular, for the panel "Jews, Poles, Communists?" I would like to thank
the following individuals who assisted me at different stages of the writing
of this work: Professor Stanisław Wellisz (Columbia University),
Professor John Micgiel (Columbia University), Professor Joseph Nagy
(UCLA), Professor Kenneth Thompson (Miller Center of Public Policy,
University of Virginia), Dr. Leo Gluchowski, Dr. Michael J. Gelb (Center
for Advanced Holocaust Studies, United States Holocaust Memorial
Museum), Professor Wacław Długoborski (Auschwitz-Birkenau State
Musuem), Dr. John Radziłowski, Richard Tyndorf, Brian Brown (Oxford
University), John Sack, Anna Gräfin Praschma, Dan Currell, Leszek
Żebrowski, Wojciech Jerzy Muszyński, Mariusz Bechta, Sebastian
Bojemski, Bibi Wellisz, Peter Gajewski, Patti and Guy de Gramont, Zofia
and Zdzisław Zakrzewski, and my sister Anna.

The mistakes and opinions contained in this work are mine alone.

Los Angeles-Santa Barbara-San Francisco, Charlottesville, VA
March 1999-July 2001

Notes

1   Dariusz Stola, *Nadzieja i Zagłada: Ignacy Schwarzbart – żydowski przedstawiciel w Radzie Narodowej RP (1940-1945)* (Warszawa: Oficyna Naukowa, 1995), 275 [afterward *Nadzieja i Zagłada*].

2   Okólnik Ministerstwa Informacji i Propagandy nr 1, 21 April 1945, in *Pierwsza próba indoktrynacji: Działalność Ministerstwa Informacji i Propagandy w latach 1944-1947*, ed. by Andrzej Krawczyk (Warszawa: ISP PAN, 1994), 74-75.

3   Marek Jan Chodakiewicz, Piotr Gontarczyk and Leszek Żebrowski, eds., *Tajne oblicze GL-AL i PPR: Dokumenty, 1942-1945, Volume 3* (Warszawa: Burchard Edition, 1999), 3: 9, 21, 200 [afterward *Tajne oblicze*]. The first two volumes appeared in 1997.

4   "PRESS CONFERENCE held by M. Bierut at the Polish Embassy in Moscow on April 23, 1945," in *Soviet-Polish Relations: A Collection of Official Documents and Press Extracts, 1944-1946* (London: "Soviet News," 1946), 30.

5   Krystyna Kersten, "Polityczny i propagandowy obraz zbrojnego podziemia w latach 1945-1947 w świetle prasy komunistycznej," *Wojna domowa czy nowa okupacja?: Polska po roku 1944*, ed. by Andrzej Ajnenkiel (Wrocław, Warszawa, and Kraków: Wydawnictwo Zakładu Narodowego imienia Ossolińskich, 1998), 140-50 [afterward "Polityczny" in *Wojna domowa*]. See also a much more detailed work by Marek Michalik, "Wizerunek Zrzeszenia 'Wolność i Niezawisłość' w wybranych tytułach prasy centralnej z lat 1945-1947: Część I," *Zeszyty Historyczne WiN-u* 12 (March 1999): 5-42.

6   Exceptionally only such Polish-Jewish anti-Communists as Henryk Aschkenazy, Henryk Landau, and Rudolf Rathaus spoke out publicly in the USA against the Communist propaganda. See Joseph Tenenbaum, *In Search of a Lost People: The Old and the New Poland* (New York: The Beechhurst Press, 1948), 208-10, 215-16, 224, 227 [afterward *In Search of a Lost People*]; Joseph Tenenbaum, *Underground: The Story of a People* (New York: Philosophical Library, 1952), 498-502 [afterward *Underground*]; Marian Turski, "Pogrom kielecki w protokołach Centralnego Komitetu Żydów Polskich," *Almanach Żydowski* [Warszawa] (1996-1997): 48-62; The Society for the Promotion of Poland's Independence, "Declaration," New York, 7 July 1946 (a copy in my collection).

7   Bernard Gotfryd, *Anton the Dove Fancier and Other Tales of the Holocaust* (Baltimore and London: The Johns Hopkins University Press, 2000), 170-71.

8   Moshe Yaari Wald, ed., *Rzeszów Jews Memorial Book, Part Three: English* (Tel Aviv: Rzeszower Societies in Israel and U.S.A., 1967), 116 [afterward *Rzeszów Jews*]. See also Raport WiN [after August 1945], "Polityka narodowościowa PPR," Archiwum Akt Nowych, Komitet Centralny Polskiej Partii Robotniczej [afterwards AAN, KC PPR], file 295/VII-255, 1-3; and Alina Cała and Helena Datner-Śpiewak, eds., *Dzieje Żydów w Polsce, 1944-1968: Teksty źródłowe* (Warszawa: Żydowski Instytut Historyczny, 1997), 17 n. 20 [afterward *Dzieje Żydów*].

9   For example, according to a Jewish testimony, the head of the Jewish community in Rabka, "David Grassgreen," was assassinated by the AK in March 1946. The Communist propaganda blamed the NSZ. However, according to an underground report, the chairman "Dawid Gringras" was killed allegedly by other Jews, possibly members of the secret police, in the process of settling scores from the Nazi occupation. Regional historian Kwiek confirms that "Dawid Grungras" was killed on February 10, 1946, but fails to name the perpetrators. See Michael Walter Fass, ed., *Nowy-Targ and*

Vicinity: Zakopane, Charni Dunaietz, Rabka, Yordanov, Shchavnitza, Kroshchenko, Yablonka, Makov Podhalanski (Tel-Aviv: Townspeople Association of Nowy-Targ and Vicinity, 1979), 72 [afterward *Nowy-Targ and Vicinity*]; Julian Kwiek, *Żydzi, Łemkowie, Słowacy w województwie krakowskim w latach 1945-1949/50* (Kraków: Wydawnictwo Naukowe Księgarnia Akademicka, 1998), 27 [afterward *Żydzi, Łemkowie, Słowacy*]; Zrzeszenie *"Wolność i Niezawisłość" w dokumentach*, vol. 3 (Wrocław: Zarząd Główny WiN, 1997), 3: 282-83 [afterward *Zrzeszenie WiN w dokumentach*]; Yehuda Bauer, *Flight and Rescue: Brichah* (New York: Random House, 1970), 338 n. 29 [afterward *Flight and Rescue*].

10   See Simon Segal, "Eastern Europe," *The American Jewish Yearbook, 5705*, vol. 46: *September 18, 1944 to September 7, 1945*, ed. by Harry Schneiderman (Philadelphia: The Jewish Publication Society of America, 1944), 240-44 [afterward "Eastern" in *American* with a volume number]; Raphael Mahler, "Eastern Europe," *The American Jewish Yearbook, 5706*, vol. 47: *1945-46*, ed. by Harry Schneiderman and Julius B. Maller (Philadelphia: The Jewish Publication Society of America, 1945), 391-408 [afterward "Eastern"]; Harry Schneiderman, "Eastern Europe," *The American Jewish Yearbook, 5707*, vol. 48: *1946-47*, ed. by Harry Scheiderman and Julius B. Maller (Philadelphia: The Jewish Publication Society of America, 1946), 334-49 [afterward "Eastern"]; Ann Vachon, ed., *Poland, 1946: The Photographs and Letters of John Vachon* (Washington, D.C. and London: Smithsonian Institution Press, 1995), 82-83 [afterward *Poland, 1946*]; Raymond Arthur Davies, *Odyssey Through Hell* (New York: L.B. Fischer, 1946), 83 [afterward *Odyssey*]; S.E. Schneiderman, *Between Fear and Hope* (New York: Arco Publishing Company, 1947), 117, 176; Henryk Frankel, *Poland: The Struggle for Power* (London: Lindsay Drummond Ltd., 1946); Wald, *Rzeszów Jews*, 116; Tenenbaum, *In Search of a Lost People*, 208-10, 215-16; Tenenbaum, *Underground*, 498-502.

11   See *Encyclopaedia Judaica*, vol. 13 (Jerusalem and New York: Encyclopaedia Judaica and the Macmillan Company, 1971), s.v. "Poland," 13: 783.

12   See Shmuel Krakowski, "Narodowe Siły Zbrojne," in *Encyclopedia of the Holocaust*, ed. by Israel Gutman, vol. 3 (New York and London: MacMillan Publishing Company and Collier MacMillan Publishers, 1990), 3: 1031-32.

13   See Eric Joseph Epstein and Philip Rosen, *Dictionary of the Holocaust: Biography, Geography, and Terminology* (Westport, CT, and London: Greenwood Press, 1997), 212.

14   See Richard Lourie, "Translator's Foreword," in Henryk Grynberg, *The Victory* (Evanston, Illinois: Northwestern University Press, 1993), ix.

15   See Bauer, *Flight and Rescue*, 115.

16   See Marc Hillel, *Le Massacre des survivants: En Pologne après l'holocauste (1945-1947)* (Paris: Plon, 1985), a picture between pp. 180 and 181, and 202-3 [afterward *Le Massacre des Survivants*].

17   Bernard Weinryb was perhaps the first scholar to distinguish critically between the post-war Communist propaganda and practice in regard to the Jewish minority. See Bernard D. Weinryb, "Poland," in Peter Meyer et al., *The Jews in the Soviet Satellites* (Syracuse, NY: Syracuse University Press, 1953), 207-326 [afterward "Poland" in *The Jews in the Soviet Satellites*].

18   Leon Shapiro, "Poland," *The American Jewish Yearbook, 5708*, vol. 49: *1947-48*, ed. by Harry Schneiderman and Morris Fine (Philadelphia: The Jewish Publication Society of America, 1947), 383-84 [afterward "Poland"].

19 However, there are at least two instances of Jewish witnesses critically approaching the official news, alas both published only after 1989. A Jewish physician perceptively noted that "I was extremely disappointed about the attitude of the Russian authorities toward the Jewish survivors of the Holocaust... The Soviets were not interested in the truth, only in what could serve their propaganda." See Samuel Drix, *Witness to Annihilation: Surviving the Holocaust. A Memoir* (Washington, D.C., and London: Brassey's, 1994), 231 [afterward *Witness to Annihilation*]. The eminent mathematician of Jewish origin Hugo Steinhaus occasionally pointed out the pervasive influence of official propaganda on the perception of the post-war reality in Poland. For instance, he described how, probably in December 1945, student riots broke out in Łódź after a body of a female student had been found near a local Soviet military installation. "The students organized a demonstration at her funeral. 'Security' [i.e. the secret police] spread a rumor that the NSZ were responsible for the killing but it forgot about the rumor and started shooting at the demonstrators." Moreover, Steinhaus suggested the possibility that common crime was also behind violence in Poland. He stressed that in Wrocław, where he resided, "robberies occur daily; every night shots can be heard discharged from all sorts of weapons. The attacks are even more frequent in the countryside. The robberies are perpetrated by demobilized soldiers, deserters, and green [i.e. military] cadres of all armies: Russians, Poles, and Germans." Nonetheless, even Steinhaus used the omnipresent bogeyman of the Communist propaganda to describe violence in Poland. In February 1946, without substantiating his claim, he wrote that "the so-called NSZ constantly kill Jews, officials, [and] secret policemen." See Hugo Steinhaus, *Wspomnienia i zapiski* (London: Aneks, 1992), 340, 342-43 [afterward *Wspomnienia*].

20 See Samuel Gringauz, "Some Methodological Problems in the Study of the Ghetto," *Jewish Social Studies: A Quarterly Journal Devoted to the Historical Aspects of the Jewish Life* [New York] 12 (1950): 65-66. In all fairness, similar reservations should be voiced about many Polish Christian memoirs of the war-time years.

21 Bogdan Brzeziński, Leon Chrzanowski, and Ryszard Halaba, eds., *Polegli w walce o władzę ludową: Materiały i zestawienia statystyczne* (Warszawa: Książka i Wiedza, 1970), 20-21 [afterward *Polegli w walce*]. This work was sponsored by the Institute of Party History of the Central Committee of the Polish United Workers Party (*Zakład Historii Partii przy KC PZPR*), which is also listed as its main "author".

22 Joanna Michlic-Coren, "Anti-Jewish Violence in Poland, 1918-1939 and 1945-1947," *Polin: Studies in Polish Jewry*, Volume Thirteen: *Focusing on the Holocaust and Its Aftermath* (London and Portland Oregon: The Littman Library of Jewish Civilization, 2000), 34-61 [afterward "Anti-Jewish Violence in Poland"; and afterward *Polin* quoted with volume number and year of publishing]; Peter Stachura, "Polish-Jewish Relations in the Aftermath of the Holocaust: Reflections and Perspectives," in *Perspectives on Polish History*, ed. by Peter Stachura, The Centre for Research in Polish History, University of Stirling, Occasional Papers, No 2 (2001): 82-96.

23 According to Romaniuk, all three Jewish victims of post-war violence in Brańsk were killed by common bandits. This includes a Jewish merchant and two Jewish women who were shot dead along with their Polish acquaintance. Kwiek blames criminals for over 30 murders in the Province of Kraków between June and August 1945. In his study of Szczecin, a port city in north-western Poland, Stankowski mentions that "in June 1946 unknown perpetrators murdered four Jews and carried out many robberies on others. The attacks could be common crimes, connected to the general lack of security in Western Pommerania." Szaynok, whose area of specialty is Silesia, has established

that out of 30 attacks on Jews between June and December 1945, robbery was the reason in eleven instances and resentment at attempts to reclaim Jewish property accounted for five attacks. The remaining 14 cases of anti-Jewish assaults are presumably unknown. See Zbigniew Romaniuk, "Brańsk and Its Environs in the Years 1939-1953: Reminiscences of Events," in *The Story of Two Shtetls Brańsk and Ejszyszki: An Overview of Polish-Jewish Relations in Northeastern Poland During World War II (Two Parts)* (Toronto and Chicago: The Polish Educational Foundation in North America, 1998), 1: 89-91, 93-96, 102 [afterward *The Story of Two Shtetls*]; Kwiek, *Żydzi, Łemkowie, Słowacy*, 23, 25; Albert Stankowski, "Emigracja Żydów z Pomorza Zachodniego w latach 1945-1960," *Studia z dziejów i kultury Żydów w Polsce po 1945 roku*, ed. by Jerzy Tomaszewski (Warszawa: Wydawnictwo TRIO, 1997), 89 [afterward "Emigracja Żydów" in *Studia*]; Bożena Szaynok, "Ludność Żydowska w Polsce," *Studia z dziejów Żydów w Polsce: Materiały edukacyjne dla szkół średnich i wyższych*, vol. 2, ed. by Elżbieta Lewczuk (Warszawa: Żydowski Instytut Historyczny and Instytut Naukowo-Badawczy, 1995), 2: 81 [afterward "Ludność" in *Studia*]. See also Cała and Datner-Śpiewak, *Dzieje Żydów*, 25-26.

24 Natalia Aleksiun-Mądrzak, "Nielegalna emigracja Żydów z Polski w latach 1945-1947, część I" *Biuletyn Żydowskiego Instytutu Historycznego*, no. 3/95-2/96 (July 1995-June 1996): 81 [afterward "Nielegalna emigracja Żydów cz. 1" in *BŻIH*].

25 David Engel, "Patterns of Anti-Jewish Violence in Poland, 1944-1946," *Yad Vashem Studies* [Jerusalem] 26 (1998): 85 [afterward "Patterns of Anti-Jewish Violence"].

26 See Plut. Sokół, Raport, no date [21 (?) March 1945], Archiwum Państwowe w Lublinie, Narodowe Siły Zbrojne, Okręg III Lublin, [afterward APL, NSZ], file 48, no page number.

27 See Odpis, Notatki z pamiętnika zabitego komendanta oddziału organizacji NSZ Korycińskiego Stefana ps. Storczyk, no date [1945?], APL, NSZ, file 48, no page number.

I

Two Occupiers, Two Revolutions, and People's Poland
(1944-1947)

Between 1939 and 1947 (and after) Poland experienced a sequence of foreign occupations and revolutions from abroad. The Nazi revolution (1939-1945) almost totally exterminated the Jews and slaughtered many Polish Christians, especially the elites. The Communist revolution (1939-1941 and 1944-1956) saw the further killing of traditional elites and the persecution of various categories of so-called "enemies of the people": political opponents, clergymen, entrepreneurs, successful farmers, and non-conforming intellectuals. In addition, the period between 1939 and 1947 saw the forced deportation and resettlement of millions of people. As the sociologist Jan Tomasz Gross observes, all this would have been impossible without a revolutionary war.[1]

The Second World War began with the joint invasion of Poland by Hitler and Stalin in September 1939. The victors quickly divided the spoils. The Soviet Union annexed the eastern half of Poland, the so-called "Eastern Borderlands" (*Kresy Wschodnie*), while the Third Reich incorporated the "Western Borderlands." Germany also controlled central Poland, which was renamed the Government General (*Generalgouvernement — GG*). Between 1939 and mid-1941 the Soviets deported at least 400,000 people to the Gulag, of whom about 40,000 died in the process. The majority of the deportees were ethnic Poles, but there were also many Jews, and smaller numbers of Ukrainians, and Byelorussians. Further, the Soviets shot about 40,000 "enemies of the people," mostly ethnic Poles. During the same period the Nazis executed perhaps three times as many "enemies of the Reich," mainly members of the Polish elite, and resettled over 365,000 people, mostly Polish Christians from the Western Borderlands, in the Government General. Additionally, between 1940 and 1944, they brought in about a million Jews from all over Europe for extermination along with the Jews of

15

Poland. Simultaneously with the onset of the Holocaust, the Germans escalated their mass slaughter of Poles and shipped out about a million and a half of them for forced labor in the Reich. Meanwhile, after the Nazi attack on the Soviet Union in June 1941, Hitler seized the eastern part of the Polish state from Stalin and held it until the return of the Red Army three years later. By March 1945 the Soviet dictator controlled all of Poland.[2]

First, Stalin reincorporated the Eastern Borderlands into the USSR and, then, undertook a massive population shift. The Soviets expropriated and expelled over 1.5 million Poles from the Eastern Borderlands to the "Recovered Territories" (that is, German lands awarded to Poland) and over 3.2 million Germans from Germany's eastern territories to western and central Germany. The occupiers also resettled in the USSR a number of Ukrainians and Belorussians from central Poland. Moreover, between 1944 and 1947, the Soviet secret police deported about 100,000 people from Poland to the Gulag. Rather inexplicably, the NKVD released about 270,000 Polish citizens, including Jewish victims of earlier deportations and refugees from the Nazis.[3]

Meanwhile, in July 1944, Stalin established a puppet Communist state in central Poland. Within a year the so-called People's Poland (*Polska Ludowa*) increased not only by the old Western Borderlands but also extensive parts of pre-war eastern Germany. The most pressing problems the country faced were the anti-Communist insurrection, political opposition to the Soviet takeover, the deportation and resettlement of the population, and economic reconstruction after the war.[4]

To secure his conquests, Stalin imposed a dual occupation structure upon "People's Poland." First, he forced upon the country a Soviet military and police occupation, with Soviet commanders and personnel stationed in every town down to the parish level (*gmina*), and Soviet military and civilian "advisors" operating in most state institutions down to the county level (*powiat*). Second, Stalin introduced the system of occupation by proxy, that is the installation in power and tight control by a foreign state of its representatives recruited from the native population. The Soviet military-political occupation overlapped with, and was reinforced by, this occupation by proxy.[5]

To staff the proxy regime, Stalin recruited the Communists of the Polish Workers Party (*Polska Partia Robotnicza — PPR*).[6] Its leadership consisted of the "Muscovites," who spent the war in the USSR, and the "natives," who experienced the Nazi occupation in Poland. Under strict supervision from Moscow, the Polish Communists entered into a sham coalition with renegade leaders of radical leftist splinter groups. These collaborators operated under the names of respectable pre-war organizations: the Polish Socialist Party (*Polska Partia Socjalistyczna — PPS*), the Peasant Party (*Stronnictwo Ludowe — SL*), and the Democratic Party (*Stronnictwo Demokratyczne — SD*). The leadership of these sham parties was thoroughly infiltrated by Communists, who also were supreme in Poland's sham parliament, the Home National Council (*Krajowa Rada Narodowa – KRN*). Moreover, the PPR controlled the state bureaucracy, which was, however, to a certain extent also composed of non-Communist and even anti-Communist technical experts.[7]

Both to reinforce the Polish Communist proxies and to increase his influence over the new regime, Stalin delegated a significant number of Soviets to serve as *ersatz* Poles. These so-called "*popy*"[8] appeared in the "people's" army and "people's" security in addition to regular Soviet advisors active there and in civilian institutions. According to the Polish scholar Edward Nalepa, in March 1945 the *popy* constituted almost 53 per cent of all commissioned officers in the "Polish" armed forces. Between 1945 and 1947, 16,460 Soviet officers were transferred to the Polish Communist army. In December 1945, 54 out of Poland's 63 generals (i.e. 86 per cent) and 228 out of 309 colonels (i.e. 74 per cent) were Red Army officers. Overall, the Soviets constituted about 40 per cent of the "Polish" officer corps. The Poles were allowed to serve mostly as junior and non-commissioned officers and draftees. Thus, it seems that the "Polish" armed forces under the Soviets can be compared to the Indian military under the British rule.[9]

Stalin considered the security establishment of particular importance. At the outset, the "Polish" military intelligence (*Informacja Wojskowa — IW*) consisted entirely of Soviet counterintelligence (*Smersh*) personnel. A number of the most trusted Polish Communists were coopted only some time later. Even after 1947, however, *Smersh* officers still occupied over 60 per cent of all command posts. In addition, Soviet NKVD personnel held all of the key technical posts in the "Polish" civilian secret police, the Public Security Office (*Urząd Bezpieczeństwa Publicznego — UBP*). Moscow's security experts also supervised the regular police force, the Citizens Militia (*Milicja Obywatelska — MO*). A Soviet general and a number of Soviet officers headed the elite police troops of the Corps for Internal Security (*Korpus Bezpieczeństwa Wewnętrznego – KBW*). Soviet superiors were in charge of 11 out of the 14 provincial security zones that Poland was divided into. Finally, Soviet personnel were also prominent in the military judiciary apparatus. Thus, the major coercive institutions of the new state operated firmly under the Soviet control.[10]

Initially the Soviets bore the brunt of the struggle against the political opposition to the new regime, including the insurgents. As the Polish

Communist leader Władysław Gomułka admitted in May 1945, "we are not able to conduct the struggle against the reaction [i.e. the Polish insurgents] without the Red Army."[11] In addition to regular Red Army units which, between 1944 and 1947, varied in strength between 200,000 and three million troops stationed in Poland, Stalin sent three NKVD divisions, including 64th Riflemen, numbering 35,000 troops, to police his largest "people's democracy." The 64th Riflemen alone arrested over 60,000 people. Of course, several other NKVD divisions operated throughout the Eastern Borderlands, fighting anti-Communists on both sides of the new Soviet-Polish border and crossing it at will. The NKVD troops were recalled from active combat duty in Poland only in the spring of 1947. The NKVD advisors with the county UBP were withdrawn at the same time. Up to that point, the Soviets had planned and led most of the major anti-insurgent operations. These included antiguerrilla pacification campaigns, kidnappings and assassinations of political opponents as well as, apparently, two sham amnesties in August 1945 and February 1947.[12]

The Soviets also masterminded the falsification of the results of the "popular referendum" of June 1946 and the parliamentary elections of January 1947, which were overwhelmingly won by the anti-Communists. Naturally, the Soviets were eagerly assisted in their activities by their Polish proxies. As their strength and ranks grew, in 1947, the Communists of Poland gradually assumed a greater share of the burden of fighting their enemies.[13]

Notes

1 See Jan Gross, "War as Revolution," *The Establishment of Communist Regimes in Eastern Europe, 1944-1949*, ed. by Norman Naimark and Leonid Gibianskii (Boulder, CO: Westview Press, 1997), 17-40 [afterward "War," in *The Establishment of Communist Regimes*]. Gross did not mention that in addition to Nazi and Soviet revolutions from above (and abroad), Europe experienced an attempted revolution from below by native Communists (1942-1944). That revolution was camouflaged as a "struggle for national liberation" against the Axis powers. Only in Poland was it nipped in the bud by the independentist underground. Elsewhere, the Communists either triumphed (Yugoslavia, Albania, and Slovakia) or came dangerously close to victory (Greece, Italy, and France). See Marek Jan Chodakiewicz, "Geneza rewolucji komunistycznej w Polsce," in Chodakiewicz, Gontarczyk, and Żebrowski, *Tajne oblicze*, 1: 13-36; David H. Close, *The Origins of the Greek Civil War* (London and New York: Longman, 1995); Tony Judt, ed., *Resistance and Revolution in Mediterranean Europe, 1939-1948* (London and New York: Routledge, 1989); Barbara Jelavich, *History of the Balkans*, vol. 2: *Twentieth Century* (Cambridge: Cambridge University Press, 1983), 247-335; Stanislav J. Kirschbaum, *A History of Slovakia: The Struggle for Survival* (New York: St. Martin's Griffin, 1995), 204-23.

2 There is no comprehensive work on Poland during the Second World War and its aftermath. For an incomplete treatment of the topic see John Coutouvidis and Jaime Reynolds, *Poland, 1939-1947* (New York: Holmes & Meier, 1986). For a comprehensive treatment of the sensitive problem of national minorities see Tadeusz Piotrowski, *Poland's Holocaust: Ethnic Strife, Collaboration with Occupying Forces and Genocide in the Second Republic, 1918-1947* (Jefferson, NC, and London: McFarland & Company, 1998) [afterward *Poland's Holocaust*]. On the first Soviet occupation see Jan T. Gross, *Revolution from Abroad: The Soviet Conquest of Poland's Western Ukraine and Western Belorussia* (Princeton, N.J.: Princeton University Press, 1988); Keith Sword, ed., *The Soviet Takeover of the Polish Eastern Provinces, 1939-41* (New York: St. Martin's Press, 1991); Ben-Cion Pinchuk, *Shtetl Jews under Soviet Rule: Eastern Poland on the Eve of the Holocaust* (London: Basil Blackwell, 1990); Tomasz Strzembosz, ed., *Studia z dziejów okupacji sowieckiej (1939-1941): Obywatele polscy na kresach północno-wschodnich II Rzeczypospolitej pod okupacją sowiecką w latach 1939-1941* (Warszawa: ISP PAN, 1997); Daniel Boćkowski, *Czas nadziei: Obywatele Rzeczypospolitej Polskiej w ZSRR i opieka nad nimi placówek polskich w latach 1939-1943* (Warszawa: Noriton and Wydawnictwo IH PAN, 1999). On the Nazi occupation see Richard C. Lukas, *The Forgotten Holocaust: The Poles Under German Occupation, 1939-1944*, rev. ed. (New York: Hippocrene Books, 1997); Jan Tomasz Gross, *Polish Society Under German Occupation: The Generalgouvernement, 1939-1944* (Princeton, N.J.: Princeton University Press, 1979); Józef Garliński, *Poland in the Second World War* (London: Macmillan Press, 1985); Czesław Łuczak, *Polska i Polacy w drugiej wojnie światowej* (Poznań: Wydawnictwo Naukowe Uniwersytetu im. Adama Mickiewicza, 1993).

3 On the mass deportations after 1944 and prisoner releases from the Gulag see Stanisław Ciesielski, ed., *Przesiedlenie ludności polskiej z Kresów Wschodnich do Polski, 1944-1947* (Warszawa: Wydawnictwo Neriton and Instytut Historii PAN, 1999); Hubert Orłowski and Andrzej Sakson, eds., *Utracona Ojczyzna: Przymusowe deportacje i przesiedlenia jako wspólne doświadczenia* (Poznań: Instytut Zachodni, 1997); Stanisław Ciesielski, Grzegorz Hryciuk, and Aleksander Srebrakowski, *Masowe deportacje radzieckie w okresie II Wojny światowej* (Wrocław: Instytut Historyczny

Uniwersytetu Wrocławskiego and Wrocławskie Towarzystwo Miłośników Historii, 1994), 26-82 [afterward *Masowe deportacje*]; Andrzej Paczkowski and Wojciech Materski, eds., *Z archiwów sowieckich*, vol. 5: *Powrót żołnierzy AK z sowieckich łagrów* (Warszawa: ISP PAN, 1995) [afterward *Powrót żołnierzy AK*]; Eugeniusz Misiło, *Akcja Wisła: Dokumenty* (Warszawa: Wydawnictwo Łódzkie DWN, 1993); Alfred-Maurice de Zayas, *A Terrible Revenge: The Ethnic Cleansing of the East European Germans, 1944-1950* (New York: St. Martin's Press, 1994); Rüdiger Overmans, "Personelle Verluste der deutschen Bevölkerung durch Flucht und Vertreibung," *Dzieje Najnowsze* vol. 26, no. 2 (1994): 51-65; Klaus-Peter Friedrich, "Wygnanie: mit niemieckiej historii," *Więź* (July 1997): 153-164; Marian Wojciechowski, "The Exodus of the Germans from the Odra and Lusatian Nysa Territories," *Polish Western Affairs* 1/2 (1990): 1-18; Krzysztof Chudy, "Ucieczka, wypędzenie i wysiedlenie ludności niemieckiej z Ziemi Wschowskiej w latach 1945-1947," *Przegląd Zachodni* vol. 55, no. 2 (April-June 1999): 205-18; Bernadetta Nitschke, *Wysiedlenie ludności niemieckiej z Polski w latach 1945-1949* (Zielona Góra: Wyższa Szkoła Pedagogiczna im. Tadeusza Kotarbińskiego, 1999).

4 The topic of the reconstruction is beyond the scope of this work. See Padraic Kenney, *Rebuilding Poland: Workers and Communists, 1945-1950* (Ithaca and London: Cornell University Press, 1997); Wacław Długoborski, Bożena Klimczak, and Elżbieta Kaszuba, eds., *Gospodarcze i społeczne skutki wojny i okupacji dla Polski oraz drogi ich przezwyciężania: Materiały z konferencji naukowej zorganizowanej przez Katedrę Historii Gospodarczej Akademii Ekonomicznej we Wrocławiu, Karpacz, 4-6 grudnia 1985* (Wrocław: Wydawnictwo Uczelniane Akademii Ekonomicznej we Wrocławiu, 1989) [afterward *Gospodarcze*]. For the general background of the period see Krystyna Kersten, *Między wyzwoleniem a zniewoleniem, 1944-1956* (London: Aneks, 1993); idem, *Narodziny systemu władzy: Polska, 1943-1948* (Warszawa: Wydawnictwo Krąg, 1985). The latter work has been translated as *The Establishment of Communist Rule in Poland, 1943-48* (Berkeley: University of California Press, 1991).

5 Officially, the Soviet Communists called this form of a system a "people's democracy." The first such state was Mongolia. During the Civil War in Spain Stalin called the anti-Nationalist coalition of the "Popular Front," under the leadership of the Communists, a "democracy of a new type." After 1944 East and Central Europe saw the establishment of "people's democracies" ruled by the Communists and their allies in the so-called "national fronts." According to the Kremlin, a "people's democracy" was the transitory stage between a "bourgeois democracy" and the "socialist system" of the Soviet Union. See E.H. Carr, *The Comintern and the Spanish Civil War* (New York: Pantheon Books, 1984), 52-65; Anthony D'Agostino, *Soviet Succession Struggles: Kremlinology and the Russian Question from Lenin to Gorbachov* (Boston: Allen and Unwin, 1988), 161-172; E. Varga, "Demokratiia novogo tipa," *Mirovoe khoziaistvo i mirovaia politika* [Moscow] (March 1947): 3-14; Władysław Gomułka, "Demokracja ludowa — droga pokojowego rozwoju Polski," *W walce o demokrację ludową (Artykuły i przemówienia)*, 2 *Volumes* (Warszawa: Książka, 1947), 2: 151-171; K. Ostrovitianov, "Lenin i Stalin ob ekonomike i politike," *Voprosy ekonomiki* [Moscow] 2 (1949): 3-29; Hilary Minc, "Concerning the basis of planning in the people's democracies," *For a Lasting Peace, For a People's Democracy!*, 18 November 1949, 2-3. For general background on the Soviet seizure of power in East Central Europe see Hugh Seton-Watson, *The East European Revolutions* (New York: Frederic A. Praeger, 1951); and Joseph Rothschild, *Return to Diversity: A Political History of East Central Europe Since World War II* (New York and Oxford: Oxford University Press, 1989), 76-123 [afterward *Return to Diversity*]. For recent historical debates on

the nature of "People's Poland" see Andrzej Paczkowski, "Communist Poland, 1944-1989: Some Controversies and a Single Conclusion," *The Polish Review*, 2 (1999): 217-225.

6   The PPR descended from the pre-war Communist Party of Poland (*Komunistyczna Partia Polski — KPP*). The KPP had about 4,000 members at its peak. The war-time Communist resistance enrolled about 6,000 members. See Henryk Cimek, *Komuniści, Polska, Stalin* (Białystok: Krajowa Agencja Wydawnicza, 1990), 106-107 [afterward *Komuniści*]; Chodakiewicz, Gontarczyk, and Żebrowski, *Tajne oblicze*, 1: 62-95. See also Jan B. de Weydenthal, *The Communists of Poland: An Historical Outline* (Stanford, CA: Hoover Institution Press, 1986).

7   See Antony Polonsky and Bolesław Drukier, eds., *The Beginnings of Communist Rule in Poland* (London, Boston and Henley: Routledge & Kegan Paul, 1980); Giennadij A. Bordiugow et al., eds., *Polska-ZSRR Struktury Podległości: Dokumenty WKP(b), 1944-1949* (Warszawa: ISP PAN and Stowarzyszenie Współpracy Polska-Wschód, 1995) [afterward *Polska-ZSRR*]; Jerzy Kochanowski, ed., *Protokoły posiedzeń Prezydium Krajowej Rady Narodowej, 1944-1947* (Warszawa: Wydawnictwo Sejmowe, 1995); Aleksander Kochański, ed., *Protokoły posiedzeń Biura Politycznego KC PPR, 1944-1945* (Warszawa: ISP PAN, 1992) [afterward *Protokoły BP*]; Bogusław Barnaszewski, *Polityka PPR wobec zalegalizowanych partii i stronnictw* (Warszawa: Wydawnictwo Naukowe Semper, 1996); Teresa Torańska, *Oni* (London: Aneks, 1985), 193-211 [afterward *Oni*], which was translated as *"Them" : Stalin's Polish Puppets* (New York: Harper and Row, 1987).

8   This acronym is a play on words. In Polish *pop* means an Orthodox priest. Native wits called a Soviet officer in Polish uniform a *"pop,"* which stood for *pełniący obowiązki Polaka*: "he who is fulfilling the duties of a Pole."

9   Although the number of senior Soviet officers in the Polish Communist army decreased after 1947, it never fell below 30 per cent until 1957. See Edward Jan Nalepa, *Oficerowie Armii Radzieckiej w Wojsku Polskim, 1943-1968* (Warszawa: Wydawnictwo Bellona, 1995), 17, 41, 48-49. The "Polish" Communist army suffered a high desertion rate and poor morale. See Elżbieta Iwaniec and Stefan Zwolniński, ed., *Polskie Państwo Podziemne i Wojsko Polskie w latach 1944-1945* (Warszawa: Wojskowy Instytut Historyczny, 1991); Ignacy Blum, *Z dziejów Wojska Polskiego w latach 1944-1948: Szkice i dokumenty* (Warszawa: Wydawnictwo Ministerstwa Obrony Narodowej, 1968); Kazimierz Frontczak, *Siły Zbrojne Polski Ludowej: Przejście na stopę pokojową, 1945-1947* (Warszawa: Wydawnictwo Ministerstwa Obrony Narodowej, 1974). For a comparison with the British *Raj* see Stanley Wolpert, *A New History of India* (New York and Oxford: Oxford University Press, 1982), 187-349.

10 See Władysław Tkaczew, *Powstanie i działalność organów Informacji Wojska Polskiego w latach 1943-1948: Kontrwywiad wojskowy* (Warszawa: Wydawnictwo Bellona, 1994), 9-16, 280-81; Mieczysław Jaworski, *Korpus Bezpieczeństwa Wewnętrznego, 1945-1965* (Warszawa: Wydawnictwo Ministerstwa Obrony Narodowej, 1984), 32-34 [afterward *Korpus*]; Henryk Dominiczak, *Organy bezpieczeństwa PRL, 1944-1990: Rozwój i działalność w świetle dokumentów MSW* (Warszawa: Dom Wydawniczy Bellona, 1997), 39; Andrzej Paczkowski, ed., *Aparat Bezpieczeństwa w latach 1944-1956: Taktyka, strategia, metody, Część I: Lata 1945-1947* (Warszawa: ISP PAN, 1994), 17; Maria Turlejska, ed., *W walce ze zbrojnym podziemiem 1945-1947* (Warszawa: Wydawnictwo Ministerstwa Obrony Narodowej, 1972) [afterward *W walce*]; Zenon Jakubowski, *Milicja Obywatelska, 1944-1948*

(Warszawa: Państwowe Wydawnictwo Naukowe, 1988) [afterward *Milicja*]; Stanisław Marat and Jacek Snopkiewicz, *Ludzie bezpieki: Dokumentacja czasu bezprawia* (Warszawa: Wydawnictwo Alfa, 1990) [afterward *Ludzie bezpieki*]; Jerzy Poksiński, ed., *"My, sędziowie, nie od Boga..." : Z dziejów sądownictwa wojskowego PRL, 1944-1956, Materiały i dokumenty* (Warszawa: Gryf, 1996).

11   Aleksander Kochański, ed., *Protokół obrad KC PPR w maju 1945* (Warszawa: ISP PAN, 1992), 42 [afterward *Protokół KC*].

12   See A.F. Noskova et al., eds., *NKVD i polskoe podpolie, 1944-1945 (Po "Osobym papkam" I.V. Stalina)* (Moskva: Institut slavianovedeniia i balkanistiki RAN, 1994) [afterward *NKVD i polskoe podpolie*]; *Pogranichnye voiska v gody velikoi otechestvennoi voiny, 1941-1945: Sbornik dokumentov* (Moskva: Izdatel'stvo "Nauka", 1968), 504-514; *Pogranichnye voiska SSSR, mai 1945-1950: Sbornik dokumentov i materialov* (Moskva: Izdatel'stvo "Nauka", 1975), 208-23, 238-44, 246-49, 257-89, 297-99, 308-309, 319-21, 326-34, 341-47, 357-58, 368, 380-81, 432-57, 490-500; Z.Z.Z., *Syndykat zbrodni: Kartki z dziejów UB i SB w czterdziestoleciu PRL* ([Paris]: Editions Spotkania, 1986); Tomasz Strzembosz, ed., *NKWD o polskim podziemiu 1944-1948: Konspiracja polska na Nowogródczyźnie i Grodzieńszczyźnie* (Warszawa: ISP PAN, 1997); Paweł Piotrowski, "Armia Czerwona na Dolnym Śląsku," *Biuletyn Instytutu Pamięci Narodowej*, 4 (May 2001); Teodor Gąsiorowski, "Smiersz i NKWD w Małopolsce," *Biuletyn Instytutu Pamięci Narodowej*, 5 (June 2001); Piotr Kołakowski, "NKWD-NKGB a podziemie polskie: Kresy Wschodnie," *Zeszyty Historyczne*, no. 136 (2001): 59-86.

13   Andrzej Paczkowski, ed., *Referendum z 30 czerwca 1946: Przebieg i wyniki* (Warszawa: ISP PAN, 1993); J.M., "Imperium wiecznie żywe," *Życie*, 17 June 1997, 10-11.

II

THE INDEPENDENTISTS AND THE ANTI-COMMUNIST INSURRECTION (1944-1947)

During the Second World War and its aftermath the Polish independentist camp consisted of all native political and military forces from right to left with the exception of the Communists. The Communists were excluded because of their complete subordination to the Kremlin. Between 1939 and 1945 the independentist camp remained underground. After the return of the Soviets in 1944 much of it gradually emerged to accommodate the new occupiers. The overt independentists attempted to take part in the political process openly only to be smashed by 1947. As mentioned, a small non-Communist minority of left-wing politicians collaborated with the Communists. The majority, however, remained in the opposition which took several forms, including political and military resistance.

The four major clandestine political parties during the Nazi occupation were the Socialists (*Polska Partia Socjalistyczna "Wolność, Równość, Niezawisłość" — PPS-WRN*), the Nationalists (*Stronnictwo Narodowe — SN*), the Populists (*Stronnictwo Ludowe — SL*), and the Christian Democrats (*Stronnictwo Pracy – SP*).[1] After 1945 only two of them were permitted to operate legally: the Christian Democrats and the Populists, who, under the émigré leader Stanisław Mikołajczyk, formed the Polish Peasant Party (*Polskie Stronnictwo Ludowe — PSL*). The Nationalists remained underground along with the Independent Polish Socialist Party (*Niezależna PPS – NPPS*).[2]

Under the Nazi occupation the largest and most powerful clandestine military force was the Home Army (*Armia Krajowa — AK*), an umbrella organization that united most of Poland's underground groups, including large parts of the right-wing National Armed Forces (*Narodowe Siły Zbrojne — NSZ*) and much of the left-wing Peasant Battalions (*Bataliony Chłopskie — BCh*). Whereas the majority of the clandestine fighters had emerged from the underground by August 1945, many stayed and struggled on. After the dissolution of the Home Army in January 1945, its leadership created a succession of secret groups: the Independence (*Niepodległość — NIE*), the Delegation of the Armed Forces (*Delegatura Sił Zbrojnych — DSZ*), and, finally, the Association for Freedom and Independence (*Zrzeszenie Wolność i Niezawisłość — WiN*). Meanwhile, as early as November 1944, the Nationalists pulled their units out of the AK and formed the National Military Union (*Narodowe Zjednoczenie Wojskowe — NZW*), which eventually absorbed the far-right National Radicals of the NSZ in 1946. In addition, hundreds of other secret organizations came into existence throughout Poland. For them, anti-Communism and anti-Sovietism were synonymous with freedom and independence. Although their aims were similar, the underground insurgency operated independently of the accommodationist political opposition headed by the PSL, both complementing and challenging it. However, as during the Second World War, the independentists falsely predicated their future success on Western assistance in liberating Poland.[3]

Faced with the return of the Red Army in 1944, the insurgents led by the AK launched Operation Tempest (*Akcja "Burza"*). The operation commenced in the winter of 1944 but reached its apex half a year later. This was an attempt by the independentists to establish against Stalin's will a free Polish administration on the territories liberated from the Germans. The insurgents planned to take advantage of the Red Army offensive against the *Wehrmacht* to seize control over Poland. In military terms, Operation Tempest was an anti-Nazi uprising. In political terms, it was the beginning of an anti-Soviet undertaking.[4]

The Poles realized but fleetingly the objectives of Operation Tempest on much of the territory of the pre-war Polish to the east of the Vistula River. A Polish civilian administration was established in provincial towns, counties, and parishes, especially in central Poland. Unfortunately, within a few days, this administration was destroyed by the Soviets. As a result, the last battles with the Nazi occupier overlapped with the first struggles against the Soviet invader.

According to the historian John Micgiel, the NKVD staged mass arrests of Polish partisans who had participated in the "Tempest." Despite their earlier tactical cooperation with the Red Army against the Nazis, they were disarmed, interned, and sent to the Gulag or inducted into the "people's" army against their will. Some were shot; many returned underground. Their subsequent efforts to reach a compromise with the Soviets ended in treachery. In March 1945, sixteen Polish clandestine leaders were granted safe conduct by the NKVD to hold talks with Stalin's emissaries. When the Poles arrived at the designated spot, they were promptly kidnapped, taken to Moscow, and subjected to a show trial.[5] This, along with a massive wave of other Communist crimes, which included assassinations, arrests, deportations, and confiscations, hardened popular attitudes against the new occupiers. In the spring of 1945, a spontaneous insurrection commenced against the Soviets in central Poland. By June 1945 the Communist power had been reduced to large cities only. To a certain extent, this uprising was a continuation of Operation Tempest so far as it sought to achieve its military and tactical objectives in the countryside. However, the anti-Communist assault lacked any coordination from above since, to prevent further bloodshed, the independentist leaders opposed it. In July 1945, the anti-Communist offensive petered out when Soviet reinforcements were rushed in to stop it. Meanwhile, the Populists under Mikołajczyk agreed to participate in a sham coalition government with the Communists and the regime proclaimed an amnesty for the insurgents.

A relative lull in the fighting followed until January 1946. Nevertheless, the subsequent increase of secret police terror caused the insurgents to step up their operations. This violated the orders of their central leaders who wanted to limit the armed struggle to necessary self-defense, if not to its outright termination. Massive police pacification efforts launched before and during the falsified referendum of June 1946 put the insurgents on a permanent defensive. Their numbers dwindled, especially after the amnesty of February 1947. Only the most hardened anti-Communist fighters remained underground. Some of them persevered until 1957; the last solitary stalwarts held out in their forest hideaways until the early 1960s.

Meanwhile, having falsified the parliamentary elections of January 1947, the Communist regime crushed the legal opposition by police terror and political means. The Stalinization of Poland continued apace. According to the scholars Maria Stanowska and Leszek Żebrowski, in People's Poland 3,000 people were sentenced to death and executed, perhaps 10,000 were tortured to death during interrogation or summarily shot, 150,000 were sentenced to jail, and about 100,000 were deported to the Gulag. In addition, 518,000 peasants were imprisoned for resisting collectivization and forced food quota extraction. Finally, between 20,000 and 50,000 people were killed during the anti-Communist insurrection.[6]

Polish historians Aleksander Gella and Ryszard Terlecki aptly dubbed the period between 1944 and 1947, "the extermination of the Second Republic" and "the dictatorship of treason." Other scholars have written in a similar vein, concentrating on the Communist terror against the underground and the destruction of voluntary institutions by the totalitarian state.[7] These scholars, however, have generally *paid very little attention* to the predicament of Poland's Jewish minority.

Notes

1   After September 1939 the independentist camp created the Polish Underground State (*Polskie Państwo Podziemne — PPP*). The PPP had its military arm, the Home Army (*Armia Krajowa — AK*), an administrative branch, the Government Delegation (*Delegatura Rządu — DR*), and a clandestine parliament, The Council of National Unity (*Rada Jedności Narodowej — RJN*), which consisted of the representatives of the main parties. Fringe elements of the independentist camp (e.g. National Radicals, revolutionary socialists, and far-left populists) often were in opposition to the political and military executives of the Polish Underground State. However, even these extremists often were members of its various institutions. See Waldemar Grabowski, *Delegatura Rządu Rzeczypospolitej Polskiej na Kraj, 1940-1945* (Warszawa: Instytut Wydawniczy Pax, 1995); Stefan Korboński, *The Polish Underground State: A Guide to the Underground, 1939-1945* (Boulder, CO and New York: East European Quarterly and Columbia University Press, 1978).

2   See Marek Latyński, *Nie paść na kolana: Szkice o opozycji lat czterdziestych* (London: Polonia Book Fund Ltd., 1985); Romuald Turkowski, *Polskie Stronnictwo Ludowe w obronie demokracji 1945-1949* (Warszawa: Wydawnictwo Sejmowe, 1992); Andrzej Paczkowski, *Stanisław Mikołajczyk: Klęska realisty (Zarys biografii politycznej)* (Warszawa: Agencja Omnipress, 1991).

3   See *Informator o nielegalnych antypaństwowych organizacjach i bandach zbrojnych działających w Polsce Ludowej w latach 1944-1956* (Warszawa: Ministerstwo Spraw Wewnętrznych, Biuro "C", 1964, Reprint Lublin: Wydawnictwo Retro, 1993) [afterward *Informator*]; *Zrzeszenie "Wolność i Niezawisłość" w dokumentach*, 3 vols. (Wrocław: Zarząd Główny WiN, 1997) (vol. 1: *wrzesień 1945-czerwiec 1946*; vol. 2: *lipiec 1946-styczeń 1947*; vol. 3: *luty-listopad 1947*) [afterward *Zrzeszenie WiN w dokumentach*]; Jerzy Ślaski, *Żołnierze wyklęci* (Warszawa: Oficyna Wydawnicza Rytm, 1996) [afterward *Żołnierze*]; Grzegorz Wąsowski and Leszek Żebrowski, eds., *Żołnierze wyklęci: Antykomunistyczne podziemie zbrojne po 1944 roku* (Warszawa: Oficyna Wydawnicza Volumen and Liga Republikańska, 1999) [afterward *Żołnierze*]. The standard published work on the WiN is Zygmunt Woźniczka, *Zrzeszenie "Wolność i Niezawisłość" 1945-1952* (Warszawa: Instytut Prasy i Wydawnictw "Novum" — "Semex", 1992). However, it was partly plagiarized from Tomasz Honkisz, "Opór cywilny czy walka zbrojna? Dylematy polskiego podziemia politycznego, 1945-1952," (Ph.D. thesis, Warszawa, Akademia Nauk Społecznych przy Komitecie Centralnym Polskiej Zjednoczonej Partii Robotniczej, 1990).

4   The first to champion the concept of the anti-Soviet and anti-Communist insurrection was the literary critic Bohdan Urbankowski, *Czerwona msza albo uśmiech Stalina* (Warszawa: Wydawnictwo Alfa, 1995), 206-207 [afterward *Czerwona msza*] (a second, expanded edition was published in 1998 in two volumes). Others dubbed the rising a "pacification", "a gigantic hunt" (Jerzy Ślaski) or even "a peasant war" (Andrzej Paczkowski), pointing out the social composition of the insurgent units. However, Paczkowski ignores the fact that the social composition of the partisan units was very similar during the Nazi occupation and that certainly was not "a peasant war." See Jerzy Ślaski, "Siły zbrojnego oporu antykomunistycznego w latach 1944-1947," in Ajnenkiel, *Wojna domowa*, 46. Communist historians talked about "a revolution," "a gentle revolution," "a civil war," and (later) about "elements of civil war." See [Stanisława Sowińska "Barbara"], *Obóz reakcji polskiej w latach 1939-45* (Warszawa: Główny Zarząd Informacji W.P., 1948); Jan Borkowski, "Walka polityczna w Polsce

w latach 1945-1947," in *Z najnowszych dziejów Polski, 1939-1947*, ed. by Władysław Góra and Janusz Gołębiowski (Warszawa: Państwowe Zakłady Wydawnictw Szkolnych, 1963), 406-30; Franciszek Ryszka, ed., *Polska Ludowa, 1944-1950: Przemiany społeczne* (Wrocław: Wydawnictwo Zakładu Narodowego im. Ossolińskich, 1974) [afterward *Polska Ludowa*]; Władysław Góra and Zenon Jakubowski, *Z dziejów organów bezpieczeństwa i porządku publicznego w województwie lubelskim, 1944-1948* (Lublin: Wydawnictwo Lubelskie, 1978), 201 [afterward *Z dziejów organów*]. The current work omits the very important problem of the Ukrainian nationalists' struggle against the Communists (essentially a dispute over territory and the resettlement of the Ukrainian population) and the relations of the Ukrainian insurgents to the Polish independentists. See Piotrowski, *Poland's Holocaust*, 234-58; Roman Drozd, ed., *Ukraińska Powstańcza Armia: Dokumenty-struktury* (Warszawa: Burchard Edition, 1998) [afterward *UPA dokumenty*]; Grzegorz Motyka and Rafał Wnuk, *Pany i rezuny: Współpraca AK-WiN i UPA, 1945-1947* (Warszawa: Oficyna Wydawnicza Volumen, 1997) [afterward *Pany i rezuny*]; Wiktor Poliszczuk, *Dowody zbrodni OUN i UPA: Działalność ukraińskich struktur nacjonalistycznych w latach 1920-1999* (Toronto: n.p., 2000).

5   This was an unprecedented event in the annals of international relations. The Soviet government kidnapped the Polish underground government and put its members on trial in a Soviet court and applying Soviet law. See John Micgiel, "'Bandits and Reactionaries': The Suppression of the Opposition in Poland, 1944-1946," in Naimark and Gibianskii, *The Establishment of Communist Regimes*, 93-110; Waldemar Strzałkowski, ed., *Proces Szesnastu: Dokumenty NKWD* (Warszawa: Rytm, 1995).

6   These figures are for the period between 1944 and 1956 but they do not include the Polish losses in the Eastern Borderlands. In the Provinces of Wilno and Nowogródek alone the NKVD arrested 13,000 Home Army soldiers, killed up to 3,000, and sent more than 20,000 people (including Polish civilians) to the Gulag. See Maria Stanowska, "Sprawy polityczne z lat 1944-1956 w świetle orzeczeń rehabilitacyjnych Sądu Najwyższego w latach 1988-1991," *Studia Juridica* [Warsaw] 27 (1995): 67; Leszek Żebrowski, "Czas liczenia, czas rozliczeń...," *Nasza Polska*, 3 March 1999, 10; Henryk Piskunowicz, "Zwalczanie polskiego podziemia przez NKWD i NKGB na kresach północno-wschodnich II Rzeczypospolitej," in Ajnenkiel, *Wojna domowa*, 70 [afterward "Zwalczanie"]; Krzysztof Szwagrzyk, *Zbrodnie w majestacie prawa* (Warszawa: ABC, 2000). See also Andrzej Paczkowski, "Poland, the 'Enemy Nation,'" in Stéphane Courtois et al., *The Black Book of Communism: Crimes, Terror, Repression* (Cambridge, Mass., and London: Harvard University Press, 1999), 363-93; and Marek Tuszyński, "Soviet War Crimes Against Poland During the Second World War and Its Aftermath," *The Polish Review*, 2 (1999): 183-216.

7   See Aleksander Gella, *Zagłada Drugiej Rzeczypospolitej, 1945-1947* (Warszawa: Agencja Wydawnicza CB, 1998); Ryszard Terlecki, *Dyktatura zdrady: Polska w 1947 roku* (Kraków: Wydawnictwo Arka, 1991); Tadeusz Żenczykowski, *Polska Lubelska 1944* (Paris: Editions Spotkania, 1987); Barbara Otwinowska and Jan Żaryn, eds., *Polacy wobec przemocy, 1944-1956* (Warszawa: Editions Spotkania, 1996); Stanisław Murzański, *PRL Zbrodnia niedoskonała: Rozważania o terrorze władzy i społecznym oporze* (Warszawa: Oficyna Wydawnicza Volumen i Wydawnictwo Alfa, 1996) [afterward *PRL zbrodnia niedoskonała*]; Roman Bäcker et al., *Skryte oblicze systemu komunistycznego: U źródeł zła* (Warszawa: Towarzystwo im. Stanisława ze Skarbmierza i Wydawnictwo DiG, 1997) [afterward *Skryte oblicze*]; Zbigniew Taranienko, ed., *Nasze Termopile: Dokumenty terroru, 1944-1956* (Warszawa:

Wydawnictwo Archidiecezji Warszawskiej, 1993); Krzysztof Szwagrzyk, ed., *Golgota wrocławska, 1945-1956* (Wrocław: Wydawnictwo "Klio," 1996) [afterward *Golgota*]; Sławomir Pająk, ed., *Straceni w polskich więzieniach, 1944-1956* (Lublin: Retro, 1994); Krzysztof Persak, ed., *Komuniści wobec harcerstwa, 1944-1950* (Warszawa: ISP PAN, 1998); Andrzej Garlicki, ed., *Z tajnych archiwów* (Warszawa: Polska Oficyna Wydawnicza "BGW," 1993); Wojciech Roszkowski, *Historia Polski, 1914-2000* (Warsaw: PWN, 2001).

III

THE JEWISH COMMUNITY AND THE COMMUNISTS
(1944-1947)

Statistics concerning the Jewish community in Poland between 1944 and 1947 are imperfect estimates. This was a period of constant flux and massive migrations that also affected the Jews. According to the most often quoted figures, between 50,000 and 100,000 Jews survived the war in Poland. A minimum of 20,000 and a maximum of 40,000 returned home from Germany and other Western countries. The figures for the repatriation of Polish Jews from the Soviet Union ranged from 100,000 to 200,000. Many Jews, 100,000 to 150,000, chose to emigrate from Poland to Palestine and the West. However, at its peak in the spring of 1946, the Jewish community numbered between 180,000 and 240,000 persons.

Between July 1944 and January 1945, Jews congregated mainly in Lublin. A minority went to smaller towns, where, for security reasons, they settled near the offices of government, police, and military. In February 1945, most of the Jewish population between the Vistula and the Bug rivers began to shift westward to large towns, the "Recovered Territories," and abroad. In June 1945, there were 10,000 Jews in Kraków, 9,000 in Warsaw, and 41,000 in Łódź. Furthermore, between 47,000 and 85,000 Jews settled in Silesia, especially in Wrocław.[1]

Jews were the only minority permitted legally to operate on the political plane. The Jewish community established its political representation, the Central Committee of Polish Jews (*Centralny Komitet Żydów Polskich — CKŻP*), by the end of 1944. It was headed by a prominent Zionist, Emil Sommerstein, who had just been released from the Gulag. The CKŻP attempted to restore Jewish life according to pre-war patterns, which meant separately from ethnic Poles. The CKŻP became involved in charitable, educational, and economic activities. By the end of 1945 it was caring for 700 Jewish children in its orphanages. It organized schools at all levels, including 36 elementary schools and 44 high schools, by June 1946. The languages of instruction were Yiddish and Polish. In addition, the CKŻP organized remedial courses. It fostered the creation of the Central Jewish Historical Commission *(Centralna Żydowska Komisja Historyczna – CŻKH)*, which in 1947 was transformed into the Jewish Historical Institute *(Żydowski Instytut Historyczny – ŻIH)* in Warsaw. The Jewish community published books and several score of Jewish papers. It operated three theaters. Finally, under the guidance of CKŻP, Jewish self-defense groups that had formed spontaneously to protect the community against common criminals and anti-Communist partisans were given an official seal of approval.

Religious and political organizations experienced rebirth as well. The pre-war religious community *(kehilot)* served as an institutional model for the followers of Judaism. All Jewish religious communities in Poland united to form the Jewish Confessional Association *(Żydowskie Zrzeszenia Religijne— ŻZR)*. Its president was Rabbi David Kahane, who also fulfilled the function of the Chief Rabbi of the Polish "people's" army.

Most of the Jewish institutions simply continued the work of their counterparts destroyed by the Nazis. These included the reborn Jewish political parties, which operated mostly under new names. The Marxist (but anti-Communist) Bund emerged from the underground as well as both wings of the Poale Zion party. The Right wing called itself the Zionist Workers Party *(Syjonistyczna Partia Robotnicza)*. The pro-Communist and pro-Soviet part dubbed itself the Zionist Workers Party of the Left *(Syjonistyczna Partia Robotnicza Lewicy)*. The centrist party of General Zionists renamed itself as the Union of Zionists-Democrats *(Zjednoczenie Syjonistów-Demokratów "Ichud")*. Religious Zionists remained with their old name – the *Mizrachi* party. However, the Communists banned the radical nationalist Zionist-Revisionist movement and greatly curtailed the Orthodox *Agudah Israel*. Therefore, the affiliates of the latter concentrated mostly on administering religious affairs. The activists of the former remained in the underground as the Jewish Military Union *(Irgun Tzvoi Leumi)*.[2]

Despite the official hostility toward the free market and private property, Jewish economic life thrived. The Polish historian Czesław Szczepańczyk has established that at that time 134 Jewish cooperatives were united in the Economic Center "Solidarity" *(Centrala Gospodarcza "Solidarność")*. The survivors opened up stores and small enterprises. Many returned to trade and crafts. Thousands found employment in industry, in Silesia in particular.[3] According to Polish scholar Marian Muszkiewicz, "it seems that as the time went on the Jewish population was returning to its traditional professions."[4] *In this respect, the conduct of the Jews was similar to that of the Poles. Wherever Communist interference was lacking, both ethnic groups reverted to pre-war, traditional customs and modes of social life.* This, of course, ended in 1947 with the government asserting its power over the economy and other aspects of life.

The relationship between the Communists and Jews was quite complex. On the one hand, the Jewish minority traditionally sought protection from any central authority to shield it from the majority population. On the other hand, the Communists used the Jewish community for a public relations propaganda blitz staged for the benefit of Western public opinion. The Communists trumpeted throughout the world their role as sole protectors of the Jews in Poland. In reality, however, the regime failed to defend the Jews effectively against violence in which its security apparatus sometimes participated.[5] As Jan Tomasz Gross put it, "Anti-Semitism was skillfully used to provoke pogroms intended to compromise anti-Communist opposition in the eyes of the Western opinion."[6] Moreover, the government covertly resolved not to return Jewish property that had been confiscated by the Nazis, while making a pretence of satisfying Jewish claims. Generally, individuals could reclaim their property unless it was claimed by the Communist state. However, the Jewish community property was much harder to regain. For instance, in Bielsko-Biała the Communist regime retained the use and ownership of the erstwhile Jewish community building despite the efforts of the rightful owners to regain it. On the other hand, in Zabłudów the Jewish community sold its center.[7]

Some Jews were gradually able to reclaim their property. According to an account from Ostrowiec, "the Jews have little-by-little begun to get settled. Many have recovered their shops and houses."[8] Evidence culled mostly from Jewish memoirs shows that successful reclamation took place in individual instances in Kraków, Gorlice, Bielanka, Mszanka, Hrubieszów, Skarżysko, Mielec, Łosice, Lublin, Nisko, Chełm, Radom, Wasilków, Brańsk, Jędrzejów, Krośniewice, Strzyżów, Drohiczyn, and doubtless many other towns. Having analyzed the issue of Jewish property in Szydłowiec, Grzegorz Miernik concluded that many rightful owners who returned to that town were able to repossess their houses but most subsequently sold the properties and moved away.[9] Probably in many cases the rightful owners received less than the market value for the property sold. This was because both the owners were eager to leave Poland as soon as possible and because they believed that private property would soon be confiscated by the Communists, the latter reason surely reinforcing the former. For example, Maryla Westreich decided to sell an apartment building she inherited in Tarnów. According to her friend,

> She could hardly expect a windfall from this property. At that time Poland was under the Soviets, and it was widely expected that private property would be nationalized. A Polish gentile decided to take a chance and buy the building. She sold an entire apartment house of at least twelve apartments and several stores for $100.[10]

Some evidence suggests that even the lowest level elective bodies, the parish (*gmina*) councils, respected the rights of rightful owners, including Jews. Composed of non-Communists, at least in some cases these councils voted to restore land as well as small- and medium-sized businesses to their owners. For example, in the Parish of Zakrzówek, the county of Kraśnik, in the Province of Lublin, the Nazis confiscated 15 small plots of land from local Jews. These were rented to Polish Christians. Within half a year after the flight of the Nazis from the area in July 1944, six Jewish legal heirs were able to reclaim the land of their relatives because of the goodwill of parish authorities, mostly independentists.[11] However, such favorable decisions were often reversed or stonewalled by the Communist authorities at a higher level. For instance, Chana Kotlarz attempted to reclaim the sawmill of her relative who had been killed in the Holocaust. Despite the backing of the local parish council in Zaklików (composed mostly of independentists) and Christian workers at the sawmill, Kotlarz was prevented from recovering the property by the Communist county authorities. Likewise, in March 1945 Itzhak Kac attempted to reclaim a mill in Kraśnik. Alas, the Communist-run Peasant Self-Aid cooperative objected with a spurious counterclaim of its own. Kac failed to win his battle against this Communist institution and his mill eventually became state property.[12]

Nonetheless, lower courts that were initially run by the pre-war, independentist judges routinely awarded property back to lawful heirs despite the fact that the Communist police and bureaucracy could and did stall the execution of court orders. An analysis of several claims of Jews from Jedwabne filed with the town court of Łomża shows that the petitioners generally were able to reclaim their property as well as property inherited from deceased relatives.[13] Available evidence suggests that the situation was similar elsewhere. The Kielce town archive contains 279 volumes of documents concerning Jewish attempts to reclaim property. According to Krzysztof Urbański, the town court (*sąd grodzki*) heard and ruled on 90 per cent of cases immediately after the claim was made. Most rulings were in favor of the claimants. Since all was according to the law, the higher Communist organ of control (*Prokuratoria Generalna*), after reviewing several score of these verdicts, was able to reverse only a few during its surprise inspection in Kielce between September 25 and October 5, 1945.[14]

Thus, it was not the Communist government but the independentists and non-Communists in the state administration and judiciary that facilitated the return of some of the Jewish property expropriated by the Nazis. Jewish scholars fail to note that when they correctly observe that in terms of the legal process, "the return of Jewish property, if claimed by the owner or his descendant, and if not subject to state control, proceeded more or less smoothly."[15] According to Mark Verstandig, who was legal counsellor in a department of the Ministry of State Security, and, thus, a high-ranking underling of a leading secret policeman, Mojżesz Bobrowicki, aka Mieczysław Mietkowski, the unofficial Communist hostility toward property restoration was palpable:

> My second run-in with Colonel Mietkowski took place over legislation for the restitution of private property which had been confiscated by the Germans – or, to put it more simply, the return of Jewish property stolen by the Nazis.... In his view, it made no sense to restore nationalised property to private ownership... [Nevertheless, Verstandig argued that] for the government to take over only Jewish property formerly expropriated by the Nazis was in effect to sanction Nazi anti-Jewish laws. But the colonel continued to argue that it was illogical to return Jewish property when very soon all private property would be nationalised... It is worth noting that, while stubbornly promoting anti-Jewish legislation, Mietkowski was himself Jewish.[16]

Even when the Communists facilitated a mass exodus of Jews from Poland in 1946, it was probably to create more havoc in the West with a wave of unexpected refugees and to stir problems for the British in Palestine. According to Iwo Cyprian Pogonowski, this was a part of Stalin's master plan to conquer the Middle Eastern oil fields, an interesting conjecture that requires further research in the Soviet archives.[17]Nonetheless, undoubtedly until as late as 1949, Jews willing to leave Poland were assisted by the Communist regime. The Communist authorities routinely maintained contacts with left-wing Zionists, including Yitzhak Zuckerman who dealt with the secret police. The regime even allowed the Zionists of the radical-nationalist *Hagana* to train in a camp at Bolkowo in Silesia and provided Communist military instructors. Also, while Poland's borders were closely guarded, especially after 1945, the Communists permitted about 100,000 Jewish refugees to slip through them between May 1946 and March 1947. Finally, the regime turned a blind eye to some of its high ranking functionaries who helped smuggle weapons and volunteers to Sweden and Czechoslovakia to fight for a Jewish State in Palestine.[18]

Nonetheless, in time, after 1947, covert harassment of Jews turned into open persecution of the religious and anti-Communist part of the Jewish community, though generally not of Jews in positions of authority, contrary to the experience in the Soviet Union and some other satellites.[19] Although no statistics are yet available, at least some Jews, especially right-wing Zionists, found themselves in Communist jails for political reasons. Most notably, the proxy regime imprisoned the chairman of the Zionists-Revisionists, Dawid Draznin. Also several leaders of the underground Jewish Military Union were arrested, including Adam Wajnryb, Leon Dojksel, and Mordechaj Mitterman.[20] However, even the members of the Marxist Bund opposed the Communists. According to a denunciation penned by a Jewish Communist against a Bundist, "Marek Edelman distinguished himself the most [in criticizing the Communists and] he even launched himself forth to beat up [the pro-Communist Solomon] Fiszgrund, accusing him of being a lackey of the PPR and that he did everything the PPR told him to."[21] There was also some grass-roots opposition in the Jewish community to the Jewish participation in the Communist regime, the security apparatus in particular. An Orthodox Jew, Zygmunt (Srul) Warszawer of Łaskarzew, averred that

> after the war it was handled wrong. So many Jews signed up for the police and for the secret police. I would shout at them: Why are you people doing this? What do you need it for? You want to beat people up and shoot people? So go to Israel. You want to be a colonel or something in the government? Do it in your own country with your own people, but not here. There's a handful left of us and still you are pushing.[22]

According to a well-educated Zionist, who refused to join the Communist party, one couldn't help but be aware of living under a regime that was controlled by Moscow. Most Poles hated it. At the expense of the Russians, a very special kind of mockery emerged, and we all thumbed our noses both at Russians and at Polish members of the Communist Party. Unfortunately, many of those installed by the Russians as powers in the new Polish government were Jewish communists who had been wartime refugees in the USSR. For example, one of the leading lights of the Party was Jacob Berman, later to serve as Poland's deputy premier. This prominence of Jews among the ranks of their oppressors caused many Poles to deflect their hatred from Russians toward Jews in general.[23]

Finally, some of the Polonized Jews and Poles of Jewish origin actively opposed the Communists, even by participating in the independentist underground. It seems that many such persons concealed their political affiliation and fled Poland as was the case with Józef Klinghofer who was involved with the independentists during the first Soviet occupation in Lwów (1939-41) and the Nazi occupation in Warsaw (1941-44). Also Dr. Roman Born-Borstein, who had belonged to a leftist clandestine group but during the Warsaw Uprising of 1944 fought in the ranks of the National Armed Forces, escaped to the West after having experienced persecution by the secret police.[24] However, some continued their struggle for Poland's liberation also after 1944.

There were a few independentists with Jewish roots who were never caught. Ludwik Ehrlich, Stefan Kisielewski, and Krystyna Modrzewska ("Kret") were active in Poland. Stanisław Aronson ("Rysiek") fought at home, fled, and later assisted the anti-Communist underground from France. Others, however, fell victim to the secret police. In November 1945 the NKVD arrested 29 leading activists of the WiN, including two Poles of Jewish origin, Kazimierz Leski ("Bradl") and Aleksander Gieysztor ("Sergiusz"). In 1947 the UB captured another Pole with Jewish roots, Maria Hulewicz. She was a Home Army soldier and, later, personal secretary to the top opposition leader Stanisław Mikołajczyk. She was tortured and received a lengthy jail sentence. In November 1948 the Communists sentenced to six years a leading Socialist activist, Ludwik Cohn, and five of his ethnic Polish comrades.[25]

Another assimilated Jew, Ludwik Fiedler, was "involved with the rightist underground" and after the war "obtained a senior post in the district government." He gathered intelligence for the underground. Among other things, Fiedler allegedly supplied the independentists with lists of Jewish Communists who had Polonized their names and were

38 AFTER THE HOLOCAUST

passing as "Aryans." Fiedler was arrested. A Polish Christian lawyer defended him, while a Jewish Communist prosecutor, Rumpler, attacked him mercilessly. "The trial lasted a single day. . . and Ludwik was sentenced to fifteen years of hard labor." Fiedler was maltreated while in jail.[26] For anti-Communist Jews and, in particular, for those with ties to the Polish independentists, there was no mercy.

The proxy regime in Poland treated Jewish Communists differently than the rest of the Jewish community. It created an official Jewish faction in the Polish Workers Party. In May 1947 the faction enrolled 7,000 members, mostly unassimilated Jews. The Polonized Jewish Communists usually joined the party as Poles.[27] This was also because the Communist leadership and rank-and-file accepted unassimilated Jews only grudgingly, and often with hostility. A top Communist leader, Władysław Gomułka, complained that "in Kraków... the head of the Personnel Department [of the party] has accepted 2,000 people (and they are Jews with bad [i.e. "Semitic"] appearance and bad pronunciation [of Polish])."[28] Many of these recruits were opportunists who found themselves in Communist ranks by force of circumstances. Their ethno-religious identity remains a source of controversy. Having researched the personnel of the Communist secret police on a local level (Katowice, Silesia), John Sack strongly disagrees that Jewish policemen lost their ethno-religious consciousness. According to Sack,

> they were 'more Communist than Jewish,' a University of California professor wrote — they were 'Communists from Jewish families,' 'Communists from Jewish backgrounds,' 'Communists of Jewish origin.' Now, I'd known these people seven years, and I'd never thought I would read that. I'd interviewed twenty-three Jews who'd been in the Office [i.e. the secret police], and one, just one, had considered himself a Communist in 1945. He and the others had gone to Jewish schools, studied the Torah, had been bar-mitzvahed, sometimes worn *payes*. In German camps, at the risk of their lives, some had made *matzo* on Pesach, and in 1945 they had lighted candles on Shabbas, held seders on Pesach, stood under *huppas* at weddings, sounded *shofars* on Rosh Hashanah, and fasted on Yom Kippur. By whose definition weren't they Jews? Not by the Talmud's, certainly not by the government of Israel's or the government of Nazi Germany's. Had they died in the Holocaust, I'd have guessed that the world would count them among the six million.[29]

Concerning such "Communists" of Jewish origin the scholar Bernard Weinryb avers that "for some years after the war, observance of such holidays as the [Jewish] New Year and Passover became something of a public affair, with thousands of Jews – *among them members of the militia and armed forces* – participating in the synagogue services and at public *Seders* [emphasis added]."[30]

According to an anti-Communist Pole of Jewish origin,

> I could not help but notice Jews in prominent and crucial posts in the military, the administration, and the leadership of the security police. The very same people who had just been telling us about the freezing cold, the hunger, the [Siberian] camps, the lice, the corruption, and ice-covered deportation transports, were now voluntarily joining to serve a system which modeled itself on the ideology and practice of the country where they had been exiled to. I noticed quite a bit of over-zealousness among them. I could not help but notice that and equally I could not understand that.[31]

One of the overzealous explains,

> I was working at the time as a journalist for a supposedly apolitical paper called *Polish Word*, published in Wrocław. In charge of its various local editions, I was in line for promotion to the post of assistant editor. It was less my talent than my being an ex-concentration camp prisoner and a Jew that had enabled me to advance so quickly. The Communist regime helped people like me to get ahead because it didn't trust the Polish-Catholic intelligentsia. The youngest of three assistant editors on the staff of *Polish Word*, one of Wrocław's two mass-circulation dailies, I had already reached the pinnacle of my profession by the age of twenty-three. The very top, of course, was for Party members alone.[32]

Nonetheless, any estimates of the numbers of Communists of Jewish origin (and Jews in general) are complicated by the fact that at least some of them continued to pass as "Aryans" under assumed Polish identities. According to a witness, "I never gave away my Jewish identity – and neither did Lutek [both non-Communist Jews]. I also found out later that the much-respected head of the Sopot hospital was Jewish. She was a colonel in the Polish army who hid her Jewishness too. Neither Lutek nor

I knew her real identity."[33] Likewise, the prominent pre-war Zionist activist Jerzy Reisler of Lwów retained his Aryan identity. As Jerzy Sawicki he became a leading state prosecutor for the Communists. Arguably one of the most notorious Stalinist prosecutors and a trusted crony of the secret police Fajga Mindla Danielak operated under an assumed name, Helena Wolińska. Her husband, Beniamin Zylberberg, under the pseudonym Włodzimierz Brus, served first as a political commissar in the "Polish" Communist army, and, then, as a Marxist economist in Warsaw. Witold Hochberg headed the Communist police in a small town outside Lublin using an assumed name Góra. There were many others like them.[34]

The exception among the Communists were "Poles of Mosaic faith." The few of them who joined the PPR were thoroughly acculturated and often had impeccable patriotic credentials, at least until 1939, including for example the first Chief-in-Command of the Communist army, General Zygmunt Berling, an erstwhile legionary of Marshal Józef Piłsudski and a career officer in Poland's pre-war military, who had listed Judaism as his faith while a law student in Kraków before 1914. Also General Marian Spychalski, who served as the Communist minister of defense, could boast of both a patriotic Polish family and a Jewish pedigree. His step-brother was a high-ranking Home Army officer killed by the Nazis. However, there were also the die-hard Communists, mostly Polonized culturally, who occupied top positions in the party.[35]

Although he left out the ethnic Pole Władysław Gomułka, the Soviet ambassador in Warsaw claimed that "the leading heart of the [Communist] party consists of [Bolesław] Bierut, [Jakub] Berman, [Hilary] Minc,... [and Roman] Zambrowski. Among them only Bierut is of Polish nationality."[36] The other three members of the Politburo were Jewish. While Minc controlled the economy, Berman supervised the secret police and culture. Zambrowski was in charge of destroying private trade, which included expropriating and dispatching "speculators" to forced labor camps, and, later, of collectivizing agriculture.

There were also other very prominent Communists of Jewish origin. According to Antoni Czubiński, one of them, General Karol Świerczewski, headed the Second Polish "people's" army. Dawid Hübner, aka Juliusz Hibner, eventually became the chief of the internal security troops. Wacław Kucyk, aka Komar, and Henryk Toruńczyk supervised military intelligence. According to Jerzy Morawski, Colonel Samuel Lewin headed the Substitute Units of Military Service (*Jednostki Zastępcze Służby Wojskowej*). In reality these were militarized slave-labor battalions created specifically for the children of the "enemies of the people," i.e. the independentists, who were drafted by force and sent to work without any protective gear in uranium and coal mining as well as other hazardous tasks.

The historian Barbara Fijałkowska has described the careers of the Goldberg brothers, Józef and Beniamin. The former as "Jacek Różański" was a high ranking officer of the UB; the latter as "Jerzy Borejsza" was a Stalinist cultural dictator in Poland. According to John Gunther, Zygmunt Modzelewski, the proxy regime's envoy in Moscow, who eventually became Foreign Minister, also had a Jewish background.[37]

Regarding these Communists of Jewish origin, sociologists Jan Tomasz Gross and Jaff Schatz have argued about the loss, or at least submergence, of their Jewish consciousness at that point in their lives.[38] Nonetheless, most people did not perceive them as Polish. Even the Soviet ambassador in Warsaw referred to these Communists as "a group of activists distinctly suffering from Jewish nationalism."[39]

Ideologically, a Polish socialist of Jewish origin divided Jewish Communists into three categories:

> The first consisted of those Communists who are so crazed by the [Marxist] doctrine that they are forgetting about the interests of the Polish nation, the Jewish nation, and Polish-Jewish cooperation. What is even worse is that they identify the doctrine with the interests of the Soviet Union which is considered a dual enemy of the Polish nation: as a representative of Russian interests and as a Communist state. This [first] Communist element... harmed Polish-Jewish coexistence the most. These are the people who, disregarding their origin, took upon themselves the fulfillment of the dirtiest political and police tasks. It is no wonder that in the general opinion the Jews rule Poland, that the Jews are lackeys of the Soviets, and that the Jews submitted Poland to Communism...
>
> The second group of Polish-Jewish Communists vacillates between the interests of the doctrine and the nation and it attempts to maintain a balance between both. It is a disproportionally very numerous group... These Jews are conscious of their Jewish origin and, with the memories about the lot of Jews in Soviet Russia before their eyes, they aim at adapting the [Marxist] doctrine to Polish conditions and to limiting [Poland's] dependence on the Soviet Union in their own interest and that of the Polish nation...
>
> Last, there is a third group, not a numerous one, fortunately. It thinks in the Jewish way, although it claims adherence to Polish Communism. These [people] have not found a balance between the

[Marxist] doctrine, Polishness, and their Jewish origin. These are revanchist elements, concentrated mostly in the security police, who would like to use the Communist doctrine to uproot and annihilate bellicose anti-Semitism.[40]

Thus it was a combination of opportunists and true believers from among the Jews who served Stalin. It seems that until at least 1947 these were a minority of the Jewish community. After the great wave of Jewish emigration from Poland, according to the historian Michael C. Steinlauf, "many of those who stayed had political reasons for doing so; their group profile ever more closely resembled the mythic Żydokomuna ['Judaeo-Commune', i.e. the alleged Jewish-Communist conspiracy].'"[41]

Israeli historians Yisrael Gutman and Shmuel Krakowski explain that even earlier

it was certainly undeniable that Jews were to be found among the upper echelons of the regime and within the government bureaucracy. By and large Jews had responded favorably to the new regime, which, in contrast to the Polish government between the wars and the major groups in the wartime resistance, had treated them with understanding and, at times, even sympathy. And the regime had accepted a relatively large number of Jews into its apparatus because it encountered difficulties in finding suitable candidates in sufficient number among the Polish intelligentsia, which had been greatly depleted during the war and many of whom either emigrated or had reservations about the government or were openly hostile to it.[42]

Gutman and Krakowski point out that the Jews worked in "civil service..., press, radio, literature, and culture-related fields."[43] However, the Jewish Communists were also prominent in the military and security establishment. They were recruited from among the Communist army in the Soviet Union, Soviet and Communist partisans in Poland, and even former prisoners of Nazi concentration camps.[44]

According to a Soviet report of July 1944 concerning the Communist Polish army,

out of 44 officers of the [Chief] Political Directorate...[there are] 34 Jews...[and] all leadership posts... are staffed with Jews. The deputy commanders of divisions and brigades are Jews, except for one Pole... In the political sections of the division, 17 out of 28 responsible political workers are Jews; on the regimental level, there are 31 Jews out of 43 political workers. In the regimental political apparatus of individual regiments... there are [Jews but] no Poles. Out of 86 deputy battalion commanders, 57 are Jews.[45]

According to an NKVD report of October 1945, "18.7% of employees in the Ministry of Public Security are Jews. 50% of the leadership posts are occupied by Jews."[46] Later, the Soviet ambassador in Warsaw claimed that "in the apparatus of the Ministry of Public Security, starting with deputy ministers going to the departmental directors, there is not a single Pole. They are all Jews. Jews only work at the Department of [Military] Intelligence."[47] Nonetheless it seems that, in time, such over-representation of Communists of Jewish origin probably was reversed by vigorous recruitment of Polish cadres.[48] In fact, between 1944 and 1947 most secret policemen at the county and province level likely were ethnic Poles.[49] The majority of the rank-and-file of the regular police and the army were also ethnic Poles. Nonetheless, because of the prominence of Soviets, Jews, and other minorities in the leadership, many of their fellow citizens perceived the new regime in Poland as alien.[50] This perception figured prominently in insurgent propaganda.

Notes

1   For the most precise estimates of Jewish returns from the USSR see Ciesielski, Hryciuk and Srebrakowski, *Masowe deportacje*, 79-81. For overall statistics see Irena Hurwic-Nowakowska, *Żydzi polscy (1947-1950): Analiza więzi społecznej ludności żydowskiej* (Warszawa: Wydawnictwo Instytutu Filozofii i Socjologii Polskiej Akademii Nauk, 1996), 24-32; Lucjan Dobroszycki, *Survivors of the Holocaust in Poland: A Portrait Based Jewish Community Records, 1944-1947* (Armonk, NY, and London: M.E. Sharpe, 1994), 12-14, 16, 21, 22-26, 67-85; Alina Cała, "Mniejszość żydowska," in *Mniejszości narodowe w Polsce: Państwo i społeczeństwo polskie a mniejszości narodowe w okresach przełomów politycznych (1944-1989)*, ed. by Piotr Madajczyk (Warszawa: Instytut Studiów Politycznych Polskiej Akademii Nauk, 1998), 245-46 [afterward "Mniejszość żydowska," in *Mniejszości narodowe w Polsce*]; Zorach Warhaftig, *Refugee and Survivor: Rescue Efforts During the Holocaust* (Jerusalem: Yad Vashem and Torah Education, 1988), 296-97; Mahler, "Eastern," in Schneiderman and Maller, *American*, 47: 399-400; Schneiderman, "Eastern," in Schneiderman and Maller, *American*, 48: 338-40, 346-49; Shapiro, "Poland," in Schneiderman and Fine, *American*, 49: 380-84; Weinryb, "Poland," in Meyer at al., *The Jews in the Soviet Satellites*, 207, 239-41, 268. Other estimates are given by Western and Polish historians cited below.

2   All Zionist parties were liquidated by the Communists between December 1, 1949, and January 1, 1950. See Ministerstwo Administracji Publicznej do Urzędów Wojewódzkich (wszystkich), oraz Zarządów m.st. Warszawy i m. Łodzi, Likwidacja żydowskich organizacji syjonistycznych, 13 December 1949, Archiwum Państwowe w Białymstoku, Urząd Wojewódzki Białostocki [afterward APB, UWB], file 690, 13. See also Rzeczpospolita Polska, Ministerstwo Pracy i Opieki Społecznej, Referat dla Spraw Pomocy Ludności Żydowskiej, "Trzynaste sprawozdanie z działalności (za miesiąc lipiec b.r.)," 31 July 1945, Archiwum Urzędu Rady Ministrów, Prezydium Rady Ministrów, Biuro Prezydialne [afterward AURM, PRM, BP], file 5/137, 20-23; Główny Rabin WP ppłk. Dawid Kahane do Ob. Starosty Grodzkiego w Kraśniku, 6 August 1945, Protokół Nr 3 z posiedzenia zarządu Żydowskiego Zrzeszenia Religijnego w Kraśniku, 12 August 1945, Archiwum Państwowe w Lublinie, Oddział w Kraśniku, Starostwo Powiatowe w Kraśniku, Stowarzyszenia i Związki, Żydowska Kongregacja Wyznaniowa, 1945-1948 [afterward APLOK, SPK, SiZ, ŻKW], file 107; Przewodniczący ["Jhudu"] Izak Giterman w Kraśniku do Starosty Powiatowego, 3 August 1945, APLOK, SPK, SiZ, Sprawy ogólne, 1945, file 81; Izrael Białostocki, "Wojewódzki Komitet Żydów Polskich w Szczecinie (1946-1950)," *BŻIH* [Warszawa] 71-72 (July-December 1969): 83-105 [afterward "Wojewódzki"]; Zygmunt Hoffman, "Związek Partyzantów Żydów," *BŻIH* 2 (94) (April-June 1975): 49-55; Leszek Olejnik, "Wojewódzki Komitet Żydowski w Łodzi – powstanie i główne kierunki działalności (1945-1950)," *BŻIH* 3 (187) (September 1998): 3-22; August Grabski, "Związek Żydów Uczestników Walki Zbrojnej z Faszyzmem (1947-1949)," *BŻIH* 2 (190) (June 1999): 23-39; Mahler, "Eastern Europe," in Schneiderman and Maller, *American*, 47: 398-404; Shapiro, "Poland," in Schneiderman and Fine, *American*, 49: 386-89; Weinryb, "Poland," in Meyer et al., *The Jews in the Soviet Satellites*, 278-89; Eugenio Reale, *Raporty: Polska, 1945-1946* (Warszawa: Państwowy Instytut Wydawniczy, 1991), 229-45 [afterward *Raporty*]; Hanna Shlomi, "The 'Jewish Organising Committee' in Moscow and the 'Jewish Central Committee' in Warsaw, June 1945-February 1946: Tackling Repatriation," *Jews in Eastern Poland and the USSR, 1939-1946*, ed. by Norman Davies and Antony Polonsky (London: Macmillan,

1991), 240-54 [afterward "The 'Jewish Organising Committee'" in *Jews in Eastern Poland*]; Rafał Żebrowski and Zofia Borzymińska, *Po-lin: Kultura Żydów polskich w XX wieku (Zarys)* (Warszawa: Wydawnictwo Amarant, 1993), 300-31 [afterward *Polin*]; Szaynok, "Ludność," in Lewczuk, *Studia*, 2: 71-88; Józef Orlicki, *Szkice z dziejów stosunków polsko-żydowskich, 1918-1949* (Szczecin: Krajowa Agencja Wydawnicza, 1983), 161-262 [afterward *Szkice*].

3   See Mahler, "Eastern," in Schneiderman and Maller, *American*, 47: 402-403; Shapiro, "Poland," in Schneiderman and Fine, *American*, 49: 389-91; Weinryb, "Poland," in Meyer at al., *The Jews in the Soviet Satellites*, 268-77; Czesław Szczepańczyk, "Wpływ wojny i okupacji na sytuację spółdzielczości polskiej i jej rola w odbudowie kraju do 1948 r.," in Długoborski, Klimczak and Kaszuba, *Gospodarcze*, 219-20.

4   Marian Muszkiewicz, "Wpływ okupacji na przemiany struktury społecznej i gospodarczej drobnomieszczaństwa polskiego," in Długoborski, Klimczak, and Kaszuba, *Gospodarcze*, 235.

5   See Shapiro, "Poland," in Schneiderman and Fine, *American*, 49: 385-86; Weinryb, "Poland," in Meyer et al., *The Jews in the Soviet Satellites*, 258-65, 282-84, 290-307.

6   Gross, "War," in Naimark and Gibianskii, *The Establishment of Communist Regimes*, 34.

7   Danuta Wiewióra, "Kilka uwag o losach społeczności żydowskiej w Bielsku-Białej po 1945 r.," *Żydzi w Bielsku, Białej i okolicy: Materiały z sesji naukowej odbytej w dniu 19 stycznia 1996 r.*, ed. by Jerzy Polak and Janusz Spyra (Bielsko-Biała: Muzeum Okręgowe i Urząd Miejski w Bielsku-Białej, 1996), 132; Szymon Datner, Wojewódzki Związek Gmin Żydowskich w Białymstoku, "Upoważnienie," 23 April 1945, concerning the reclamation and subsequent sale of Jewish community property in Zabłudów (a copy in my collection).

8   "Ostroviec Jewry exists no more!" *The Ostrowiec Memorial Book: A Monument on the Ruins of an Annihilated Jewish Community* posted at <http://www.kampel.com/ memorial/yzkor/ostrowiec/index.htm>.

9   See Sara Rosen, *My Lost World: A Survivor's Tale* (London: Vallentine Mitchell, 1993), 289; Samuel P. Oliner, *Restless Memories: Recollections of the Holocaust Years* (Berkeley, CA: Judah L. Magnes Museum, 1988), 182 [afterward *Restless Memories*]; Samuel P. Oliner, *Narrow Escapes: A Boy's Holocaust Memories and Their Legacy* (St. Paul, Minnesota: Paragon House, 2000), 153-54 [afterward *Narrow Escapes*]; Michael Korenblit and Kathleen Janger, *Until We Meet Again: A True Story of Love and War, Separation and Reunion* (New York: G.P. Putnam's Sons, 1983), 286; Diana Binder [pseud.], "Abandoned," *Heroes of the Holocaust*, ed. by Arnold Geier (Miami, FL: Londonbooks, 1993), 219 [afterward "Abandoned" in *Heroes*]; John Munro, *Białystok to Birkenau: The Holocaust Journey of Michel Mielnicki* (Vancouver: Ronsdale Press and Vancouver Holocaust Education Centre, 2000), 13, 221-22 [afterward *Białystok to Birkenau*]; Oscar Pinkus, *A Choice of Masks* (Engelwood Cliffs, NJ: Prentice-Hall, 1969), 6, 23, 75 [afterward *A Choice of Masks*]; Noach Lasman, *Wspomnienia z Polski, 1 sierpnia 1944-30 kwietnia 1957* (Warszawa: Żydowski Instytut Historyczyny, 1997), 25 [afterward *Wspomnienia*]; Alexander Bronowski, *They Were Few* (New York: Peter Lang, 1991), 42 [afterward *They Were Few*]; Stanisław Puchalski, *Partyzanci "Ojca Jana"* (Stalowa Wola: Światowy Związek Żołnierzy AK — Koło w Stalowej Woli, 1996), 459 [afterward *Partyzanci*]; Mark Verstandig, *I Rest My Case* (Melbourne: Saga Press, 1995), 204, 212 [aferward *I Rest My Case*]; Barbara Stanisławczyk, *Czterdzieści twardych* (Warszawa: Wydawnictwo ABC, 1997), 142, 251-52 [afterward *Czterdzieści twardych*]; Jerzy Niczyporowicz,

"Ciemność z jasnością," *Rzeczpospolita: Plus-Minus*, 20-21 May 2000; Sabina Rachela Kałowska, *Uciekać, aby żyć* (Lublin: Norbertinum, 2000), 236-37 [afterward *Uciekać, aby żyć*]; Abram Korn, *Abe's Story: A Holocaust Memoir* (Atlanta, GA: Longstreet Press, 1995), 169; Itzhok Berglass, "After the War and the Holocaust," in *Strzyżów, Poland: Sefer Strizhuv ve-ha-seviva (Memorial Book of Strzyzow and vicinity)*, ed. by J. Berglas and Sh. Zahalomi (Diamant) (Tel Aviv: Former Residents of Strzyzow in Israel and Diaspora, 1969), posted at http://www.jewishgen.org/yizkor/ Strzyzow/Str245.html [afterward *Sefer Strizhuv*, Internet]; Shumel Mordechai Lev, "Diary of Pain and Suffering: Pages from a Diary in the Years of the Holocaust," *Sefer Drohiczyn: Drohiczyn Book*, ed. by D. Shtokfish (Tel Aviv: n.p., 1969), posted at http://www.jewishgen.orgyizkor/Drohiczyn/Dro042e.html [afterward *Sefer Drohiczyn*, Internet]; Grzegorz Miernik, "Losy Żydów i nieruchomości pożydowskich w Szydłowcu po II wojnie światowej," *Żydzi szydłowieccy: Materiały sesji popularnonaukowej 22 lutego 1997 roku*, ed. by Małgorzata Piątkowska (Szydłowiec: Muzeum Ludowych Instrumentów Muzycznych w Szydłowcu, 1997), 135-66.

10   William Kornbluth, *Sentenced to Remember: My Legacy of Life in Pre-1939 Poland and Sixty-Eight Months of Nazi Occupation* (Bethlehem, London and Toronto: Lehigh University Press and Associated University Press, 1994), 147 [afterward *Sentenced to Remember*].

11   See Wykaz gospodarstw poniżej 50 ha należących do obywateli polskich narodowości nieniemieckiej przed 1939 w gminie Zakrzówek, 22 February 1945, APLOK, Państwowy Urząd Ziemski 1944-1947 [afterward PUZ], Akta administracji, file 62.

12   See Starosta Powiatowy Jan Pytel w Kraśniku do Obywatela Zarządzającego tartakiem "Lipa" w Lipie, 15 November 1944, Starosta Powiatowy Jan Pytel w Kraśniku do Obywatela Zarządzającego tartakiem "Lipa" w Lipie, 5 December 1944, Chana Kotlarz w Lublinie do Starostwa Powiatowego w Kraśniku, 6 February 1945, Protokół zeznania Bolesława Woźniaka i Józefa Łyszczarza, 14 June 1945, APLOK, SPK, Różne, file 495; Protokół z II posiedzenia Prezydium Powiatowej Rady Narodowej odbytego w dniu 13.III.1945 r., APLOK, Powiatowa Rada Narodowa [afterward PRN], file 31; Wykaz większych przedsiębiorstw na terenie powiatu janowskiego, no date [June? 1945], APLOK, SPK, file 138.

13   The successful claimants of Jedwabne, including Josel Lewin and Gedala London, subsequently sold their properties to their Christian neighbors. At least fifteen Christian witnesses assisted their Jewish neighbors in reclaiming their property by testifying on behalf of the petitioners at the municipal court in Łomża. Similar conditions prevailed in Łomża, Zambrów, and Kolno. See cases Co. 3/1947, 4/1947, Co. 13/1947, Co. 35/1947, Co. 49/1947, Co. 52/1947, Co. 115/1947, Co. 116/1947, Co. 147/1947, Co. 149/1947, Co. 167/1947, Co. 168/1947, Co. 176/47, Co. 180/1947, Co. 116/1948, Co. 8/1949, Co. 10/1949, Co. 12/1949, Co. 13/1949, Co. 14/1949, Co. 16/1949, Co. 17/1949, Co. 18/1949, Co. 19/1949, Co. 22/1949, Zg. 98/1947, Zg. 1677/1947, Zg. 236/1947, Zg. 129/1948, Zg. 130/1948, Zg. 165/1948, Zg. 234/1948, Zg. 235/1948, Zg. 308/1948, Zg. 334/1948, and Zg. 356/1948 in Archiwum Państwowe w Białymstoku, Oddział w Łomży, Sąd Grodzki w Łomży [afterward APBOŁ, SGŁ]. There were also unsavory dealings in Jewish property and embezzlement in Jedwabne involving a Christian, Tadeusz Zarzecki, and several Jews, including Eliasz Grądowski, Chaim Sroczko, and Eliasz Trokenheim, who was the head of the Communist secret police in Łomża. Their scheme was foiled when one of their intended victims, Jan Cytrynowicz, also of Jewish origin, blew their cover. See Akta w sprawie Józefa Grądowskiego o

wprowadzanie w posiadanie nieruchomości, Akta w sprawie Eliasza Grądowskiego o wprowadzenie w posiadanie nieruchomości, and Akta w sprawie Symy-Zeldy Kuberskiej o wprowadzenie w posiadanie nieruchomości, APBŁ, SGŁ, Co. 35/1947, Co. 49/1947; Co. 10/1949; Danuta and Aleksander Wroniszewscy, "Odkrywanie tajemnicy," *Kulisy*, 7 June 2001, 24-25.

14 See Krzysztof Urbański, *Kieleccy Żydzi* (Kraków: Małopolska Oficyna Wydawnicza, [1993]), 183-91 [afterward *Kieleccy Żydzi*]. For favorable rulings by lower courts and unanswered petitions to higher judicial authorities in the county of Kraśnik see Zawiadomienie o wszczęciu egzekucji, 25 June 1948, Petycja do Prokuratury Generalnej w Warszawie, 7 October 1947, APLOK, SPK, Referat Rolnictwa i Reform Rolnych, Mienie porzucone i opuszczone pożydowskie, 1948, file 672. For Jewish-Polish property disputes in the county of Kraśnik, the Province of Lublin, see cases number 643, 644, 657, and 666 in APLOK, Sąd Grodzki w Kraśniku, Rejestr spraw, file 99. More broadly on property issues in Poland see Marek Jan Chodakiewicz, "*Restytucja*: The Problem of Property Restitution in Poland (1939-2001)," forthcoming in Marek Jan Chodakiewicz, John Radziłowski, and Dariusz Tołczyk, eds. *Polish Transformation: A Process Completed or Still in Progress?*. And see Leonid Smilovitsky, "The Struggle of Belorussian Jews for the Restitution of Possessions and Housing in the First Postwar Decade," *East European Jewish Affairs*, vol. 30, no. 2 (2000): 53-70. For a different conclusion concerning Jewish property after the war see the seriously underresearched work of Richard Z. Chesnoff, *Pack of Thieves: How Hitler and Europe Plundered the Jews and Committed the Greatest Theft in History* (New York: Doubleday, 1999), 180-81 [afterward *Pack of Thieves*].

15 See Shapiro, "Poland," in Schneiderman and Fine, *American*, 49: 390. See also Schneiderman, "Eastern," in Schneiderman and Maller, *American*, 48: 342-46; Weinryb, "Poland," in Meyer et al., *The Jews in the Soviet Satellites*, 244-45, 263-65, 267.

16 Verstandig, *I Rest My Case*, 216.

17 See Iwo Cyprian Pogonowski, *Jews in Poland: A Documentary History*, rev. ed. (New York: Hippocrene Books, Inc., 1998), 317-18, 351-52 [afterward *Jews in Poland*]; Iwo Pogonowski, interview by the author, Blacksburg, VA, 26 February 1999.

18 See Schneiderman, "Eastern," in Schneiderman and Maller, *American*, 48: 338-40; Weinryb, "Poland," in Meyer et al., *The Jews in the Soviet Satellites*, 254-57, 308-311; Cała and Datner-Śpiewak, *Dzieje Żydów*, 82-83, 130-31, 133; Ronald J. Berger, *Constructing A Collective Memory of the Holocaust: A Life History of Two Brothers' Survival* (Niwot, CO: University Press of Colorado, 1995), 96-97; Yitzhak Zuckerman ("Antek"), *A Surplus of Memory: Chronicle of the Warsaw Ghetto Uprising* (Berkeley, CA: University of California Press, 1993), 587, 651-52, 659-61, 665-77 [afterward *A Surplus of Memory*]; Michael Checinski, *Poland: Communism, Nationalism, Antisemitism* (New York: Karz-Cohl, 1983), 13 [afterward *Poland Communism*]; Michał Rudawski, *Mój obcy kraj* (Warszawa: Agencja Wydawnicza Tu, 1996) [afterward *Mój obcy kraj*], 178-197; Maurice Shainberg, *Breaking from the KGB: Warsaw Ghetto Fighter, Intelligence Officer, Defector to the West* (New York: Shapolsky Books, 1986), 209-14 [*Breaking from the KGB*]; Józef Adelson, "W Polsce zwanej ludową," *Najnowsze dzieje Żydów w Polsce w zarysie (do 1950 roku)*, ed. by Jerzy Tomaszewski (Warszawa: Wydawnictwo Naukowe PWN, 1993), 412-13 [afterward "W Polsce" in *Najnowsze*]; Jarosław Lipszyc, "Przystanek Dolny Śląsk," *Midrasz* [Warszawa], 7-8 (July-August 1998): 10-13; Natalia Aleksiun-Mądrzak, "Emigracja Żydów z Polski w latach 1945-1949," (M.A. thesis, University of Warsaw,

1995); Natalia Aleksiun, "Ruch syjonistyczny wobec systemu rządów w Polsce w
latach 1944-1949," in *Komunizm: Ideologia, System, Ludzie*, ed.
by Tomasz Szarota
(Warszawa: Wydawnictwo Neriton and Instytut Historii PAN, 2001), 233-51
[afterward "Ruch syjonistyczny wobec systemu rządów w Polsce w latach 1944-1949,"
in *Komunizm*]; and Arieh J. Kochavi, *Post-Holocaust Politics: Britain, the United
States, and Jewish Refugees, 1945-1948* (Chapel Hill and London: University of North
Carolina Press, 2001), 42, 46, 52, 136-37, 140, 157-81.

19   According to Andrzej Paczkowski, "In Moscow, they apparently ignored the opinion of
[the Soviet] ambassador [in Warsaw], who in February 1952 demanded the purge of the
leadership of the MBP [i.e. the Ministry of Public Security]. Nothing like that took
place. Even the anti-Semitic purge, which effected seriously the Soviet security
services and those of some other Communist states (Czechoslovakia, Rumania),
generally did not affect the security apparatus [in Poland]." See Andrzej Paczkowski,
"Wstęp," in Antoni Dudek and Andrzej Paczkowski, eds., *Aparat bezpieczeństwa w
Polsce w latach 1950-1952: Taktyka, strategia, metody* (Warszawa: Dom Wydawniczy
Bellona, 2000), 17.

20   These arrests occurred in 1947 and after. See *Informator*, 171; Bernardetta Gronek and
Irena Marczak, eds., *Biuletyny Informacyjne Ministerstwa Bezpieczeństwa
Publicznego, 1947* (Warszawa: Ministerstwo Spraw Wewnętrznych, 1993), 166
[afterward *Biuletyny 1947*]; Stankowski, "Emigracja Żydów," in Tomaszewski, *Studia*,
112. See also Bożena Szaynok, "Walka z syjonizmem w Polsce (1948-1953)," in
Szarota, *Komunizm*, 252-71.

21   Cała and Datner-Śpiewak, *Dzieje Żydów*, 132. Marek Edelman was a deputy
commander of the Jewish Fighting Organization in the Warsaw Ghetto Uprising in 1943.

22   See the interview with Zygmunt (Srul) Warszawer in Małgorzata Niezabitowska,
Remnants: The Last Jews of Poland (New York: Friendly Press, Inc., 1986), 125.
Warszawer was addressing a query about the persistence of anti-Semitism after the war.

23   Moshe Prywes as told to Haim Chertok, *Prisoner of Hope* (Hanover and London:
Brandeis University Press and University Press of New England, 1996), 174.

24   Klinghofer was a translator of the BBC service into Polish for the underground press.
See Irvin Klinghofer, "Joseph Klinghofer," *The Globe and Mail* [Toronto], 18 October
2000; Roman Born-Bornstein, *Powstanie Warszawskie: Wspomnienia* (London: Poets'
and Painters' Press, 1988), 77-78 [afterward *Powstanie Warszawskie*].

25   Cohn and one of his collaborators were soon released because of an amnesty. Aronson
moved to Israel, where he died recently. See Tatiana Cariewskaja et al., eds., *Teczka
specjalna J.W. Stalina: Raporty NKWD z Polski, 1944-1946* (Warszawa: ISP PAN, IH
UW, Rytm i APFR, 1998), 430-31 [afterward *Teczka specjalna*]; Stefan Kisielewski,
Dzienniki (Warszawa: Iskry, 1996), 364, 844; Krystyna Modrzewska, *Trzy razy Lublin*
(Lublin: Wydawnictwo Panta, 1991), 70 [afterward *Trzy razy Lublin*]; Murzański, *PRL
zbrodnia niedoskonała*, 123; Henryk Skwarczyński, interview by the author, Chicago,
12 October 1998.

26   See Henry Armin Herzog [aka Adam Budkowski], *...And Heaven Shed No Tears* (New
York: Shengold Publishers, Inc., 1995), 293, 303 [afterward *And Heaven*].

27   Maciej Pisarski, "'Na żydowskiej ulicy': Szkic do dziejów żydowskiej Frakcji PPR i
Zespołu PZPR przy CKŻP, 1945-1951," *BŻIH* 2 (182) (April-June 1994): 35-48.

28   Kochański, *Protokół KC*, 43.

29   See John Sack, *An Eye for an Eye* (New York: Basic Books, 1995), ix [this is the

paperback edition; all future references are to the hardback edition of 1993 cited as *An Eye for an Eye*].

30 Weinryb, "Poland," in Meyer et al., *The Jews in the Soviet Satellites*, 281.

31 Modrzewska, *Trzy razy Lublin*, 93.

32 Roman Frister, *The Cap or the Price of a Life* (London: Weidenfeld & Nicolson, 1999), 34, 227 [afterward *The Cap or the Price of a Life*].

33 Jack Klajman, *Out of the Ghetto* (London and Portland, OR: Vallentine Mitchell, 2000), 134.

34 Sometimes the Communists persuaded "Aryan-looking" Jewish comrades to conceal their ethnic origins and, "for the good of the cause," the latter became "statistical Poles." See Rudawski, *Mój obcy kraj?*, 143-44. See also Isaac J. Vogelfanger, *The Life of a Surgeon in the Gulag* (Montreal, Kingston, London, and Buffalo: McGill-Queen's University Press, 1996), 205; Ewa Berberyusz, *Książę z Maisons-Laffitte* (Gdańsk: Wydawnictwo Marabut, 1995), 39; Jerzy Sawicki, *Przed polskim prokuratorem: Dokumenty i komentarze* (Warszawa: Iskry, 1958); Tadeusz M. Płużański, "Polski Pinochet," *Tygodnik Solidarność*, 13 June 2001; Tadeusz Kowalik, "Włodzimierz Brus: W czyśćcu historii," *Gazeta Wyborcza*, 24 August 2001; Sprawozdanie Instruktora Wydziału Okr. Org. K.C. Brodzińskiego St. z przeprowadzonej inspekcji od dnia 12.8.45r. do dnia 18.8.45.r. na terenie miasta Łodzi, AAN, Komitet Centralny Polskiej Partii Robotniczej [afterward KC PPR], file 295/VII-51, vol. 3, 46; Leszek Żebrowski, "Ludzie UB – Trzy pokolenia," *Dekomunizacja i rzeczywistość* (Warszawa: Wydawnictwo Amarant, 1993), 51-60; Marian Fuks, "Prasa PPR i PZPR w języku żydowskim ('Fołks-Sztyme' 1946-1956)," *BŻIH* 3 (111) (July-September 1979): 21-35; Shainberg, *Breaking from the KGB*, 120-27; Harold Werner, *Fighting Back: A Memoir of Jewish Resistance in World War II* (New York: Columbia University Press, 1992), 232 [afterward *Fighting Back*]; Mark Kurlansky, *A Chosen Few: The Resurrection of European Jewry* (Reading, Mass.: Addison-Wesley Publishing Company, 1995), 68, 71, 133, 187,192 [afterward *A Chosen Few*].

35 Berling's religious faith is a mysterious issue. As a student, he listed Judaism twice in two separate questionnaires which are preserved in his file at the Jagiellonian University. However, his biographer claims that Berling was also baptized by his parents at a Catholic church but fails to provide any reference to the pertinent entry in the parish register. Siemaszko also fails to annotate his revelations about Spychalski's background adequately. Nonetheless, according to Zuckerman, Spychalski was his main ally in the Communist regime as far as expediting Jewish emigration from Poland was concerned. See Stanisław Jaczyński, *Zygmunt Berling* (Warszawa: Książka i Wiedza, 1993), 33; Z.S. Siemaszko, "Płk. Prawdzic-Szlaski organizator AK na Nowogródczyźnie," *Zeszyty Historyczne* [Paris] 67 (1984): 18 *n* 2; Zuckerman, *A Surplus of Memory*, 665-68.

36 Aleksander Kochański et al., eds., *Polska w dokumentach z archiwów rosyjskich, 1939-1953* (Warszawa: IS PAN, 2000), 41 [afterward *Polska w dokumentach*].

37 Antoni Czubiński, *Polska i Polacy po II wojnie światowej* (Poznań: Wydawnictwo Naukowe Uniwersytetu im. Adama Mickiewicza w Poznaniu, 1998), 145; Jerzy Morawski, "Niewolnicy PRL," *Rzeczpospolita*, 2 February 2001; Barbara Fijałkowska, *Borejsza i Różański: Przyczynek do dziejów stalinizmu w Polsce* (Olsztyn: Wyższa Szkoła Pedagogiczna, 1995), 12 [afterward *Borejsza i Różański*]; John Gunther, *Behind the Curtain* (New York: Harper and Brothers Publishers, 1949), 271; Krystyna Kersten,

Polacy, Żydzi, komunizm: Anatomia półprawd 1939-1968 (Warszawa: Niezależna Oficyna Wydawnicza, 1992) [afterward *Polacy i Żydzi*].

38 See Jan Tomasz Gross, *Upiorna dekada: Trzy eseje o stereotypach na temat Żydów, Polaków, Niemców i komunistów, 1939-1948* (Kraków: TAiWPN Universitas, 1998), 93-94 [afterward *Upiorna dekada*]; Jaff Schatz, *The Generation: The Rise and Fall of the Jewish Communists of Poland* (Berkeley: University of California Press, 1991), 48, 126-27, 218, 225-27, 314 [afterward *Generation*].

39 Kochański, *Polska w dokumentach*, 47.

40 Feliks Mantel, *Stosunki polsko-żydowskie: Próba analizy* (Paris: Księgarnia Polska, 1986), 10-11.

41 Michael Steinlauf, "Poland," in *The World Reacts to the Holocaust*, ed. by David S. Wyman and Charles H. Rosenzveig (Baltimore and London: The Johns Hopkins University Press, 1996), 113 [afterward "Poland" in *The World Reacts*]. See also Michael C. Steinlauf, *Bondage to the Dead: Poland and the Memory of the Holocaust* (New York: Syracuse University Press, 1997), 52 [afterward *Bondage to the Dead*].

42 Yisrael Gutman and Shmuel Krakowski, *Unequal Victims: Poles and Jews During World War Two* (New York: Holocaust Library, 1986), 367 [afterward *Unequal Victims*].

43 Gutman and Krakowski, *Unequal Victims*, 368.

44 For a case of an Auschwitz survivor who became a top secret policeman (the chief of the Political Division of the Central Command of the Citizens Militia) in Poland see Seweryn Bialer, "I Chose Truth: A Former Leading Polish Communist's Story," *News From Behind the Iron Curtain* vol. 5, no. 10 (October 1956): 3-15; Nick Eberstadt, "The Latest Myths About the Soviet Union," *Commentary* (May 1987): 17-27.

45 Bordiugow, *Polska-ZSRR*, 76. A deputy battalion commander was a political commissar.

46 Cariewskaja, *Teczka specjalna*, 421. It is unclear if 50% of leadership posts applies just to the Ministry of Public Security in Warsaw, or to the entire security apparatus, including its provincial branches.

47 Kochański, *Polska w dokumentach*, 46. The ambassador made his statement in 1949. Although no comprehensive, in-depth statistical studies of the security apparatus after 1944 have been published, the assertion that "only Jews" headed the terror machine must surely be an exaggeration. The ambassador completely disregarded the Soviet advisors and ethnic Polish Communists who occupied some leadership positions. See below.

48 See the internal publication of the secret police *Służba Bezpieczeństwa Polskiej Rzeczypospolitej Ludowej w latach 1944-1978* ([Warszawa:] Ministerstwo Spraw Wewnętrznych, Biuro "C" [1978?]). According to Andrzej Paczkowski and Leo Głuchowski, there were 25,600 personnel in the UB in November 1945. However, "there was a constant movement of lower-level cadres in and out of the UB between 1945 and 1946. At this time, approximately 25,000 employees left the UB; about the same number of cadres that were employed by the UB at the end of 1946. The majority had been released from the UB for drunkenness, theft, abuse, or for a lack of discipline." See Leo Gluchowski and Andrzej Paczkowski, "Stalin's security officers in Poland," *Times Literary Supplement*, 28 March 1997. The subject of the Jewish participation in the Communist regime, the secret police in particular, is very controversial. It still awaits solid research and dispassionate presentation. See Steinlauf, "Poland," in Wyman and Rosenzveig, *The World Reacts*, 112; Włodzimierz

Rozenbaum, "The Road to New Poland: Jewish Communists in the Soviet Union, 1939-46," in Davies and Polonsky, *Jews in Eastern Poland*, 224 [afterward "The Road to New Poland"]; Joan S. Skurnowicz, "Soviet Polonia, the Polish State, and the New Mythology of National Origins, 1943-1945," *Nationalities Papers* (Special Issue), Vol. XXII, Supplement No. 1 (Summer 1994): 93-110; Checinski, *Poland Communism*, 11; Sack, *An Eye for An Eye*, 176, 219; Piotrowski, *Poland's Holocaust*, 58-65, 131, 313-15; Stefan Korboński, *The Jews and Poles in World War II* (New York: Hippocrene Books, 1989), 71-86; Andrzej Paczkowski, "Żydzi w UB: Próba weryfikacji stereotypu," in Szarota, *Komunizm*, 192-204.

49 This certainly follows from the research of Krzysztof Szwagrzyk in Silesia and my own work in the county of Kraśnik, the Province of Lublin. See Szwagrzyk, *Golgota*, 37-71; Marek Jan Chodakiewicz, "Accommodation and Resistance: A Polish County During the Second World War and in Its Aftermath, 1939-1947," (PhD diss., Columbia University, 2000), 312-20. See also lists of secret policemen in "Lista bezpieczniaków," *Gazeta Polska*, 6, 13, 20, and 27 June, 18 and 25 July, 1 August and 26 September 1996; and "Lista sędziów i prokuratorów wojskowych z lat 1944-1956," *Gazeta Polska*, (July 1993): 10.

50 Poland's leading liberal of impeccable philosemitic credentials lamented that "the UB, [and] the judiciary are entirely in Jewish hands. In the past two years or more not one Jew faced a political trial. Jews arrest Poles and surrender them to be executed. And how can there be no vile anti-Semitism spreading in Poland?" See Maria Dąbrowska, *Dzienniki powojenne, 1945-1965*, vol. 1 (Warszawa: Czytelnik, 1996), 1: 146. Another philosemitic liberal recalled that "during the Stalinist times Communists and para-Communists of Jewish origin played an important role in the apparatus of repression [i.e. the secret police] and — perhaps foremost — in propaganda." See Anna Tatarkiewicz, "Prawda, tylko cała prawda," *Więź* (October 1999): 135. A Jewish source confirms the presence of Jews in the propaganda apparatus. See Alicja Zawadzka-Wetz, *Refleksje pewnego życia* (Paris: Instytut Literacki, 1967), 46-52 [afterward *Refleksje*]. For more information on the Jewish Communists in Poland see *Encyklopedia "Białych Plam"*, vol. 2: *Armia Polska na Wschodzie — Bernanos Georges* (Radom: Polskie Wydawnictwo Encyklopedyczne, 2000), s.v. "'Autorytety' w Polsce," 151-55, by Jerzy Robert Nowak; and Mirosław Malański, "'Słynny wydawca' antypolskiego *Maus*," *Nasza Polska*, 12 July 2000, 14.

IV

THE INDEPENDENTIST PROPAGANDA

After 1944 the Polish independentist (anti-Communist) underground was rather hostile toward the Jews. This enmity was engendered by the perception of the Jewish minority as apparently friendly toward, or even corresponding with, the Communists. To a certain extent, this attitude was a continuation of a similar war-time stance, exacerbated however by the Soviet occupation of Poland. The anti-Jewish animus was fully reflected in the propaganda of the underground but to a much lesser extent in its deeds, which were mostly a function of anti-Communism as determined by local conditions. Anti-Semitism on the part of Polish insurgents was not the primary motivation for the deaths of Jews.

As mentioned, the independentist camp consisted of all political forces in Poland, except the Communists. The insurgents were anti-German, anti-Soviet, and anti-Communist. Many of those independentists who remained underground after the arrival of the Soviet Army in the summer of 1944 were also hostile toward national minorities, including Jews. Their anti-Semitism, however, was mostly "Christian-conservative" rather than "racialist," according to standards introduced by the liberal scholar Peter Pulzer. He has shown that "the two cleavages overlap to a considerable degree," but the "Christian-conservative" brand of anti-Semitism did not advocate extermination of the Jews.[1] In Poland, "Christian-conservatives," or more properly "national-Christians," at the extreme advocated the expulsion of Jews and the ghettoization of those who remained. Moreover, of the two dominant orientations of the Polish post-war underground, the patriotic followers of the late Marshal Józef Piłsudski were much less hostile toward Jews and other minorities than were the nationalist supporters of the late Roman Dmowski.[2] To describe their Soviet and Communist enemies, however, the Polish post-war underground employed a generic catch phrase of "*żydokomuna*" (Judaeo-Commune). This term denoted a "Jewish Communist conspiracy," thus expressing anti-Communism in anti-Semitic terms.

53

The underground press and its dispatches reflected the strong nationalistic animus of the insurgents. Their message was predicated on a dichotomy of "true Poles" against "aliens." Already during the Nazi occupation the independentists regarded even ethnic Polish Communists as "non-Poles." For them, the only true Pole was an anti-Communist one (and an anti-German one of course). According to the main organ of the Home Army, "each worker, peasant, [and] member of the intelligentsia who gives in to the Communist propaganda [and] collaborates with the Communists becomes a traitor just like a *Volksdeutsche* [i.e. a Polish citizen of ethnic German origin who was a Nazi collaborator].... A Pole cannot be a Communist because he ceases to be a Pole."[3] At least some in the Polish underground, however, did conflate Jews and Communism. A contemporary Home Army report stressed:

It is universally known that the KPP [the Communist Party of Poland], as well as the Communist movement in general, was infused with Jewish elements and led by jews [sic], who displayed a hostile attitude against Poland. But also now the Jewish influence in the PPR is enormous. The Warsaw Ghetto is still the site of the Communist center in Poland. Among the Communist agents bustling about in the country, there are many jews [sic] passing as Poles, Ukrainians, Belorussians, or Russians. Jewish intelligentsia is Communized and displays an anti-Polish attitude to a degree not less than the Jewish proletariat does. The Communists have been defending Jews politically and have been promising them in the future Poland, which according to their designs will be a Soviet one, not so much equal rights but a leading position. We must be mindful of the stance of the Jewish masses in the tragic days of the fall of 1939 and later under the bolshevik [sic] occupation [when Jews allegedly collaborated with the Soviets]. *Antisemitism continues to be a very effective weapon in the struggle against Communism* [emphasis added].[4]

Certainly, all minorities were considered to be hostile to Poland because, as the American sociologist Tadeusz Piotrowski argues, the highly visible and dynamic extremists among them were disloyal toward the Polish majority and the Polish state during the war. According to Piotrowski, with limited encouragement from the occupying powers, the extremists spearheaded the separatist efforts. These apparently attracted considerable popular support (and, in the case of Ukrainian nationalists, unleashed a campaign of ethnic cleansing of the Polish population). Therefore, Poles projected the actions of the extremists onto their ethnic groups of origin. Thus, the Ukrainians and Belorussians earned Polish enmity because of their collaboration with both the Nazis and the Soviets. As far as the Jews were concerned, they were widely believed to have collaborated with Stalin in the Eastern Borderlands between 1939 and 1941 and with the Communist underground from 1942 to 1944.[5] Moreover, Jews were tied to war-time banditry since, to survive, they were often forced to seize food and provisions from Polish peasants.[6] After 1944, it was charged that Jewish partisans and Jewish soldiers of the Polish army created by Stalin in the USSR were appointed to many important positions in the proxy government of Poland. Additionally, the ethnic roots of some in the leadership of the new regime further reinforced the pre-war and war-time stereotype of the "Jewish-Communist conspiracy" (żydokomuna).[7]

Accordingly, in May 1945 a top Home Army officer ordered:

> The entire effort of the AK, both [armed] self-defense and propaganda, should be directed to derail the argument of Russia which attempts to announce to the world that in Poland there are a powerful Communist party, currently called 'democratic', and a small 'reactionary' group. We represent the Polish Nation; we want to create a division: Poles vs. Soviets. Today we can already say that the aim has been achieved to a great extent.... To be prepared [for the struggle] means to... cleanse the area of all 'snitches' [informers] because it will be too late the moment the NKVD arrives... [and to] prepare the [Polish] society [for that task] with all possible means (diversion, [and] propaganda); [we must] convince this society that the entire Nation is with us and [that] on the other side there are only soviets [sic] and Jews. This is our most immediate and most important task.[8]

The dichotomy of "us" versus "them" was a continuation of a similar trend from the period between 1939 and 1944 which proved durable beyond the Second World War. Nevertheless, the anti-minority (including anti-Jewish) thrust of the independentist propaganda was only one aspect of the insurgent ideology. The insurgents talked more often about the clash of Poland, the bulwark of the West, with the Soviet "Asiatics," who were supported by Polish traitors. According to an underground leaflet,

> We who have endured such sacrifices cannot allow the Asiatics to rampage in our State and to impose their laws on us through their lackeys in the persons of [the Communist president Bolesław] Bierut, [the radical socialist renegade prime minister Edward] Osóbek [sic Osóbka-Morawski], and others like them.
>
> We want Poland to be ruled by the Poles devoted to the cause [of independence] and elected by the whole Nation, but we have such people [in the government] who cannot speak up loudly because the UB and a clique of Soviet officers is alert.
>
> Therefore we have proclaimed a life-and-death struggle against those who, for Soviet money or [government] posts, have been murdering the best Poles who demand freedom and justice.... We are not a band, as the traitors and bastard sons of our fatherland call us. We are from Polish towns and villages. Some of your fathers, brothers, and friends are with us.
>
> We are fighting for the sacred cause, for a free, independent, just, and truly democratic Poland!...
> LONG LIVE FREEDOM AND FRATERNITY!!!
> DOWN WITH THE TRAITORS!
> who sold the Country and the Polish Nation to the Soviets [capitalized in the original].[9]

Historian Rafał Wnuk stresses that anti-Communism was the main feature of the independentist propaganda because the insurgents were convinced that "the Communist ideology was totally evil, and the aim of the Communists was not only to turn Poland into a vassal of the Soviet Union, or into its seventeenth republic but, even worse, it was to destroy Polish national culture, to affect the annihilation of traditional values, [and] to smash the institution of family." Nonetheless, Wnuk admits that, even if it largely failed to translate into anti-Semitic acts, most of the anti-Jewish propaganda emanated from the lower ranks of the underground. According to this scholar

> In its publications and documents the AK-DSZ-WiN devotes relatively much space to materials concerning the Jewish minority (about 10% of the newspapers and 40% of the leaflets contain texts depicting Jews in a negative light.). The lower the level of the [underground] cell publishing the press, the more

frequent the anti-Semitic references. Therefore one can surmise that the anti-Semitic attitudes in the independentist underground reflected the contemporary social feelings [among the Poles]. The post-AK underground unequivocally judged in a negative way the role that the Jews were playing in Poland during the period of "the struggle for people's power." It is interesting to note, however, that this verbal anti-Semitism translated itself into deeds only to a minimal degree. Merely about 1% of armed actions of the AK-DSZ-WiN units were aimed at Jews.[10]

The presence of an anti-Jewish element in the insurgent propaganda and rhetoric is undeniable. A poster displayed in Kraśnik in fall 1944 read: "Death to the bandits [and] liars under the Communist-Jewish banner."[11] In September 1944 the Rzeszów district command of the Home Army printed a bill that asked: "Do you know that the PKWN [i.e. the proxy regime] is secretly led by the Jews, who have always badmouthed and betrayed Poland which harbored them?"[12] In a leaflet of the Clandestine National Army (*Konspiracyjna Armia Narodowa* – *KAN*) distributed to the rank-and-file of the Communist military in the spring of 1945, the authors exclaimed: "SOLDIERS... We are divided by your commanders – Jews, Russians, and a few Poles, traitors... Turn your weapons against the true enemy of the Fatherland. The time of our victory, the day of the defeat of the *żydokomuna*, is already near."[13] In one of its declarations, the National Military Union (NZW) referred to the government of Poland as "lackeys of the *żydokomuna*."[14] In August 1945, in Kraków a bill was posted that read, "Germans are our enemies, the bolsheviks also, and the Jews are the third enemy... There is no room in Poland for Germans, bolsheviks [sic], and Jews. Poland for the Poles."[15] In December 1945, the underground newssheet *Echa Leśne* (Sylvan Echoes) of the Siedlce region referred to the provincial Communist governor as "a Jewish lackey" and warned that "the mendacious Jewish-Russian policy will fail to wrestle [Polish] culture away from us just as the brutal Hitlerite hand failed to."[16] Although "its attitude toward Jews can be termed as marked by moderate prejudice [*umiarkowana niechęć*]," the paper *Ku Wolności* (To Freedom) of the Freedom and Independence (WiN) in the Rzeszów area reinforced "the stereotype of a Jew-Communist and secret policeman," for instance writing in May 1946 about "Jewish and Soviet activists trained in Russia" and "Jews and Jew-boys [*Żydzi i Żydziaki*]" in the security police.[17] According to an internal memo of the WiN of July 1946, Poland was under the domination of the "Soviet *żydokomuna*."[18] In September 1946, the town of Skarżysko and its environs were covered with bills saying "Down with the *żydokomuna*" and "Down with the PPR."[19] In January 1947, an underground paper of the National Military Organization in Rzeszów referred to the Communist regime as "the Jewish government."[20]

Nevertheless, as mentioned, the identification of Jews with Communism in propaganda did not constitute the main foundation of the insurgent rhetoric. For example, Professor Władysław Chojnacki lists 1,278 bills, posters, and leaflets of the underground from the period between 1944-1953. Only 57 of them mention Jews, albeit for the most part in a negative light and nearly always in conjunction with Communism. Moreover, at least five of these leaflets are regional reprints of a master copy, which further limits the number of anti-Jewish bills to 52. Exceptionally, one leaflet of June 1946 is positive, forbidding Poles to acquire "post-Jewish" property.[21] Furthermore, it is possible that at least some of the anti-Jewish leaflets were the work of the Communist secret police. For instance, in the fall of 1945 in Jasło the Communists secretly put up "posters inciting the [Polish] population against the jews [sic]."[22] At least in certain instances the underground press differentiated between Communists and Jews. In August 1946, the clandestine WiN paper *Honor i Ojczyzna* appealed to the leaders of the Jewish community publicly

> to speak out against and expose the criminals and psychopaths of Jewish nationality in UBP [secret police] uniforms.
> Otherwise we will be forced to blame for the crimes committed [by the Jewish Communists] all of the Jews of Poland, as a single entity, hostile toward us. We are not anti-Semites [but] we elevate the interest of our Nation above everything.[23]

Finally, the underground did not discriminate between Communists depending on their ethnic origins. In a proclamation aimed at "the Soldiers of the W.P. [Polish Communist army] and the U.B. [secret police]," the insurgents warned that "we shall ruthlessly carry on [our struggle] against every enemy – even if he is a Pole. So help us God!"[24]

Nonetheless, a combination of anti-Communism and anti-Semitism (or perhaps anti-Communism expressed in anti-Semitic terms) permeated the rank-and-file insurgents and their officers.[25] One of the most valiant insurgent commanders, Captain Zenon Broński ("Uskok"), penned a poem entitled "Slavery" which accurately reflects precisely those sentiments:

Stay alive, slave
Chain your neck faster
Surrender your will, knave
And crawl to your master.

Grovel like a faithful dog
Underneath the Jewish boot
patted like a scornful hog
Brown-nose the Commie hood

My righteous heart, be free
fight and suffer terribly
Turn my soul to the future brave
Live proud, and not a slave.[26]

In September 1946, after having fought its way out of an encirclement by a joint NKVD-UB-KBW pacification expedition, the AK-WiN unit of Major Hieronim Dekutowski ("Zapora") clashed with a Communist-led group of the Volunteer Reserve of the Citizens Militia (*Ochotnicza Rezerwa Milicji Obywatelskiej — ORMO*) in Moniaki near Kraśnik, the Province of Lublin. The insurgents quickly routed the Communist militia auxiliaries. They shot one of them, disarmed the rest, and burned part of the village. According to a secret police interview with the vanquished, "there was singing and accordion playing during the shooting and they [i.e. the insurgents] were shouting that 'Moscow is burning;' 'Let Stalin come and help;' 'For Siberia and Katyń!'" Others called the defeated "Jewish and Soviet lackeys." They berated the ORMO members for having "voted three times yes [i.e. for the Communists] in the [falsified] referendum [of June 1946]; so now you get what you deserve because you wanted a Jewish government." Major Dekutowski gave a speech explaining that the insurgents "were fighting for Poland; so there would be no jews [sic] and soviets [sic]." Furthermore, he stated that "we shall not shoot you... [even though] you want a [Communist party] cell, a Jewish government, and collective farms. We shall endeavor not to allow that."[27]

However, anti-Jewish rhetoric did not automatically translate into anti-Jewish practice. According to Communist court records, during the Nazi occupation Major "Zapora" had under his command "three jews [sic]: two who fled from Warsaw, and one, a Belgian citizen [sic subject], who escaped from a camp."[28] These men were saved from the Holocaust thanks to the Polish AK partisans. Nonetheless, one can guess that even at that time "Zapora" and his Christian Polish soldiers subscribed to the popular theory of *żydokomuna*. After the arrival of the Soviets, this abstract notion of a link between Jews and Communism was reinforced.[29]

The concept of *żydokomuna* certainly persisted among the insurgents. However, most surviving independentist veterans flatly reject the notion that they were gripped by an anti-Semitic obsession. Ryszard Mikołajczuk ("Ryś") was an eighteen-year-old high school student when he joined a partisan unit of the National Armed Forces in 1947. According to his recollections,

> During our free time Captain "Bronisz" [Stanisław Okiński ("Zych")] would tell us jokes, most often Jewish jokes, which were the funniest. He'd also tell us about the partisan deeds of Captain "Remisz" [Jan Morawiec], and of the [forest] units of "Zenon," "Młot" [Capt. Władysław Łukasiuk], and others. We were mesmerized by him because he was a magnificent storyteller and joker. I mention this here to dispel the myth of the alleged extreme nationalism and anti-Semitism of the NSZ in particular and the Poles in general. During my two years in the NSZ I never heard any anti-Semitic pronouncements in any of the remarks of my superiors and colleagues. When Captain Okiński told us Jewish jokes, he did this to show the specific aspects of Jewish humor, without any [malicious] subtext. The family of Captain "Bronisz" hid Jews during the Hitlerite occupation and saved some of them. The same "anti-Semitic" deed was perpetrated by my family and the families of our colleagues [of the NSZ] who harkened from the countryside... For example, during [the Nazi] occupation the uncle of Captain Okiński "Zych" [who was also involved with the independentist underground] hid Jews – Dr. Turski and his family – at his estate of Stanisławów-Drupie [where Capt. Okiński hid occasionally as well]. My family saved many Jews, giving them temporary shelter in buildings owned by us adjacent to the ghetto in Siedlce. Among others, we saved the prominent storekeeper of Siedlce Leon Goldman, his daughter, and his brother Jonte Goldman... Sure [after 1944 under the Soviet occupation] there was talk [in the partisan unit] about Jews who were faithful lackeys of Stalin. Without generalizing [about all Jews], particular persons and names would be mentioned as for instance Berman, Różański, Landsberg, Borejsza, Brystygierowa, and in Siedlce, Alberg, the

Blumsteins, Kwiatek, and others. We would condemn their
bestiality and bandit-like behavior toward the Poles, [and] their
animalistic Polonophobia [*polakożerstwo*]. Similarly, there was
no xenophobia among us toward the Russian nation but only
toward the bolshevik [sic Soviet] leaders [and] the functionaries
of the NKVD and SMERSH. We had nothing against... the
Russian or Ukrainian people. However, we could not consent to
the conquest and despoliation of Poland regardless of whether it
was carried out by the Germans, Russians, or their Polish and
Jewish lackeys. We desired an independent and free Poland that
would be ruled by the Poles elected in free elections. We desired
to save ourselves and others from being sent as slaves into the
depths of Russia and from arrest and jail at home. We desired
simply to survive, preserving our dignity and honor.[30]

The above demonstrates the attitude of a typical anti-Communist
insurgent toward the post-war reality in Poland. Even in the most extreme
case of the National Armed Forces (NSZ), this anti-Jewish animosity did
not amount to a genocidal animus. According to the leftist Polish scholar
Krystyna Kersten, "Did the NSZ murder Jews? From what we know
today during the war and also in its aftermath the killing of Jews as Jews
was not included in their program... Undoubtedly, there is a link between
anti-Semitic ideology and [anti-Jewish] deeds, but that is not enough to
regard the NSZ as an organization that programmatically murdered
Jews."[31] According to the available military documents of the National
Armed Forces issued after 1944, the so-called "Jewish problem" never
appeared in partisan field instructions and orders. For professional
officers, as opposed to ideologues, there were two enemies: the Germans
and the Soviets.[32] This was also the case with the Home Army. If
anything, central and provincial insurgent commanders attempted to limit
military actions, including those against the Jews. According to an order
of October 1945 by the commander of the Rzeszów District of the
National Military Organization (NOW-NZW), "All actions against Jews,
Ukrainians, or bolsheviks [sic Soviets] are forbidden, with the exception
of self-defense or in an emergency... Each action carried out without
orders will be considered as banditry."[33] Finally, despite the defection of
many of the émigré Jewish leaders to the pro-Soviet side,[34] the Polish
Government in Exile in London and Polish émigré politicians in the West
were rather sympathetic to Jews in Poland and aghast at anti-Jewish
violence, pogroms in particular. Also, as early as February 1945, in order
to stop the hopeless bloodshed, the émigré authorities vainly appealed to

the insurgents to cease fighting.[35] Similarly, the Catholic Church in Poland appealed to end guerrilla warfare and spoke out against the anti-Jewish violence.[36]

Notes

1   Peter Pulzer, *The Rise of Political Anti-Semitism in Germany and Austria* (Cambridge, MA: Harvard University Press, 1988), xiii.

2   See Włodzimierz Mich, *Obcy w polskim domu: Nacjonalistyczne koncepcje rozwiązania problemu mniejszości narodowych, 1918-1939* (Lublin: Wydawnictwo Uniwersytetu Marii Curie-Skłodowskiej, 1994); Krzysztof Kawalec, *Narodowa Demokracja wobec faszyzmu, 1922-1939: Ze studiów nad dziejami myśli politycznej Obozu Narodowego* (Warszawa: Państwowy Instytut Wydawniczy, 1989); Szymon Rudnicki, *Obóz Narodowo-Radykalny: Geneza i działalność* (Warszawa: Czytelnik, 1985); Marek Jan Chodakiewicz, *Narodowe Siły Zbrojne: "Ząb" przeciw dwu wrogom* (Warszawa: Fronda, 1999) [afterward *Narodowe*]; Wojciech Jerzy Muszyński, *W walce o Wielką Polskę: Propaganda zaplecza politycznego Narodowych Sił Zbrojnych (1939-1945)* (Warszawa and Biała Podlaska: Rekonkwista-Rachocki i ska, 2000).

3   See "Komunizm — narzędziem podbojów Rosji," *Biuletyn Informacyjny* 38 (23 November 1943): 1.

4   "Materiały do akcji przeciwkomunistycznej," May 1942, AAN, AK, file 203/VII-62, 27-28 in Chodakiewicz, Gontarczyk, and Żebrowski, *Tajne oblicze*, 3: 61. In the Polish language it is customary to spell followers of a religion with a lower case letter. Hence, *katolik* and not *Katolik* (Catholic) and *żyd* rather than *Żyd* (Jew). To stress one's ethnic origin, an upper case spelling was used. Thus, only sometimes the word "Jew" spelled with a lower case "j" was meant to be derogatory. Contemporary Jewish authors also adhered to this convention. See for instance, "Szopka satyryczna pt. 'Sylwetki znakomitych mężów Służby Porządkowej' z 1941 roku," Appendix IV, in Aldona Podolska, *Służba Porządkowa w getcie warszawskim w latach 1940-1943* (Warszawa: Wydawnictwo Fundacji "Historia Pro Futuro", 1996), 111-22.

5   See Piotrowski, *Poland's Holocaust*, 35-75; Jerzy Robert Nowak, *Przemilczane zbrodnie: Żydzi i Polacy na Kresach w latach 1939-1941* (Warszawa: Wydawnictwo von Borowiecky, 1999); Mark Paul, *Neighbors on the Eve of the Holocaust: The Polish Minority and Jewish Collaboration in Soviet-Occupied Eastern Poland, 1939-1941* (Toronto: PEFINA Press, 2001), posted online at <http://www.kpk.org/KPK/toronto/sovocc.pdf>; John T. Pawlikowski, "The Nazi Attack on the Polish Nation: Towards a New Understanding," in *Holocaust and Church Struggle: Religion, Power and the Politics of Resistance*, ed. by Hubert G. Locke and Marcia Sachs Littell (Lanham, New York, and London: University Press of America, 1996), 33-44; Bogdan Musiał, "Stosunki polsko-żydowskie na Kresach Wschodnich R.P. pod okupacją sowiecką 1939-1941," *Biuletyn Kwartalny Radomskiego Towarzystwa Naukowego* 34, no. 1 (1999): 103-26; and Jerzy Robert Nowak, *Polacy i Żydzi na Kresach w latach 1939-1941*, 2 vols. (Warszawa: von borowiecky, 2001); Marek Wierzbicki, *Po drodze do Jedwabnego: Stosunki polsko-żydowskie na Zachodniej Białorusi (Ziemie Północnowschodnie II Rzeczypospolitej) pod okupacją sowiecką 1939-1941* (Warszawa: Fronda, 2002).

6   For the only English language account of this controversial topic see Mark Paul, "Anti-Semitic Pogrom in Ejszyszki? An overview of Polish-Jewish Relations in Wartime Northeastern Poland," in *The Story of Two Shtetls, Brańsk and Ejszyszki: An Overview of Polish-Jewish Relations in Northeastern Poland During World War II*, Part Two (Toronto and Chicago: The Polish Educational Foundation in North America, 1998), 85-106, 110-123 [afterward "Anti-Semitic Pogrom in Ejszyszki?" in *The Story of Two Shtetls*].

7   Piotrowski, *Poland's Holocaust*, 6.

8   Colonel Mieczysław Liniarski ("Mścisław"), Konspekt propagandowy nr. 14, BiP Białostockiego Okręgu AK, 15 May 1945, in Kazimierz Krajewski and Tomasz Łabuszewski, *Białostocki Okręg AK-AKO, VII 1944-VIII 1945* (Warszawa: Oficyna Wydawnicza Volumen i Dom Wydawniczy Bellona, 1997), 145 [afterward Konspekt in *Białostocki*].

9   See Tomasz Łabuszewski and Kazimierz Krajewski, eds., *Od "Łupaszki" do "Młota", 1944-1949: Materiały źródłowe do dziejów V i VI Brygady Wileńskiej* (Warszawa: Oficyna Wydawnicza Volumen, 1994), 127 [afterward *Od "Łupaszki"*].

10 Rafał Wnuk, "Zorganizowany opór wobec państwa komunistycznego na przykładzie Okręgu Lublin AK-DSZ-WiN (1944-1945)," *Dzieje Najnowsze* 4 (1999): 183. The Home Army (AK) converted itself first into the Delegation of the Armed Forces (Delegatura Sił Zbrojnych — DSZ) and then the Association for Freedom and Independence (WiN).

11 Władysław Chojnacki, ed., *Bibliografia polskich publikacji podziemnych wydanych pod rządami komunistycznymi w latach 1939-1941 i 1944-1953: Czasopisma, druki zwarte, druki ulotne* (Warszawa: Literackie Towarzystwo Wydawnicze, 1996), 119 [afterward *Bibliografia*].

12 A bill "Żołnierze," no date [September 1944], signed by "Dowództwo Armii Krajowej," in my collection.

13 Odpis, ŻOŁNIERZE ARMII ROLI-ŻYMIERSKIEGO, no date [1945?], the collection of Wojciech Jerzy Muszyński, Gdańsk [afterward CWJM].

14 Narodowe Zjednoczenie Wojskowe, "Do b. członków bratnich organizacji A.K. i WiN," no date [1947?], CWJM.

15 Cariewskaja, *Teczka specjalna*, 363-64. Advanced chiefly by the National Party (SN), the slogan "Poland for the Poles" enjoyed some currency already before the war.

16 *Echa Leśne*, no. 51, 12 December 1945, in Archiwum Państwowe w Białymstoku, Komitet Wojewódzki Polskiej Partii Robotniczej w Białymstoku [afterward APB, KW PPR], file 1/V/22, 1-2.

17 *Ku Wolności*, 24 May 1946 quoted in Tomasz Balbus, *Major Ludwik Marszałek "Zbroja" (1912-1948): Żołnierz polski podziemnej* (Wrocław: Gajt Wydawnictwo s.c., 1999), 117.

18 *Zrzeszenie WiN w dokumentach*, 2: 192.

19 Wanda Chudzik, Irena Marczak and Marek Olkuśnik, eds., *Biuletyny Informacyjne Ministerstwa Bezpieczeństwa Publicznego, 1946* (Warszawa: Ministerstwo Spraw Wewnętrznych, 1996), 34 [afterward *Biuletyny 1946*].

20 *Głos Jedności Polskiej*, 10 January 1947, quoted in Stanisław Janicki, "Działalność i likwidacja Rzeszowskiego Okręgu 'Narodowej Organizacji Wojskowej' w latach 1944-1947," in Turlejska, *W walce*, 249 [afterward "Działalność"].

21 Chojnacki, *Bibliografia*, 216.

22 Odpis, *Informator* 3-4 (November-December 1945): 2, AAN, KC PPR, file 295/VII-192, 55.

23 *Honor i Ojczyzna*, 9-10 (October 1946): 6, CWJM.

24 Chojnacki, *Bibliografia*, 311.

25 According to one historian, "fascist and semi-fascist dissidents [i.e. the independentists] used the issue of Jews-in-government to rally the antisemitic masses against an extremely

unpopular regime. For many Poles, Jew was synonymous with Communist. Thus, antisemitism became a vehicle for anticommunism, and anticommunism could be disguised as antisemitism." See Leonard Dinnerstein, *America and the Survivors of the Holocaust* (New York: Columbia University Press, 1982), 108-109.

26 See Urbankowski, *Czerwona msza*, 2nd ed., 2: 175.

A kto chce być sługą, niechaj sobie żyje,
Niechaj sobie powróz okręci na szyje,
Niechaj swoją wolę na wieki okiełza
Pan niedaleko, niech do niego pełza

Niechaj jak pies wierny czołga się bez końca,
za żydowskim butem, który nim potrąca
i najpierw głaskany, a potem wzgardzony,
niechaj bolszewikom wybija pokłony

lecz kto chce być wolnym i prawe ma serce,
niech walczy, niech cierpi, choćby w poniewierce
niech ducha pokrzepi myślą o przyszłości
i czoła nie zniża w podłej służalczości.

27 Protokoły przesłuchania świadków Józefa Wacha, Bronisława Traczyka, Władysława Stojka, Stanisława Czernela, 25-29 September 1946, APLOK, PRN, Sprawy różne, Sprawozdania i protokóły zeznań świadków w sprawie spalenia wsi Moniaki przez bandę dywersyjną, 1946, file 250.

28 Henryk Pająk, ed., *"Zaporowcy" przed sądem UB* (Lublin: Wydawnictwo Retro, 1997), 231 [afterward *Zaporowcy*].

29 For an exhaustive account of the activities of the "Zapora" unit during the Nazi occupation see Ireneusz Caban, "Oddziały partyzanckie Armii Krajowej 8 PP Leg.," (Ph.D. diss., Uniwersytet im. Marii Curie-Skłodowskiej in Lublin, 1991); and Ireneusz Caban, *8 Pułk Piechoty Legionów Armii Krajowej: Organizacja i działania bojowe* (Warszawa: Wydawnictwo Bellona, 1994), 123-53 [afterward *8 Pułk*]. For a succinct description of the "Zapora" unit during the Soviet occupation see Plan operacji grupy operacyjno-propagandowej wojsk W.B.W. wojew. Lubelskiego, w celu likwidacji bandy WIN "Zapory" dzialajacej [sic] w rejonie pow! [sic] Krasnik [sic] i czesciowo [sic] w pow! [sic] puławskim i w pow. lubelskim na okres od dnia 25.XI.46 r. do dnia 22.XII.46r., no date [November 1946], Centralne Archiwum Wojskowe in Warsaw [afterward CAW], file IV/111 507, 103-105; *Informator*, 82.

30 Ryszard Mikołajczuk, "Przyczynek do historii XII Okręgu Podlaskiego Narodowych Sił Zbrojnych w okresie okupacji sowieckiej, 1944-1950 r.," *Narodowe Siły Zbrojne na Podlasiu*, vol. 2: *W walce z systemem komunistycznym w latach 1944-1952*, ed. by Mariusz Bechta and Leszek Żebrowski (Siedlce: Związek Żołnierzy Narodowych Sił Zbrojnych, 1998), 2: 266-67 [afterward "Przyczynek" in *NSZ na Podlasiu*].

31 "Oblicza prawdy: Z prof. Krystyną Kerstenową rozmawia Anna Baniewicz," *Rzeczpospolita: Plus Minus*, 8-9 May 1993, I.

32 See Leszek Żebrowski, ed., *Narodowe Siły Zbrojne: Dokumenty, struktury, personalia*, 3 vols. (Warszawa: Burchard Edition, 1994-1996) (Vol. 1 was published in 1994; and both vol. 2: *NSZ-AK* and vol. 3: *NSZ-ONR* in 1996) [afterward *NSZ dokumenty*].

33 Rozkaz nr 1, 26 October 1945, Archiwum Państwowe w Rzeszowie, Wojewódzki Sąd Rejonowy [afterward APRz, WSR], file Sr. 6/49, in Dionizy Garbacz, *Wołyniak:*

Legenda prawdziwa (Stalowa Wola: Wydawnictwo "Sztafeta", 108 [afterward *Wołyniak*].

34 See Stola, *Nadzieja i Zagłada*, 60, 272-78.

35 Naturally, the émigré Poles were concerned about the issue of Jewish Communists in Poland but official reports never overestimated the problem. See Tadeusz Wolsza, *Rząd RP na obczyźnie wobec wydarzeń w kraju 1945-1950* (Warszawa: Wydawnictwo DiG, 1998), 128-39, 239-46 [afterward *Rząd*].

36 For the most exhaustive treatment of the subject in English see Mark Paul, "The Catholic Church and the Kielce Tragedy," in *Kielce — July 4, 1946: Background, Context and Events* (Toronto and Chicago: The Polish Educational Foundation in North America, 1996), 108-14 [afterward "Catholic" in *Kielce*]. See also John Micgiel, "Kościół katolicki i pogrom kielecki," *Niepodległość* [New York], 25 (1992): 134-72; Jan Żaryn, *Kościół a władza w Polsce (1945-1950)* (Warszawa: Towarzystwo im. Stanisława ze Skarbimierza i Wydawnictwo DiG, 1997); Jan Śledzianowski, *Ksiądz Czesław Kaczmarek biskup kielecki, 1895-1963* (Kielce: n.p., 1991) [afterward *Ksiądz Czesław Kaczmarek*]. For a somewhat dissenting opinion, albeit based on very limited evidence, see Michał Borwicz, "Polish-Jewish Relations, 1944-1947," in *The Jews in Poland*, ed. by Chimen Abramsky, Maciej Jachimczyk, and Antony Polonsky (London: Basil Blackwell, 1986), 194-97. For a very critical assessment of the role of the Church vis-á-vis the Jewish community, see Warhaftig, *Refugee and Survivor*, 299-300.

V

JEWISH SELF-DEFENSE OR JEWISH REVENGE?

The Polish-Jewish confrontation occurred only gradually. The Jews, for the most part, minded their own business and either attempted to return to their pre-war life or to emigrate from Poland. However, Jews also faced a more general hostility which drew on traditional prejudices reinforced by the post-war political situation under the Soviet occupation. According to a Jewish witness, "after te [sic the] liberation I went back to our house in Szydłowiec. However, on account of the cruel behavior of the Poles we left very soon."[1] In particular, conflict developed over the reclamation of Jewish property that had been confiscated by the Nazis and rented by them to Christian Poles or simply appropriated by Poles. Occasionally, Jews and Poles quarreled over Jewish children saved by Christians who were reluctant to return them to their relatives.

Aside from reclaiming their children and property, some Jews wanted revenge. Their manifold reasons were grounded chiefly in the Jewish experience before and, especially, during the Holocaust. In certain instances they or their relatives fell victim to Polish bandits and criminals, often part-time perpetrators who were hard to distinguish from the rest of the peasantry, thus broadening the scope of the Jewish backlash. Other Jews perished at the hands of Polish partisans (both independentists and Communists), who might have killed them for a multitude of reasons, including as suspected Nazi spies, bandits, and Communists. It is safe to assume that all survivors resented purveyors of anti-Semitism, which, in its Nazi variety, became genocidal, and, therefore, after the war at least some Jews lashed out at anyone perceived as harboring any anti-Jewish animus. Finally, it seems that certain survivors blamed Polish Gentiles in general and various right-wingers, conservatives, and Catholic activists in particular for the Holocaust.[2]

Following the arrival of the Red Army, serious clashes broke out over the conduct of certain Poles toward Jewish fugitives during the Nazi occupation. In many instances the survivors sought the assistance of the Soviet and Polish Communist authorities to bring the guilty to justice.[3]

According to Alina Cała,

> the most dramatic and conflict-engendering cases involving Jews and Poles were reflected in the interventions undertaken by the Legal Department of the CKŻP [Central Committee of Polish Jews], where Jewish lawyers were available to help. First of all, these cases concerned the [alleged Nazi] collaborators, who participated during the [German] occupation in the Holocaust, denouncing or murdering Jews. Basing themselves upon written denunciations of both Jewish and non-Jewish witnesses, these cases were forwarded to the courts or the UBP [secret police]. The first trials took place in 1944 in Lublin and their number was not small.[4]

A few Jews, however, took justice into their own hands. Having already assaulted some Poles for their alleged collaboration with Nazis during the war, such Jewish avengers continued their punitive strikes also afterward.[5] According to a Jewish witness from the Białystok area, Jews "worked in the U.B. [secret police], which was the organization for saving Jewish children from Poles. They punished non-Jews who were known to have killed Jews prior to the liberation and after the liberation."[6] It further appears that the Communist security forces encouraged Jews to provide intelligence services in exchange for protection and support. Separately, the Jewish members of the Communist guerrilla squads, along with their Gentile comrades, joined Soviet security forces and lashed out at insurgents. This continued a mutual struggle that had begun under the Nazi occupation and ended in defeat for the anti-Communists. Lastly, it seems that a small number of Jews carried out robberies against Poles. (This phenomenon will be discussed in a subsequent chapter.)

All these developments occurred while the Communists were conducting a vigorous recruitment drive to staff their regime, enlisting some Jews. Many of them firmly believed that Communism was the only viable alternative to "fascism." One such recruit recalled that she and her friends joined the Communist party because of "the personal experiences during the [Nazi] occupation, the still existing idealism of our youth, and foremost the desire to prevent the rebirth of fascism."[7] Marcel Reich-Ranicki signed up for the party and the secret police because of his gratitude for the Soviets for saving his life, his faith in Communism, and his conviction that only the proxy regime was capable of maintaining order in Poland since it enjoyed the backing of Stalin and the West.[8] For leftist Zionists the affinity for the Communists straddled ideologies and cemented ties for which the groundwork had already been laid during the German occupation.[9] Yitzhak Zuckerman, for example, while enjoying the protection of the Home Army after the collapse of the Warsaw Uprising of August-October, 1944, cast his lot with its adversaries and the Soviet-imposed Communist regime:

> In those [first] weeks [after the Soviet entry] in Grodzisk, we performed a very important function for the AL [Armia Ludowa]. That was an historic opportunity to repay our debt to them. We created contact with [the Communist government in] Lublin for them: we sent two people to Lublin, Kazik [Simha Rotem aka Ratajzer] and Irka Gelblum, who got through to there. We helped them with money. We put them on the list of those we supported. We did all we could for them. I think that was our *moral obligation* to them, and they appreciated it; and, thanks to that, a lot of our misfortunes were solved after the war, because they remembered what we had done for them. Our messengers reached Lublin and created contacts with the AL, which had been crushed and was impotent. By then, the Communists governed Lublin, but in the German occupation zone, they had been murdered and punished severely. Communist Poland already existed, but the Russians didn't help the Uprising and abandoned the rebels to their fate. We knew the "great love" in Poland for the Communists throughout the years, so we were their saving grace. Nevertheless, we shouldn't say that the Jews lost anything by helping the Polish Communists with money and deeds.[10]

Historian Natalia Aleksiun amplifies the nature of the relationship between the Zionists and the Communist regime as follows:

> The leaders of all of the legal Zionist parties and organizations expressed their support for the governing system in Poland, but the activists of the extreme Leftist Zionist parties and youth organizations did so in an emphatic manner. For the activists of the Poale Zion-Left [far left Socialist Zionists], Haszomer Hacair [Young Guard], Borochow Jugent [Borochow Youth] and Dror, the takeover of

power in Poland by the Communists opened the door to carrying out a radical social program.

The declarations emanating from the circles of organizations like Haszomer Hacair or Poale Zion-Left can be explained by ideological considerations. On the other hand, the position of the leaders of parties that distanced themselves from Marxism, such as Ichud [General Zionists], Mizrachi [religious Zionists], Poale Zion-Right [moderate Socialist Zionists], and Hitachdut, whose activists also expressed support for the Communist camp, was tied to their assessment of the situation of the Jewish community in post-war Poland and had a pragmatic character. In the years 1944-49 a declaration of loyalty was a necessary precondition for obtaining permission from the authorities to carry on their legal activities in Poland and to realize their Zionist postulates, above all to educate Jewish youth according to the ideological tenets of Zionism and to organize the mass emigration of Jews to Palestine. Another factor that influenced the Zionist activists to support the Lublin government was the conviction that the favor of the Polish authorities on the central and local level was indispensable to obtaining material assistance for the Jewish survivors, to securing their safety, and to organizing the repatriation of Polish Jews from the interior of the USSR.[11]

Qualified support for the Communist regime was also expressed at the first post-war Bund conference in Lublin and, for tactical reasons, by Agudah Israel, although the latter party nonetheless failed to gain official recognition.[12] Declarations of support for the "democratic" regime by the leaders and activitists of the organized Jewish community led naturally and in turn to the condemnation of the independentists – the so-called "reaction," "dark forces," and "fascist bands."[13] The attitude of the political leaders of the Jewish community reflected the mood of many of the rank-and-file. Not surprisingly, many Jews were dismayed by displays of Polish anti-Sovietism and related to it in a similar manner as they did to anti-Semitism. A Jewish witness reported in shock that "a similar hate [as toward the Jews] they [the Poles] showed toward the Red Army, an army that lost thousands of soldiers when they sacrificed their lives to liberate Poland. The marble monument that was erected to the memory of the liberators of the city [of Lublin] was violated daily."[14]

While the issue of Polish anti-Sovietism as a factor in Jewish attitudes toward the Poles has been downplayed in the scholarship, the topic of Jewish anti-Polonism has been virtually ignored by historians. Nonetheless, a popular perception persisted about Jewish collusion with the Communists on the basis of their alleged "anti-Polonism." In fact, there have been allegations about Jewish "anti-Polonism" as a significant factor behind Jewish actions in Poland after 1944. At least some sources tied such impulses to "Jewish nationalism."[15]

These allegations functioned not only among ethnic Poles but also Poles of Jewish origin and even among some Jewish Communists. Already in 1942 a conflict broke out between General Zygmunt Berling, the first Commander-in-Chief of the Polish Communist army, who had been an erstwhile adherent to Judaism, and Jewish Communists, including the future security boss Jakub Berman, whom the military leader accused of anti-Polonism which, Berling hinted, stemmed from Jewish prejudice.[16]

An American scholar commented that Berling was reacting to "the hostility that Polish Communists of Jewish origin in Moscow evidently displayed towards anyone they regarded as a Polish patriot" but nonetheless warns that Berling's memoirs are peppered with "numerous anti-Jewish statements."[17] However, the veteran Jewish Communist activist Teofila Weintraub affirms that a top security official, Colonel Józef Goldberg, aka Jacek Różański, "was a Pole-hater [Polakożerca]. He hated [the Polish] people."[18] A Jewish pundit called paradoxical, when he meant pathological, "a situation where a Jewish officer of the Security Service tortured a Polish officer, who had been one of the most distinguished rescuers of Jews during the war. I mean Różański interrogating Kazimierz Moczarski."[19]

There were others like Różański. For example, the commander of the penal camp in Jaworzno, Shlomo Morel, routinely yelled in a Nazi fashion at his anti-Communist juvenile prisoners: "You Polish pig!" (ty polska świnio).[20] Threats tainted with ethnic prejudice were also noted by civilian Communist authorities in October 1945: "the functionaries of the security police in Kielce do not express themselves in an appropriate manner to the Polish population, for example [they have been heard saying] 'I will shoot everyone of you Poles here.'"[21] Elsewhere, "many members and sympathizers of the National Party were imprisoned. They experienced brutal interrogation, during which the officers of the UBP, who were of Jewish origin, were avenging themselves for the pre-war [anti-Jewish] program of the endecja." The Jewish Colonel of the UB Józef Światło told the prisoners: "Now you will remember what anti-Semitism is." One of the victims retorted: "Unlike your anti-Polonism, our anti-Semitism never led to torture."[22]

It is even alleged that anti-Polonism transcended the divisions within the Communist party. On October 28, 1947, the liberal assimilationist Ludwik Hirszfeld wrote to a leading Jewish Communist, Jerzy Borejsza, that "the Jewish objections are directed against the assimilationist tendencies [among Polish Jews] and they prove one thing, namely, that Jewish nationalists hate the Poles more than they do the Germans."[23]

A Jewish officer in the Polish "people's" army exclaimed that "I hated the Poles almost as much as I hated the Germans. I took out my anger and bitterness on the poor cadets, demanding strict discipline from them." When 40 cadets and an officer deserted, the Jewish officer participated in the pursuit organized by the Soviet colonel in charge of his "Polish" regiment. "All forty deserters were condemned to death by a military tribunal. Thirty-nine were shot by the firing squad."[24]

Thus, property disputes, Jewish revenge, banditry, anti-fascism, anti-Semitism, anti-Polonism, and anti-Communism exacerbated the Jewish conflict with the Polish population and insurgents, playing itself out in the framework of a much more serious and widespread Soviet-Polish independentist confrontation. The struggle between the main adversaries broke out as soon as the Soviet security forces commenced their assault on the Polish underground. The assault varied in ruthlessness according to the level of resistance offered and to the locality. It seems that the Communists applied a somewhat more moderate approach in the Polish territories than they did in the Soviet areas cleansed from German forces.

A Jewish lieutenant colonel of the NKVD recalled that

> I was also assigned to a mission behind enemy lines, as part of a group of 200 people who interrogated the local people to identify collaborators. When I returned to the area under Russian control, life was brutal. Most of the Ukrainians were pro-Nazi. If somebody fired a shot at us, we would kill everyone in the village.
>
> There were a lot of collaborators. When we found them, we set up a court, held a hearing, and hung collaborators right in the center of the village. I appointed villagers as judge and juries. All this to personally avoid an execution. I hope nobody will ever again see the things I saw then.
>
> I was storming certain villages when I was picked up by a local court for brutality and put on trial. I stated that if anyone

fired on us, we returned fire because one of our men was more valuable than a hundred villagers. The villages that did not attack us were turned over to the regular army, to the local [NKVD] brigades without being harmed. I was coming there in the name of liberation, to liberate the Soviet people.[25]

In Poland, according to a Jewish witness of the events, the Soviets

> launched a ruthless persecution of all unauthorized [i.e. insurgent] underground groups. Their special aim was to destroy the powerful forces of the A.K. Many people were arrested only because they had been associated with the Home Army during its anti-Nazi days. Many of those arrested had nothing to do with postwar illegal operations. Because all former A.K. members were in danger, some tried to conceal their wartime affiliations. A virtual witch hunt ensued.[26]

From the point of view of the Polish anti-Communist insurgents the most important aspects of Jewish behavior after the entry of the Red Army were informing and participating in the institutions of the new regime, the security apparatus in particular. Mark Verstandig recalled that "Jews were offered jobs and careers which surpassed their wildest expectations."[27] Another Jewish witness likewise remembered that the "newly created Polish government offered the Jewish partisans jobs in the government administration in Lublin. We were also given positions in local police forces."[28] According to Mark Hillel, some Jewish partisans in the environs of Białystok automatically joined the police.[29] Jakob Rotenberg, aka Friedmann, who fought with the Communist guerillas near Włodawa became the militia commander in a small town outside of Szczecin.[30]

Such contentions are seconded by various insurgent sources from other localities. On August 12, 1944, a local Home Army command radioed London that in "Przemyśl [there is] a Soviet commander, [and] a mayor. Jews [are enrolled] in the militia."[31] On September 1, 1944, Polish underground operating in the Rzeszów subdistrict informed their superiors that "PPR, or the Party of Soviet Politicians [*Partia Polityków Radzieckich*], has been selecting its members [and] it derives support for its work from old Communists and Jews."[32] More specifically, it was reported that "a Jew, the lawyer Reich from Rzeszów, became legal advisor of the investigative section" of the secret police.[33] In August 1945 an underground leaflet in Kielce announced that "Jews and

Bolsheviks...rule Poland" and that the head of the provincial Office for Public Security was "a Jewish major [*major Żyd*]."[34]

Unlike in many other instances, where such claims have not yet been independently verified, two regional historians researched quite carefully the local power structure in Kielce, where perhaps 250 Jews, many of them from the Soviet Union, settled temporarily after the war. According to Krzysztof Urbański and Danuta Blus-Węgrowska, until 1946 the commander of the provincial UB in Kielce was Major Dawid Kornhendler, aka Adam Kornecki, a trusted NKVD operative. The deputy head of the County Office of the UB in Kielce was Albert Grynbaum. Captain Moryc Kwaśniewski, Eta Lewkowicz-Ajzenman, and Natan Bałanowski, a physician, were also high-ranking Jewish employees of the secret police. Wolf Zalcberg held the crucial post of interpreter with the Soviet military command in Kielce. Among the civilian bureaucrats in Kielce, the following were only the most prominent Communist activists of Jewish origin: the first secretary of the Province Committee of the PPR, Jan Kalinowski, the town mayor Tadeusz Zarecki, and the chief of the Organization Department of the PPR, Julian Lewin. In addition, a number of Jewish Communists worked very closely with the provincial governor, who was an ethnic Polish Communist.[35]

Nevertheless, in many instances, on the lower level, perhaps most Jewish individuals were not strictly speaking Communists in their ideology but rather pro-Soviet. According to a Jewish account from Ejszyszki, the county of Troki, the Province of Wilno,

> Those [Jews] who had fought in Russian partisan units were able to help by working with the NKVD (the Russian secret police) and the militia. Considered a great asset by the [Soviet] military [security], since they were so familiar with the local language, populace, and countryside, many of the Jewish partisans were drafted into prominent positions where their knowledge of local politics and personalities could be put to use. It was men like these whom the Russians trusted to identify and track down their mutual enemies: members of the anti-Communist White Poles [i.e. Home Army] (in areas that were largely Polish) and Green Partisans in areas that were largely Lithuanian); civil officials and others who had collaborated with the Germans; Nazi sympathizers who had been responsible for the murder of Jews.[36]

The recruitment of Jews by the secret police was not always entirely voluntary. For instance, in September 1944 an erstwhile Soviet partisan Szulim Sznycer joined the Polish Communist military in Wilno. He became a company scribe but was expected to detect "reactionaries" and "fascists" from among the Polish troops who were drafted under duress. Sznycer was threatened by the NKVD to turn the "pro-Nazi" Poles in, a request he complied with hastily, albeit after some anguish. According to his memoirs,

> Most of the soldiers had previously been in the ruthless AK, and were patriotic nationalists who had fought against the Soviet soldiers and partisans, as well as the Nazis. A special recruiting base was established, and the units were formed to go to the surrounding towns and villages. According to lists acquired at the town or village halls, the soldiers went from house to house to search for the men, and brought them to the camp. Another group of soldiers had to guard them, to prevent them from attempting to escape.... I was in charge of registering all those who were chosen for our company.... I grilled them about their activities during the German occupation. They were frightened, and I needed to use my intuitive skills to draw out the information, to calm them down, to play on their national patriotism.... About the week after the recruitment, I was called one evening to the regimental headquarters and told to appear before the chief intelligence and security officer [of the NKVD] in Polish uniform with the rank of captain [who] was a Russian.
>
> He told me in Russian to sit down, and came straight to the point. He knew that I had been a Soviet partisan, fighting for Stalin and the homeland, so he could speak openly to me. He lectured me about spies, traitors, and counter-revolutionaries, especially among the Poles, who should be carefully watched and distrusted, even though they were in the Polish Army fighting alongside the Soviets. He then bent toward me across the table, and, looking me straight in the eyes, said, "By tomorrow you will bring me a list and the files of all the spies of counter-revolutionaries in your company." Looking back at him, I answered that, had I known of anyone like that in my company, I would have immediately taken care of him myself. Leaning even closer to me, he said, "I know that there are such men in your company."

I thought, "What does this man think of me? I am fighting the Nazis, and anybody helping them is my enemy. Would I leave them be, if I knew of any such people?"

I smiled and said, "We are on the same side." Suddenly I felt a whack on my face. The captain grabbed his revolver, shoved his face even closer, and, after swearing at me, said, "Do you want me to make you look so that even your mother won't recognize you? Now get out, and be here tomorrow morning with your list!"

I was stunned and worried. Even the [Soviet] colonel in charge of the regiment was afraid of him [i.e. the NKVD captain]. Nobody could help me.

I returned to the company headquarters, went straight to the files, and started reading through each one. I worked all night. Although I did not know these men, I agonized over each name, wondering whether the men really were staunch supporters of the Germans... By morning I had put together the names of five men...

I took their files, went to the NKVD officer, and explained that these files should be further examined. He came around the table toward me and patted me approvingly on the shoulder. "I see that you are a quick learner. If you have any further suspicions of anybody, come directly to me." I saluted smartly and left, hoping never to see the man again. I never found out what happened to the men on the list after they were taken in for interrogation.[37]

Some Jews refused to heed the siren call of the Communists to join the secret police. After the arrival of the Red Army in July 1944, Berl Kagan joined the Soviet militia in Nowogródek. His superiors wanted to send him to the NKVD training center in Minsk. Instead, Kagan left for central Poland.[38]

Abraham Wunderboim survived the war as a Communist partisan in the environs of Parczew. After the arrival of the Red Army, Wunderboim briefly "was active in capturing Germans and their cooperators" but did not join the secret police. Instead, he became an officer of the Communist armed forces and participated in the storming of Berlin.[39]

The Jewish partisan Haim Frimmer, aka Aharon Carmi, "was integrated into the militia" automatically and soon wore "the uniform of the UB." His friend, a left-wing Zionist, who closely cooperated with the Communists, and the secret police in particular, to expedite the Jewish exodus from Poland, ultimately did not join the terror apparatus. Nonetheless, he recalled that

> I went through two different experiences: that of Polish Communism, as I saw it in those years, including the two years I stayed in Poland after the war. If I had been Polish, I would have joined them [the Communists] wholeheartedly, and not the other forces. The other experience was the *Zionist, Eretz-Israeli line* [emphasis in the original]. . . . There was no need to explain to us that this was no longer Poland, but one big cemetery, with no room for Jewish life. . . . True, we, the active cadre, were at a crossroads. Some of us thought we should leave at once, or devote ourselves to vengeance and [then] escape from Poland.[40]

Jan Dawid Landau, a Zionist-Revisionist, and a veteran of both the Warsaw Ghetto Uprising (1943) and the Warsaw Uprising (1944), was arrested by the Communists in 1945 for illegal possession of weapons. While in jail, an UB officer "told me that now I would be able to avenge myself for everything I had suffered from the [Polish] people during the war." Then, the officer encouraged the prisoner to join the secret police and released him. Landau immediately ran away to the West.[41]

Another Zionist-Revisionist, Maurice Shainberg, aka Mieczysław Prużański, joined the Communist intelligence quite willingly. According to his account,

> My section was responsible for discovering persons or groups who were hostile to the new Polish government or to the Soviets. We arrested Gestapo collaborators like members of the Polish Fascist Home Army, and we uncovered the names of individuals who had worked with the Nazis. Although [*Smersh*] Captain Kochetov was my superior in order of rank, I was actually working as adjutant to Colonel Gregory Zaitzev, who was the overall head of Soviet military intelligence for the Polish Second Army. I had fought alongside Russians, and looked up to them. They treated the Jewish officers in the Polish Army as brothers, and I saw them as our possible salvation. True, they had arrested some Polish nationalists. But I really didn't care what happened to them.
>
> During my first day at this new assignment, I learned that my initial investigation of Captain Olshewski [Olszewski] had mushroomed, implicating several hundred Poles still living in the

Poznan [Poznań] area. They had all been involved with fascist groups before the war and served the Germans as informers and undercover agents during the occupation. In 1945, orders were issued for certain Polish soldiers and civilians to leave for Russia. They were not really going there; instead, this was just another massive transport of people with questionable loyalties to the Polish town of Brezescz [Brześć?], which the Soviets had turned into a labor camp. Who were these latest deportees? They were physicians, lawyers, specialists, and surprisingly, many laborers who had never had anything to do with capitalistic regimes or rightist parties.[42]

Of course the alleged "fascists" and "German informers" seem to have been simply anti-Communist Poles, often soldiers of the war-time underground. Why were they pursued by persons of Jewish origin?

The journalist John Sack argues that "revenge" was an important factor that influenced Jewish participation in the Communist security apparatus.[43] Although Sack stresses the anti-German factor of "revenge," other sources show that Jewish retribution also had an anti-Polish edge. This is not to suggest that "all Jews" thought about nothing but vengeance. For example, after receiving death threats from several Poles who had acquired his property, a Jewish man sought assistance from the Soviet town commander of Jędrzejów. The Soviet officer told him to file an official complaint so that the guilty could be arrested and deported to the Gulag. Despite the fact that the Jewish victim was also prompted by his local Christian friends to punish the offenders, he refused: "Why don't you do it yourselves? Do you want the people to be saying that a Jew avenged himself? I shall not seek vengeance."[44] Nonetheless, Poland had its share of Jewish avengers.

Adina Blady Szwajgier, who worked for the Central Committee of Polish Jews, stated that one should "not forget about the role of the Jews in Poland following the war, when one considers Stalinist crimes... I cannot say that Jews were not involved in them. Do not think that there was no revenge in their actions. Jews are not angels."[45] Simon Wiesenthal, in turn, drew the following comparison: "I know what kind of role Jewish communists played in Poland after the war. And just as I, as a Jew, do not want to shoulder responsibility for the Jewish communists, I cannot blame 36 million Poles for those thousands of *szmalcownicy*" (i.e. blackmailers of Jews during the Nazi occupation).[46]

Jonathan Kaufman interviewed a Jewish functionary of the UB who had escaped from Auschwitz. Having been turned away by the independentist partisans wary of strangers, he therefore joined the Communist guerrillas. After the war,

> When he returned to his hometown in search of his family, he learned they had been wiped out by the Germans. The Poles seemed happy they were gone. Indeed, every Jew in his town had been killed; the Poles had moved into their houses. At this point the Communists asked him if he wanted to become a member of the secret police. He agreed.
>
> When I asked him why he had joined the secret police, the man uttered a single word: 'Revenge.'
>
> Especially in places like Poland, the annihilation of the Jews and the pogroms that erupted after the war confirmed for many Jewish Communists that these societies were so infiltrated with Fascism that extreme measures were required to extirpate it. The collaboration of Poles in the crimes against the Jews astounded and infuriated these Communists. Their reactions were, of course, understandable in young men returning home to find everything they knew and loved wiped out. But instead of sympathy, the Communists handed many of these angry young Jews guns and truncheons, urging them to root out the enemies of Communism — in essence to do the Communists' dirty work.[47]

Another Holocaust survivor,

> Ben Kass, who spent most of the war years in the forests with [Soviet] partisans, spoke with relish of the wrath he exacted both during and after the official hostilities. Having fought for several years with a Russian partisan group of eighteen thousand men and women, Ben was in Poland during the closing years of the war. He arrested many Poles from the AK who had previously murdered Jews, and handed them over to the Russian authorities for imprisonment.[48]

A Jewish witness from Ejszyszki recalled that

> When the Russians returned [in 1944], I went back to Aishishok [Ejszyszki] I enlisted in the N.K.W.D. [sic NKVD] troop which operated in Aishishok and the vicinity to purge the area of the Hitler collaborators and the White Polish partisans

[i.e. the AK] who we had learned to know during our 'hot' 'encounters' with them in the forests. Moshe Sononzon [Sonenson] and myself, thirsty for revenge belonged to an armed unit which, while pretending to search for Germans and traitors took reprisals on the evil goys as they richly deserved.

We terrorized the goys. We collected many articles and clothes robbed from Jews we had known and made those goys pay, if only a fraction for what they had done to us and our children. Thus, we continued to terrorize the 'German collaborators' and those who had 'enjoyed' the spectacle of Jewish murder.[49]

The son of Moshe Sonenson, Yitzhak, confirmed that

my father joined the Russian police, the NKVD, and when they traveled to look for Polish people he went with them. There were days that they killed about fifteen to twenty people and brought them to the Eishishok market. And they put them in the middle of the market to let other people see what is going to happen. It was like that for a month and a half without mercy.[50]

Leon Kahn described his participation in the anti-independentist raids both during the Nazi occupation and afterward and, in particular, how he avenged himself on a Pole who allegedly had been indirectly responsible for the death of Kahn's father during a skirmish between a Jewish-Soviet partisan unit and a Home Army detachment:

We came up to his house and I kicked the door and he was standing there and right away he started denying "I had nothing to do with it! I wouldn't do it to your father!" and so on. Anyway I told him to say his prayers. And I wasn't going to shoot him. I bayoneted [him], you know, maybe, I don't know, maybe 50 times. I really, really felt the time had come to payback. I didn't do it enough. I am only sorry I didn't do it more.[51]

Another Jewish survivor admitted that

When the Russians returned in 1944 and liberated Poland, I joined the regular Red Army. I returned to Biala Podleska [sic Biała Podlaska] and was there assigned as chief of the department of criminal offenders in the Distruict [sic District]

Police. I served there for half a year till I felt that I could no longer stand being in Poland. The chief of Police hinted to me that I must leave for there were many complaints about me from the personal vengeance I took on the White Poles (of the 'Armia-Krayova' [sic]) and on the other anti-Semitic hooligans who had showed excessive cruelty to the Jews under the German rule. I understood the hint. I also had a strong desire to leave Poland which was soaked in so much Jewish blood. In a Russian military car I crossed the border and entered Austria. From there I reached Italy and then Israel.[52]

In August 1944, in a village between Siemiatycze and Drohiczyn Kesil Karshenstein (Karszensztejn) took justice into his own hands and punished collectively the guilty and the innocent alike. Earlier, in March 1943, a Polish man allegedly denounced the sylvan hideaway of the Karshensteins to the Nazis who murdered them. Subsequently, according to a memorial book, "a week after the Red Army recaptured Bialistok [Białystok], the oldest son Kesil [Karshenstein], avenged the blood of his murdered family, shooting the treacherous Pole's entire family."[53]

After August 1944 in Lublin a group of former Jewish partisans, led by Simon Wiesenthal of Drohobycz, and Tuvia Friedman of Radom, Abba Kovner of Wilno, and Yitzhak Zuckerman (Icek Cukierman) of Warsaw allegedly formed a clandestine organization ominously called *Nekama* ("Revenge"). Its activities are unknown but its alleged targets were persons who had harmed Jews during the Nazi occupation.[54] An NKVD functionary, who happened to be a former Jewish partisan, affirmed that "revenge" also motivated his actions. Joseph Riwash recalled that "I looked for survivors of the Vilna [Wilno] ghetto and enlisted their help in uncovering Lithuanians and Poles who had denounced Jews to the Germans. We reported these individuals to the Soviet occupation authorities, who (be it said to their credit) dealt with them swiftly and summarily."[55]

Some other Jewish participants also claim rather disingenuously that they targeted only those members of the underground who had killed or otherwise harmed Jews. Nevertheless, any member of the underground seized for whatever reason could be (and often was) tortured by the NKVD to reveal the whereabouts of his confederates. Nearly anyone considered to be anti-Soviet faced retribution, although admittedly anti-Semites had more to fear from Jewish informers. Yet, if it is maintained that anti-Semitism was allegedly all-pervasive in Polish society, who was immune from denunciation?

Unscrupulous individuals also used the struggle against anti-

Semitism as an excuse to settle private scores. The head of the Communist movie industry Aleksander Ford, who was Jewish, baselessly denounced Jerzy Gabrielski, a film director, to the NKVD as a "reactionary" and an "anti-Semite." Gabrielski was arrested and tortured.[56] The definition of "a Nazi collaborator" was infinitely flexible. In Wilno, for instance, after many Lithuanian collaborators fled with the Nazis, "in the fall of 1944, the NKGB [NKVD] tracked down 'collaborators' among the remaining population, that is among the Poles. The concrete proof [of guilt] would be stretched beyond belief so that, as one unverifiable rumor had it, it was enough to posses in one's collection postage stamps from the Ostland [i.e. the Nazi-occupied Eastern Territories] or the GG [i.e. central Poland] with the likeness of Adolf Hitler on them to be accused of pro-fascist sympathies at the least and even of 'collaboration'." In fact, stamps bearing Hitler's likeness were practically the only ones available during the Nazi occupation. Therefore anyone would have had them, including philatelists.[58]

Even Jewish sources acknowledge how easy it was to be branded an anti-Semite and repressed. A Ukrainian woman in Lwów named "Parysia" (NN) saved two Jewish women during the Nazi occupation. In order to support herself and her cares, this woman frequently stole confiscated Jewish clothes from German warehouses. After the arrival of the Soviets someone must have denounced her as a Nazi collaborator. When the NKVD found Jewish items in her possession, she was shipped off to the Gulag. A similar fate befell another Christian rescuer of Jews. A Polish servant girl who had saved her Jewish mistress made some stereotypical, but in her opinion complimentary, remarks about Jews. She was overheard by a Soviet Jew, denounced, arrested, and dispatched to the Gulag. Both women most likely died in the camps. According to a Jewish account,

> A very close friend of mine and her sister were hidden, one in the space of a double ceiling, the other under a bed in the small apartment of the woman who cleaned their house before the war. Parysia, the cleaning woman, worked to support all three of them in a German warehouse where the clothes confiscated from the Jews of Lvov were cleaned, stored, and packaged for shipment to Germany, where they would be distributed. She would steal some items of clothing, sell them in the black market, and use the money to support herself and the two Jewish women.
>
> After the liberation the Russians suspected all Ukrainians and Poles of collaboration with the Germans, especially those who had a reputation of dealing on the black market with goods taken from Jews. The police came and searched her apartment

and found a piece of velvet from a Jewish "Talit bag." This was just what the Russians needed to arrest her. Velvet was the most expensive cloth on the black market.

Parysia was taken to the railroad station to be loaded into a boxcar and shipped to Siberia. Parysia was never heard from again.

Mrs. K. was from a well-to-do Jewish family and had a law degree before the war. Her servant girl from before the war, the daughter of a prostitute, became her rescuer. She did everything that she could for Mrs. K., often risking her life...

The girl spoke in the language and slang of her milieu, such as, "Jews are the business people." "They are the doctors." "They stick together." "You should know. You have a Yiddish head." Such phrases were often used by Jews themselves, but when used by Poles they became 'anti-Semitic.' The servant often meant them with love and respect for Mrs. K., or in some cases simply believed them. Her use of such phrases proved to be her downfall...

[After the arrival of the Red Army in July 1944], Mrs. K. and the servant went to work for a Russian hospital... There she was overheard making some of her "anti-Semitic" remarks by a Russian doctor, who happened to have been Jewish. He reported her as being a pro-Nazi and an anti-Semite. She was not only fired, but was sent to Siberia and, like so many others, was never heard of again.[57]

It seems then that informal cooperation was much more common than official service in the secret police. Probably in April 1944 in Trembowla, Shmercio Halpern denounced to the NKVD a local woman, Anna Bartetska (Bartecka), "who had betrayed the eight members of my family [to the Nazis] for some sugar two days later she was arrested by the Russians for collaborating with the enemy and was then sent to Siberia."[59]

Most likely in the summer of 1944 in Włodzimierz Wołyński, the Province of Volhynia, a Jewish woman, Irena Franziak, who had been sheltered with her baby by Ludwik Janiak, informed the NKVD about the Home Army group her benefactor belonged to. Janiak and five other insurgents were sent to the Gulag. The AK soldier died as a result of forced labor.[60]

Probably in the fall of 1944, in the village of Sąsiadka near Szczebrzeszyn, in the Province of Lublin, "Jews, who had been sheltered during the war by one of the farmers, put this farmer in [the Communist] jail in Zamość for belonging to the AK and for having cached weapons [for the underground]."[61] In the village of Dropie near Radzymin in eastern Mazovia, local Jews denounced a young Home Army soldier to the Communists despite the fact that his father facilitated their survival during the war. The AK man was arrested and never returned home.[62] In the spring of 1945, in Gorlice the leader of the local community of Jewish survivors informed the Soviets about two Poles who allegedly had denounced local Jews to the Germans. At least one of the alleged Polish informers was promptly tortured to death by the NKVD.[63]

After the arrival of the Red Army in Rożyszcze, the Province of Volhynia, in June of 1944, Jewish teenagers struck out against the locals who had allegedly harmed Jews. According to Zwi Roiter, "A group of seven of us who had still been children when the Nazis came, formed a revenge organization. We were encouraged by Bukin, a Jew from Kiev who was the [NKVD] deputy commander of Rozhishch [Rożyszcze]. With his informal approval we borrowed horses from the NKVD, and at nights we would hound those whom we knew had been especially vicious to the Jews, burning their houses and forcing them into hiding."[64] This was also the case in Luboml in Volhynia. Nathan Sobel recalled that "while I lived under the Soviets who were in Libivne [Luboml], I helped the Russians seek out the murderers of the Jews, and I was there long enough to see some revenge. After that, I left for Poland."[65]

In July 1944, in a forest near Raduń, in the Province of Nowogródek, Yankele Stolnicki and another Jewish man detected a unit of the AK hiding from the Soviets. They promptly informed the Red Army which took the Polish partisans prisoner and intended to shoot them. Their subsequent fate is unknown.[66]

Informal affiliation with the authorities sufficed to exact vengeance. At times, however, it led to formal employment with the secret police or the Communist military. Aba Gefen survived the war in the northern part of Poland's Eastern Borderlands. According to his account, "after my liberation for the next year I served the N.K.V.D., the Russian Police, as an interrogator of Nazis and their collaborators. In August 1945, I learned that the Soviet authorities were about to arrest me for 'complicity' in acts of revenge against Lithuanian Nazi collaborators, so I escaped to [central] Poland."[67] According to his secret police colleague, Leon Kahn, Gefen worked directly under a Soviet NKVD colonel in Alytus (Olita) and Orany (Varėna), where he interrogated prisoners. Gefen also took part in summary executions of suspected insurgents.[68]

In August 1944 in Mielec, the Province of Rzeszów, Mark Verstandig informed the NKVD about several Home Army men who allegedly had murdered Jews during the Nazi occupation. He later began working for the UB on the central level but continued to press for "retribution" against the killers on the local level. At least two of them paid with their lives.[69]

Also in August 1944, to the north of Lublin, an erstwhile Jewish partisan joined the NKVD. About his motives Mieczysław Grajewski, aka Zamojski, aka Martin Gray, stated that "I knew the N.S.Z. *I was a Jew with a private score to settle* [emphasis added]."[70] The Soviets encouraged him to "do your best, find us the N.S.Z., the informers, the denouncers, the collaborators, *the people who don't like us* [emphasis added]."[71]

The Jewish agent was sent to Zambrów and its environs, where he infiltrated the underground. A wave of arrests followed but Zamojski had to flee an assassination attempt. Soon, he continued his tasks elsewhere. According to his recollections,

> I arrived in Zambrow [Zambrów] one morning in civilian clothes, a peasant. I went from village to village, and mingled with the peasants. I found some N.S.Z. men, and an N.K.V.D. car came and picked them up in the morning. We had to purge the countryside; it was their turn to pay. I went from village to village, tracking them down in a pitiless, bitter spirit of revenge. In Zambrow they were waiting for me. Some men appeared before me. Three of them were barring my way, arms outstretched. I leaped aside and made off through a cornfield. They were behind me. I gradually outstripped [i.e. outdistanced] them. They'd given up the chase but the warning was clear: I was of no further use in the Zambrow area. The N.S.Z. had spotted me. I slept in the [NKVD] *Kommandantura*, revolver in hand, and the next day the captain in charge at Zambrow decided to send me back to Lublin.
>
> At the *Kommandantura* [in Lublin], the gray-haired [Soviet] colonel had me attached to an N.K.V.D. unit that followed up the front line troops purging Russian-occupied territory of suspicious elements.[72]

In the fall of 1944 and later, Ephraim Schwarzmann, a Volhynian Jew who spent the Nazi occupation in the Soviet Union, was transferred from the Red Army to head a special task force of the Polish Communist military in the Kowel area in the Eastern Borderlands. According to his recollections,

I was put in charge of a special unit which was to act as a liaison between the Polish and Russian Armies. For my unit I chose Poles who had suffered at the hands of the Germans and I selected former underground characters [i.e. Communist partisans]. I knew what I intended to do — to be revenged at all costs... My only inclination was to stay as close to the front as possible to take my revenge on the Germans and their Polish and Ukrainian collaborators. In the villages of Golova [Hołoby], Midniovka [?], and Groskovka [Gruszówka] (near Kovel) I gave the underworld characters in my unit a free hand to deal with any collaborators and they did their work so thoroughly that I received a severe reprimand from General Headquarters.[73]

In January 1945, in a village near Kraków, Naftali Saleschutz, an ex-Communist partisan who served as a liaison with the Red Army, shot a Polish peasant who had supposedly confessed to killing Jews during the war. As Tadeusz Zaleski, Saleschutz soon became a colonel in the Communist army.[74]

Probably in February 1945, Isadore Hollander volunteered for an informal Jewish revenge group that consisted of some soldiers of the Red Army and the Polish "people's" army. The group operated in Łódź and its environs. It seems that the Communist secret police supplied the group with lists of alleged Nazi collaborators (of course accused of having harmed Jews), and the Jewish death squad carried out the assassinations believing that they were avenging themselves on the anti-Semitic perpetrators. At least some, if not most, of their victims must have been Polish independentists who had nothing to do with any anti-Jewish actions. According to Hollander, his group targeted the Poles who

tried to help the Germans destroy the Jews and we found out about them. The time came for revenge. It was an illegal procedure [but] I had a little bit of power. I wore a [Polish "people's" army] uniform and I found more Jewish soldiers already in the army. I [also] found Jewish officers in the Russian army and they already knew [what] Hitler did and they started to feel with us. I think I started to feel better [when I took] the revenge which I did.

We went out every night for a little bit of a ride. We had a list, Poles [i.e. secret police] giving us lists of all those names. They were glad to give us details because their civilians couldn't do much. We went out, three soldiers at night. We did use guns but I had to close my eyes and ask God for forgiveness [for] what I have to do. Because of being a Jew it was a hard bite. It was the worst thing in my life to see what I have to do. It was my commitment. That's why I enlisted myself [in the military]. I didn't have to enlist myself to become a volunteer [in the death squad] but I did it because of revenge. I wanted to do it and I did it. As it went on, I felt satisfied. We didn't touch German [civilians].[75]

On March 24, 1945, the secret police tracked down and shot the Home Army soldiers Tomasz Hołownia and Jeruzalski in Beliny near Huszcza, the county of Biała Podlaska. A Jewish functionary of the UB, Golczer, allegedly inspired the hunt and participated in the shooting in revenge for Hołownia's self-defense activities during the Nazi occupation.[76]

Most likely in June 1945 in Warsaw a lieutenant colonel, who happened to be Jewish, attempted to avenge himself on Dr. Jerzy Filip ("Biga") of the AK. A year earlier, in the south of Lublin, this Jewish man was captured by the AK unit of Captain Edward Błaszczak ("Grom"), who suspected him of being a Nazi spy. The partisans would have shot him had it not been for the intercession of Dr. Filip who recommended a whipping to extract information. The captive eventually confessed to being a Jew in hiding and, to prove the truthfulness of his confession, described a clandestine forest camp, where Dr. Filip often administered to the health of the Jewish fugitives. His identity established, the captive was released. After the war, however, upon accidentally meeting Dr. Filip in Warsaw, the Jewish man, now an officer in the Communist military, arrested the Home Army physician. Fortunately, Dr. Filip managed to overpower his guard and escape.[77]

On April 24, 1946, a Communist militiaman summarily shot a Pole in Będzin after the latter had been "recognized by a Jewish woman." She claimed that this man had allegedly abused Jews during the Nazi occupation.[78]

In the summer of 1946 in Białystok, after a chance encounter, Dawid Lipnicki denounced the AK soldier Wacław Misiuro to the NKVD. At the behest of Father (Lieutenant Colonel) Gedymin Pilecki, the head AK chaplain for the Province of Nowogródek, Misiuro had sheltered Lipnicki for several years during the Nazi occupation in Hermaniszki, the county of Lida. After the Soviet arrival, Lipnicki joined the Red Army. Clearly, in this case, loyalty to the Soviet liberators outweighed any obligation toward his Polish rescuer.[79]

It is obvious that extrajudicial undertakings in pursuit of justice invited abuse. It is also clear that the intelligence provided to the NKVD was sufficient to harm not only those Poles who had allegedly wronged Jews but also any member of the underground, his family, friends, and even casual acquaintances. After all, at the time the Communists were persecuting, arresting, deporting, and killing tens of thousands of members of Polish clandestine organizations, most of whom probably had not harmed Jews, and at times even assisted them. Thus, the informers were resented by the Polish population in general and the insurgents in particular. Aggression against the Jewish community as a whole sometimes followed. That, in turn, forced all Jews to seek protection from the Communists. In addition, the insurgents felt that at least in certain cases the killing of the Jews that had occurred during the German occupation was justifiable self-defense against alleged bandits, Nazi agents, and Communists.[80]

For example, in October 1944, in Tarnobrzeg the underground was alarmed that "denunciations occurred against the AK [soldiers] for the alleged participation in the murder of the Jews."[81]

Most likely acting just on such tips, in 1946 the secret police initiated an investigation of Lieutenant Marian Sołtysiak ("Barabasz") and his AK partisans of the "Wybraniecki" unit, who were accused of burning six Jews and their Polish rescuer alive in Zagórze near Kielce on February 16, 1944. "Barabasz" and his men drew lengthy jail sentences.[82]

Because unfounded Jewish allegations must have mingled with justified Jewish complaints which nonetheless, if inadvertently, assisted the secret police in identifying the independentists, it seems that all manner of denouncing further increased the popular resentment against Jewish (and other) informers. Finally, the crimes of individual Jewish Communists were immediately projected onto the Jewish community at large. In Raciąż, for example, in response to the abusive ways of "Szymek" (NN), probably a Jewish security man, a group of unknown perpetrators, likely the insurgents, struck at his quarters in the spring of 1945. According to a Jewish witness, the culprit was absent but the attackers kidnapped six Jews in his stead and killed them. The circumstances of this assault remain unexplored yet it appears that victims most likely had nothing to do with the Communists.[83]

Against this violent background, the leaders of the organized Jewish community at the center and their rank-and-file followers in the countryside differed somewhat in their attitudes toward the Communists and the insurgents. Initially, the leadership of the Central Committee of Polish Jews refrained from actively and directly taking sides in the struggle between the Communists and the insurgents. The obvious exception was its open endorsement of the regime and its propaganda, thus helping to maintain the fiction, mostly for the benefit of the West, that the Communist government of Poland was "democratic." However, on the provincial level, Jewish self-defense forces appeared spontaneously in the wake of the Soviet arrival. Most seem to have instantaneously secured the unofficial blessing of the Communists, although at least some of them were involved in secret Zionist work.[84] Sociologist Jan Tomasz Gross argues, however, that it was only after a great wave of pogroms and attacks in the spring and summer of 1946 that the Jewish leadership decided to organize a formal institution that would work with the secret police. Between July 1946 and March 1947, a number of the so-called Special Commissions (*Komisje Specjalne — KS*) operated under the guidance of the Central Special Commission (CKS) with the Central Committee of Polish Jews.[85] Most likely they were based upon the informal self-defense groups created locally as early as 1944. One of the Jewish leaders recalled that "the authorities regarded them as a kind of popular militia for the defense of Jews. The Poles [i.e. Communists] did not interfere, and no one supervised us. The weapons were given to us in full trust."[86] Many, if not most volunteers were also members of the Jewish war veterans' association that was firmly under Communist control. In some places, Silesia in particular, the KS units were amalgamated into the Volunteer Reserve of the Citizens Militia (ORMO). According to the regional historian Julian Kwiek, about 2,500 men enrolled in 200 local cells of the CKS.[87] These bodies formalized and institutionalized free-lance informing by members of the Jewish community on the Polish population, the underground included. According to its final report,

> The chief duty of the C.K.S. was to aid the [Communist] authorities, through the proper organization of the security and defense of Jewish institutions, to protect the lives of the Jewish population of the country, to prevent panic, and to enable the Jewish society to [carry on] peaceful [and] constructive work... to rebuild its life. The first step of the C.K.S. was establishing a close contact with the Security Authorities of Democratic [i.e. Communist] Poland. The [security] authorities reacted to our plans favorably and supported our efforts, granting us universal help.
>
> The contact of the K.S. in the entire country with the Organs of the M.B.P., M.O., and O.R.M.O. [i.e. the Communist security forces] was close and the collaboration yielded good

results. *In the period of their activity the K.S. undertook over 2,000 interventions with the [security] Authorities throughout the country.*
The work of our apparatus [of informers] was universal. We had our people in factories, market squares, schools, universities, etc. Our people even attended [Christian] churches [emphasis in the original].[88]

The activities of the agents of these Special Commissions varied from infiltrating the underground to looking for manifestations of anti-Semitism in public life. According to the final report quoted above, "thanks to our information the [security] Authorities have liquidated four bands of the N.S.Z. and W.I.N. ([in] Wrocław and Szczecin)."[89] Another reported success of the CKS was the denunciation to the secret police of the manager of a public library in Włocławek in December 1946. It seems that she was unaware that there was an allegedly anti-Semitic book in the collection. As Gross put it, "unfortunately in those times even denunciations by half-illiterates about books had severe consequences and as a result of the intervention [with the UB] by the Łepek siblings [i.e. by Icek and Helcza Łepek] the [public] library in Włocławek was shut down and the completely innocent manager was arrested."[90] The Special Commission in the Province of Kraków, however, intervened very rarely. Once a Jewish self-defense group repelled an attack in Rabka. It intervened four times in Kraków itself to prevent provocations involving the alleged kidnapping of Christian children by Jews, which routinely was invoked as a reason to incite mobs to stage pogroms.[91]

In self-defense or in revenge some persons of Jewish origin denounced, arrested, and even killed a large number of Poles, at least some of whom were not guilty of any anti-Semitic deeds. Some witnesses recalled quite precisely how many Poles were affected and how many Jews were involved. However, many cases are open to interpretation. Most still need to be confirmed and elaborated upon.

For example, the Special Commissions alone are credited with 2,000 "interventions" with the secret police. Such "interventions" included complaints and denunciations, at least some of which resulted in arrests. Next, it is very probable that members of Jewish self-defense participated as auxiliaries in the operations of the secret police, including apprehending suspects and perhaps pursuing the insurgents.[92] As for Jewish denunciations, they affected anywhere from one person (e.g. the librarian in Włocławek) to entire underground groups ("four bands" in Szczecin and Wrocław). Between 1944 and 1947 an autonomous (local) underground group could have as few as ten members and as many as several hundred. National groups had easily thousands of affiliates. Thus, if the Jewish Commission boasted that "four bands" were destroyed thanks to its work, that could mean the arrest of a few score or even several hundred Poles. It is entirely possible that if a Jewish agent denounced even a single independentist, the ensuing investigation, expedited by the ruthless interrogation methods of the secret police, resulted in many further arrests. After all, as Maurice Shainberg admitted, his investigation of Captain Olszewski led to the implication of "several hundred" of Poles, who were doubtless apprehended by the Soviet military intelligence.[93] How many victims should Shainberg be given credit for: one or "several hundred"? Most Jewish sources are even less precise, listing "many" Poles or alleged "Nazi collaborators" (which was often, but not always, a byword for independentists) denounced, imprisoned, despoiled, beaten, abused, or shot.

Finally, only some of the deeds against the Poles could be described as "purely Jewish," namely where a Jew, for his own private or broader Jewish reasons, initiated hostile actions against a specific Pole or a specific group of Poles considered anti-Jewish. But even in the case of a "purely Jewish" deed the line between Jewish self-interest and the Communist cause is blurry. For example, although he was a high ranking Communist policemen, Shneor Glembotzky openly admitted that he took "personal vengeance" on the AK and "anti-Semites." On the one hand, his actions had nothing to do with Communism. On the other, to complicate things, by eliminating enemies of the Soviet Union, Glembotzky expedited Stalin's aims in Poland. Likewise, individuals like Alter Michelovsky and Moshe Sonenson, acting on specific Jewish grievances, attacked Polish independentists together with the NKVD men, who had their own unrelated reasons to target the Poles.

In sum, some Jewish actions against the Poles appear to have been perfectly justifiable, for example Frydzia Baldinger's search for redress that led her to denounce the man who allegedly had turned her family in to the Nazis. Some Jewish actions were plainly damnable, for example Maurice Shainberg's activities in the Soviet secret police. Most anti-Polish activities carried out by Jews fell in between the clearly understandable and clearly damnable categories, leaning in each individual case more toward one or the other side.

Although the acts of revenge often defy a clear-cut categorization, it is important to stress that they arose in a spontaneous manner from below among individual Jews. *Pace* conspiracy theorists, there was no nationwide "Jewish conspiracy," which does not mean that some Jews did not act in concert. Some of them formed secret groups and organizations, most notably *Nekama*, to carry out retribution on alleged Polish anti-Semitic perpetrators. Their deeds combined with much more numerous unorganized Jewish acts of revenge and self-defense. In the eyes of the Poles, since the Communists apparently did not punish the Jewish avengers and, in some instances, even encouraged them, all violent Jewish actions and their results contributed to the reinforcement of the stereotype of *żydokomuna*.

The following is a list of Poles affected by Jewish actions based only upon Jewish accounts mentioned in this chapter.

Table 1
Poles affected by Jewish actions

Source	Action
Frydzia Baldinger	1 Pole denounced
Mark Verstandig	5 Poles denounced, 2 killed
Szulim Sznycer	5 Poles denounced and arrested
Chaim Shapiro	39 Poles arrested and shot
Maurice Shainberg	"several hundred" Poles arrested
Abraham Wunderboim	some Nazi "cooperators" arrested
Mieczysław Grajewski	some NSZ members denounced and arrested
Ben Kass	"many Poles" arrested
Alter Michelovsky	revenge on "evil goys" and the AK
Moshe Sonenson	15 to 20 "Polish people" killed daily
Naftali Saleschutz	1 Pole killed
Leon Kahn	1 Pole killed
Aba Gefen	"Nazi collaborators" arrested and killed
Kesil Karshenstein	"entire [Polish] family" killed
Joseph Riwash	individual Poles denounced
Ephraim Schwarzmann	Polish "collaborators" killed
Samuel Oliner	2 Poles denounced and one of them killed
Yankele Stolnicki	"Polish partisans" denounced and arrested
Isadore Hollander	a number of Poles killed

Thus, nineteen Jewish witnesses describe their part in the denunciation, arrest, and killing of several hundred Poles in at least 23 localities. Of course, each case needs to be carefully verified but some preliminary thoughts on the raw data are possible. Depending on the area affected (e.g., three villages), the circumstances of the events (e.g., a whole partisan unit denounced), and the rank (and hence his capacity for damage) of the person of Jewish origin involved in anti-Polish actions, I estimate conservatively that around 300 Polish victims were involved, including perhaps 70 killed. If Jan Tomasz Gross's data about the Jewish Commission and nine Polish sources cited in this chapter are included, the number of Poles affected will increase significantly (other sources concerning the issue will be analyzed later in this work).

Accordingly, the following preliminary rough estimate can be made.

Table 2
Jewish involvement against the Poles: A Sample Estimate No. 1[94]

Poles:	minimum	maximum
denounced	2,080	6,148
arrested	2,145	6,625
killed directly	23	73
caused to be killed	65	220

Thus, for a variety of sometimes complex reasons, persons of Jewish origin were responsible for harming up to 7,000 Poles as established on the basis of a very limited sample of accounts. Although few in number, these sources are very useful in suggesting trends in Polish-Jewish relations rather than in providing precise statistics. We must remember, however, that the true extent of Jewish actions against the Poles will only be known if the secret police files and other pertinent records are made available.

Notes

1   Max Ostro, "The last deportation," *Memorial Book Szydłowiec*, ed. by Berl Kagan (New York: Published by Shidlowtzer Benevolent Association of New York, 1989), 329.

2   See Marek Jan Chodakiewicz, *Żydzi i Polacy, 1918-1955: Współistnienie, Zagłada, Komunizm* (Warszawa: Fronda, 2001); Marek Jan Chodakiewicz, "Dialektyka cudzego nieszczęścia: Teoria i praktyka polityki PPR w stosunku do Żydów w okresie II wojny światowej w świetle dokumentów i badań naukowych," in Chodakiewicz, Gontarczyk and Żebrowski, *Tajne oblicze*, 2: 21-42; Chodakiewicz, *Narodowe*, 113-18.

3   For example, in Warsaw Frydzia Baldinger, aka Sława Szymańska, denounced to the Communists Tadeusz Zawada, who had allegedly informed the Nazis about the woman's mother and sister. After the war Baldinger tracked Zawada down in Lublin where he served as a captain in the Polish "people's" army. It is unclear whether Baldinger's actions resulted in the arrest of Zawada. She recalled that after confronting him, the man threatened her and, thus, "I fled from Lublin, glad to have escaped with my life." See Diane Armstrong, *Mosaic: A Chronicle of Five Generations* (Sydney: Random House, 1998), 343-44, 352-53. In Jędrzejów an alleged denouncer of Jews called Gajos was unremorseful when confronted by a friend and rescuer of the victims, Tola Grzywnowiczówna-Leszczyńska, but subsequently he went into hiding and even was thought to be responsible for an unsuccessful assassination attempt on Tola. Reportedly, Gajos went unpunished. See Kałowska, *Uciekać, aby żyć*, 231, 233.

4   Cała, "Mniejszość żydowska," in Madajczyk, *Mniejszości narodowe w Polsce*, 259.

5   For accounts by Jewish avengers who commenced their activities already during the Nazi occupation see Hillel, *Le Massacre des survivants*, 151; Werner, *Fighting Back*, 167-69, 178-79; Eliezer Tash (Tur-Shalom), ed., *The Community of Semiatych* (Tel Aviv: Association of Former Residents of Semiatych in Israel and the Diaspora, 1965), xii–xiii. At times Jewish avengers, inadvertently, worked hand-in-glove with the independentists. For instance, according to an underground dispatch, during the German occupation in March 1944, a hit squad of the NSZ assassinated a Nazi collaborator, Pazdruk from Blinów, the county of Kraśnik. "The Communists suspected that he had informed the [Nazi] police about the movement of Jewish bands. Therefore already last fall the jews [sic] kidnapped him and attempted to kill him in the forest but, although wounded, he ran away and went into hiding. A few days ago Sosna's [NSZ] men killed him. . . It was easy because Pazdruk was only hiding from jews [sic] and Communists." Nazi collaborators often constituted as much of a danger to the independentists as they did to fugitive Jews. See Pismo "Warmińskiego" do Komendy Okręgu NSZ, 23 March 1944, APL, NSZ, file 47.

6   Chana Fuks, "The Battle for Life: Memories from the time of the Holocaust," in *Stawiski: Sefer yizkor; Stawiski Memorial Book*, ed. by I. Rubin (Tel Aviv: Stavisk Society, 1973). This is a translation posted on the Internet at <http://www.jewishgen.org/yizkor>.

7   Zawadzka-Wetz, *Refleksje*, 40.

8   Marcel Reich-Ranicki, *Mein Leben* (Stuttgart: Deutsche Verlags-Anstalt, 1999).

9   After surveying the Jewish underground press published in the Warsaw ghetto, historian Teresa Prekerowa noted the existence of strong pro-Soviet sentiments among certain Zionist factions. Leftist Zionists saw their future linked with the Communists, whom most Poles considered to be an enemy on par with the Nazis. The Hashomer Hatza'ir faction regarded the Soviet-German Non-Aggression Pact of August 1939,

which partitioned Poland between those two invaders, to be a "wise and justified move." Mordechai Anielewicz, who became the commander of the Jewish Fighting Organnization (ŻOB), to which Yitzhak Zuckerman also belonged, was the editor of a periodical (*Neged Hazerem*) that openly embraced Communism over capitalism and the Soviet Union over Poland. See Teresa Prekerowa, "The Jewish Underground and the Polish Underground," in *Polin: Studies in Polish Jewry*, vol. 9, *Poles, Jews, Socialists: The Failure of an Ideal* (London: The Littman Library of Jewish Civilization, 1996), 151–53.

10 Zuckerman, *A Surplus of Memory*, 556–57.

11 Natalia Aleksiun, "Ruch syjonistyczny wobec systemu rządów w Polsce w latach 1944–1949," in Szarota, *Komunizm*, 234–35.

12 ibid., 235 *n.* 8.

13 ibid., 238, 244–45.

14 David Zabludovsky, "Horrors, Death and Destruction (Experiences of a Holocaust Survivor)," *Zabludow: Dapim mi-tokh yisker-bukh*, ed. by Nechama Shmueli-Schmusch ([Tel Aviv:] Former Residents of Zabludow in Israel, 1987), transl. by Ziva Rosenhand and posted online at <www.jewishgen.org/yizkor> [afterward *Zabludow*, Internet].

15 The Soviet ambassador in Warsaw accused three leading Polish Communists of Jewish origin of "Jewish nationalism." See Kochański, *Polska w dokumentach*, 47. According to the prominent Jewish Communist secret policeman Roman Romkowski concerning a Jewish defector from the security service, "beginning in 1952, in various statements of [Colonel Józef] Światło before me and [Colonel Anatol] Fejgin [a Communist secret policeman of Jewish origin], there emerged ever stronger Jewish-nationalist tendencies in reactions to various personnel decisions in our state and other people's democracies." Simply, Światło must have expressed his displeasure at purges of Jewish Communists. See Roman Romkowski quoted in Marat and Snopkiewicz, *Ludzie bezpieki*, 23.

16 See Zygmunt Berling, *Wspomnienia: Przeciw 17 Republice* (Warszawa: Polski Dom Wydawniczy Sp. z o.o., 1991), 283-85.

17 See Daniel Blatman, "Polish Anti-Semitism and 'Judeo-Communism': Historiography and Memory," *East European Jewish Affairs*, vol. 27, no. 1 (1997): 30.

18 See Teofila Weintraub quoted in Ruta Pragier, *Żydzi czy Polacy* (Warszawa: Oficyna Wydawnicza Rytm, 1992), 91.

19 Krzysztof Srebrny in "Dyskusja: Wnuki 'żydokomuny,'" *Idełe: Żydowskie pismo otwarte, Wydanie specjalne: Żydzi komunizm* [Warsaw] (Spring 2000): 166.

20 Mateusz Wyrwich, *Łagier Jaworzno: Z dziejów czerwonego terroru* (Warszawa: Editions Spotkania, 1995), 36-37.

21 "Ja tu was Polaków wszystkich powystrzelam." Quoted in Urbański, *Kieleccy Żydzi*, 191-92. This complaint concerned either Jewish or Soviet secret policemen, or both. For the ethnic composition of the secret police leadership in Kielce see below.

22 Czesław Leopold and Krzysztof Lechicki, *Więźniowie polityczni w Polsce, 1945-56* (Paris: Editions Spotkania, 1983), 15.

23 See Hirszfeld quoted in Fijałkowska, *Borejsza i Różański*, 139.

24 See Chaim Shapiro, *Go, My Son* (Jerusalem and New York: Feldheim Publishers, 1989), 492, 503.

25	Irving Zahn, "Life as a Russian Soldier," in *We Shall Not Forget! Memories of the Holocaust*, 2nd ed., ed. by Carole Garbuny Vogel (Lexington, Mass.: Temple Isaiah, 1995), 297-98. Irving Zahn was a Zionist and a Polish citizen who joined the Soviet secret police after the Red Army invaded Poland in 1939.

26	Nechama Tec, *Dry Tears: The Story of a Lost Childhood* (New York: Oxford University Press, 1984), 230 [afterward *Dry Tears*].

27	Verstandig, *I Rest My Case*, 218.

28	Werner, *Fighting Back*, 232.

29	Hillel based himself upon an interview with a Jewish witness testifying under the pseudonym "Ignacy Borkowski." The witness was most likely Paweł Korzec, who had joined the Soviet partisans during the Nazi occupation and later became the deputy head of the Citizens Militia in Białystok. See Hillel, *Le Massacre des survivants*, 46.

30	Rotenberg defected to West Germany in 1950. See Christian Schmidt-Häuer, "Jakob und seine Geschwister," *Die Zeit*, 19 June 2001.

31	Franciszek Gryciuk and Piotr Matusak, eds., *Represje NKWD wobec żołnierzy podziemnego Państwa Polskiego w latach 1944-1945*, vol. 1: *Wybór źródeł* (Siedlce: WSRP, 1995), 1: 138 [afterward *Represje NKWD*].

32	Gryciuk and Matusak, *Represje NKWD*, 1: 206.

33	Raport sytuacyjny Inspektoratu AK Rzeszów do Podokręgu, 26 October 1944, quoted in Zbigniew K. Wójcik, *Rzeszów w latach drugiej wojny światowej: Okupacja i konspiracja, 1939-1944-1945* (Rzeszów and Kraków: Instytut Europejskich Studiów Społecznych w Rzeszowie and Towarzystwo Sympatyków Historii w Krakowie, 1998), 297.

34	Tadeusz Wiącek, ed., *Zabić Żyda: Kulisy i tajemnice pogromu kieleckiego, 1946* (Kraków: Oficyna Wydawnicza "Temax," 1992), 144.

35	Urbański, *Kieleccy Żydzi*, 191; Danuta Blus-Węgrowska, "Atmosfera pogromowa," *Karta* 18 (1996): 101; Chodakiewicz, Gontarczyk, and Żebrowski, *Tajne oblicze*, 2: 19-20, 119-20, 126, 188-89.

36	Yaffa Eliach, *There Once Was A World: A Nine-Hundred-Year Chronicle of the Shtetl of Eishyshok* (Boston: Little, Brown and Company, 1998), 669-70 [afterward *There Once Was a World*].

37	Shalom Yoran, *The Defiant: A True Story* (New York: St. Martin's Press, 1996), 237, 242-45 [afterward *Defiant*].

38	Jack Kagan and Dov Cohen, *Surviving the Holocaust with the Russian Jewish Partisans* (London and Portland, OR: Vallentine Mitchell, 1998), 96-98.

39	Abraham Wunderboim, "In the hands of fate," in *The Lomaz Book: A Memorial to the Jewish Community of Lomaz*, ed. by Yitzhak Alperovitz (Tel Aviv: Published by the Lomaz Society in Israel with the Participation of the Lomaz Society in the United States of America, 1994), 40 [afterward *The Lomaz Book*].

40	Zuckerman, *A Surplus of Memory*, 477, 582, 656.

41	Jan Dawid Landau, "Byłem ochroniarzem Karskiego," *Losy żydowskie: Świadectwo żywych*, ed. by Marian Turski (Warszawa: Stowarzyszenie Żydów Kombatantów i Poszkodowanych w II Wojnie Światowej, 1996), 147 [afterward "Byłem" in *Losy żydowskie*].

42	Shainberg, *Breaking from the KGB*, 124-25, 158, 164. Shainberg was a Zionist-Revisionist before and during the war. Afterwards, in the ranks of the Communist counterintelligence, he continued secretly to aid the cause of Israel. All the while, between February and April 1946, in the environs of Krotoszyn, Shainberg also hunted down "two active anti-Soviet Polish partisan groups" codenamed "Bór" and "Cień" which were subordinated to the insurgent Major Zygmunt Szendzielarz ("Łupaszko"). *Smersh* Colonel Zaitsev and Shainberg employed two agents: "Zając" and Lieutenant Świderski ("Cukier"). See ibid., 194-96.

43   Understandably, not only Jewish secret policemen hated the Germans and their collaborators of various ethnic groups. For a story of a Jewish avenger who pursued alleged Belorussian collaborators hiding in Poland see Aharon Moravtchik, "My Small Revenge from the Heinous Crime, May 1946," *Memorial Book of David-Horodok* posted online at <http://davidhorodok.tripod.com/8a.html>. Civilian Jews also avenged themselves on German and autochthonous inhabitants of Silesia, the Sudetenland, Austria, Hungary, and elsewhere. See Sack, *An Eye for an Eye*, 100-11; Jacob Egit, *Grand Illusion* (Toronto: Lugus, 1991), 52-53 [afterward *Grand*]; Donald L. Niewyk, ed., *Fresh Wounds: Early Narratives of Holocaust Survival* (Chapel Hill, NC, and London: The University of North Carolina Press, 1998), 133-34 [afterward *Fresh Wounds*]; Abraham H. Biderman, *The World of My Past* (Sydney: Random House, 1995), 19, 331-32 [afterward *World*]; Jack Kuper, *After the Smoke Cleared* (Toronto: Stoddart, 1994), 6-7; Leon Kahn, *No Time to Mourn: A True Story of a Jewish Partisan Fighter* (Vancouver: Laurelton Press, 1978), 205-6 [afterward *No Time*]; Henry Friedman, *I'm No Hero: Journeys of a Holocaust Survivor* (Seattle and London: University of Washington Press, 1999), 56, 60, 63, 65 [afterward *I'm No Hero*]; Laszlo Karsai, "The People's Courts and Revolutionary Justice in Hungary, 1945-46," *The Politics of Retribution in Europe: World War II and Its Aftermath*, ed. by István Deák, Jan T. Gross, and Tony Judt (Princeton, N.J.: Princeton University Press, 2000), 245-47 [afterward "The People's Courts" in *The Politics of Retribution*]. According to *The Canadian Jewish News* (17 February 2000), there was even a plot by a clandestine Jewish group, the Avengers, to poison more than 2,000 imprisoned SS-men. This story is confirmed by Beckman and Segev, who reveal also other acts of Jewish retribution on the Germans. See Morris Beckman, *The Jewish Brigade: An Army with Two Masters, 1944-1945* (Staplehurst: Spellmount, 1998), 126-27; Tom Segev, *The Seventh Million: The Israelis and the Holocaust* (New York: Hill and Wang, 1993), 140-49 [afterward *The Seventh Million*]. For an account of Jewish prisoners of a Nazi concentration camp killing a Jewish kapo after the liberation see Joe Rosenblum and David Kohn, *Defy the Darkness: A Tale of Courage in the Shadow of Mengele* (London and Westport, Conn.: Praeger, 2001), 286-87. A Jewish soldier in the Polish Communist army recalls that he and his gentile colleagues, after liberating a concentration camp, avenged themselves upon innocent German civilians. See Lasman, *Wspomnienia*, 49. In April 1946, in the British zone of occupation, Lt. Feliks Rohatyn, an officer of the 24th Lancers, 1st Polish Armored Division (and later in the Israeli army), led his underlings in destroying German property in reprisal for allegedly celebrating Hitler's birthday. Namely, at the head of 80 Polish tanks, he pulverized freshly plowed and planted fields of over a dozen square kilometers. Allegedly, Polish (Christian) counterparts and superiors of Rohatyn abused German civilians as ruthlessly. See Wojciech Cioromski, interview by the author, 10 March 1997, Chicago.

44   Kałowska, *Uciekać, aby żyć*, 229.

45   Adina Blady Szwajgier, "Tak naprawdę – w 1942 roku wyszłam z domu i nigdy do niego nie powróciłam," in Anka Grupińska, *Po kole: Rozmowy z żydowskimi żołnierzami* (Warszawa: Wydawnictwo Alfa, 1991), 180.

46   Interview with Simon Wiesenthal, Radio Free Europe (Munich), January 7, 1989, as cited in Wladyslaw T. Bartoszewski, *The Convent at Auschwitz* (London: The Bowerdean Press, 1990), 30.

47   Jonathan Kaufman, *A Hole in the Heart of the World: Being Jewish in Eastern Europe* (New York: Viking, 1997), 110 [afterward *A Hole in the Heart*].

48   Aaron Hass, *The Aftermath: Living With the Holocaust* (New York: Cambridge University Press, 1995), 170.

49   Alter Michelovsky, "The White Partisan Attack on Aishishok," *"Aishishuk"* — *Its History and Its Destruction: Documentaries, Memories and Illustrations*, ed. by Peretz Alufi and Shaul Kaleko (Barkeli) and transl. by Shoshanna Gavish ([Jerusalem?]: n.p. 1980), 79-80 [afterward "The White Partisan" in *Aishishuk*]. This is a translation of Peretz Alufi and Shaul Kaleko (Barkeli) eds., *Eishishok, koroteha ve-hurbanah: Pirke zikhronot ve-'eduyot (be-tseruf temunot) liket* [Ejszyszki, its History and Destruction] (Jerusalem: Committee of the Survivors of Ejszyszki in Israel, 1950).

50   Yitzhak Sonenson in the documentary film "There Once Was a Town," WETA TV (PBS), Washington, shown in October 2000.

51   Leon Kahn in the documentary film "There Once Was a Town," WETA TV (PBS), Washington, shown in October 2000. It is unclear whether Kahn perpetrated his deed before or after the arrival of the Red Army in 1944. However, in his memoris Kahn relates the story of a Jewish family camp, which included his father, in the Lipiczański forest, that apparently experienced no problems with Polish independentists until the arrival of some Soviet and Jewish partisans of the Lenin Komsomol Brigade and the Davidov unit. Using the Jewish family camp as their staging point, they carried out a number of anti-Polish independentist attacks, including supply raids against Polish peasants. Therefore, a Pole named Nowicki allegedly revealed the whereabouts of the Jewish family camp to the AK, which ambushed some Jewish fugitives, killing Kahn's father. Subsequently, Kahn confesses that "we detoured to Nowicki's farm. I had no definite proof that he had betrayed us, but every indication pointed at him. But Nowicki's pleas fell on deaf ears. Repeatedly, I stabbed him over and over again with my bayonet. For the moment I was glad. But Nowicki was not dead. I had inflicted something far more horrible on him: he was blinded and maimed. He lived out the rest of his life unable to see, speak, or function in any normal way." See Kahn, *No Time*, 142-44, 158. For the chronology of Polish-Soviet fighting in the area of the Lipiczański forest see Zygmunt Boradyn, Andrzej Chmielarz and Henryk Piskunowicz, eds., *Armia Krajowa na Nowogródczyźnie i Wileńszczyźnie (1942-1945) w świetle dokumentów sowieckich* (Warszawa: Instytut Studiów Politycznych PAN, 1997), 146.

52   Shneor Glembotzky, "From a Prisoner's Camp to a Partisan Troop," in Alufi and Kaleko, *Aishishuk*, 77-78.

53   See Shumel Mordechai Lev, "Diary of Pain and Suffering: Pages from a Diary in the Years of the Holocaust," *Sefer Drohiczyn*, Internet.

54   The existence of *Nekama* and its founding meeting in Lublin are confirmed also by Jewish sources, which mostly talk about its anti-German edge. However, although he would have supported it, Zuckerman claims that the topic of revenge was not debated in Lublin but, later, in Rumania and that it concerned Germans only. Nonetheless, in 1960 Bernard Mark, who headed the Jewish Historical Institute in Warsaw, claimed that the former Jewish partisans who participated in *Nekama* in Poland contributed to the capture of the Nazi Adolf Eichmann in Argentina. See Anna Kornacka, "Utworzona po oswobodzeniu Lublina grupa b. partyzantów żydowskich działająca pod kryptonimem 'Zemsta' przyczyniła się do ujęcia Eichmanna," *Express Wieczorny*

[Warszawa], 14 June 1960; Segev, *The Seventh Million*, 141; Zuckerman, *A Surplus of Memory*, 579. A Hindu scholar alleged that *Nekama* was responsible for the kidnapping and murder of a teenage son of a notorious radical nationalist leader Bolesław Piasecki. See Peter Raina, *Mordercy uchodzą bezkarnie: Sprawa Bohdana P.* (Warszawa: Wydawnictwo von borowiecky, 2000).

55   Joseph Riwash, *Resistance and Revenge, 1939-1949* (Montreal: No publisher, 1981), 66 [afterward *Resistance*].

56   See Jerzy Robert Nowak, *Zagrożenia dla Polski i polskości*, 2 vols. (Warszawa: Inicjatywa Wydawnicza "ad astra," 1998), 1: 49.

57   See Aleksander Achmatowicz, "Wilno w latach wojny i okupacji w pamięci i według badań źródłowych," *Kwartalnik Historyczny* 2 (1998): 111.

58   See Leon W. Wells, "The Righteous Gentiles," in *Holocaust Literature: A Handbook of Critical, Historical, and Literary Writings*, ed. by Saul S. Friedman (Westport, CT: Greenwood Press, 1993), 149-50.

59   Initially, Halpern attempted to shoot the woman himself but was physically prevented from doing so by his Polish Christian friend and savior: "One day as I was walking through Trembowla with Jan Gorniak [Górniak], I saw Anna Bartetska [Bartecka] I recognized her immediately and walked right over to her. She tried to walk away, but I blocked her path. 'I'm going to kill you,' I said to her, taking out my pistol. 'Everyone here knows you betrayed my family for five kilos of sugar.' I held my pistol higher, aiming at her heart. Jan grabbed my arm and pulled me back. He was seven years older than me, stronger, and like my older brother Avrum Chaim, his childhood friend, an authority figure for me. 'Shmercio,' he said to me sternly, 'you lived through such a terrible war. You want to go to prison for killing her? For this piece of –? Don't ruin your life for her. Let her go to hell.' He spat on the street by her feet and pulled me away. I let him overpower me because he was right." See Sam Halpern, *Darkness and Hope* (New York: Shengold Publishers, Inc., 1996), 145 [afterward *Darkness and Hope*].

60   Wacław Zajączkowski, *Martyrs of Charity*, part 1 (Washington, D.C.: St. Maximilian Kolbe Foundation, 1988), 1: 270 [afterward *Martyrs of Charity*].

61   Czesław Stanisław Bartnik, *Mistyka wsi: Z autobiografii młodości, 1929-1956* (Źrebce: n.p., 1999), 300.

62   Henryk Grynberg, *Dziedzictwo* (London: Aneks, 1993), 49-50.

63   The NKVD officers were of Jewish origin; the alleged Polish informers were Lega and Krupa. See Oliner, *Restless Memories*, 185-86; and Oliner, *Narrow Escapes*, 155-56.

64   Gershon Zik, ed., *Rożyszcze: My Old Home* (Tel Aviv: The Rozhishcher Committee in Israel, 1976), 41 [afterward *Rożyszcze*]. These raids presumably targeted Ukrainians since the author speaks favorably of his treatment by local Poles, and few of them remained in that province after the ethnic cleansing campaign conducted by the Ukrainian Insurgent Army.

65   Nathan Sobel, "The Annahilation: Chronology of Destruction," in *Luboml: The Memorial Book of a Vanished Shtetl* (Hoboken, New Jersey: Ktav Publishing House, Inc., 1997), 253. These activities also most likely affected Ukrainians.

66   Stolnicki survived the Nazi occupation because he was hidden by a Polish peasant. See Kahn, *No Time*, 168-69.

67   [Aba Gefen], *Hope in Darkness: The Aba Gefen Diaries* (New York: Holocaust Library, 1989), 3.

68   Kahn advanced to become head of the NKVD in Orany. See Kahn, *No Time*, 179, 183, 186-88.

69   See Verstandig, *I Rest My Case*, 204-209, 212, 221-22.

70   Martin Gray, *For Those I Loved* (Boston and Toronto: Little, Brown, and Company, 1972), 238 [afterward *For Those I Loved*].

71   Gray, *For Those I Loved*, 205.

72   Gray, *For Those I Loved*, 233-38. The activities of Grajewski as an NKVD man were discussed by Cezary Chlebowski in *Tygodnik Solidarność*, 19 May 1995; Jerzy Robert Nowak, "Dzieje grzechów (3): Za co Żydzi powinni przeprosić Polaków," *Nasza Polska*, 11 April 1996, 1, 8-9; and Jerzy Robert Nowak, *Spory o historię i współczesność* (Warszawa: von borowiecky, 2000), 359-61.

73   Ephraim Schwarzmann, "With the Red Army from Stalingrad to Berlin," *Horchiv Memorial Book*, ed. by Yosef Kariv (Tel Aviv: Horchiv Committee in Israel, 1966), 73. As mentioned earlier, these raids presumably targeted Ukrainians since few Poles remained in the province of Volhynia after the ethnic cleansing campaign conducted by the Ukrainian Insurgent Army. Two of the villages mentioned, Hołoby and Gruszówka, were Ukrainian villages-bases from which Ukrainian partisan units struck at Jews and, more often, ethnic Poles. See Władysław Siemaszko and Ewa Siemaszko, *Ludobójstwo dokonane przez nacjonalistów ukraińskich na ludności polskiej Wołynia 1939-1945*, vol. 1 (Warszawa: Wydawnictwo von borowiecky, 2000), 1: 333, 353-54.

74   See Norman Salsitz [Naftali Saleschutz] and Amalie Petranker Salsitz, *Against All Odds: A Tale of Two Survivors* (New York: Holocaust Library, 1990), 36-41 [afterward *Against All Odds*].

75   Isadore Hollander in *The Persistence of Youth: Oral Testimonies of The Holocaust*, ed. by Josey G. Fisher (Westport, CT: Greenwood Press, 1991), 117. Hollander hailed from Będzin. He was a member of a Zionist youth group (*Noar Tsioni*). The Polish underground helped him escape from a forced labor detail near Równe in Volhynia and Hollander joined a Jewish partisan group. After the arrival of the Red Army, he enlisted with an anti-aircraft unit of the Polish "people's" army.

76   According to Mariusz Bechta, Hołownia had organized a vigorous self-defense against anyone trying to rob the peasants, including bandits, Communists, and Jewish fugitives during the Nazi occupation. Golczer had been a ghetto policeman in Łomazy. Eventually, he escaped and survived the war in the forest by robbing Polish peasants. Afterward, Golczer joined the UB in Biała Podlaska and avenged himself on those who had defended themselves from the supply raids by the fugitive Jews. See Mariusz Bechta, *Rewolucja, mit, bandytyzm: Komuniści na Podlasiu w latach 1939-1944* (Warszawa and Biała Podlaska: Rekonkwista-Rachocki i ska, 2000), 96 n. 89; Mariusz Bechta to MJCh, 25 October 2000.

77   A letter of Dr. Jerzy Filip ("Biga") to the editor, *Głos Polski* [Toronto], 21 December 1978, 6.

78   The victim, the Pole Andrejew, had earlier been imprisoned by the UB twice but fled from jail each time. See *Zrzeszenie WiN w dokumentach*, 1: 527.

79   Father Pilecki was arrested by the NKVD earlier, in February 1945, but no details are available. See Wiktor Noskowski, "Czy Yaffa Eliach przeprosi Polaków?" *Myśl Polska* [Warsaw], 20-27 July 1997, 1, 7-9; Kazimierz Krajewski, *Na Ziemi Nowogródzkiej: "Nów" — Nowogródzki Okręg Armii Krajowej* (Warszawa: Instytut Wydawniczy PAX, 1997), 50 [afterward *Na Ziemi Nowogródzkiej*]; Jarosław Wołkonowski, *Okręg*

Wileński Związku Walki Zbrojnej Armii Krajowej w latach 1939-1945 (Warszawa: Adiutor, 1996), no page number (a photograph at the end) [afterward *Okręg Wileński*]; *Zrzeszenie WiN w dokumentach,* 1: 324.

80 See for example Marek Jan Chodakiewicz, "Akcja Specjalna NSZ na Lubelszczyźnie: Część I," *Wojskowy Przegląd Historyczny* 2 (1993): 68-71.

81 Gryciuk and Matusak, *Represje NKWD,* 1: 301.

82 This is an extremely complex case. According to a Polish historian, the Home Army sent a few Jews to Stefan Sawa to hide them. However, later AK intelligence determined that Sawa was also collaborating with the Nazis, namely the *Kriminalpolizei.* An underground military court sentenced him to death along with everyone in his household. As was customary, the superiors passed the sentence down
·   to be executed by a guerrilla squad that was not briefed in depth but only told to carry out its assignment. The squad members shot Sawa and four Jewish adults. Then, they set the house on fire unaware that a Jewish woman with two children, including the six-year-old Frynusia Frydman, were hiding in the attic. They burned alive. See Krzysztof Urbański, *Zagłada ludności żydowskiej Kielc, 1939-1945* (Kielce: Kieleckie Towarzystwo Naukowe, 1994), 156-57. According to a Jewish source, "Barabasz" allegedly found the Jews, including the 12-year-old Dina (Danuta) and her aunt Sofia Selinger (Zalinger), hiding in the house in Brzechowice (and not Zagórze), and told Stefan Sawa, "to have them expelled;" otherwise "the Germans would exact punishment on the whole village." Since Sawa ignored the order, his house was torched sometime later. See Mordecai Paldiel, *Saving the Jews: Amazing Stories of Men and Women Who defied the "Final Solution"* (Rockville, Maryland: Schreiber Publishing, 2000), 161-63.

83 Helena Bodek, *Jak tropione zwierzęta: Wspomnienia* (Kraków: Wydawnictwo Literackie, 1993), 149-50 [afterward *Jak tropione zwierzęta*]; Yoran, *Defiant,* 253. For further information about the Jews of Raciąż see E. Tsoref, ed., *Gal-Ed: Memorial Book of the Community of Racionz, Selected Chapters* (Tel Aviv: Former Residents of Racionz, 1965).

84 For an account of underground activities of the Hagana, including illegal purchases of weapons in Grodno, Kaunas, and Białystok by Zionist emissaries from Łódź in May 1945 see Felix Zandman, *Never the Last Journey* (New York: Schocken Books, 1995), 156-59 [afterward *Never the Last Journey*].

85 Gross, *Upiorna dekada,* 94.

86 Zuckerman, *A Surplus of Memory,* 671.

87 August Grabski, "Żydowski ruch kombatancki w Polsce w latach 1944-1947," *BŻIH* 2 (190) (June 1999): 21-32; Kwiek, *Żydzi, Łemkowie, Słowacy,* 46.

88 Sprawozdanie z działalności C.K.S. przy C.K.Ż.P., Archiwum Żydowskiego Instytutu Historycznego in Warsaw, Centralny Komitet Żydów w Polsce, Centralna Komisja Specjalna [afterward AŻIH, CKŻP, CKS], pudło (box) No 3-7, 1,3-4, in Gross, *Upiorna dekada,* 94-95, 105-106. The presence of Jewish informers during Catholic services was also noted by the underground. See *Zrzeszenie WiN w dokumentach,* 1: 328. See also Maurycy Zielonka, Komitet Żydowski w Płocku, Oświadczenie, 30 September 1946, AURM, PRM, BP, file 5/133, 61; and Urząd Wojewódzki Białostocki, Wydział Społeczno-Polityczny, Tajne, Sprawozdanie Wydziału Społeczno-Politycznego za miesiąc październik 1945 roku, APB, UWB, file 94, 19.

89 Gross, *Upiorna dekada,* 111.

90   Gross, *Upiorna dekada*, 112. On the situation in Włocławek see Hillel, *Le Massacre des survivants*, 25-26.

91   Kwiek, *Żydzi, Łemkowie, Słowacy*, 46-47; Rzeczpospolita Polska, Ministerstwo Pracy i Opieki Społecznej, Referat dla Spraw Pomocy Ludności Żydowskiej, "Czternaste sprawozdanie z działalności (za miesiąc sierpień roku 1945)," 31 August 1945, AURM, PRM, BP, file 5/133, 68; Raport WiN, "Polityka narodowościowa PPR," [no date, after August 1945], AAN, KC PPR, file 295/VII-255, 1-2; *Zrzeszenie WiN w dokumentach*, 1: 435. Peretz Hochman, *Daring to Live* (Tel Aviv: Ministry of Defense Publishing House, 1994), 227-28.

92   This was for example the case in Siedlce. See Grażyna Dziedzińska, "Tej zbrodni dokonali Żydzi z UB," *Nasza Polska*, 12 June 2001, 14; and see below.

93   Shainberg, *Breaking from the KGB*, 124-25, 158, 164.

94   The rubric "Poles denounced" concerns specific denunciations and general complaints to the Communist authorities. The rubric "Poles arrested" includes direct and indirect actions of the Jewish security men in the Communist employ. The rubric "Poles killed directly" concerns Jewish perpetrators acting alone. The rubric "Poles caused to be killed" includes the victims of the Jewish denunciations or other actions that resulted in Polish deaths, including the activities of Jewish security men acting in concert with their Polish and Soviet counterparts.

VI

Jews in the Eyes of the Insurgents

The involvement of some Jews with the Communists, so amply
described in Jewish testimonies, is also confirmed in the insurgent reports.
In fact, some individual Jewish accounts can be specifically verified,
corrected, and elaborated upon with evidence from the underground
archives. Not surprisingly, the Polish insurgents paid attention to the
conflict with the Jewish community and, more specifically, to the deeds of
Jewish supporters of the Soviets.

As seen from the independentist side, the activities of Jewish
collaborators were lethal. For the insurgents, the Jewish partisans who had
fought together with the Communists figured prominently and adversely
in the first period following the arrival of the Red Army.[1] According to a
dispatch of July 1944 for the Government Delegate,

> After Grodno was occupied by the bolsheviks [sic], Jewish
> bands entered the town in conjunction with the band of
> Wasilewski, who is paid and armed by the bolsheviks [i.e.
> Soviets]. Both bands conduct themselves aggressively against
> the Poles; they murder [people]. The same thing has been
> occurring in the environs of Białystok.[2]

In January 1945 the AK command of Bielsk reported that

> The Jews collaborate with the NKVD and almost all are
> armed with pistols. They spy on the local population and on
> the outsiders. In Drohiczyn the Soviets accidently killed a
> jew [sic]. Convinced that the Poles had done it, the Jews
> murdered 9 Poles.[3]

According to a report of February 1945, in the Wilno and
Nowogródek Provinces, "the NKVD with the assistance of the remaining

Jews has been carrying out bloody orgies. The [Polish] population under
the leadership of the AK has been resisting heroically and it trusts in the
urgent assistance of the legal [Polish] government" in London.[4]
.   In that same region, a female liaison of the AK, who was seized by
the NKVD, recalled that the Soviets

> carried out enormous sweeps. This is how it happened: they
> would arrive around two or three o'clock in the morning,
> surround a hamlet, and conduct house-to-house searches. They
> looked for arms and took men away. The prisons in the nearby
> towns of Raduń and Ejszyszki were overflowing. The
> interrogations by the NKGB were ruthless; they were mainly
> undertaken at night. The numerous informers were mainly
> recruited from among the Jews who secured posts in the military,
> NKVD, and NKGB as well as worked as confidence men.
> Guerrilla units [of the AK], not wanting the civilian population
> to suffer because of such denouncing, liquidated Soviet agents.
>   I was arrested. They took us to Raduń. On the first night I
> was interrogated seven times. The interrogations were simple: [I]
> was beaten. Their [i.e. the NKVD] purpose was to elicit
> information about AK detachments. The men were treated much
> worse. They were tortured, beaten, their ribs were broken, their
> teeth knocked out. In towns, the prisoners were detained for
> about two weeks, then they were taken to Wilno or Lida to stand
> trail. Every two weeks, trains departed for Siberia.[5]

Another local AK soldier, Witold Andruszkiewicz, confirms the
above account, naming the former Jewish-Soviet partisans Alter
Michelovsky (Michałowski) and Moshe Sonenson as the most ruthless
members of the NKVD in Ejszyszki.[6] In Lida, the Province of
Nowogródek, during the trial of four Home Army soldiers before a Soviet
military court, one of them demanded to be transferred to the jurisdiction
of a Polish court. "The colonel judge, a Jew, laughed and said that next
time we would be tried by a polar bear" in Siberia. The AK man was
sentenced to 15 years in the Gulag.[7]
    Initially, however, the Polish underground reports distinguished
between the Jewish community as such and the Jewish collaborators.
Indeed, some of the evidence from the underground sources confirms that
immediately after the Soviet arrival the Jews were rather neutral toward
the Polish insurgents in certain localities. According to an underground
report of October 1944 from the Białystok region,

thanks to the kind care of the Christian Polish population about 3,000 Jews survived in the area. All of them decided to abandon their current domicile and to emigrate to America. They will not allow us to draw them into work for the Underground Poland. Very few of them work in the offices of the PKWN [Polish Committee of National Liberation, i.e. the proxy regime].[8]

A Jewish witness corroborates that during the first few weeks after the expulsion of the Nazis there was a Polish-Jewish symbiosis and he characterized the independentist Poles in Lublin as "friendly" toward the Jewish survivors.[9]

In early spring of 1945, shortly after the Red Army occupied the area, a clandestine activist from western Poland confirmed the fact of Jewish neutrality. "The Jews remaining in the little towns of the eastern 'Wartegau' [*Warthegau*]: out of 1,000 Jews in 1939, [there are] maybe between 5 and 10 per little town in 1945. They do not participate actively in the undertakings of the [Communist] Lublin government."[10] As late as September 1945, the underground noted, doubtless with approval, the case of two Jewish deserters from the security police unit in Białystok.[11]

After the initial period, however, in certain localities the involvement of Jews in anti-insurgent activities imperceptibly set in. In November 1944, the Home Army command of the Białystok District reported that "the attitude of the Jews, who remained in the Sarna area [i.e. code name for Białystok] – all the Jews *gradually* engage themselves in intelligence work for the NKVD [emphasis added]."[12] A month later the underground informed its superiors that

The Jews who survived are concentrated in county towns. So far, the number of jews [sic] in the Białystok district is probably between 1,000 and 2,000. Almost all of them are engaged in the PKWN [i.e. the Communist proxy regime], especially in the militia. Most serve the NKVD.[13]

It seems that at times the insurgents became unable to differentiate between the passively neutral members of the Jewish community, on the one hand, and the actively hostile, on the other. This was probably because for security reasons the Jews tended to live together in close quarters and also because the most highly visible members of the Jewish community did cooperate with the Communists.[14] This did not only entail Jewish secret policemen and militiamen. After all, in order to get anything accomplished formally, one had to deal with the authorities. This was perhaps the main reason behind the frequent peregrinations of the people to the local centers of Communist power. Alas, in the Jewish case, these peregrinations seem to have reinforced the perception of the alleged Jewish collaboration with the Communists.

Nonetheless, the underground also realized that the Polish-Jewish animosity focused on war-time affairs, including property disputes. According to a Home Army dispatch from Wysokie Mazowieckie,

> The Jews allegedly keep away from everything but in fact they are confidence men of the NKVD. They denounce those who have any items that had belonged to the jews [sic]; frequently they [i.e. the Jews] blackmail [the Poles] demanding even for allegedly used up items from 10 to 15 [cubic] meters of grain. They [the Jews] do not spare even those [Poles] who hid them [during the Nazi occupation] but took a significant amount of money from them.[15]

After the initial period the underground reports showed a tendency to lump together all parties considered hostile to Poland. According to an underground dispatch, undoubtedly exaggerated, in September 1945 "it has been established that all Jews without any exception in the counties of Augustów and Sokółka [in the Province of Białystok] remain in the service of the NKVD."[16] In October 1945, the command of the Citizen Home Army-Freedom and Independence (*Armia Krajowa Obywatelska — AKO-WiN*) reported:

> National minorities. All Jews are collaborators of the UB and NKVD as agents, confidence men, and informers. Almost all leadership posts in the UB are occupied by the Jews... In Białystok all Jewish merchants were granted a city tax exemption.
> Belorussians, employees of the UB and MO, are characterized by a hostile attitude toward the Poles. The personnel of the UB consists of the most terrible social scum — thieves, bandits, Gestapo snitches, Communists, and the national minorities which are hostile toward us: Jews and Belorussians.[17]

According to an assessment by the central WiN leadership of January 1946,

> The Jews are busy almost in all walks of political and economic life. Almost all of them are informers for the soviets [sic] and the UB. Therefore they are also under special protection of the [Communist] party.[18]

In January 1947, the WiN reported an increase in "the recruitment of new members into the ranks of the UB. The enlistment takes place mainly among the youth and the criminal element, or degenerates, and above all the Jews."[19]

Of course, there were also specific reports concerning the activities of the Jewish secret policemen, their underlings, and other Communist functionaries of Jewish origin.[20] For instance, in September 1945, the author of an underground report stated that "the UBP [i.e. the Office of Public Security] uses Jews (!) to monitor sermons in Catholic churches. They can be seen during every mass."[21] The veracity of the dispatch is confirmed by Jewish and Communist sources.[22] Nonetheless, most other clandestine reports and recollections of witnesses still need to be verified against Communist or Jewish documents.

The participation of secret police officers of Jewish origin in anti-insurgent operations was real enough. However, we must remember that Polish and Soviet personnel took part in them as well. The responsibility for any crimes committed must be thus assessed individually.

In spring 1945 in Sierpc, the Province of Warsaw, the leader of the local secret police was Zołtogórski,[23] "a Jew from eastern Poland." It is unclear whether his underlings were ethnic Poles, Soviets, or Jews. According to a Polish witness, whose family's house was occupied by the security men, "terrible terror commenced. People disappeared; persons were drowned in the septic tank of our house; at night the soil in our garden was dug up" to bury clandestinely the corpses of the Polish victims. As a consequence, "deadly hatred prevailed toward the Jews in Sierpc."[24]

After 1945, the head of the UB in Białogard was allegedly Zdzisław Stolzman. According to a witness, he cooperated closely with the NKVD outposts in Białogard and Borne-Sulinowo. Stolzman and his men allegedly conducted joint operations with the NKVD against the insurgents, including the units of Major Zygmunt Szendzielarz ("Łupaszko") of the Fifth and Sixth Wilno Brigades. In one instance, Stolzman participated in the interrogation and the show trial of three Home Army soldiers who "confessed" their crimes. Jerzy Łoziński, Stanisław Subortowicz, and Witold Milwid "were shot in the presence of comrade Stolzman." In another instance, the UB man took part in the trial of five high school students with ties to the independentists. Bogdan Szczucki, Marian Baśladyński, Feliks Stanisławski, Pszczółkowski, and Tracz "received long prison sentences [of hard labor] in the coal mines."[25]

On July 10, 1946, a public hanging of three insurgents of the NSZ unit of Lieutenant Józef Stefko ("Mściciel" – Avenger) took place in Dębica, the Province of Rzeszów.[26] According to an independentist document,

> First the MO, the UB, and the military occupied the execution square holding their machine guns ready to fire. Then, a car came with uniformed individuals who placed the noose on the hook. After a short time the same car brought three condemned men in white shirts. Their hands and legs were tied with barbed wire. A Jewish prosecutor read the sentence and passed the condemned into the hands of the executioner. Before the execution, one of the condemned yelled:
>
> "Long live the Home Army. Long live General Anders and General Bór-Komorowski. Down with the commies. Brothers persevere or you'll die like us. I swear before God that I have never been a bandit [that is what the Communist propaganda called the insurgents — MJCh]. I am dying for the Motherland. Lord forgive them [the executioners] because they know not what they are doing."[27]

Also in the summer of 1946 the secret police resolved to stage a provocation to destroy the NSZ unit of Captain Henryk Flame ("Bartek"), operating in the Beskid Mountains. Two ethnic Polish secret policemen, Henryk Wendrowski ("Lawina") and Czesław Krupowiec ("Korzeń"), infiltrated the unit posing as émigré couriers. They lured about 200 NSZ soldiers into a trap with promises of safe passage to the West. On September 1, 3, 5, and 7 several groups of insurgents reported in the environs of Łambinowice in Silesia to be transported to the American zone in Germany. However, they were disarmed, drugged, and summarily executed in batches. Hundreds of police troops must have participated in the operation which is still veiled in secrecy. Nonetheless, according to Grzegorz Wąsowski and Leszek Żebrowski, the plan was allegedly masterminded by four prominent secret policemen of Jewish origin: General Roman Romkowski, who was deputy minister of public security, Colonel Józef Czaplicki, who supervised the Third (anti-insurgent) Department at the ministry, Lieutenant Colonel Józef Kratko, who headed the provincial security office in Katowice, and Captain Marek Fink, who headed the Third Bureau (*wydział*) of the UB in Katowice.[28]

In another case, an underground source described a massive police sweep in the county of Kraśnik, which was led putatively by Communist officers of Jewish origin, between February 17 and 24, 1946:

> Pacification actions, arrests, [and] terror meted out to the population and the detainees have intensified ever more. On February 17 a pacification commenced on the territory of the Waterways Management Number 1 [the underground cryptonym of the county of Kraśnik and the adjacent areas]. The pacification is carried out by the UB and KBW [internal security troops] from Rzeszów. The strength of the latter is around 100 men. The pacification action started in the Parish of Urzędów. On the staff of the pacification team there are several captains in Polish uniforms who speak Polish very poorly, but Russian well.
>
> The commander of the expedition is a Second Lieutenant, a Jew, who is aided by several other Jewish officers. He has been directing the operation together with a Soviet NKVD officer, who is permanently stationed in Kraśnik. The mode of conducting arrests is as follows: the UB and the military arrive at night and surround a particular locality. For instance, they came to Urzędów with a certain list containing [names of] people who had been arrested by the UB already back in [19]44. These people are either dead or are beyond the Urals [i.e. in the Gulag]. This [list] is a trick because the security authorities know very well where these people are. However, there are also other persons on the list who still live around here. They often belong to the PSL [the Polish Peasant Party] or are its sympathizers. They [i.e. the police] often take two or three people from [each] household. Everyone is accused of [illegal] possession of weapons.
>
> In the present month there have been arrests in the parishes of Urzędów, Dzierzkowice, Trzydnik, Batorz, Wilkołaz, Gościeradów, Modliborzyce, Zaklików, and Zakrzówek. So far several hundred persons have been arrested. The detainees are interrogated on the spot and then driven to the UB [jail] in Kraśnik, where the interrogation continues. The facilities and basements of the UB and MO [i.e. the militia] in Kraśnik are overcrowded. Everyone is accused of [illegal] possession of weapons. However, because they do not have any weapons, no one confesses to possessing any. The UB tries to force an inculpatory confession. Namely, the detainee is laid out on a

bench. Two UB-men or bolsheviks [i.e. NKVD] sit on him. One sits on his head and the other on his back. The third beats him on the heels of his feet with a walking stick. On average one receives 1,000 hits on the heels. After such an interrogation, the prisoner is unable either to walk or to stand because his bones are shattered. Another way [to extract confessions] is to pour water into one's nose. Apart from this they wave a gun before the prisoner's eyes and threaten to shoot him. In one instance, while issuing such threats, a shot was fired and shattered the knee of the person under interrogation.

In Urzędów the population was informed that an execution would take place at the market square. [However,] the execution did not take place because of a fear that it would have an effect contrary to that intended [i.e. that the people would not be cowed but would resist more]. Four persons were to be executed. One was released with his veins slit.

On February 24, one Jan Smok attended a wedding in the neighborhood of Urzędów. On his way back from the wedding he happened upon a unit of the UB and he started to flee. The soldiers [i.e. internal security troops] shot him in the back. Seriously wounded, Smok begged to be taken to the hospital. The functionaries of the UB threw him on a sleigh and covered his face with straw; they sat on him and brought him to Kraśnik. Of course, the wounded man died and his funeral took place on February 26 with a massive participation of the local population. His coffin was carried by his colleagues in military uniforms, who are army men on furlough. Immediately afterwards they were called in to the UB to explain why they had carried the coffin of a bandit. [At any rate,] a wave of arrests has been sweeping the entire county. Former members of the AK are targeted because they are now accused of belonging to the PSL.[29]

Such pacification actions were quite frequent, although the ethnicity of their leadership was not always mentioned. For instance, another one took place in the very Parish of Urzędów in December 1946 and January 1947. According to a sanitized Communist report,

the W.B.W. group [i.e. internal security troops] operating on the territory of the Parish of Urzędów deserves gratitude for its work because of enlightening the citizens there who were infected with fascist propaganda. That operation gave positive results by bringing the local citizens on the road of cooperation in the reconstruction of Democratic People's Poland. I must mention that the citizens of the Parish of Urzędów totally succumbed to the underground propaganda. Thanks to the educational work of the officers and soldiers of the W.B.W. of Lublin the situation in the territory of the aforementioned parish has changed for the better. The PSL which used to be very well organized throughout the parish has been smashed and the [Communist-puppet] Peasant Party, the [Communist] Peasant Self-Aid, and the [Communist-controlled youth] Beacon Fire have been established there.[30]

Likewise, in the Province of Rzeszów, according to an underground account,

> on April 28, [1946,] a Gestapo-like pacification took place in Leżajsk. Thirty-one trucks came from Rzeszów carrying the KBW, UB, MO, and NKVD. The entire city was encircled; all streets were closed. There were heavy machine guns placed in the fields and on the streets. Groups of soldiers from 5 to 8 people walked from house to house bringing men aged between 14 and 60 to the marketplace. The captives waited between 6 and 14 hours in uncertainty. The UB and the Soviets dressed in Polish uniforms ruled the city. There were also many Jews – officers speaking Polish very poorly. [Finally,] twenty-nine persons were shipped away.[31]

It seems, however, that the interaction between the secret police, including Jewish officers, and persons critical of the Communist regime and its terror apparatus were not always bloody and violent. Andrzej Kownacki recalled his ordeal with the UB in Silesia. After he was held for two weeks in jail with no charges, Kownacki was invited to see the head of the local secret police "a strikingly handsome young Jew." The security supervisor very courteously asked Kownacki to become a police collaborator. The Polish man refused politely and he was promptly released.[32] In another case, according to an underground report of the spring of 1946,

> On March 3, the UB arrived in Kłoczew [in the Province of Lublin] to organize a propaganda meeting. A few women and children attended the meeting. After a speech by a functionary of

the UB, who was a Jew, a woman spoke up. She accused the UB
that whenever they caught a real bandit he could soon be seen in
the service of the UB, but a decent human being would get
deported to Siberia.[33]

There is no evidence that the woman was punished for her defiant
frankness. Nonetheless, the veracity of the report regarding the putative
Jewish officer of the UB should be verified against secret police files.

The allegations of Jewish participation in the NKVD and the Polish
Communist secret police should be treated very carefully. As mentioned,
the lower ranks of the secret police were mostly Polish. They not only
followed orders of their superiors, who set the general agenda and tone
of the policy of terror, but the lower ranking secret policemen just as
often initiated and perpetrated crimes themselves. Moreover, the notion
of mass denunciations by the Jews needs to be verified in newly
accessible archives. True, just as under the Soviets (1939-1941) and the
Nazis (1939-1944), informing was rampant in Poland but it is nonsense
to maintain that it was "only" (or "mainly") the Jews who collaborated
with the Communist secret police.[34] It is important to note, however, that
in postwar Poland political denunciations appear to have been directed
almost exclusively at Poles. Some of the collaborators were of course
Communist sympathizers like, for instance, Mojżesz Lewinkopf, aka
Mieczysław Kosiński, in Rzeczyca Okrągła, the Parish of Radomyśl, the
county of Nisko, the Province of Rzeszów, who allegedly denounced
Polish insurgents to the NKVD after they had saved his life during the
Nazi occupation. However, even in Rzeczyca Okrągła there were several
Gentile collaborators. Lewinkopf was the sole Jew, albeit the only
educated man in the village and thus considered a leader. Yet, despite
allegedly denouncing others, he is said to have saved at least one Home
Army soldier from the clutches of the NKVD.[35] In Wilno, in the
leadership of the so-called "Union of Polish Patriots" (*Związek Patriotów
Polskich – ZPP*), which collaborated with the Soviet authorities, there
was at least one activist of Jewish origin, Benedykt Scherman-
Szymański. He was put in charge of military affairs and promoted to the
rank of a colonel, while allegedly working hand-in-glove with the
NKVD. As a pre-war member of a pro-government veterans' association,
this erstwhile Piłsudskite used his contacts to de-conspire those units of
the AK which remained underground.[36]

According to the data analyzed in this chapter, and following the
criteria for estimates established in the previous chapter, about 800 Poles
were victimized by various Jews.

Table 3
Jewish involvement against Poles: A Sample Estimate No. 2[37]

Poles:	minimum	maximum
denounced	48	90
arrested	263	800
killed directly	24	28
caused to be killed	110	215

The Jewish avengers and informers constituted only a minority of the Jewish community. Alas, as the most dynamic members of their group, they were also the most highly visible. This further reinforced the stereotype of *żydokomuna*. Yet, it is undeniable that among the Jews at large there was an enormous and profound gratitude toward the Red Army for saving them from the Nazis. A Jewish partisan of the Home Army recalls the events of the summer of 1944 outside of Lwów:

> As the Russians approached, we prepared ourselves as a military unit. We wore a red-white band on the left arm, with the symbol of the Polish eagle embroidered on it and, underneath, the letters A.K. We captured fleeing German units and disarmed them. We confiscated military equipment, carriages, stores and supplies. I was wearing German uniform.
>
> A few days before Lvov and its suburbs were taken over by the Russians, at the end of July 1944, our unit made contact with a frontal reconnaissance unit of the Red Army. The image of the first Russian soldier is imprinted in my memory. This moment which I had dreamt of for years — and I had had my doubts whether it would ever be realized — became real in front of my eyes I had to stop myself from embracing him... We were given an order to abandon the small Russian unit. I was outraged and bewildered. Deeper bewilderment was to be mine a few days later when it was decided, contrary to instructions from the new, temporary [Communist] regime, to refuse to hand over all the arms. I was a witness to the decision to hide arms and to the carrying out of the order. *The extent to which I identified with the Red Army at that time, the army which symbolized the main force fighting the Germans, was complete. I felt I had to do something but, illogically, my heart would not let me inform on my comrades in arms* [emphasis added].[38]

How many Jews, without any affinity for the AK, gave in to the temptation to show loyalty to their Soviet saviors? Further research in former Soviet and Polish secret police archives should clarify this issue.

Some Jewish secret policemen used their power to settle scores with Christians who had dealt with them under various circumstances during the Nazi occupation. In the Białystok region, Jewish police informers denounced to the NKVD those Poles who had illicitly acquired Jewish property. In Bielsk, some Jews even blackmailed their war-time rescuers if the latter had taken money for their services. In Łódź, the secret policeman Gedala (NN), who was the brother-in-law of Stanisław Rotholc, either denounced or arrested his war-time rescuer. Fearing the Nazis would kill his family, the Pole had once threatened violently to evict the Jewish man and his relatives from a clandestine shelter, though he did not follow through with the threat. In Chełm Lubelski, a Jewish lieutenant denounced a peasant for his abusive language and excessive monetary demands while the Jew and his family had been hiding with him. A subsequent Communist police investigation revealed, however, that the peasant did not benefit monetarily from the rescue and the abusive language was employed to quiet down the Jews in hiding lest Nazi informers hear them and bring death to all. The enormous psychological stress connected with hiding and being hidden from the Nazis must have exacted an enormous toll on both the rescuer and the rescued in many more ways than we can imagine.[39]

The issue of alleged Jewish collaboration with the Communist security forces went beyond the presence of a few high-profile individuals whether on the central or local rungs of power. Its complexity revealed itself on many levels and in various interdependent and overlapping processes. Its mechanism can be reconstructed with some accuracy in the case of Jedwabne and Radziłów, in the county of Łomża, the Province of Białystok. In both towns, Jewish complaints and denunciations led to a police investigation and allegedly to extrajudicial killings, both official and unofficial, as well as to torture and imprisonment of the real and alleged perpetrators.

In both Jedwabne and Radziłów some local Poles participated in the murder of several hundred Jews in July 1941.[40] A few persons survived the war and at least two of them, Menachem Finkielsztejn (Finkelstein) and Szmul Wasersztejn (Wasserstein), aka Stanisław Całka, undoubtedly informed the Communist security forces about the pogrom and its perpetrators. They also testified about the crime before the Jewish Historical Commission in Białystok. Hence, the Jewish leadership found out about the events in Jedwabne and Radziłów and subsequently sought justice from the Communist judiciary.[41]

Meanwhile, already at the end of 1945 or at the beginning of 1946, according to a Polish witness, a special secret police team, allegedly headed by "a Jewish prosecutor" (*prokurator Żyd*), arrived in Łomża and launched its investigation. "Many [extrajudicial] executions" occurred, as the UB pursued real and alleged perpetrators.[42] "Jews" were even falsely suspected of the revenge killing of the wife of a Polish official implicated in the pogrom.[43] Nonetheless, many persons were seized for interrogation. For example, in Radziłów, "after the 'liberation' many local Poles were arrested by the security forces (UB) in connection with the pogrom and taken to the jail in Grajewo, where they were beaten and tortured; they faced trials in Grajewo and Ełk and were imprisoned. Józef Kosmaszewski, who was beaten with chains and therefore admitted to anything and everything, was imprisoned in Wronki for many years."[44] Likewise, the real and alleged pogromists of Jedwabne were seized, interrogated, and tortured. At least some of them drew lengthy jail sentences.

Nonetheless, at this point it is nearly impossible to disentangle the security police actions against the local underground from its undertakings against the suspected pogromists of Jedwabne and Radziłów. It must have been convenient for operational and propaganda purposes to lump both categories together as "fascists" and "reactionaries." Finally, it is doubtful that justice was served because the extrajudicial killings, interrogation methods, and the nature of the trials themselves were blatant Stalinist violations of all civilized norms of conduct.[45] We certainly cannot be sure if all of the accused were guilty, and to what extent, and how many real perpetrators were let off the hook because they collaborated with the Communist secret police. Thus, the outcome of the police and judicial actions on behalf of the victims was less than satisfactory. However, the Jewish search for redress certainly infuriated those Poles who had nothing to do with the pogromists but who nonetheless experienced the fury of the secret police directly or indirectly.[46] Undoubtedly, both the guilty and the guiltless blamed Jews and Communists for their misfortune.

There were also other factors exacerbating the situation. A few Jews (and many Poles) used their contacts with the secret police as a badge of immunity to stage common robberies. According to Jankiel Kac of Białystok,

A few months after the liberation my cousin went once with Icie [Itzhak] to steal two cows from the peasants. The farmers caught them, my cousin escaped, but they killed Icek [Itzhak].

When we emerged from the forest [after the arrival of the Soviets], I lived by Josif and Brache. I boiled potatoes [and] some kasha; but they had meat. I could not fathom where they got so much meat from. I also want to eat meat. My cousin tells me where they get it from: they steal it.

They give me an offer. A group gathers. We shall go and steal a calf from Popławy. I, Niomko, and Wolf are walking but my heart starts pounding. This is the first time I am going on a thieving expedition. After a while I tell them that I'm going back. What are they going to say, if they catch me? That the son of David also steals? I will eat my potatoes and will not defile the memory of my honest father. They returned with a calf in a few hours.

In 1945 we lived on Kupiecka [Street] in Białystok. One night, someone knocked on my window. It was my cousin Pejsach Brojcman and Josif with bicycles. They had backpacks filled up clothes and shoes. Brojcman was dressed in a Polish uniform with the patches of corporal and a military cap.

I ask them: "Where are you coming back from?" They answer: "We did a little job near Knyszyn and we robbed a teacher." I thought to myself that when [during the Nazi occupation] they had been in the forest and robbed, it was different because they wanted to survive. But why do they go thieving after the war! If Icek did not go stealing, he'd be alive. He did not need to rob.[47]

On the night of December 5, 1944, about five months after the return of the Soviets, Jewish bandits led by Szloma and Dawid Gruda allegedly carried out two successive attacks on two peasant farmsteads in the environs of Siemiatycze. In Miłkowice Maćki, in addition to three unknown female Polish refugees, the bandits killed sixty-year-old Michalina Maksymiuk, thirty-year-old Stanisław Maksymiuk, and eleven-year-old Marian Bojara. In Kłyzówka, most likely the same robber group assaulted the Jarocki farmstead. The attackers killed twelve-year-old Halina Jarocka and thirty year old Maria Jarocka. They seriously wounded two more women, Maria (junior) Jarocka and Felicja Jarocka, and left them for dead. In both instances the raiders despoiled the farmsteads and burned them to the ground.[48]

In another case, the Polish Oppenheim family of prominent business executives saved a young Jewish man from the ghetto in Warsaw and for several years afterwards sheltered him in their residence outside of the city. After the Red Army appeared in January 1945, the young man "returned with a rifle and a [militia] armband together with several uniformed and armed people driving a truck. He robbed the villa of its furniture and accoutrements, but when confronted by Mrs. Oppenheim with accusations of ingratitude, he threatened to shoot her and told her to be happy that she was not arrested."[49] Perhaps the most prominent bandit of Jewish origin was Izrael Ajzenman-Kaniewski. He had been a criminal already before the war, victimizing mainly Jewish artisans and merchants in Radom and Kielce. During the war he became a particularly bloody Communist partisan and a collaborator of the NKVD. After the Soviet arrival, Ajzenman joined the UB. Aside from persecuting and killing the independentists, he indulged in a large number of private robberies.[50]

It is important to stress, however, that Jewish banditry at this point must have been a fringe phenomenon. Although no research has been done on the topic, it is safe to assume that the Jewish criminals constituted a tiny minority. Nonetheless, they also were a source of conflict with the Polish community, including the insurgents, in the same way as Polish robbers were viewed through ethnic criteria by Jews. And so too were numerous property disputes.[51] Just one witness recalled the conflict generated by various Jewish attempts to reclaim a house appropriated by Polish artisans in Łosice; a case of a flour mill repossessed by its Jewish owner; and anti-peasant expeditions by armed Jews who, to make a living, confiscated property (furniture, clothes, and so on) they suspected had belonged to Jewish victims of the Nazis.[52]

Again, the key to Polish vexation seems to have been the Communist involvement in cases which in independent Poland would have been automatically adjudicated in favor of the rightful Jewish owners. Perversely, for some Poles under the new regime, resisting the return of Jewish property meant resisting the government, hence Communism. In this case anti-Jewish sentiment did not surface because, as the popular opinion held, "Jews were Communists" but because Communists were seen as protecting the Jews. Unable or unwilling to confront the Communists, and the security forces in particular, some Poles chose to confront the alleged protégés of the Communists, the Jews.

In March 1945 Chaim Fajgenbaum, his wife, and five children, who had survived the war in hiding, returned to reclaim his farm in Swoszowa near Tarnów, the Province of Kraków. A Polish peasant, who had, meanwhile, occupied the land and the farmstead, refused to move. Fajgenbaum complained to the Communist Citizens Militia but his complaint was ignored. The Jewish man then asked the local Red Army command to intercede on his behalf. The Soviets forcibly evicted the Polish peasant and the Fajgenbaum family returned home. On April 2, unknown perpetrators machine-gunned the Fajgenbaum farmstead, seriously wounding their thirteen-year-old daughter. The Jewish family immediately left their property and fled to Tarnów. There is no proof the underground was involved but that possibility cannot be excluded.[53] Likewise, it is unknown whether the underground was behind the killing "of a Jewish family in Sowin near Jasło, who returned to reclaim their land from the peasants" in early August 1945.[54]

Most of the time, however, the perpetrators of such anti-Jewish deeds were likely Poles who were using the property during the absence of the Jewish owners, for instance in Wasilków near Białystok, where a Jewish heir to a house was shot at to scare him off.[55]

Some Jewish testimonies suggest that local Poles often took matters into their own hands without bothering to get the underground involved. For instance, when Sam Berry returned home to Sosnowiec, he "found that the grandparents left some property there, land and buildings and everything. But going back was foolish. The [Polish] neighbors surrounded the house and wanted to kill me. I had to jump through a window to get away."[56] In Jędrzejów, Sabina Rachela Kałowska and her uncle Henryk Landschaft attempted to reclaim some family possessions from Wawrzyniec Wesołowski, who had acquired them during the Nazi occupation, but the Pole sought assistance of the mayor and a Communist secret policeman who threatened the Jewish heirs with his gun and chased them away. Another Jewish man mysteriously disappeared after he had attempted to reclaim his property in Sędziszów. The background of these events still remains unexplored.[57]

Aside from the disputes over property, conflict developed concerning Jewish children, thousands of whom had been sheltered by Polish Christians during the Nazi occupation. After 1945, Jewish organizations and individuals zealously traversed Poland back and forth in search of their lost relatives and co-religionists. The most energetic effort was sponsored by the Jewish Committee. Its emissaries visited private households and even Catholic convents. Many of the Jewish emissaries had little patience to appreciate the bond of love that developed between the rescued and the rescuers, who in essence had become their foster families. Accusations of anti-Semitism were answered with charges of anti-Polonism and "Jewish" callousness. In the extreme, some kidnappings and counter-kidnappings of Jewish children occurred as both sides fought for custody, additionally embittering Jewish-Polish relations.[58]

Finally, undergirding all other factors, there was a widespread perception among many Poles that the Soviets and their proxy regime in Poland favored Jews on the political, social, and economic fields. Of course, the reality was much more complicated. Nonetheless, this was no time for a nuanced analysis. Many Poles juxtaposed the allegedly friendly conduct of the Communist authorities toward the Jews with the bitter treatment accorded to the independentists. For instance, it was widely commented that after 1944 only Poles were deported to the Gulag, while mostly Jews, including those formerly from the Eastern Borderlands, were permitted to return home from the USSR. (On the other hand, more than 200,000 ethnic Poles who had registered for "repatriation" from territories incorporated into Soviet Lithuania and Soviet Belorussia were denied permission to leave.) The widespread conviction about the alleged favoritism was most certainly reinforced by the instances when Polish perpetrators of anti-Jewish deeds were prosecuted, while Jewish trespassers were apparently left alone.[59] Chafing and bleeding under the NKVD and UB terror, the independentists in particular bristled at the instances of Jewish-Soviet fraternity and suspected a secret collusion of the Jews with the Communists.

After all, it was easy to notice the comraderie of at least some Jews with Communist officials. The prominent Zionist leader Zorach Warhaftig successfully solicited the assistance of the top supervisor of the Polish Communist secret police, Jakub Berman, to expedite the Jewish exodus from Poland. As Warhaftig put it, their pre-war acquaintanceship, their common ethno-religious background, and their shared concern for the lot of the Jewish community in Poland "may have affected the Jewish element in him [Berman]. Then and there he instructed her [a high-ranking bureaucrat, who was also Jewish] to double the daily quota of passports."[60] On a lower level, for instance, in June 1945, the erstwhile Communist partisan Nachemia Wurman hobnobbed not only with Jewish secret policemen but also with a particularly repugnant ethnic Polish Communist security commander, Jan Byk, aka Czesław Borecki ("Brzoza").[61]

Undeniably, at least some Jewish Communist secret policemen felt a certain kinship with their fellow Jews. For example, a religious Jewish petitioner at the NKVD headquarters in Łódź swayed his interrogator, a Soviet major, who looked Jewish, by unexpectedly reciting "in a loud and clear voice the Hebrew profession of faith *Shema Yisrael*."[62] Afterward the Jewish man's petition was treated favorably. We have not been able to find a comparable account of a propitious outcome of dealings with the Communist secret police for a Christian reciting the Lord's Prayer before his interrogators. In another instance, a Jewish man was arrested by the Soviets on suspicion of being a Nazi spy. After he prayed aloud in Hebrew, he was released with cordial apologies.⁶³ More prosaically, in Białystok a Zionist emissary was released from a Communist jail for a substantial bribe.⁶⁴ In 1945 in Łódź, a Jewish informer, Dr. Wiesenfeld, aka Ciosnowski, and a Polish stool pigeon, "the nurse Kowalska," denounced Dr. Roman Born-Borstein to the UB because he had fought in the NSZ during the Warsaw Uprising of 1944. However, the UB refused to believe that a Jew could have been involved with Polish nationalists. They "showed a great deal of tolerance. I was only shadowed discreetly for a year."⁶⁵ In Lwów, a rabbi who must have had connections to the NKVD warned a Jewish dentist about his impending arrest for "dealing in gold." Dr. Henryk Kamiński and his family promptly fled to central Poland and, later, to the West.⁶⁶

Nonetheless, it is true that it would come as a surprise to most Poles that some Jews were also harassed by the Communists and sometimes even persecuted. Yet, there is ample evidence to attest to that. In Lwów, in November 1944, an NKVD inspector gratuitously accused Samuel Drix, a Jew, of being a Ukrainian nationalist. The same inspector charged Dr. Lewenheck of being "a Polish nationalist, a Fascist" because the physician, a Pole of Jewish origin, refused to change his nationality to "Jewish" in his documents. The accused men barely escaped repression.⁶⁷

On June 5, 1945, in Szczecin, a group of Red Army soldiers attacked a Jew. Polish militiamen intervened. One of the perpetrators explained that "the victim is a Jew to which they [the Polish militiamen] responded, 'if a Jew, must you kill him?', and they chased the attackers away, killing one of them while he was fleeing."⁶⁸ In Parczew, a Soviet commander menacingly harassed a local Jewish man, who, however, managed to propitiate the officer with vodka.⁶⁹

In the summer of 1945, in Częstochowa, fifteen-year-old Ben Helfgott and another Jewish boy were assaulted by two Communist (Polish) militiamen, who stole their belongings and appeared to want to shoot them. Fortunately, the militiamen changed their minds because of the boys' age. In another instance, in the summer of 1945 near Chodecz, the Jewish teenager Roman Halter was accosted by a Soviet soldier, who robbed him, made him undress to check for circumcision, and attempted to shoot him. Halter survived because the soldier's gun misfired.⁷⁰

In Ligota near Katowice, Carl Horwitz and some Polish militiamen came to the rescue when "a group of Russian soldiers who were obviously drunk" attempted to break into an apartment apparently to rape women, including his fiancée Irene Mendel.⁷¹ In the fall of 1944 in Kraśnik,

Communist policemen (acting on the orders of Wacław Raś, aka Czyżewski) kidnapped a member of the local Jewish Committee and later shot him in Lublin. This deed was carried out because the Jewish man had been a witness to the killing of a number of Jews by Communist partisans during the Nazi occupation. Raś and his comrades wanted to prevent him from testifying against them.[72] On August 17, 1945, in Lublin, a second lieutenant of the Communist militia and a security plainclothesman robbed and killed Symcha Lejb Fajnzylber. On August 28, 1945, in Kozienice, the Province of Radom, local militiamen and secret policemen from Gniewoszów falsely imprisoned, tortured, and extorted money from a local Jewish man. He was re-arrested and blackmailed again on September 5. Meanwhile, a day earlier, in Gniewoszów, a group of blackmailers (in all likelihood connected to the police) killed five local Jews after they failed to pay ransom.[73] Finally, some persons of Jewish origin were imprisoned by the Communists for political reasons. At least one of the prisoners, suspected of aiding the insurgents, was tortured to death by the secret police in Zamość in 1946.[74]

Unfortunately, on the popular plane, such instances of conflict between Jews and Communists were often overlooked perhaps because the official propaganda was silent about them, because the Polish community tended to concentrate on its own troubles with Stalin's followers, and because they undermined the conviction about the power of żydokomuna over Poland. This conviction, in turn, informed the attitude of the insurgents toward the Jewish community at large. Yet, it was neither the only nor the principal factor that determined the independentist reactions toward the Jews.

Notes

1   Already before the Soviet arrival, as early as 1943, in the Province of Lublin a few military planners of the Home Army exceptionally advocated repressive measures against the pro-Soviet elements to preempt the Communist threat. These recommendations were firmly rejected by the leadership of the AK. According to "my own conclusions" of a counterintelligence officer, "because of the possibility of the arrival of the bolsheviks [sic] for a possible revolution in Lublin, just as [occurred] in Równe and Łuck [where pro-Soviet elements attacked the Poles in 1939], I believe that the regional command [komenda obwodu] should be moved to the countryside. This would provide me with the freedom to act; it would allow for direct assessment of the situation in the countryside and, thus, for the liquidation of the Communist-Jewish bands." See Raport KW za miesiąc grudzień 1943, no date, APL, Armia Krajowa, Okręg Lublin "Orbis" [afterward AK, OL] file 1, vol. I, 67. Thinking along the same lines another junior officer proposed "an operational battle plan" to "create conditions that would be most favorable for the struggle through elaborating on the ways of liquidating or neutralizing hostile or unreliable elements (traitors, [criminal] bands, jews [sic], bolsheviks [sic], [and] local communists)." See Komenda Powiatu, Instrukcja odnośnie opracowania planu mob.[ilizacyjnego] i operac.[yjnego], no date [1943], APL, AK, OL, file 1, vol. II, 242.

2   Referat Komunistyczny, Załącznik nr. 1, 19 July 1944, AAN, Delegatura Rządu [afterward DR], file 202/II-58, 76. A Jewish witness confirmed the presence of the Jewish partisans in Grodno without, however, elaborating on the atrocities they allegedly perpetrated against the Poles. See Zandman, Never the Last Journey, 143-45.

3   Raport sytuacyjny i wywiadowczo-polityczny nr. 11 za grudzień 1944, Komenda Okręgu AK Sarna [Białystok], 5 January 1945, Dokumenty i materiały Archiwum Polski Podziemnej, 1939-1956 [Warszawa] 2 (April 1994): 80 [afterward Raport nr. 11 in Dokumenty].

4   Gryciuk and Matusak, Represje NKWD, 2: 24-25.

5   Wanda Lisowska, "Wspomnienia 'Grażyny'," Zeszyty Historyczne [Paris] 36 (1976): 30-32.

6   According to Andruszkiewicz, Michelovsky and Sonenson were involved in both anti-Polish and anti-German atrocities after the arrival of the Soviets in 1944. These consisted of executing German POWs, capturing Home Army members, and raiding Polish civilians. In his immediate post-war testimony Michelovsky fully corroborated Andruszkiewicz's claim, which was also substantiated by Professor Eliach albeit in a more general vain. See Witold Andruszkiewicz, "Holocaust w Ejszyszkach," Zeszyty Historyczne [Paris] 120 (1997): 93-95; Michelovsky, "The White Partisan Attack on Aishishok," in Alufi and Kaleko, Aishishuk, 79-80; Eliach, There Once Was a World, 669-70.

7   Edward Dragun, "Życie i jego ciernista droga," Wspomnienia Sybiraków: "Polsza budiet kakda woron zbieliejet", vol. 1 (Warszawa: Wydawnictwo Pomost, 1989), 1: 52.

8   Raport sytuacyjny nr 8 Komendy Okręgu AK Białystok, 10 October 1944, Białostocczyzna 1944-1945 w dokumentach podziemia i oficjalnych władz, ed. by Jan Kułak (Warszawa: ISP PAN, 1998), 45 [afterward Raport nr 8 in Białostocczyzna].

9   Samuel Gruber, I Chose Life (New York: Shengold Publishers, Inc., 1978), 155 [afterward I Chose Life].

10   Raport, no date [May? 1945], AAN, DR, file 202/III-36, 64.

11   Privates Kohn and Lewin escaped along with the Pole Kaczmarek and were immediately sentenced to death *in absentia* by the Communists. See *Zrzeszenie WiN w dokumentach*, 1: 323.

12   Raport sytuacyjny nr 9 Komendy Okręgu AK Białystok, 5 November 1944, in Kułak, *Białostocczyzna*, 49.

13   Raport sytuacyjny nr 10 Komendy Okręgu AK Białystok, 5 December 1944, in Kułak, *Białostocczyzna*, 80.

14   See Cała and Datner-Śpiewak, *Dzieje Żydów*, 184; Janet Singer Applefield, "Lost Childhood: Autobiographical Recollections," in *Resisters, Rescuers, and Refugees: Historical and Ethical Issues*, ed. by John J. Michalczyk (Kansas City: Sheed & Ward, 1997), 206-207 [afterward "Lost Childhood" in *Resisters*]; Pinkus, *A Choice of Masks*, 14, 22, 24-25; Lasman, *Wspomnienia*, 39.

15   Raport sytuacyjny nr. 11 Komendy Okręgu AK Białystok, 5 January 1945, in Kułak, *Białostocczyzna*, 98.

16   *Zrzeszenie WiN w dokumentach*, 1: 309.

17   Raport sytuacyjny Komendy Okręgu AKO-WIN Białystok za październik 1945, 22 November 1945, Aneks 16, in Krajewski and Łabuszewski, *Białostocki*, 795, 797.

18   *Zrzeszenie WiN w dokumentach*, 1: 361.

19   *Zrzeszenie WiN w dokumentach*, 2: 434.

20   The leadership of the underground compiled reports on all aspects of life in Poland, which included its Jewish minority. Although the Jewish attitude toward the Communists was of particular interest to the insurgents, often other aspects of Jewish life were noted as well. See *Zrzeszenie WiN w dokumentach*, 1: 240, 308-309, 313, 318-19, 328, 333, 341, 345, 361, 369-71, 374, 381-82, 425, 431, 435, 440-41, 444, 450-52, 455-56, 471-72, 508, 520-21, 524, 527, 530, 538-39, 541-42, 546-54, 594, 596, 598, 601, 603, 607, 612, 620-24; 2: 81, 138-40, 151, 154, 191-192, 261-265, 273-275, 278, 281, 286, 326, 336-37, 340-41, 347, 360-61, 432, 434, 438, 447, 477; 3: 64, 73-74, 195-96, 221, 247, 281, 323, 339, 348.

21   *Zrzeszenie WiN w dokumentach*, 1: 328.

22   See Sprawozdanie z działalności C.K.S. przy C.K.Ż.P., AŻIH, CKŻP, CKS, pudło (box) No 3-7, 1, 3-4, in Gross, *Upiorna dekada*, 95. See also Maurycy Zielonka, Komitet Żydowski w Płocku, Oświadczenie, 30 September 1946, AURM, PRM, BP, file 5/133, 61; Urząd Wojewódzki Białostocki, Wydział Społeczno-Polityczny, Tajne, Sprawozdanie Wydziału Społeczno-Politycznego za miesiąc październik 1945 roku, APB, UWB, file 94, 19.

23   More than a year later, in June 1946, Second Lieutenant W. Złotogórski (and not Zołotogórski) was the listed as the county head of the secret police in Sztum but it is unclear whether that was the same officer. There was also Second Lieutenant Modest Złotogórski, who served with the Communist militia in Kraśnik in the fall of 1944, but he was a local man who had worked during the Nazi occupation as a court clerk in Janów Lubelski, and was not "a Jew from eastern Poland." See Łabuszewski and Krajewski, *Od "Łupaszki"*, 176; Kierownik Wydziału Śledczego PKMO Modest Złotogórski do PRN w Kraśniku, 14 November 1944, APLOK, Starostwo Powiatowe w Kraśniku, Referat Społeczno-polityczny, Różne, 1944, file 146; Józef Zaręba, "Janów Lubelski w latach okupacji hitlerowskiej," (M.A. thesis, UMCS, Lublin, 1977), 40.

24   Jerzy K. Malewicz to editor, *Nowy Dziennik, Przegląd Polski on-line*, 9 February 2001.
25   Jan Krawiec, "Towarzysz Stolzman?" *Gwiazda Polarna* [Chicago], 9 March 1996. This is an extremely contentious allegation because it concerns putatively the father of the current post-Communist president of Poland, Aleksander Kwaśniewski. The allegation should be treated with the utmost caution because no available original documentary material supports the charges and because no scholarly research has been conducted on the topic. The rumor first surfaced before the presidential campaign in Poland. Compare a letter of an alleged witness to the editor of the libertarian-conservative *Najwyższy Czas!*, 1 July 1993; and the official statement of President Kwaśniewski at <http://www.president.pl/prezydent/w_rodowod.html>
26   The victims were Józef Grębosz, Józef Kozłowski, and Franciszek Noster. Their execution was clandestinely photographed by Józef Stec ("Joda"), who headed the WiN intelligence in Dębica and who most likely penned the original report quoted below. See Wąsowski and Żebrowski, *Żołnierze*, 342.
27   *Zrzeszenie WiN w dokumentach*, 2: 291.
28   The secret policeman Wendrowski had been a prominent officer of the AK in the Białystok area. He was arrested by the NKVD in July 1944 and saved himself by denouncing his superiors and soldiers. Later, he joined the UB, where he eventually achieved the rank of a colonel. Afterwards, he became a Communist diplomat, serving as Poland's ambassador to Iceland and Denmark. Whereas Romkowski and Czaplicki died in Poland, Kratko and Fink emigrated to Israel. This account is based largely on Jan Kantyka, an author who deals with secret police matters, who described the operation in some detail. See Wąsowski and Żebrowski, *Żołnierze*, 244-45; Jarosław Szurek, "Zbrodnia prawie doskonała," *Gazeta Polska*, 13 January 1999, 14; and Jan Kantyka, *Na tropie "Bartka" , "Mściciela" , i "Zemsty" : Z dziejów walki o utrwalenia władzy ludowej* (Katowice: Śląski Instytut Naukowy, 1984), 165.
29   "Meldunek sytuacyjny," [no date, February 1946], in *Zbrodnie UB-NKWD*, ed. by Henryk Pająk (Lublin: n.p. [Retro], 1991), 242-44 [afterward "Meldunek" in *Zbrodnie UB-NKWD*].
30   See Starosta Powiatowy Jan Pytlak, "Ocena pracy politycznej grup prop.[agandowych] W.B.W Lublin dla Dowództwa Wojsk W.B.W," 10 March 1947, APLOK, SPK, Referat Ogólno Organizacyjny, Tajne, 1947, file 1350.
31   *Zrzeszenie WiN w dokumentach*, 1: 524.
32   Andrzej Kownacki, *Czy było warto?: Wspomnienia* (Lublin: Towarzystwo Naukowe Katolickiego Uniwersytetu Lubelskiego, 2000), 548. An erstwhile officer in the Polish army and a technical expert, Kownacki was re-arrested soon after on the spurious charge of being a saboteur. While Jewish and Polish Communists tried and accused him, state-appointed lawyers, who happened to be Jewish, defended him. "The [military] judge was a Jew, and also seven out of eight lawyers defending us were Jews. Among the experts there were no Jews and, what is strange, the prosecutor also was not a Jew but a Pole with a typically peasant last name." Ibid., 629.
33   "Raport wywiadowczy za marzec-kwiecień 1946 r.," in Pająk, *Zbrodnie UB-NKWD*, 248-49 [afterward "Raport"].
34   For example, an underground dispatch of August 1945 for the Inspectorate of Puławy lists 27 security agents, including three Jews. These included the following inhabitants of Puławy: Zdzisław Frajt ("a very harmful individual"), Jakub Edelman ("a very dangerous confidence man"), and Chil Edelman ("torments workers"). See

"Inspektorat [WiN] Puławy, Meldunek za sierpień 45," in Pająk, *Zbrodnie UB-NKWD*, 231-34.

35   Siedlecka, *Czarny ptasior*, 122; James Park Sloan, *Jerzy Kosinski: A Biography* (New York: Dutton-Penguin, 1996), 49, 53 [afterward *Jerzy Kosinski*].

36   Already before the war, Scherman-Szymański was ostracized by the Jewish community in Wilno for his political opportunism. See Stanisława Lewandowska, *Życie codzienne Wilna w latach II wojny światowej* (Warszawa: Wydawnictwo Neriton and Instytut Historii PAN, 1997), 339-40.

37   The rubric "Poles denounced" concerns specific denunciations and general complaints to the Communist authorities. The rubric "Poles arrested" includes direct and indirect actions of Jewish security men in the Communist employ. The rubric "Poles killed directly" concerns Jewish perpetrators acting alone. The rubric "Poles caused to be killed" includes the victims of Jewish denunciations or other actions that resulted in Polish deaths, including the activities of Jewish security men acting in concert with their Polish and Soviet counterparts.

38   Yitzhak Sternberg, *Under Assumed Identity* ([Tel Aviv?]: Hakibbutz Hameuchad Publishing House and Ghetto Fighters' House, 1986), 102-103 [afterward *Under Assumed Identity*].

39   Raport sytuacyjny nr. 11 Komendy Okręgu AK Białystok, 5 January 1945, in Kułak, *Białostocczyzna*, 98; "Czterdzieści twardych: Wspomina Zdzisław Mańkowski," in Stanisławczyk, *Czterdzieści twardych*, 41; Zbigniew Małyszycki, "Wspomnienia o Żydach," TMsS, Gdynia, 23 November 1997, 15-16 (a copy in my collection).

40   The case of Jedwabne is still under investigation by Poland's Institute of National Remembrance. Currently, there are three major schools of thought. The first maintains that the murder was perpetrated by a large contingent of Nazi Germans with minimal Polish participation. The second claims that the Polish half of the town spontaneously murdered their Jewish neighbors by burning them in a barn with virtually no German involvement. The third holds that, although some Poles indeed participated in rounding up Jews in the market square, their role in the burning of the Jews in the barn is unclear. According to this last scenario, direct German participation was significant, if not pivotal, to the unfolding of the events. While recent research allows us to dismiss the first school and to doubt the second, more evidence is needed to determine the extent of Polish and German involvement. We do know, however, as a result of a recent exhumation, that the number of victims was closer to 300, rather than the widely publicized 1,600 alleged by a Jewish source. See Marek Jan Chodakiewicz, "Kłopoty z kuracją szokową," *Reczpospolita*, 5 January 2001. For an impassionate, but controversial, argument about the alleged spontaneity of the murderers see Jan Tomasz Gross, *Sąsiedzi: Historia zagłady żydowskiego miasteczka* (Sejny: Pogranicze, 2000), translated as *Neighbors: The Destruction of the Jewish Community in Jedwabne, Poland* (Princeton, NJ: Princeton University Press, 2001) [afterward *Neighbors*]. See also *Thou Shalt Not Kill: Poles on Jedwabne* (Warsaw: Więź, 2001), available on the Internet at <http://free.ngo.pl/wiez/jedwabne/index.html> and <http://www.polandembassy.org/jedwabne/jedwabne_thou_shall/main.html>; Tomasz Strzembosz, *Jedwabne 1941* (Melbourne: Biblioteka Tygodnika Polskiego, 2001); Jerzy Robert Nowak, *100 kłamstw J.T. Grossa o Jedwabnem i żydowskich sąsiadach* (Warszawa: Wydawnictwo von borowiecky, 2001); Thomas Urban, "Sie kamen – und sie sprachen Deutsch: Neue Fakten dafür, dass SS-Hauptsturmführer Hermann Schaper die 'Judenvernichtungsaktion' in Jedwabne geleitet hat," *Süddeutsche Zeitung*, 1

September 2001; Bogdan Musiał, "Tezy dotyczące pogromu w Jedwabnem: Uwagi krytyczne do książki 'Sąsiedzi' autorstwa Jana Tomasza Grossa," *Dzieje Najnowsze*, vol. 33, no. 3 (2001): 253-80; Alexander B. Rossino, "Polish 'Neighbors' and German Invaders: Contextualizing Anti-Jewish Violence in the Białystok District during the Opening Weeks of Operation Barbarossa," forthcoming in *Polin: Studies in Polish Jewry*, vol. 16 (2003), posted online at <http://pogranicze.sejny.pl/ jedwabne/angielskie/rossino.html>; Marek Wierzbicki, *Po drodze do Jedwabnego: Stosunki polsko-żydowskie na Zachodniej Białorusi (Ziemie Północnowschodnie II Rzeczypospolitej) pod okupacją sowiecką 1939-1941* (Warszawa: Fronda, 2002); Marek Jan Chodakiewicz, *The Massacre in Jedwabne, 10 July 1941: Before, During, and After* (forthcoming). Most of the articles that have appeared in Polish and English on this topic are posted on the Internet at <http://pogranicze.sejny.pl/ jedwabne/index.html>. A compilation of selected articles in English, including the important articles by historian Tomasz Strzembosz, are available at <http://www.kpk.org/KPK/toronto/jedwabne_update.pdf>.

41   Szmul Wasersztejn, Archiwum Żydowskiego Instytutu Historycznego [afterward AŻIH], file 301/152; Menachem Finkielsztejn, AŻIH, file 301/1846. Finkielsztejn's account was also published in *Grayevo Memorial Book*, ed. by George Gorin (New York: United Grayever Relief Committee, 1950). See also Jan T. Gross, "Lato 1941 w Jedwabnem. Przyczynek do badań nad udziałem społeczności lokalnych w eksterminacji narodu żydowskiego w latach II wojny światowej," in *Europa nieprowincjonalna: Przemiany na ziemiach wschodnich dawnej Rzeczypospolitej (Białoruś, Litwa, Łotwa, Ukraina, wschodnie pogranicze III Rzeczpospolitej Polskiej) w latach 1772-1999. Non-Provincial Europe: Changes on the Eastern Territories of the former Polish Republic (Belarus, Latvia, Lithuania, Ukraine, eastern borderlands of the III Republic) in 1772-1999*, ed. by Krzysztof Jasiewicz (Warszawa and London: ISP PAN, Rytm, and Polonia Aid Foundation Trust, 1999), 1097-1103.

42   Stanisław Dąbrowski, "Mordowali 'nasi' i nie nasi," *Gazeta Wyborcza*, 12 December 2000. Allegedly, the name of the "Jewish prosecutor" was Eliasz Trokenhajm or Trokenheim. Although ruthless, he was also famous for accepting bribes. See Małgorzata Rutkowska, "I z nami tak będzie," *Nasz Dziennik*, 24-25 March 2001. According to another source Trokenheim was a high ranking officer with the UB in Łomża. In 1949 Trokenheim was tried by a military court for embezzling and appropriating real estate belonging to Jewish Holocaust victims. Another Communist secret policeman of Jewish origin involved in the case of Jedwabne was Jakub (Jankiel) Stupnik. See Danuta and Aleksander Wroniszewscy, "Odkrywanie tajemnicy," *Kulisy*, 7 June 2001, 24-25.

43   According to police records, Julia Karolak, the wife of the German-appointed mayor who participated in the mass murder of Jews in July 1941, was killed by "unknown attackers" on November 1, 1945. In fact, she was assassinated by the independentists for collaborating with the Communist security forces. Thus, one should be careful before blaming "Jewish avengers" or the secret police for all extrajudicial killings in the area. See Raport za czas od 1.11.45r. do 30.11.45r., APBOŁ, Raporty sytuacyjne Komendy Powiatowej MO o stanie bezpieczeństwa, 1944-1948, file 59, subfile 9, 12; Leszek Żebrowski to MJCh, 20 November 2000.

44   See Wacław Bagiński, interview by Richard Tyndorf, 21 October 2000.

45   For example, the police "preparations" of the witnesses and the accused before the trail of the Jedwabne pogromists took merely two weeks. During the trial, some of the

accused withdrew their earlier "confessions," claiming they were beaten during interrogation and thus compelled to make incriminating depositions. See Gross, *Neighbors*, 28,

46   For example, one of the Poles sentenced for his alleged part in the Jedwabne slaughter was Roman Górski, who had sheltered the Jewish Serwetarz brothers in the aftermath of the massacre. See Protokół rozprawy głównej, Sprawa Bolesława Ramotowskiego i 21 innych, 16 May 1949, Archiwum Instytutu Pamięci Narodowej (a copy in my collection); Danuta and Aleksander Wroniszewscy, "Odkrywanie tajemnicy," *Kulisy*, 7 June 2001, 24-25.

47   Quoted in Piotr Szczepański [Zbigniew Romaniuk], "Pogromy i pogromiki," *Kurier Poranny* [Białystok], 12 April 1996, 6.

48   Very little is known about these events. On the one hand, violence was a way of life at the time and killing women, children, and the elderly was rather frequent even by common bandits, who would thus get rid of witnesses. On the other hand, the ruthlessness of the assaults suggests that these may have been revenge killings for anti-Jewish deeds committed during the Nazi occupation. However, that line of reasoning is weakened by the fact that between 1942 and 1943 the Jarocki family had sheltered a Jewish family from Drohiczyn. As in other cases, we have precious little evidence to reconstruct the events. The underground assassinated the Gruda brothers within two months following the assaults, though further evidence is required to establish conclusively that the Grudas were indeed responsible for the massacre. See Andrzej Olędzki, "Hersz Szebes – morderstwa w Czartajewie – marzec 1944, oraz podobne w Miłkowicach, Maćkach i Kłyzówce," *Głos Siemiatycz* on line, posted at <http://box.zetobi.com.pl/glos_siemiatycz/histor_zydzi_1944.htm>. According to a Jewish source, a Shloyme Grude was active in a Jewish group in that area that terrorized the Polish population and exacted revenge against alleged wrongdoers. See *The Community of Semiatych*, ed. by Eliezer Tash (Tur-Shalom) (Tel Aviv: Association of Former Residents of Semiatych in Israel and the Diaspora, 1965), xii–xiii [afterward *The Community of Semiatych*].

49   Tadeusz Bednarczyk, *Życie codzienne warszawskiego getta: Warszawskie getto i ludzie (1939-1945 i dalej)* (Warszawa: Wydawnictwo Ojczyzna, 1995), 308-309 [afterward *Życie codzienne*].

50   Ajzenman served time in prison before the war. His most famous exploit during the war was a raid on Drzewica, where his Communist partisans robbed the settlement and killed seven independentists in January 1943. After the war he was arrested for robberies by his own Communist comrades but released in 1947, ironically, because of an amnesty intended for the independentists. He was rearrested again sometime later for embezzling. A constant embarassment for the Communist party, Ajzenman ended up at a scientific institute. See Piotr Gontarczyk, "Powstawanie elit politycznych PRL: Przypadek Ajzenmana-Kaniewskiego," (MA thesis, University of Warsaw, 1997); Chodakiewicz, *Narodowe*, 80-81.

51   It is important to note that impoverished Poles also often took over properties of expropriated or absent Polish (Christian) owners. At least in some cases peasants were reluctant to appropriate Jewish and Polish property, for instance in the county of Kraśnik. See Zygmunt Bryczek, Instytut Historii Polskiej Akademii Nauk [afterward IHPAN], Wspomnienia chłopów, file 389. In Biała Rawska, Jewish homes remained empty throughout the war but afterward, with the encouragement of the Communists, they were taken over by the local poor. For an example of a Jewish woman refusing to

return property appropriated during the war to its rightful Polish owner see Stanisławczyk, *Czterdzieści twardych*, 59, 178.

52   See Pinkus, *A Choice of Masks*, 5-6, 8-10.

53   See Cała and Datner-Śpiewak, *Dzieje Żydów*, 25-26.

54   See Steinhaus, *Wspomnienia*, 323.

55   See Munro, *Białystok to Birkenau*, 220.

56   Sam Berry in *Voices from the Holocaust*, ed. by Sylvia Rothchild (New York and Scarborough, ON: Nal Books, 1981), 221, 226 [afterward *Voices*].

57   Kałowska, *Uciekać, aby żyć*, 88, 227-28, 232-33.

58   One of the kidnap victims was Abraham Fucksman (Foxman), who was snatched from his parents by his war-time rescuer only to be "kidnapped back" by his parents. Both sides denounced each other to the NKVD and Polish Communists. See André Stein, *Hidden Children: Forgotten Survivors of the Holocaust* (New York: Viking and Penguin, 1993), 210-217. There is no scholarly monograph concerning the immediate post-war fate of Jewish children rescued by Christians. See Richard C. Lukas, *Did the Children Cry? Hitler's War Against Jewish and Polish Children, 1939-1945* (New York: Hippocrene Books, 1994), 219-20; Ewa Kurek, *Your Life is Worth Mine: How Polish Nuns Saved Hundreds of Jewish Children in German-Occupied Poland, 1939-1945* (New York: Hippocrene Books, 1997), 111-21; Alvin Abram, *The Light After the Dark* (Scarborough, Ontario: Abbeyfield Publishers, 1997), 105-10; Alexander Donat, *The Holocaust Kingdom: A Memoir* (London: Secker & Warburg, 1965), 353-54; Lena Küchler-Silberman, *One Hundred Children* (Garden City, NY: Doubleday, 1961), 125.

59   For example, six members of the Jewish Miedziński family hid with the Polish peasant Mróz near Jędrzejów. After some time, in 1943, Mróz and a number of other peasants killed the Miedzińskis. Local guerrillas, most likely Jews, found out about the murder and assassinated Mróz in reprisal, along with his innocent wife and two toddlers. After the war, the rest of the peasants involved in the killing of the Miedzińskis were denounced, prosecuted, and punished. The killers of the Mróz family were not. To the outside observers it must have appeared that one could murder Polish children with impunity. See Kałowska, *Uciekać, aby żyć*, 124-25, 247-48. On the night of March 30, 1944, Hersz Szebes and his Jewish partisans attacked the farmstead of the Wiliński and Siemieniuk families in Czartajew near Siemiatycze. The following eight Poles were killed: fifty-year-old Jan Siemieniuk, his pregnant wife Stanisława, their three-year-old child, seventy-year-old Stanisław Wiliński, his seventy-year-old wife Maria, and their sons: thirty-year-old Adam and fifteen-year-old Jan. The reason for the killing remains unknown, although it was probably a revenge raid. After the return of the Soviets, the NKVD issued Szebes and his group with new weapons and allowed him to establish a local militia, or a self-defense force, in Siemiatycze. His deed went unpunished by the Communists. In contrast, the Soviets immediately arrested several local Poles in Siemiatycze who were alleged to have assisted the Nazis against Jews and Soviet collaborators in the summer of 1941. The Polish perpetrators were jailed in Brześć, where they perished. See Tash (Tur-Shalom), *The Community of Semiatych*, x–xiii; Andrzej Olędzki, "Hersz Szebes — morderstwa w Czartajewie — marzec 1944, oraz podobne w Miłkowicach, Maćkach i Kłyzówce," *Głos Siemiatycz* on line, posted at <http://box.zetobi.com.pl/glos_siemiatycz/histor_zydzi_1944.htm>.

60   See Warhaftig, *Refugee and Survivor*, 301.

61   See Nachemia Wurman, *Nachemia: German and Jew in the Holocaust* (Far Hills, N.J.:

New Horizon Press, 1988), 233-39. On Byk see Chodakiewicz, *Narodowe*, 85, 437 *n.* 258.

62 See Michael Skakun, *On Burning Ground: A Son's Memoir* (New York: St. Martin's Press, 1999), 218.

63 See Abe Argasinski, "Instant adulthood," in Geier, *Heroes*, 60.

64 See Zandman, *Never the Last Journey*, 159.

65 Born-Bornstein, *Powstanie Warszawskie*, 77-78.

66 Dr. Kamiński used gold for dental work which was illegal according to the Soviet authorities. See Ann Kazimirski, *Witness to Horror* (Montreal: Devonshire Press, 1993), 106-107.

67 See Drix, *Witness to Annihilation*, 227-28.

68 See Raport MO, 5 June 1945, Archiwum Państwowe w Szczecinie, Urząd Wojewódzki Szczeciński [afterward APSz, UWSz], file 1213, 413 in Aleksiun-Mądrzak, "Nielegalna emigracja Żydów, cz. 1," 80 *n.* 77

69 Benjamin Mandelkern, *Escape from the Nazis* (Toronto: James Lorimer & Company, Publishers, 1988), 209-210.

70 See Martin Gilbert, *The Boys: Triumph over Adversity* (Vancouver and Toronto: Douglas & McIntyre, 1996), 263-65, 267-68 [afterwards *The Boys*].

71 See Irene and Carl Horowitz, *Of Human Agony* (New York: Shengold Publishers, Inc., 1992), 174-75.

72 See Zeznanie Edwarda Gronczewskiego in AAN, Prokuratura Generalna, file 21/99, 281-340; Piotr Gontarczyk, "Dał rozkaz aby wymordować: Bojownicy AL, w tym późniejszy generał LWP [Grzegorz Korczyński] mają na sumieniu zabójstwa Żydów," *Życie*, 15-16 March 1997, 15.

73 Odpisy protokołów zeznań świadków, 19 September 1945, AURM, PRM, BP, file 5/133, 17-18.

74 See Jerzy Morawski, "Kat Zamojszczyzny," *Rzeczpospolita*, 20 February 2002; and see Chapter Three.

VII

INSURGENT SELF-DEFENSE OR POLISH ANTI-SEMITISM?

There were several factors that bore directly on the independentist animus toward and aggression against the Jews. Since in the complex setting of post-war Poland these factors often overlapped with considerations unrelated to anti-Semitic attitudes, it is pertinent to explore the circumstances of anti-Jewish violence. Better still, to overcome the dominant stereotype of "Polish anti-Semitism," we should inquire about what conditioned Jewish-insurgent relations.

The first and most important factor was Jewish participation in the institutions of the Communist regime, especially the secret police, as manifested in concrete anti-insurgent deeds. The second factor militating against the Jews was free-lance informing, which often took the form of squaring accounts with anti-Semitic perpetrators, real or alleged, with the assistance of the NKVD and the UB. This also tended to broaden the scope of denunciations to any person and organization of independentist character. Third, insurgent reactions toward enemies and bystanders, including Jews, were conditioned by the intensity of the secret police terror against the independentists.

Fourth, anti-Jewish animus was conceivably a reaction of the underground to the complaints of the civilian population concerning property disputes with the Jews and persecution of the Poles by the Communist authorities acting at the behest of often legitimate Jewish claimants. The fifth reason behind some instances of anti-Jewish violence was the protection of the Polish civilian population from robbers, their ethnic roots notwithstanding. The sixth reason that could conceivably cause harm to Jews (as well as any other stranger) was a universal paranoia of the underground concerning spies and agents. The seventh reason involved those tragic cases where anti-Communist operations of the underground inadvertently harmed innocent Jewish bystanders. The eighth reason concerned the possibility of revenge on family members of Jewish Communist perpetrators. Ninth, potentially, a high level of decentralization, lack of supervision, and infrequent contacts with the underground superiors could adversely influence the fate of strangers, including Jews, coming into contact with the rank-and-file insurgents. Tenth, mutual relations between Jews and insurgents were conditioned by the level of intimacy on the individual plane; where personal cordiality existed, Jews needed not to fear but, otherwise, suspicion on both sides was palpable. Eleventh, anti-Jewish animus could and did manifest itself in attempts to induce Jews to leave a locality under threat or through the application of force. Twelfth, the stereotype of *żydokomuna* influenced the insurgents to consider the Jewish community collectively as adversarial and pro-Communist and (*however, only in combination with any of the eleven factors listed above*) a legitimate target of retribution, which could range from assaults and property confiscation to outright killing of Jews.

Relations between the Polish insurgency and the Jewish community were exacerbated when Jewish partisans returned with the Red Army and NKVD as policemen and soldiers to undertake the purge of the enemies of Communism. Next, the Soviet terror and violence increased when Jewish avengers began retribution against real and alleged perpetrators of crimes against the Jews during the Nazi occupation. Some of the avengers came from the ranks of Jewish Communist partisans, who operated by means of institutionalized violence; other Jews acted privately, albeit often enlisting Soviet assistance.

The Communists and private avengers were clearly a minority in the Jewish community. However, even those Jews who eschewed revenge and involvement with the Communists encountered serious problems when they attempted to reclaim their own property that had been either appropriated by the Poles or rented to them by the Nazis. The rightful owners pressed their legitimate property claims and, faced with the resistance of illegal Polish occupants, were forced to turn to the Communist authorities, including the Soviet occupiers, for assistance. At times, the Communists resorted to force to aid the rightful owners. This, of course, intensified the police terror and, hence, the conflict between the Poles and Jews. The latter recoiled and sought more protection from the Soviets. Drawing closer to the Communists, the Jewish community thus inadvertently continued to alienate the Poles.

In Polish eyes, the activities of Jewish Communists, Jewish avengers, and Jewish property owners at large appeared to be coordinated and complementary. For the insurgents and other Christian Poles this was a manifestation of *żydokomuna*, an unholy collusion of the entire Jewish community with Communism. Incapable of disentangling this complicated web, they regarded the Jews (as well as other "non-Poles") as enemies. This occurred gradually and mirrored similar generalizations about Poles on the part of the Jewish community.

First of all, the insurgents undertook operations against highly visible Jewish Communist secret policemen. Then, they targeted agents, true and imagined. The insurgents applied a similar mechanism of retribution to their ethnic Polish enemies, real and alleged. The Polish partisans would kill family members in reprisal for activities of a Communist relative, however, but would not target all the Poles in a locality, as they sometimes did with Jews or Ukrainians. The Polish underground fighters usually took action to avenge earlier denunciations, arrests, or killings of insurgents. In that way, anti-Semitism was a secondary factor. However, it was certainly present whenever the rule of collective responsibility was applied to innocent Jewish civilians as punishment for the deeds of Jewish collaborators or the Communists. Even then, it seems, this was hardly different from anti-Ukrainianism, when Polish insurgents struck back at the Ukrainian Insurgent Army (UPA) strongholds by burning villages and killing people, and likewise anti-Polonism, when Ukrainian partisans perpetrated similar deeds against the Poles, albeit much more frequently. Alas, collectivistic thinking produced collectivistic reprisals.[1]

Fighting the Communists was legitimate. Attacking innocent Jews was not. Therefore we must keep in mind that the crimes perpetrated by Jewish security men, Jewish secret police informers, and Jewish robbers absolutely do not excuse attacks by the underground on the Jewish community as a whole. Presently we shall examine a number of examples of, for the most part, armed actions of the insurgents which involved Jews.

In at least one instance the killing of a Jew was attributed to his conduct before the arrival of the Red Army. Probably in early June 1945, allegedly the National Armed Forces assassinated Siudek Meryl in Rzeszów. According to a Jewish source, this was a revenge killing. Meryl had been a ghetto policeman during the Nazi occupation and allegedly had denounced Polish rescuers and Jewish fugitives to the Nazis. His case seems to have been an exception, however.[2]

Perhaps the easiest to understand are the straightforward assaults on Communist security men, who happened to be Jewish. In September 1944, a patrol from the NSZ unit of Second Lieutenant Zbigniew Góra ("Jacek II") disrupted a ceremony marking the establishment of a Communist party cell in the village of Kozice Górne near Lublin. The insurgents disarmed a group of Communists and militiamen whose leader, a second lieutenant, was of Jewish origin. The members of the group were forced to eat their party identification cards. According to a participant, "after eating their IDs, they all had to drink half a liter of strong moonshine per person, and before that the Jew and the [village party] secretary received 15 lashes on their naked a...[sses]. We took the Jew with us." It does not take a vivid imagination to guess the subsequent fate of this Communist activist.[3]

Between August and November 1944, a Communist secret police agent, Hersz Blanke, aka Holc, denounced more than a dozen Home Army soldiers to the NKVD and the UB in Lublin. The District Command of the AK passed a death sentence on him. On November 4, 1944, a hit squad from the AK unit of Lieutenant Czesław Rosiński ("Jemioła") assassinated this agent.[4]

On February 5, 1945, the Home Army soldiers Tadeusz Niedźwiecki ("Sten") and Bolesław Jóźwiakowski ("Huzar") assassinated the commander of the Communist militia in Zwierzyniec, Dawid Biberman, who happened to be Jewish.[5]

There were also instances of group killings of alleged secret police collaborators of various backgrounds, some of whom were Jews. In the Province of Białystok, "on March 24, 1945, the self-defense unit [of Second Lieutenant Kazimierz Kamieński ("Huzar")] entered Czyżew, where it liquidated 13 individuals. Nine persons of Jewish nationality were killed [because] they were accused of collaborating as agents with the Soviets, [as well as] three agents of Polish origin – Józef M., Józef O. and Józef M., and a Soviet lieutenant."[6] The insurgents also attacked a militia post unsuccessfully. Finally, several Soviet soldiers were disarmed and a Polish child was seriously wounded in the cross-fire.[7]

On the night of March 25, 1945, the AK units of Lieutenant Konrad Bartoszewski ("Wir"), Lieutenant Marian Warda ("Polakowski"), and Second Lieutenant Antoni Kusiak ("Bystry") attacked the forced labor camp in Błudek in the county of Biłgoraj in the Lublin area. The insurgents disarmed a garrison of 120 troops but failed to free any political prisoners because they had been transferred elsewhere by their captors several hours prior to the assault. Finally, the guerrillas executed three officers, including two ethnic Poles and the camp commander, Captain Vladimir Konovalov (Włodzimierz Konowałow), who was reportedly Soviet Jewish.[8]

On the night of July 24, 1945, a squadron of Major Zygmunt Szendzielarz ("Łupaszko") took over Narewka in the Białystok Province. The Communist militia surrendered without a shot. Subsequently, the insurgents executed two NKVD collaborators: the ethnic Polish militiaman Władysław Jeleniowski and Lucjan Zakrzewski, who was Jewish.[9]

In August 1945 a hit squad of the Conspiratorial Polish Army (*Konspiracyjne Wojsko Polskie – KWP*), an organization headed by Major Stanisław Sojczyński ("Warszyc"), carried out a death sentence on a Jewish secret policeman. "[Jan] Cukierman was one of the most cruel torturers and the chief of the investigative section of the Security Office in Radomsk."[10] His ethnic Polish comrade, Józef Krauze, was shot at the same time as well.[11]

On March 19, 1946, in Lublin the Secret Military Organization (*Tajna Organizacja Wojskowa*), a high-school youth group with links to the AK-WiN, assassinated the secret policeman Chaim Hirszman. The squad was led by Edmund Wołodkiewicz ("Włodek").[12]

On May 12, 1946, a WiN patrol of Second Lieutenant Antoni Kopaczewski ("Lew") shot the Communist militiaman Mordechai (Mordka) Chomik near Piaski, the Province of Lublin.[13]

Not all attempts were equally successful. In January 1945, Abram Tauber, an erstwhile Communist partisan and subsequently the commander of the militia in Chodel in the Lublin area, discovered and shot four unarmed Home Army soldiers: Edmund Pogoda ("Rubita"), Bolesław Pogoda ("Bolek"), Stanisław Wójcik ("Etażerka"), and Teofil Rejkiewicz ("Abo-Piotruś"). The victims were hiding from the NKVD. Ironically, their commanding officer, Lieutenant Stanisław Wnuk ("Opal"), had sheltered Tauber during the Nazi occupation. Within a few days, the AK unit of Major Hieronim Dekutowski ("Zapora") launched an attack on the militia post in Chodel. The AK captured its personnel except for Tauber, who had fled never to reappear in the area. The militiamen were disarmed and released.[14]

In March 1945, the NKVD and UB kidnapped and assassinated a group of Poles in Mińsk Mazowiecki.[15] Most likely, Jewish Communist militiamen were also involved in the crime. According to a Jewish witness, "one night seven Poles were shot at once. Among them were a number of well-known anti-Semites and even one Communist [sic]. The town militia included four Jewish youths who had survived the Warsaw Ghetto revolt. [After the killing] they were so frightened that they fled the town."[16] Thus, they successfully escaped retribution by the underground.

On the night of April 12, 1945, a UB death squad which included Jewish secret policemen kidnapped and killed between 16 and 24 mostly inactive soldiers of the underground in Siedlce. Their bodies were displayed for several days on the street to intimidate the local population and the insurgents. Before the anti-Communists were able to organize a counterstrike, most of the perpetrators, including Braun (Bronek) Blumsztajn and Hersz Blumsztajn, were transferred to other localities.[17]

Most likely in the spring of 1945, the underground attempted to assassinate the deputy chief of the Office of Public Security in Białystok, who was Jewish. The attempt failed but the secret policeman was seriously wounded. As a Polish historian put it, "if an *ubowiec* [a secret policeman] of that rank had been not Jewish but a Spaniard or an Australian, he would also have been shot at."[18]

Nevertheless, the moral impetus behind the anti-Communist activities became compromised when apparently innocent acquaintances or family members of Jewish secret policemen were either targeted for revenge or fell victim to lethal mistakes of the underground.[19] This was the case, for instance, with an operation conducted by the Citizen Home Army (AKO) in the county of Wysokie Mazowieckie, the Province of Białystok. According to Polish historians,

> On the evening of February 17, 1945, the patrols of "Huzar" [Second Lieutenant Kazimierz Kamieński] and "Zemsta" [NN] headed for Sokoły to carry out four death sentences on the 'NKVD snitches' of Jewish nationality. The sentenced persons were taking part in a meeting at a house in Sokoły. Although they were surprised, they [i.e. the NKVD informers] resisted. In the ensuing melee, an oil lamp was toppled. [In the darkness] the executioners began shooting blindly, killing seven out of 20 participants of the meeting (including a child).[20]

On March 12, 1945, in Ostrowiec, two Home Army soldiers, Ludwik Krzymiński and Kazimierz Markwita, walked into the apartment of Fajgla Korngold, aka Felicja Kwiatkowska. Their objective was to seize a list of Gentiles who had allegedly harmed Jews during the Nazi occupation and whose names were reportedly compiled by Korngold with the intention of passing them on to the Communist secret police. Apparently because of faulty intelligence, instead of finding Korngold alone, the Home Army soldiers stumbled upon a meeting of at least a dozen Jews. A melee ensued. Bewildered, the insurgents opened fire with submachine guns killing four persons and wounding several others.[21]

In early March 1945, the AK sent a bomb to Second Lieutenant Chil (Yekhiel) Grynszpan, who headed the County Office of Public Security in Hrubieszów (and later in Włodawa). This was in revenge for the group killing of at least nine Poles, only some of whom were tenuously connected to the underground. The secret policeman was wounded but survived. On March 30, 1945, another bomb killed his Gentile successor, the UB Sergeant Jacenty Feliks Grodek, who was also involved in the assassination. Soon after, in Sławatycze unknown perpetrators attempted to assassinate Chil Grynszpan, while he was visiting his father, Wolf, a sixty-year-old merchant. Taking advantage of the cover of darkness, the secret policeman fled. His father was shot. It is unclear whether this was an accident or revenge for having missed the son.[22] In another instance, the son of a Jewish NKVD agent survived an assassination attempt in Wasilków near Białystok. So hated did his father become that "because I was Chaim Mielnicki's son, I found myself the target of Polish bullets when I returned to Bialystok [sic Białystok] after the War."[23] According to Mendel Mielnicki, "I have no proof of this, but I have always believed this attempt on my life to be the work of some local fascist that the NKVD, on my father's recommendation, sent to a labour camp in Siberia."[24] Clearly, one did not have to be a "fascist" or an "anti-Semite" to harbor ill-will toward anyone connected in any way to the NKVD, even if the son was perfectly innocent of the father's crimes.

Attacks against both Communists and Jews truly walked a fine line between anti-Communism and anti-Semitism, and sometimes crossed over into the realm of clearly anti-Jewish deeds. On the night of February 18, 1945, a part of the NOW unit of Józef Zadzierski ("Wołyniak") launched a surprise attack against secret policemen and their alleged collaborators in Leżajsk. The main target was the adjacent buildings that housed both the NKVD and most of the Jewish inhabitants of the town. The Polish insurgents failed to capture the Soviet quarters, which were well defended with machine guns. However, the NOW partly blew up and successfully stormed the more exposed Jewish building. Meanwhile, two other Jewish homes were attacked elsewhere in Leżajsk. According to the regional historian Dionizy Garbacz, "Jews collaborating with the NKVD were liquidated."[25] Fourteen people perished in the fighting, including two NKVD men and "one soldier in a Polish uniform." Israeli historians Yisrael Gutman and Shmuel Krakowski affirm that Jews were killed, including women and children, but fail to mention the anti-Soviet factor in the attack. So far no research has been conducted to verify the veracity of the insurgent claims about the alleged Jewish informers.[26]

That is also the case with another guerrilla action that involved Jews. On May 27, 1945, in Przedbórz, the Province of Kielce, an NSZ unit killed 8 Jews. Its commanding officer, Captain Władysław Kołaciński ("Żbik"), claimed that he had singled the victims out of perhaps 300 local Jewish residents because they were Soviet agents.[27] However, the

American historian David Engel established that there were only nine Jews in Przedbórz at the time of the assault. Engel concluded that "the attack actually resulted in at least the temporary liquidation of the entire Jewish settlement in the town. Unlike in the case of Parczew [where the underground targeted Jewish militia auxiliaries only], and Kołaczyński's [sic Kołaciński's] assertion to the contrary, the killing in Przedbórz appears to have been indiscriminate and wholesale, much more akin to a pogrom than a surgical strike against specific known enemies."[28] It may come as surprise then that Kołaciński spared Dr. Juliusz Kamiński, a Jew who resided in Przedbórz at the time. According to Father Zygmunt Maj, Kamiński continued to express "very positive" opinions about the NSZ commander well into the 1960s. Would an eminent and respected Jewish physician cherish a Jew-killer? Clearly, the case of Przedbórz requires further research.[29]

Even more mysterious is the attack that occurred in Żelechów on June 11, 1945. David Engel quotes a contemporary Jewish paper, *Dos Naje Leben*, that "a NSZ unit fell upon a group of 'Polish democratic activists' that included several Jews" ("democratic activists" was an official euphemism for Communists and their supporters).[30] However, in her subsequent testimony, one of the survivors of the assault, Khanke Ashlak, mentioned neither Communist nor Gentile victims of the attack, which occurred at night. Ashlak also claimed that three Jews were killed, while the Jewish Press Agency confirmed only two deaths: both of them Jews.[31] Was the report in *Dos Naje Leben* a concoction of Communist propaganda? After all, the Communists always endeavored to characterize all civilian victim of violence as supporters of the regime and to depict the insurgents as genocidal anti-Semites, thus linking them with the Nazis. Furthermore, was the NSZ responsible for the attack? If so, which unit? Who was the commander? In fact, there is no independent confirmation that the NSZ (or any other insurgent group) launched the attack. We certainly can presume insurgent involvement but only after we have established the presence of Communists or secret police agents, Gentile and Jewish, among the victims. Until then we may just as well claim that this was a common bandit attack. It is premature to rule, as Engel did, that the Jews were killed in Żelechów "because of their political association."[32] It is also hasty to blame the NSZ based on the available evidence.

Whereas most of such assaults on Jews have not been satisfactorily investigated, at least some work has been done to clarify the events in Parczew, the county of Włodawa, the Province of Lublin. On February 5, 1946, the WiN units under the command of Leon Taraszkiewicz

("Jastrząb") attacked Parczew. The raid lasted from 5:30 p.m. to 11:00 p.m. First, the insurgents besieged the local Citizens Militia and secret police command post. Next, during their advance, the WiN partisans captured, disarmed, and shot three militia auxiliaries of the town's Jewish self-defense. Then, the insurgents broke into Jewish stores and apartments. Local Poles joined them in looting and mistreating the Jews. The insurgents appropriated store merchandise and other items (especially boots) and distributed some of the spoils to the civilian Poles. During their prolonged stay in Parczew the insurgents set up checkpoints and sent out patrols which searched people and demanded their documents. That was to flush out the Communists and their supporters.

According to the deputy commander of the insurgents, their task was "to ravage [rozgromić] the local Jews who grabbed the entire trade in their hands [i.e. monopolized it] and would not let live [i.e. prosper] other small merchants and traders, who were Poles."[33] Was the partisan officer suggesting that the attack on the Jews was connected to the perception that the local Communist authorities allegedly favored the Jewish community on the economic field? Or were these simply resurrected pre-war resentments aimed at Jewish skill in economic matters?[34] It is impossible to verify either possibility at this point.

About 150 insurgents took part in the assault on Parczew. At the time, according to the Central Committee of the Polish Jews, perhaps 200 Jews lived in this town. Of course, some of them managed to hide. However, the rest were at the mercy of the independentists.[35] Nonetheless, the only Jews who lost their lives were the aforementioned three militia auxiliaries, including the secret policeman Abraham Zysman ("Bocian"). In addition, one other Jewish man was wounded.[36]

The attack on Parczew of February 1946 is significant for several reasons. First, it is important to note that during an earlier raid on that town, on September 20, 1944, the insurgents assassinated the Polish Communist Mayor Aleksander Moskalik-Danielski and other "comrades" of the PPR. However, almost certainly no Jews were killed.[37] Second, the assault of February 1946 is the only example where an insurgent officer explicitly admitted that the Jews were his primary target, although the Communist secret policemen were also attacked, thus making the tactical-military aspect of this case apparently similar to the earlier assault on Leżajsk. Third, the mass participation by civilian Poles in anti-Jewish activities differentiated this attack from others. Thus, the raid of February 1946 shows the growth of anti-Jewish animosity on the part of the underground and local population and warrants, according to Alina Cała and Helena Datner-Śpiewak of the Jewish Historical Institute in Warsaw, the label "pogrom," even though it did not result in any deaths of Jews *qua* Jews.[38] Fourth, unlike the attack on Leżajsk, which had allegedly been ordered by a superior officer, the assault on Parczew was a local initiative, demonstrating the growing independence of the local commanders.[39] Fifth, the raid on Parczew caused relatively few deaths. In comparison to Polish-Belorussian and especially Polish-Ukrainian struggles, where inhabitants of entire villages were slaughtered, the WiN unit showed considerably more restraint in Parczew.[40] This suggests that the Polish insurgent brand of anti-Semitism, although vicious and at times lethal, was not genocidal.

In at least two instances, albeit poorly substantiated, both criminality and anti-Semitism came into play. According to Rafał Wnuk, in late spring 1945, some underlings of Lieutenant Tadeusz Kuncewicz ("Podkowa") of the ROAK caught two Jewish men near Krasnystaw. They forced them to beat each other up and then shot them for fun. In March 1946, a patrol from the WiN unit of Kazimierz Harmida ("Lech") attacked and looted a household near Biała Podlaska. They shot two Jews inside, including a soldier of the Polish "people's" army. Next, the perpetrators kidnapped a Polish woman and her child as well as three other Jewish men, killing them shortly afterward. Thus, Wnuk argues, anti-Jewish violence was perpetrated by a few degenerate partisans who combined banditry with anti-Jewish prejudice.[41]

The intensity of the aggression against the Jews, and the violence in general, seems to have been directly proportional to the degree of control exercised by the higher insurgent authorities over their units in the field. The closer the supervision, the fewer the victims of armed activity. The insurgent unit blamed for the highest number of Jewish deaths was completely unaffiliated with any national organization. The detachment operated in southern Poland under the command of Józef Kuraś ("Ogień" –Fire) and was erroneously identified by numerous Jewish sources as being a part of the NSZ.[42]

According to regional scholar Julian Kwiek, the "Fire" unit was responsible for the deaths of about 50 Jews. Some of them seem to have been murders perpetrated for anti-Semitic reasons. The circumstances need further clarification, however. For example, it is important to verify the identity of the perpetrators of two grenade and machine-gun attacks on a Jewish orphanage in Rabka on August 12 and 27, 1945. Both were blamed on "Fire," the second one probably correctly. However, the first one was supposedly carried out by a local anti-Communist youth group "Chimera." The only bright side to these horrifying episodes is that no one was killed.

Often the circumstances of such violence remain murky. For example, the killing allegedly by the "Fire" unit of a Polish guide and thirteen members of the General Zionist "Gordonia," who attempted to escape from Poland on May 3, 1946, has been variously (but insufficiently) explained as a secret police provocation and an altercation among border smugglers. Some blame it on the "Fire" unit, while others angrily reject the charge. In another case, on April 20, 1946, in Nowy Targ a patrol of Second Lieutenant "Żbik" (NN) of the "Fire" unit attempted to stop a car. The driver accelerated and his passengers started shooting at the partisans. The patrol returned fire, disabling the car and killing the passengers, one of them a secret policeman, after they had surrendered. Was this coincidence, a routine road block, a successful assassination of a security man, or a pre-planned assault on Jews? Were the passengers shot in the heat of the battle or killed in cold blood? Was this done for anti-Semitic reasons? It no longer suffices just to count and identify the victims. Scholars need to study in depth the circumstances of their deaths.[43]

For example, it was rather unlikely that anti-Semitism caused the deaths of two Jews in Ejszyszki, the county of Troki, the Province of Wilno. On the night of October 19 and 20, 1944, the AK unit of Cadet Officer Michał Babul ("Gaj") attacked Ejszyszki. Its aim was to seize Soviet official seals and caputure supplies from the municipal storehouses. During the operation the AK also resolved to kidnap a captain of the Red Army counterintelligence (*Smersh*) and his archive. In the process two Soviets met their deaths, including the captain. Unfortunately, an innocent Polish woman was wounded and, in a separate location, two blameless Jewish bystanders were killed in the firefight: a mother and her baby son. Alas, the Soviet officer had been billeted in their house and at least two Jewish auxiliaries of the NKVD lived there as well. Although there were about 30 Jews in Ejszyszki at the time of the operation, no one else was harmed. Nonetheless, it is reasonable to assume that the Jewish (or any other) NKVD auxiliaries would have been targeted if found. The raid in Ejszyszki is the single most publicized, most contentious, most controversial, and best researched episode in the Polish anti-Communist uprising. The daughter and sister of the Jewish victims, Professor Yaffa Eliach née Sonenson, stubbornly continues to maintain, against all evidence, that this was a premeditated Polish assault on Jews. Most other scholars disagree.[44]

When analyzing the relations between the insurgents and the Jewish community, we must be mindful of the widespread perception of Jews as friendly toward the Soviets and of the suspicious nature of the underground fighters who lived under constant threat of spies and infiltrators. Perhaps the most dangerous were the so-called "fake bands" (*bandy pozorowane*), or sham partisans, fielded by the NKVD and UB. These groups, disguised as insurgents, murdered political opponents and even burned villages.[45] Secret police agents were ubiquitous. According to a confession of a Polish (Christian) agent of the NKVD from Białystok, who himself unsuccessfully tried to infiltrate the underground, "a whole bunch of [secret police] snitches travel between villages [disguised] as beggars, merchants, and salesmen."[46] The author of an underground dispatch of February 1946 from the Lublin area informed his superiors that "the methods of the work of both the NKVD and the UB continue to be based upon trick, lie, and crime. There are known instances of impersonating by individual agents of the UB and MO of forest [i.e. insurgent] units, [and of] disguising [themselves] as beggars, traders, singers, etc."[47] This is confirmed by several Jewish testimonies mentioned earlier, and in particular by Martin Gray's account.

The increasing immediate threat from the secret police was directly proportional to the escalation of violence by the insurgents. The guerrillas considered it self-defense. According to an NKVD report referring to the period between 21 March and 16 April 1945:

> In the last days of this week, the members of the underground formations of the Home Army, NSZ (National Armed Forces), and UPA (Ukrainian Insurgent Army) have stepped up their bandit activities in many counties of [the provinces] of Rzeszów, Lublin, and Białystok. The bandits busy themselves with robbing food from the peasants, they kill the local inhabitants, *especially persons of Jewish nationality suspected of collaboration with our oper[ational] group of the NKVD,* [and] they kill the local parish [Communist government] employees of the militia, the organs of public security, and PPR members.
>
> We have also noted the instances of killing of the Red Army soldiers staying in those counties for food acquisition for the troops at the front.
>
> *At this time we have conducted many operations to pursue and liquidate the bands of the AK, NSZ, and UPA, during which more than 900 bandits were killed and 1,300 captured* [emphasis added].[48]

Yet, despite a flood of NKVD agents, UB infiltrators, and Communist terror, it is important to stress that the insurgents did not automatically kill a person simply for being Jewish. Exceptionally, even a member of the Communist security forces who happened to be Jewish was not always killed if captured by the independentists. In March 1945, a Home Army unit of Second Lieutenant Jerzy Pawełczak ("Jur") attacked a train on the Lublin-Rozwadów line near Kraśnik. The insurgents kidnapped four UB officers, who were Jewish. After disarming, terrorizing, and disrobing the officers, the partisans forced them to sing Jewish songs and dance around a fire. Afterward the officers were released, which was an unprecedented display of mercy on the part of the insurgents toward secret police personnel.[49]

It seems that the severity of the measures varied depending on the degree of individual guilt. Sometimes the alleged Jewish collaborators of the secret police were only targeted for expropriation but not for assassination. For example, on August 31, 1945, a team led by Second Lieutenant Jerzy Pawełczak ("Jur") attempted to expropriate a jewelry store in Łódź whose Jewish owner was alleged to be a secret police collaborator. No Jew was harmed during the operation which was, in any event, unsuccessful.[50]

Usually, the underground was ruthless toward the security men. However, it appears that the insurgents tended to spare innocent bystanders, especially if nothing unpredictable happened in the course of carrying out a clandestine assignment.

In November 1944, a Home Army squad entered an apartment in Lublin to assassinate a secret police agent, Hersz Blanke, who was Jewish. In addition to the agent, there were five other Jews in the apartment: a man, two women, and two children. The informer was killed; the remaining Jews were left unharmed because they neither aided the informer nor attempted to defend themselves.[51]

Probably in March 1945, a Polish underground team assassinated an alleged Jewish informer of the NKVD at his home in Sambor, which by then had been already incorporated into Soviet Ukraine. The agent's wife was spared despite the fact that she attempted to defend her husband and a melee ensued after the informer tried to reach for a gun.[52]

On March 24, 1945, the AKO unit of Second Lieutenant Kazimierz Kamieński ("Huzar") raided Czyżew, where the insurgents executed thirteen Soviet collaborators, including nine Jews. However, the bulk of the Jewish population was unharmed and, later, allowed to depart unmolested to Wysokie Mazowieckie.[53]

In April 1945, a guerrilla squad burst into the household of the NKVD collaborator Mojżesz Lewinkopf, aka Mieczysław Kosiński, in Rzeczyca Okrągła. Lewinkopf was absent. The insurgents departed, leaving his wife, a son, and another Jewish boy unharmed.[54] Kosiński and his family experienced another close call on the road from Jelenia Góra to Warsaw sometime in 1946. Despite the fact that they were distinctly "Jewish looking," an insurgent patrol left everyone unharmed. According to James Park Sloan,

> The two [Jewish] men, Kosinski [sic Kosiński] and Urban [Urbach], both had business there and they had taken the boys along to see the capital. Somewhere on the road they were stopped by "white" guerrillas, probably a vestigial unit of the Home Army, who were making a final thrust of counterrevolutionary terrorism against the victorious Communists. Fathers and sons alike sat in the car and trembled as the guerrillas looked over their documents. Finally the guerrilla leader returned the documents and waved them on. Perhaps they were looking for someone else, someone specific. Nevertheless, had they realized the position of the men in the car [who were prominent supporters of the Communist regime], the senior Kosinski and Urban would almost certainly have been shot on the spot.[55]

Even when the independentists harbored hostile intentions toward Jews targeted in their operations, they did not usually kill them. On June 25, 1945, in Kraśnik, six insurgents arrived at the local railroad station. With the assistance of Polish railway guards, they selected several Jewish passengers, separating them from the rest. Three of the Jews were members of the Communist military. They were disarmed and promptly stripped of their uniforms. Other Jews had their wares and money confiscated. However, no one was physically harmed in the process and the Jewish passengers were quickly released, including the military men who were forced to depart in their underwear.[56]

In July 1945, the NSZ unit of Captain Stanisław Okiński ("Zych") "levied and collected a contribution [i.e. ransom] from the Lewin enterprise (a steam mill)." The partisans took 100,000 złoty but there is no evidence that anyone was harmed, including the Jewish owner.[57] According to a Communist report, "on November 16, 1945, in the evening, an armed band [i.e. the insurgents] took from Chaim Finkelsztejn who was on the road, his horse and a cart with things in it." Finkelsztejn was left unharmed.[58] Mark Hillel claims that, on September 12, 1945, a unit of "the NSZ" arrived in Białobrzegi at the house of the chairman of the local Jewish Committee, Mayer Hajdera. The NSZ men levied a contribution of 24,000 złoty on the Jewish community and demanded that all Jews leave Białobrzegi within three days. The Jews departed unmolested almost immediately; none of the thirty-four persons was harmed despite the fact that the Communists failed to protect them in any way.[59]

At least in one instance the insurgents went out of their way to ascertain that a Jew they had captured was an innocent man in no way connected to the Communist regime and subsequently spared him. According to the recollections of a Jewish witness, who found himself most likely in the northern area of the Province of Lublin in the spring of 1945:

> Though I was no longer condemned to death for being Jewish, there were now new dangers on every side. There was a local war between the Polish nationalists and those who were coworking [sic] with the Communist regime. No sooner had the Nazi occupation finished, than the Communist occupation began. The people of Poland had had enough occupation of any sort, and many of them had regrouped to fight the Communists.
>
> I was now walking or traveling by horse cart from village to village, and it happened one day that I was ironically brought again to the point of death, this time not for being Jewish but for being a suspected Communist. I was in the company of an older believer who was wearing a white patriarchal beard. *We were detained by nationalist troops [i.e. insurgents] who demanded to know if we were Jewish Communists.* We denied it, of course, but I had Jewish Bibles with me and my [companion] was suspected of being a Jew because of his beard. It was no longer illegal to be Jewish, strictly speaking, but it was not a good thing either.
>
> *The soldiers were going to kill us, but they decided at length that they would simply hold us until they inquired about our true political leanings.* They confiscated our documents and all of our possessions and went to their headquarters to check on us. Three men remained with us and held their guns pointed at us. *After midnight the others returned and all was well. They accompanied us to the next village and told us never to come back or tell anyone about their outpost* [emphasis added].[60]

Also during a potentially dangerous late night encounter in Gliwice in Silesia, the Jewish side emerged unscathed, although the persons involved might have been common bandits rather than the independentists. According to Henry Friedman,

Gliwice was not a safe place. Germans were still in the area. Poles were moving in and taking over possessions from the Germans by legal and illegal means. The middle of the night was the most dangerous time. Bandits would hold you up and take everything you had. Those guys did not care if you were a Pole or a German. We used to protect ourselves and our money by putting our valuables in our boots. I was carrying two empty suitcases and a rucksack on my back that night, when I was stopped by a couple of Polish bandits.

"Where are you going?" they demanded.

"I'm being repatriated from Russia," I said. "I was delayed because of a train wreck."

"What's your address?" they said.

I told them.

They pointed me in the direction of my house and let me go.[61]

Were these exceptions? We cannot say for certain. Yet, these cases suggest that the insurgent attitudes toward the Jews were very different from the anti-Semitic animus of the Nazis. Nonetheless, it is undeniable that the insurgents harmed Jews, including killing them. The data analyzed above suggests that, over time, the insurgents' anti-Jewish animus and the severity of measures they applied collectively against the Jewish community increased after the news of Jewish participation in high profile group assassinations of Polish independentists spread throughout the countryside. In this chapter we have been able to document between 36 and 44 further Polish victims of four Communist assassinations with Jewish participation and even leadership. As the data presented in Chapter Five suggests, this was just the tip of the iceberg. The response of the independentists was predictably severe.

Five Soviet, twenty-three Jewish, and thirty-five Polish sources analyzed in this chapter show that the independentists interacted with Jews in over 30 situations in at least 36 localities. In some instances Jews were unharmed. Nonetheless, most encounters were hostile and ended in violence. As a result, 132 Jews were killed, including at least 25 innocent bystanders. The single largest identifiable category of Jewish victims (53 persons) allegedly had connections to the Communist security, including a minimum of 36 suspected agents. However, no data is available to determine the status of the remaining 54 victims of the insurgents.

Table 4
Jewish deaths by the insurgents:
Victims by category

Jews

Security forces		
	Soviet	3
	Polish Communist	10
	police agents	36
Military		
	Soviet	1
	Polish Communist	3
Civilian by-standers		25
Undetermined affiliation		54
Total		132

Contrary to the reigning stereotype, the National Armed Forces were not the single largest killer of Jews.[62] The insurgent unit allegedly responsible for the death of the largest number of Jews, the "Fire" detachment, was unaffiliated to any national organization. Only a few Jewish victims registered in this chapter fell at the hands of unknown perpetrators. This category of victims will be analyzed much more in-depth later.

Table 5
Jewish deaths by the insurgents:
Organizations responsible

AK-WIN	34
NSZ-NZW	25
Others	52
Unknown perpetrators	21
Total	132

To summarize, the killing of Jews by the insurgents usually occurred in self-defense to real and perceived threats and in revenge for alleged and real denunciations, as well as very often in conjunction with actions against the Communist security forces.

NOTES 149

Notes

1 At times, the line between individual assassinations and collective reprisals became increasingly blurry. For example, according to a Communist report, in January and February 1945, "a few political killings occurred (of jews [sic] and PPR members) perpetrated mostly in the county of Bielsk Podlaski." See Sprawozdanie sytuacyjne z terenu Województwa Białostockiego za styczeń i luty 1945, 27 February 1945, APB, Urząd Wojewódzki Białostocki [afterward UWB], file 231, 2. However, in March 1945, when the insurgents stepped up their opperations, a Communist official alarmed his superiors that "an action is under way obviously aimed at murdering Jews." See Sprawozdanie sytuacyjne z terenu Województwa Białostockiego za marzec 1945, 4 April 1945, APB, UWB, file 231, 9.

2 In fact, it is doubtful that the NSZ carried out the death sentence. It was probably the National Military Organization (NOW) which was very strong in Rzeszów. At any rate, according to Herzog, the assassination caused panic among local Jews and, along with anti-Jewish riots, prompted them to leave the town. See Herzog, *And Heaven*, 301.

3 Marian Bobolewski to the author, 27 November 1992.

4 The squad was headed by Romuald Szydelski ("Paweł"). In January 1945 five members of the squad were arrested, quickly tried, and shot. Seven of their superiors received lengthy jail sentences. See Anna Grażyna Kister, "Koniec donosiciela," *Gazeta Polska*, 14 September 1995, 7 [afterward "Koniec donosiciela"]; Ireneusz Caban and Edward Machocki, *Za władzę ludu* (Lublin: Wydawnictwo Lubelskie, 1975), 157 [afterward *Za władzę*]; Thomas (Toivi) Blatt, *Sobibor: The Forgotten Revolt. A Survivor's Report* (Issaquah, WA: H.E.P., 1997), 109 [afterward *Sobibor*].

5 Brzeziński, Chrzanowski, and Halaba, *Polegli w walce*, 89; Rafał Wnuk, *Konspiracja akowska i poakowska na Zamojszczyźnie od lipca 1945 do 1956 roku* (Zamość: Zakład Poligraficzny "Attyla," 1993), 83-84 [afterward *Konspiracja*].

6 Krajewski and Łabuszewski, *Białostocki*, 241.

7 Starosta Powiatowy w Wysokiem Mazowieckiem do Ob. Wojewody w Białymstoku, 26 March 1945, APB, UWB, file 285, 27.

8 Urbankowski claims that Konovalov was a Soviet Jewish "prosecutor." Another source reveals that Konovalov held the rank of captain in the Polish Communist military, but that he often dressed in the uniform of a major of the NKVD. Both authors can be right. See Urbankowski, *Czerwona msza*, 2nd ed., 1: 564; Władysław Ćwik, *Dzieje Józefowa* (Rzeszów: Krajowa Agencja Wydawnicza, 1992), 176-77.

9 Łabuszewski and Krajewski, *Od "Łupaszki"*, 77.

10 Urbankowski, *Czerwona msza*, 2nd ed., 1: 603.

11 See Maciej Roman Bombicki, ed., *Księża przed sądami specjalnymi, 1944-1954* (Poznań: Polski Dom Wydawniczy Ławica, 1993), 30, 37.

12 Martin Gilbert incorrectly averred that Hirszman "was murdered, because he was a Jew." Ironically, according to a contemporary Jewish account, Hirszman had quit his job shortly before the assassination. The underground was not aware of that fact and, besides, the sentence was carried out for Hirszman's deeds while in the UB and not for the mere fact of employment with the secret police. See Martin Gilbert, *The Holocaust: The Jewish Tragedy* (Glasgow: William Collins, 1986), 817 [afterward *Holocaust*]; Henryk Pająk, *Konspiracja młodzieży szkolnej, 1945-1955* (Lublin: Wydawnictwo Retro, 1994), 130-31 [afterward *Konspiracja*]; Cała and Datner-Śpiewak, *Dzieje Żydów*, 43; Brzeziński, Chrzanowski, and Halaba, *Polegli w walce*, 174.

13 Henryk Pająk, *Oni się nigdy nie poddali* (Lublin: Wydawnictwo Retro, 1997), 178 [afterward *Oni*].

14 See Ewa Kurek, *Zaporczycy 1943-1949* (Lublin: Wydawnictwo Clio, 1995), 190-91 [afterward *Zaporczycy*].

15 According to a Home Army dispatch intercepted by the NKVD, "5 persons, including 2 U.S. citizens" were killed in Mińsk. See Cariewskaja, *Teczka specjalna*, 275. For further information on the Communist terror in Mińsk Mazowiecki see Magdalena Chadaj, "Na hańbę i potępienie oprawcom," *Nasza Polska*, 1 September 1999, 4.

16 "The City Without Jews: Sefer Minsk-Mazovyetsk," in *From a Ruined Garden: The Memorial Books of Polish Jewry*, 2nd expanded ed., ed. by Jack Kugelmass and Jonathan Boyarin (Washington, D.C., Bloomington and Indianapolis: United States Holocaust Memorial Museum and Indiana University Press, 1998), 257 [afterward "The City," in *From a Ruined Garden*, 2nd ed.].

17 Two of the intended victims, Marian Pilarczyk and Edward Prachnio, survived despite serious wounds. According to a brief of the chief prosecutor in Siedlce, the UB death squad was led by "Bronek" Blumsztajn and consisted of the following Polish, Ukrainian, and Jewish Communists: Mikołaj Meluch ("Kolka"), Marian Reduch, Hersz Blumsztajn, Czesław Sągol, Marian Więckiewicz, Surowiec, and Adamiak. The secret police officer Alberg, who served as the deputy chief of the county UB office in Siedlce, was involved as well. Alberg and his immediate superior Lieutenant Edward Słowik, aka Kwiatek, also allegedly of Jewish origin, were even briefly detained following the killings. This was most likely because of international pressure. Churchill intervened with Stalin on behalf of the AK, specifically asking about the crime in Siedlce. Stalin angrily responded that nothing of the sort had taken place and that the whole thing was baseless propaganda of the Polish Government-in-Exile to smear the Soviet Union. It must be remembered, however, that the crime could not have occurred without the knowledge and, perhaps, inspiration of the Soviet "advisor" in Siedlce, the NKVD Major Timoshenko. Meanwhile, the underground assassinated at least two secret policemen involved in the crime, Marian Więckiewicz (14 April 1945) and Czesław Sągol (8 July 1945), both ethnic Poles. See Prokurator Anna Dańko-Roesler, "Postanowienie o umorzeniu śledztwa," 18 December 1992, Prokuratura Wojewódzka w Siedlcach, file Ds. 30/92/S, 7-8 (a copy in my collection); Gryciuk and Matusak, *Represje NKWD*, 2: 101, 121, 136; Cariewskaja, *Teczka specjalna*, 275, 280; Mikołajczuk "Przyczynek," in Bechta and Żebrowski, *NSZ na Podlasiu*, 2: 191-92; Wąsowski and Żebrowski, *Żołnierze*, 335; *Korespondencja Stalin — Roosevelt, Truman* (Warszawa: Wydawnictwo M.O.N., 1960), 221-23; Leszek Żebrowski, "Rozstrzelano siedemnastu," *Gazeta Polska*, 8 June 1995, 10. Of course, this was not the only crime of the Communist security forces in Siedlce. Already on August 22, 1944, the erstwhile Communist guerrilla and, later, the local militia commander Bolesław Drabik ("Bolek Bimberek") arrested and killed Sergeant Stefan Kosobudzki ("Sęk") of the NSZ-AK. Other victims followed. See Chodakiewicz, Gontarczyk, and Żebrowski, *Tajne oblicze*, 2: 193-94; Piotr Kosobudzki, "Partyzancka działalność NSZ na Podlasiu," *Narodowe Siły Zbrojne na Podlasiu*, vol. 1: *Materiały posesyjne*, ed. by Mariusz Bechta and Leszek Żebrowski (Siedlce: Związek Żołnierzy Narodowych Sił Zbrojnych, 1997), 1: 122-23; Piotr Jakucki, "Tajemnice siedleckiego UB," *Gazeta Polska*, 9 February 1997, 7. According to a journalistic account, about 20 out of 50 persons employed by the secret police in Siedlce were Jews. See Grażyna Dziedzińska, "Tej zbrodni dokonali Żydzi z UB," *Nasza Polska*, 12 June 2001, 14.

18 Ślaski, *Żołnierze*, 189-90.

19 For example, a member of the Board of the Jewish Community in Białystok, Szloma Szuster, complained to the Communist authorities that "after the curfew hour I do not open the door to anyone because of several terrorist attacks by the NSZ bands against my family caused by the fact that my brother, who lives with me, works in the Public Security [Office] in Białystok." See Szloma Suster do Ob. Wojewody Białostockiego, 20 November 1945, APB, UWB, file 531, 8. Szloma's brother was the UB functionary and Communist party member Szepsel Szuster ("Saszka"), who was assassinated by the insurgents in Sokółka on December 3, 1945. See Szepsel Szuster, Karta Ewidencyjna członka Polskiej Partii Robotniczej, APB, PPR, file 30, 2. In the official list of the fallen Communists he is mistakenly listed as "Szepsel Alperm." See Brzeziński, Chrzanowski, and Halaba, *Polegli w walce*, 75.

20 Krajewski and Łabuszewski, *Białostocki*, 240-41.

21 Fajgla Korngold and Chaja Sznajder née Szpigel survived the war passing as Christians. The casualties included seventeen-year-old Leib Lustig and a Jewish woman from Ćmielów. A Jewish memorial book (*Yizkor Bukh*) claims that the AK killed 5 Jews. The Communist propaganda immediately classified the perpetrators as "fascists." According to Urbański, the Communist "press blamed the National Armed Forces and 'fascist elements in the AK.'" See Urbański, *Kieleccy Żydzi*, 192; Regina Renz, "Żydzi w Ostrowcu w Polsce Odrodzonej," in Waldemar R. Brociek, Adam Penkalla, and Regina Renz, *Żydzi ostrowieccy: Zarys dziejów* (Ostrowiec Świętokrzyski: Muzeum Historyczno-Archeologiczne, 1996), 117; *Ostrowiec: A Monument On The Ruins of An Annihilated Jewish Community*, ed. by Gershon Silberberg ([Tel Aviv]: The Society of Ostrovtser Jews in Israel, no date [1970s?]), 95-96 [afterward *Ostrowiec*].

22 Caban and Machocki, *Za władzę*, 171, 206; Brzeziński, Chrzanowski, and Halaba, *Polegli w walce*, 168; Michał Grynberg, "W trud-armii i na froncie," in Turski, *Losy żydowskie*, 235-36 [afterward "W trud-armii"] (the author fails to note the UB connection); Cariewskaja, *Teczka specjalna*, 216; Werner, *Fighting Back*, 233; Marek Jan Chodakiewicz, "W służbie Ojczyzny (Wspomnienie o 'cichociemnym,' Kawalerze Virtuti Militari, płk. Marianie Gołębiewskim ps. 'Irka,' 'Ster,' 'Korab'," *Dziennik Związkowy* [Chicago], 8-10 November 1996, 11, 26; Maciej Podgórski, "Zbrodnia UB w Hrubieszowie," *Rzeczpospolita*, 26 May 1998, 1, 14.

23 Munro, *Białystok to Birkenau*, 10. On the activities of his father, which consisted chiefly of compiling list of Poles to be deported to the Gulag during the first Soviet occupation of the Eastern Borderlands, see pp. 10, 82-83.

24 Munro, *Bialystok to Birkenau*, 222.

25 Garbacz, *Wołyniak*, 97.

26 According to most witnesses and court records, "Wołyniak" did not participate in those events. Only one Polish witness claims improbably that "Wołyniak" had secured Soviet neutrality to attack the Jews only. Engel incorrectly states that the attack occurred on August 7, 1945. See Garbacz, *Wołyniak*, 117-18; Engel, "Patterns of Anti-Jewish Violence," 73; Gutman and Krakowski, *Unequal Victims*, 220. Gutman and Krakowski relied solely on *Lizhensk: Sefer zikaron le-kedoshei Lizhensk she-nispu be shoat ha-natsim* [Memorial Book of the Martyrs of Lezajsk who Perished in the Holocaust], ed. by H. Rabin (Tel Aviv: Former Residents of Lezajsk in Israel, [1970]), 93-94, 130. Tragically, the killing of women and children in collective reprisals against their male adult relatives was rather frequent. During the Nazi occupation, on June 1, 1944, a Home Army unit in the Puławy area killed an entire Polish (Christian) family of six,

because its head had allegedly denounced "members of the underground and others," presumably Jews, to the Nazis. In June 1945, the AK-WiN shot the Polish bandit Mamert Jankowski of Mrozy, who had been robbing local peasants. To avenge his death, Jankowski's family began informing to the secret police about the independentists. In November 1945 an NSZ unit executed the entire Jankowski family to stop its activities. On August 24, 1946, a National Military Union detachment under Zygmunt Kacprzak, aka Zdzisław Piotrowski ("Błysk"), killed nine members of a Polish (Christian) family, including an infant, because some of them allegedly had informed the Communist secret police about the insurgents. See Sprawozdanie za czerwiec 1944, 30 June 1944, APL, AK, OL, Inspektorat Puławski [afterward IP], file 12, vol. 1, 471; Remigiusz Markwart, "Komenda Rejonu Narodowych Sił Zbrojnych Mrozy (1944-1948)," in Bechta and Żebrowski, *NSZ na Podlasiu*, 2: 164-165; Garbacz, *Wołyniak*, 132-33; *Informator*, 104; Caban and Machocki, *Za władzę*, 368-69. So too did Soviet and Jewish partisans massacre Polish civilians, including women and children, for example in May 1943 in Naliboki (128 dead) and in January 1944 in Koniuchy (between 34 and 300 dead). See Chodakiewicz, *Narodowe*, 81; Krajewski, *Na Ziemi Nowogródzkiej*, 387-88, 511-12; Sulia Wolozhinski Rubin, *Against the Tide: The Story of an Unknown Partisan* (Jerusalem: Posner & Sons, Ltd., 1980), 126-27; Chaim Lazar, *Destruction and Resistance* (New York: Shengold Publishers and The Museum of Combatants and Partisans in Israel, 1985), 174-75; Isaac Kowalski, *A Secret Press in Nazi Europe* (New York: Central Guide Publishers, Inc., 1969), 333-34; Wacław Nowicki, *Żywe Echa* (Komorów: Wydawnictwo "Antyk", 1993), 87-88, 99-101; and *The Story of Two Shtetls, Bransk and Ejszyszki*, Part Two, 110-116. For more information about the massacres at Naliboki and Ejszyszki, which are under investigation by Poland's Institute of National Remembrance, see <http://www.kpk.org/KPK/toronto/koniuchy.pdf>.

27   In his memoirs Kołaciński claims to have killed 14 Communist agents between January and July 1945. However, in his letter of July 24, 1945, to the secret police, this officer admits to executing seven persons who were German agents and a further five for robberies, including two partisans from his own unit. There is no mention of Przedbórz in the letter. The letter was a successful ruse to allow him to escape to the West. See Władysław Kołaciński, *Między młotem a swastyką* (Warszawa: Wydawnictwo "Słowo Narodowe," 1991), 219 [afterward *Między młotem*]; Tomasz Lenczewski, ed., "Zaginiony list kpt. NSZ Władysława Kołacińskiego – 'Żbika' do władz bezpieczeństwa z lipca 1945 r.," *Mars* [Warszawa] 2 (1994): 323-26. According to an early Jewish account, "In Przedborz [sic] near Lodz [sic], nine Jews were kidnapped and shot in the nearby forest." See Mahler, "Eastern," in Schneiderman and Maller, *American*, 47: 405.

28   Engel, "Patterns of Anti-Jewish Violence," 72.

29   Dr. Juliusz Kamiński was saved from the Nazis by Kołaciński. Subsequently, under the *nom de guerre* "Migoń," Kamiński fought in Kołaciński's unit. Heavily wounded by the Germans in March 1944, he lost his hand but recuperated in hideaways of the NSZ and AK. Kamiński then served as a physician in the Holy Cross Brigade of the NSZ. He remained in Poland after the war. Kołaciński and his siblings also saved the family of Jakow Torenberg, aka Jakub Tomaszewski, of Piotrków Trybunalski. See Kołaciński, *Między młotem*, 234-36; Zbigniew S. Siemaszko, *Narodowe Siły Zbrojne* (London: Odnowa, 1982), 156-57 [afterward *Narodowe*]; Antoni Bohun-Dąbrowski [Szacki-Skarbek], *Byłem dowódcą Brygady Świętokrzyskiej Narodowych Sił Zbrojnych: Pamiętnik dowódcy, świadectwa żołnierzy, dokumenty* (London: Veritas

Foundation Publication Centre, 1984), 147-48 [afterward *Byłem dowódcą Brygady*]; Father Zygmunt Maj, Ubly, Michigan, to Władysław Kołaciński, Chicago, Illinois, 12 September 1962, a copy of the letter in the collection of Leszek Żebrowski in Warsaw [afterward CLŻ].

30 "Di Mord-Bandes vern oisgerisn mitn Vurtsl," *Dos Naje Lebn*, 20 June 1945, 1 cited in Engel, "Patterns of Anti-Jewish Violence," 75 and *n.* 75 also on p. 75.

31 Cała and Datner-Śpiewak, *Dzieje Żydów*, 29; Khanke Ashlak, "My tragic night in Zhelekhov," in *From a Ruined Garden: The Memorial Books of Polish Jewry*, ed. by Jack Kugelmass and Jonathan Boyarin (New York: Schocken Books, 1983), 218-20; and also ibid., idem, 2nd ed., 246-48.

32 Engel, "Patterns of Anti-Jewish Violence," 75 *n.* 75.

33 Dziennik Edwarda Taraszkiewicza ("Żelazny"), APL, AK, OL, Inspektorat Chełmski, Obwód Włodawa [afterward ICh, OW], file 101, vol. II, 19-23.

34 No study of the post-war relations between Communists and Jews in Parczew has been written. However, in Białystok the alleged favoritism accorded to the Jews by the Communists on the economic field caused resentment on the part of the underground. According to a report of October 1945, "in B[iały]stok all Jewish traders have been exempt from town taxes." Nonetheless, there are no independent studies yet to verify such allegations. See Raport sytuacyjny Komendy Okręgu AKO-WiN Białystok za październik 1945, 22 listopada 1945, Aneks 16, Krajewski and Łabuszewski, *Białostocki*, 795.

35 A memorandum of the Jewish Committee in Lublin, quoted by Engel, erroneously stated that these three men were unarmed. Compare Cała and Datner-Śpiewak, *Dzieje Żydów*, 38-40; and "Memoriał w sprawie bezpieczeństwa życia i mienia żydostwa lubelskiego," 25 March 1946, AAN, Ministerstwo Administracji Publicznej [afterward MAP], file 787, 116, quoted in Engel, "Patterns of Anti-Jewish Violence," 70; Pająk, *Oni*, 103-104.

36 According to a Jewish source, Zysman and others served with the Communist partisans during the Nazi occupation and later collaborated with the new regime, including its security forces. "Abram Bochian [Zysman], together with some other Parczew Jews felt secure because they were familiar with the members of the newly appointed left-wing government there and the local police chief." See Werner, *Fighting Back*, 233. The WiN deputy commander noted that Abram Zysman ("Bocian") was "a sergeant of the UB, and he was a pretty awful old Jew [*Żydzisko*] in his attitude toward the Poles." See Dziennik Edwarda Taraszkiewicza ("Żelazny"), APL, AK, OL, ICh, OW, file 101, vol. II, 19-23. While the auxiliary militiamen Dawid Tempy and Mendel Turbiner were shot to death, Lejb Krajnberg was wounded. See Protokół, 8 February 1945, AURM, PRM, BP, file 5/133, 66.

37 Kochański, *Protokoły BP*, 27.

38 Cała and Datner-Śpiewak, *Dzieje Żydów*, 37.

39 "Żelazny" admitted that his commanding officer, Captain Klemens Panasiuk ("Orlis"), refused to participate in and give orders for the assault on Parczew. Garbacz claims that "Wołyniak" was issued orders to attack Leżajsk by Captain Ludwik Więcław ("Śląski") from the NOW provincial command. See Dziennik Edwarda Taraszkiewicza ("Żelazny"), APL, AK, OL, ICh, OW, file 101, vol. II, 19-23; Garbacz, *Wołyniak*, 97.

40 The UPA burned 160 Polish villages in the Province of Rzeszów alone. The Polish independentists burned some Ukrainian villages, and the NZW slaughtered Ukrainian

peasants in at least three localities. On Polish-Ukrainian battles see Piotrowski, *Poland's Holocaust*, 242-54; Garbacz, *Wołyniak*, 69-86; Motyka and Wnuk, *Pany i rezuny*, 53-71, 139-54; Brzeziński, Chrzanowski, and Halaba, *Polegli w walce*, 25; Wiktor Poliszczuk, *Bitter Truth: The Criminality of the Organization of Ukrainian Nationalists and the Ukrainian Insurgent Army (The Testimony of a Ukrainian)* (Toronto: n.p., 1999), 177-209, 260-73, 279-84; Grzegorz Motyka, *Tak było w Bieszczadach: Walki polsko-ukraińskie, 1943-1948* (Warszawa: Oficyna Wydawnicza "Volumen," 1999); Tadeusz Piotrowski, *Genocide and Rescue in Wołyń: Recollections of the Ukrainian Nationalist Ethnic Cleansing Campaign Against the Poles During World War II* (Jefferson, NC: McFarland and Company, 2000); Wiktor Poliszczuk, *Dowody zbrodni OUN i UPA: Działalność ukraińskich struktur nacjonalistycznych w latach 1920-1999* (Toronto: n.p., 2000), 421-92, 538-47, 556-63, 615-50. The Polish-Belorussian conflict was limited mostly to the Province of Białystok but it has not been yet studied comprehensively. The independentists targeted some Belorussian villages for confiscation and burned a few, killing a number of Belorussian peasants for alleged collaboration with the NKVD and UB. According to the Belorussian scholar Eugeniusz Mironowicz, the Belorussians of the Province of Białystok were overrepresented in the local agencies of the Communist proxy regime, the terror apparatus in particular. For example, "at the beginning of 1945 Belorussians constituted 10% of the militiamen in the province and 50% of the secret police functionaries." In May 1945, in the county of Białystok, which was no more than 25% Belorussian, representatives of that minority accounted for over 75% of the membership of the Polish Workers Party (175 Communists out of 228). In the county of Bielsk Podlaski, which was 45% Belorussian, Belorussian Communists dominated the local party structure (84.3% or 437 persons). See Protokół w związku z napadami bandy i spalenia wsi Zaleszany, 31 January 1946, Protokół strat wsi Szpaki, 3 February 1946, Protokół strat wsi Zanie, 5 February 1946, APB, UWB, file 496, 42-62; Rejonowy Przedstawiciel Rządu Jedności Narodowej do Spraw Ewakuacji na rejon Siemiatycze, Bielsk Podlaski, do Głównego Przedstawicielstwa Rządu Jedności Narodowej do Spraw Ewakuacji w Białymstoku, 1 February 1946, Powiatowa Rada Narodowa w Bielsku Podlaskim, Telefonogram do Urzędu Wojewódzkiego w Białymstoku, 6 February 1946, APB, UWB, file 55, 2-3; Jerzy Kułak, "Pacyfikacja wsi białoruskich w styczniu 1946 roku," *Biuletyn Instytutu Pamięci Narodowej* no. 8 (September 2001): 49-54; Eugeniusz Mironowicz, "Białorusini," in Madajczyk, *Mniejszości narodowe w Polsce*, 15. Even the Communist authorities remarked that "the attitude of the Belorussian population is very bad toward the Polish people and authorities." See Sprawozdanie sytuacyjne z terenu Województwa Białostockiego za listopad 1945, 17 December 1945, APB, UWB, file 231, 28.

41 Wnuk based the first incident on a single undated testimony (probably from the 1990s). As to the second incident, he failed to address the fact that the perpetrators killed not only five Jews but also two Poles. Greed and desire to cover their tracks must have been at least as strong as, if not stronger than, anti-Semitism. See Rafał Wnuk, "Problem bandytyzmu wśród żołnierzy antykomunistycznego podziemia w Polsce," in Szarota, *Komunizm*, 76-77.

42 During the Nazi occupation, Józef Kuraś was involved with the populist underground group Tatra Confederation (*Konfederacja Tatrzańska*), which later became a part of the BCh and AK. He was eventually expelled from the AK for lack of discipline, raised his own partisan unit, and started cooperating with Soviet, Jewish, and Polish Communist guerrillas. After the arrival of the Red Army, Kuraś ("Fire") joined the secret police and

became the UB commander in Nowy Targ. In the spring 1945 he deserted, restored his old partisan unit, and accepted new recruits. Until 1947, his insurgents controlled the area, ruthlessly defending themselves against the Communists. See *Informator*, 37; Wąsowski and Żebrowski, *Żołnierze*, 289-304; Bolesław Dereń, *Józef Kuraś" Ogień" : Partyzant Podhala* (Kraków: Secesja, 1995), 123-24 [afterward *Józef Kurań*]; Grzegorz Mazur, Wojciech Rojek, and Marian Zgórniak, *Wojna i okupacja na Podkarpaciu i Podhalu na obszarze Inspektoratu ZWZ-AK Nowy Sącz, 1939-1945* (Kraków: Wydawnictwo Naukowe Księgarnia Akademicka, 1998), 317-19; Julian Krzewicki, "Wspomnienia," *Zeszyt historyczny: Fundacja Studium Okręgu AK Kraków* no. 3 (September 1998): 82-83 n. 15; Maciej Korkuć, "'Ogień' bez odwrotu," *Życie* [Warszawa], 22 and 23 February 1997, 16; Grażyna Dziedzińska, "Bo nic nie było takie jak trzeba," *Nasza Polska*, 12 June 2001, 18. For the misidentification in Jewish testimonies of the "Fire" unit as belonging to the NSZ see Tenenbaum, *In Search of a Lost People*, 137; Tenenbaum, *Underground*, 469; Niewyk, *Fresh Wounds*, 151-60; Fass, *Nowy-Targ and Vicinity*, 71-73; Lena Küchler-Silberman, *My Hundred Children* (New York: Laurel-Leaf/Dell, 1987), 176 [afterward *My Hundred*]. One second-hand witness and one historian incorrectly stated that "Fire" was at the time in the AK. See Kornbluth, *Sentenced to Remember*, 156-57; Gilbert, *Holocaust*, 817-18.

43 See Rzeczpospolita Polska, Ministerstwo Pracy i Opieki Społecznej, Referat dla Spraw Pomocy Ludności Żydowskiej, Czternaste sprawozdanie z działalności (za miesiąc sierpień roku 1945), 31 August 1945, AURM, PRM, BP, file 5/133, 68; Kwiek, *Żydzi, Łemkowie, Słowacy*, 27-29, 47; Pająk, *Konspiracja*, 260; Tenenbaum, *Underground*, 469; Fass, *Nowy-Targ and Vicinity*, 71-73; Niewyk, *Fresh Wounds*, 155-56; Bauer, *Flight and Rescue*, 147; Küchler-Silberman, *My Hundred*, 176; Cała and Datner-Śpiewak, *Dzieje Żydów*, 32, 185; Cariewskaja, *Teczka specjalna*, 364; Gilbert, *Holocaust*, 817-18; Hillel, *Le Massacre des survivants*, 131-32, 136-37, 226-29; Singer Applefield, "Lost Childhood," in Michalczyk, *Resisters*, 206; Lucjan Dobroszycki, "Restoring Jewish Life in Post-War Poland," *Soviet Jewish Affairs*, 2 (1973): 67 [afterward "Restoring Jewish Life"]. As late as September 1998 a journalist incorrectly claimed that eight children were kidnapped from the orphanage in Rabka and killed. The sources listed above either stress that no one died in the attacks, or fail to discuss the question of victims, thus implicitly admitting that no one died. See Adam Rok, "Kto, komu i co imputuje?" *Słowo Żydowskie, Dos Jidisze Wort: Dwutygodnik społeczno-kulturalny* [Warsaw], 18 September 1998, 4, 6. Nonetheless, the secret police alleged that in April 1946, near Białka, the "Fire" unit killed seven Jews. According to one source, they were six Jewish children and their chaperon from the orphanage in Rabka, trying to escape illegally from Poland. However, according to an investigative journalist, there is no solid proof "Fire" was involved or that this killing truly took place. See Paweł Smoleński, "Koszmar był, odszedł i go nie ma?" *Gazeta Wyborcza*, 14 November 2001.

44 See Yaffa Eliach, "The Pogrom at Eishyshok," *The New York Times*, 6 August 1996, 15; Eliach, *There Once Was a World*, 663-68; Piotrowski, *Poland's Holocaust*, 91-94; John Radzilowski, "Yaffa Eliach's Big Book of Holocaust Revisionism," *Journal of Genocide Studies* 1, no. 2 (1999): 273-80; John Radzilowski, "Ejszyszki Revisited, 1939-1945," forthcoming in *Polin: Studies in Polish Jewry*, vol. 15 (2002); Paul Gottfried, "Polonophobia," *Chronicles* (January 1997): 12-14; "Celem akcji był radziecki kapitan: Rozmowa z dr. Jarosławem Wołkonowskim," *Gazeta Wyborcza*, 8 August 1996, 2; Jarosław Wołkonowski, "Ejszyszki – zniekształcony obraz przeszłości," *Kurier Wileński*, 6 September 1996, 3; Leszek Żebrowski, "Sprawa Yaffy

Eliach," *Gazeta Polska*, 22 August 1996, 12-13; Michał Wołłejko, "Opowieści chasydzkie," *Gazeta Polska*, 15 August 1995, 11; Krajewski, *Na Ziemi Nowogródzkiej*, 619; Mark Paul, "Anti-Semitic Pogrom in Ejszyszki?" in *The Story of Two Shtetls*, 9-172; Anna Ferenc, "Głowy na wietrze," *Gazeta Wyborcza*, 27-28 May 2000, 14-19. See also Icchak Sonensohn, "Protokół zeznania świadka," Yad Vashem Archive [afterward YVA], file 03/2743, 8; Witold Andruszkiewicz to Richard Tyndorf, 28 July 1999 (a copy in my collection); and the NKVD documents and Polish testimonies in *Kurier Wileński* serialized as "Z gminy Ejszyskiej: Przyczynek do dziejów AK na Wileńszczyźnie po lipcu 1944 r.," 11, 14, 15, 16, 17, 18, 21, 22, 23, 24, 25, 28, 29, 30 and 31 July and 4, 5, 7, 8, 11, 12, 13, 14, 15, 18, 19, 20, 21, 22, 25, 26, 27 and 28 August 1992.

45   See Leszek Żebrowski, "Działalność tzw. band pozorowanych jako metoda zwalczania podziemia niepodległościowego w latach 1944-1947," in Bäcker, *Skryte*, 75-90 [afterward "Działalność"]; Maciej Korkuć, "Oddziały prowokacyjne UB i KBW w Małopolsce," *Zeszyty Historyczne WiN-u* 8 (1996): 97-108; Marcin Zaborski, "Zbrodnia nie popełniona przez NSZ," *Gazeta Polska*, 15 September 1994, 8-9; Marek Jan Chodakiewicz, "Nieznani czy nie ukarani sprawcy?" *Słowo: Dziennik katolicki*, 14-15 June 1995, 11; and for a sanitized version by a participant see Edward Gronczewski, "Trudne dni: Wspomnienia z lat 1945-1946," *Wojskowy Przegląd Historyczny* 4 (October-December 1976): 131-54. For an individual case see [Stanisław Milczarczyk to the PSL leadership in Warsaw], [no date, December 1945], Archiwum Zakładu Historii Ruchu Ludowego in Warsaw, Polskie Stronnictwo Ludowe [afterward AZHRL, PSL], file 166, 67. For a list of murdered populist leaders see "Uprowadzenia członków PSL," AZHRL, no file name, no page number (uncatalogued notebook).

46   See Protokół przesłuchania "Papierosa," 17 May 1945, in Kułak, *Białostocczyzna*, 142.

47   See "Meldunek sytuacyjny," no date [February 1946], in Pająk, *Zbrodnie UB-NKWD*, 242.

48   See Cariewskaja, *Teczka specjalna*, 248.

49   More specifically, after the dissolution of the AK, Pawełczak's unit belonged to the Resistance Movement of the Home Army (*Ruch Oporu Armii Krajowej – ROAK*). See Kurek, *Zaporczycy*, 210. A Communist document, based upon Jewish reports, confirms that on June 23, 1945, at 5:30 am the insurgents attacked a train at the Kraśnik railroad station. Jewish passangers were despoiled of money and merchandise and "three Jewish military men" were disrobed and left in their underwear only. Nonetheless, all Jews were released unharmed. It is possible that this may be the same action as described by Kurek. See below; and see Ministerstwo Pracy i Opieki Społecznej, Referat dla Spraw Pomocy Ludności Żydowskiej, Trzynaste sprawozdanie (za miesiąc lipiec b.r.), 31 July 1945, AURM, PRM, BP, file 5/137, 22.

50   The attack on the jewelry store was undertaken by Second Lieutenant Jerzy Pawełczak ("Jur") of the ROAK on his own initiative after a bitter quarrel with his superior officer, Major Heronim Dekutowski ("Zapora"). The latter had ordered most of his soldiers to give up the armed struggle. Pawełczak and his followers needed the funds to continue the fight. Acting upon the intelligence supplied by another Home Army soldier, Marian Grabski ("Spec"), they picked "the jewelry store of Welt, which belonged to a Jew who worked in the UB," according to Kurek. Jerzy Pawełczak ("Jur") and Platoon Leader Władysław Winogrodzki ("Modrzew") were caught by the UB during the expropriation action and executed on October 23, 1945. The third member of the squad, Private Janusz Pawełczak ("Głaz"), managed to save himself. He returned to the Province of Lublin to continue the struggle. See Kurek, *Zaporczycy*, 267-68; Wąsowski and

Żebrowski, *Żołnierze*, 99-100; Sławomir Pająk, ed., *Straceni w polskich więzieniach* (Lublin: Wydawnictwo Retro, 1994), 123, 159 [afterward *Straceni*]; Andrzej Zagórski, ed., "Wyrok w sprawie rtm. Władysława Nowickiego 'Stefana', mjr. Hieronima Dekutowskiego 'Zapory' i towarzyszy," *Zeszyty Historyczne WiN-u*, 9 (December 1996): 166 *n.* 16.

51 Later, the same Jewish witnesses, including Zofia Rosen née Burstein, who had been spared, testified against the AK soldiers involved in the assassination. Five of them were sentenced to death; seven were incarcerated for a long time. Basing himself on a single second-hand account, Kopcikowski claims that another Jewish man, Leon Feldhendler, was killed as well at the time — by mistake. However, the author admits that no trace of the alleged second victim exists in the very detailed court and police records concerning the case. See Adam Kopcikowski, "Problemy bezpieczeństwa," posted online at <http://ktf.umcs.lublin.pl/stona/lublin_po_1944_bezpeczenstwo.html>; Kister, "Koniec donosiciela," 7; Caban and Machocki, *Za władzę*, 157.

52 Later, the woman testified against the attackers at their trial. Nonetheless, the details of this episode are unclear. The assassination was carried out by Henryk Urbanowicz and Edward Buca. Urbanowicz entered the Jewish household alone because the informer's wife barricaded the door before Buca could walk in. Both Polish teenagers belonged to the Podhale Eagle Cubs (*Orlęta Podhalańskie*) of Sambor. Led by Tadeusz Bukowy, this youth group had connections to the Home Army. The NKVD destroyed the Eagle Cubs in May 1945. A score of people were arrested. Urbanowicz, who was the shooter, spent 14 years in the Gulag for his deed. Edward Buca was sentenced to death, which was later commuted to long-term imprisonment. Several Polish witnesses have given conflicting testimonies concerning the assassination. According to some, this was ordered from above; others claim that Urbanowicz and Buca acted on their own initiative. Bukowy stresses that there was no death sentence passed on the alleged informer; that Urbanowicz was just to deliver a warning; but that the Jewish man attempted to reach for a gun and was shot. One second-hand source claims that this was not an assassination but an expropriation assignment to acquire money for weapons. Others vehemently deny this. These testimonies are a classic example of Rashomon-like memories of people, who were in various ways directly or indirectly connected to Urbanowicz. See Małgorzata Strasz and Tomasz Gleb, eds., "Henryk Urbanowicz: Człowiek na krze," *Karta* 12 (1994): 5-7, 30-31.

53 See Krajewski and Łabuszewski, *Białostocki*, 227, 241.

54 Siedlecka, *Czarny ptasior*, 118.

55 Park Sloan, *Jerzy Kosinski*, 59.

56 "Memoriał Wojewódzkiego Komitetu Żydowskiego w Lublinie do wojewody lubelskiego," 11 July 1945, quoted in Rzeczpospolita Polska, Ministerstwo Pracy i Opieki Społecznej, Referat dla Spraw Pomocy Ludności Żydowskiej, Trzynaste sprawozdanie z działalności (za miesiąc lipiec b.r.), 31 July 1945, AURM, PRM, BP, file 5/137, 22.

57 Mikołajczuk, "Przyczynek," in Bechta and Żebrowski, *NSZ na Podlasiu*, 2: 200.

58 See Sprawozdanie sytuacyjne z terenu Województwa Białostockiego za listopad 1945, 17 December 1945, APB, UWB, file 231, 36.

59 The story has not been confirmed by any other sources and thus it is unknown whether the NSZ or other insurgent group was involved. According to Hillel, a few days before the arrival of the insurgents in Białobrzegi with the anti-Jewish ultimatum, allegedly the NSZ had shot a cousin of the chairman of the Jewish committee. However, there

had been no reports of conflict between the insurgents and the local Jewish community prior to the killing. It is unclear if the Jewish man was connected to the Communists in general and their security forces in particular. If so, that would have at least partly explained why the insurgents issued their ultimatum, alas holding the whole community accountable. However, only one witness, writing in the memorial book of Białobrzegi, recalled that the decision to depart was made both because of the local conditions and, especially, because of the massacre in Kielce in July 1946. "Shortly after our return to Biyalabgige [sic] the Poles showed great hostility towards us. At that period the pogrom at Klotzer [Kielce] took place were [sic where] 50 Jews, Holocaust survivors, were brutally massacred by the Poles. We therefore decided to leave for Germany." Did the flight occur in September 1945 because of the insurgents? Or did it take place after the Kielce massacre of July 1946? This incident requires further research. See Hillel, *Le Massacre des survivants*, 237-38; *Book of Remembrance of the Community of Bialobrzeg,* ed. by Rabbi David Avraham Mendelbaum (Tel Aviv: The Council of Bialobrzeg, 1991) at <http://www.mathsci.appstate.edu/sjg/yizkor.html>.

60   Rachmiel Frydland, *When Being Jewish Was A Crime* (Nashville and New York: Thomas Nelson Inc., 1978), 145-46.

61   Friedman, *I'm No Hero*, 60.

62   This mirrors the stereotype about the NSZ that has emerged in relation to the German occupation, even though historians at Yad Vashem have identified the AK as the alleged perpetrators in most of the incidents that they have detailed. See Yisrael Gutman and Shmuel Krakowski, *Unequal Victims: Poles and Jews During World War Two* (New York: Holocaust Library, 1986), 215-18.

VIII

Unknown Perpetrators
and Murky Circumstances

In many instances of anti-Jewish violence the evidence is insufficient to reach firm conclusions. The following analysis considers individual assassinations, mob attacks, and threats of violence against Jews. The main feature of these occurrences is that the perpetrators, their motives, and even the circumstances remain unknown. Therefore, it is difficult to judge them conclusively.

In certain cases, the perpetrators are misidentified as insurgents. In April 1945, in Katowice, according to Izaak Goldberg, "five young Poles entered my apartment. They were armed with knives, sticks and clubs." The intruders identified themselves as Home Army soldiers and attempted to kidnap Goldberg. However, they were prevented from executing their plan by the local Jewish self-defense which disarmed them and notified the Communist security forces. "The perpetrators were taken away by the police, and as usual released afterwards," recalls Goldberg.[1] This detail alone suggests strongly that the intruders were impostors. No Home Army soldier could count on the mercy of the Communist secret police, especially if caught red-handed during an operation. Moreover, according to the journalist John Sack, the security office in Katowice was heavily staffed with Jewish Communist officers at the time. It is doubtful that they would have spared perpetrators that were not Communists.[2]

At times, the information available is too vague to identify the perpetrators. According to a Home Army report, on "October 14 [1944] in B-stok [Białystok], unknown perpetrators killed a standard bearer [*chorąży*] of the A.B. [the Berling Army] Hirsz Brawa [sic Brau] (a jew [sic]); they [i.e. the Communists] are making him a victim of the AK."[3] Obviously, someone else was responsible other than the AK. Who? Why?

Similarly, according to the testimony of Nuchim Rozenel, in August 1944 two Jewish men were shot in unknown circumstances in Kraśnik. Communist historians claim that these two were "former members of the

159

AL," the Communist guerrilla "People's Army" (*Armia Ludowa – AL*). Were they also militiamen? Who killed them? After all, the local AK and NSZ units had fled the area to avoid disarmament and imprisonment by the Soviets. Soon after, other mysterious killings took place in the county of Kraśnik; for example sometime before January 1945 twelve Jews were allegedly massacred in Janów Lubelski all on the same day. However, recounting the allegation, David Engel neither confirmed the crime nor described its circumstances. So far it has been impossible to verify the event, despite an extensive search in local, provincial, and national archives.[4]

Fortunately, there is more information about another case that took place in the same area. According to a Communist dispatch, on October 14, 1944, "six killings took place in the county, namely two poles [sic] and four jewesses [sic], who walked around the villages in the environs of Kawęczyn, trading."[5] The authorities gave no reason for the killings. Presumably, the Jewish women had merchandise for sale, which could have been a reason for bandits to attack them. David Engel, however, contends that "one man and three Jewish women were pulled from two separate carts traveling on the road to Kraśnik in Lublin province; in both cases the victims had been riding together with Christian passengers, who were unharmed."[6] We still do not know who killed them.

Likewise, information provided by the late Lucjan Dobroszycki fails to explain the events in Połaniec satisfactorily. According to this senior expert in Jewish-Polish affairs, approximately forty Jews returned to that town after the arrival of the Soviets in August 1944. Half a year later, "on April 10, 1945, an armed band came to the town. Five Jews were murdered, two wounded. The next day the rest of the Jewish population left."[7] Why were those five targeted? How did the rest of the Jewish community survive the assault? What group carried out the attack?[8]

The methodology of the religious Zionist activist Zorach Warhaftig unfortunately suffers from similar shortcomings as that of Dobroszycki and others. Warhaftig mentions a number of Jewish deaths, including forty-six in the Province of Białystok, but he usually fails to delve into their intricacies, treating these tragedies uniformly as manifestations of Polish anti-Semitism. As his "proof" and without elaborating, Warhaftig points to the prevalent anti-Jewish animosity which was allegedly fueled by suspicions of Jewish involvement in the so-called "ritual murders." Yet, at least one anti-Jewish act of violence described by this scholar seems to have been simply a common criminal deed. Namely, in Chełm "a couple was taken hostage and axed to death when the Jewish community failed to meet the demand for ransom."[9]

In at least several instances, we are faced with competing allegations and guesses. According to an investigative journalist, in April 1945 a number of Jews died violently in Klimontów near Sandomierz. Historian Eugeniusz Niebelski claims that at least one of the victims, Abram Złotnik, was an NKVD agent. A local Christian witness recalls that Złotnik was no confidence man but, rather, "had big mouth" and threatened some of the locals with denunciations. There is no consensus on the number of Jewish victims killed either. Basing himself on a single testimony, Niebelski mentions eight Jews shot. A local peasant claims that there were twelve. Another swears that the perpetrators killed twenty-five Jews, including a pregnant woman. The author of a contemporary report at the Jewish Historical Institute in Warsaw was more precise: "on April 18 of this year [1945], five Jews were murdered in Klimontów. The remaining Jews had to move to Sandomierz." However, there are also divergent versions concerning the identity of the perpetrators. A few local peasants allege that it was "the Home Army," naming a few names. However, at least one of the alleged AK assassins was not even around at the time of the deed. He had been seized by the Soviets in 1944 and sent to the Gulag for several years. Further, the AK veterans flatly reject the accusations aimed at them, pointing their fingers at the underground populist Peasant Battalions or an "unaffiliated robber band." It appears not to have been a political assassination, but rather a common robbery combined with murder. The allegations about the victims and perpetrators are yet to be cross-checked against local administration documents, insurgent reports, and secret police archives.[10] Likewise, the accounts from Wasiliszki, the county of Szczuczyn, Province of Nowogródek, regarding from one to four Jewish victims killed between July 1944 and January 1946 are quite baffling.[11]

In certain other instances the only information describing violence against Jews comes from Communist secret police scholars and is thus very unreliable. For example, Stanisław Janicki claims that on November 25, 1945, the NOW unit of Bronisław Gliniak ("Radwan") attacked the township of Kańczuga and killed "a group of Jews." The author failed to provide any details or describe the circumstances. Did the attack even take place? If so, why?[12]

Likewise, Anatol Leszczyński offers no explanation why, on his way back home, "the members of the reactionary underground of the 'Iskra' group shot Majer Sznajder near Ostrołęka."[13] Such flawed scholarship is routine. The Communist authors of an omnibus compilation of victims of the underground who were killed in the process of "the solidification of the people's power" (utrwalanie władzy ludowej) limit themselves simply to listing the names and, occasionally, institutional affiliation of the fallen. Thus, we simply learn that "Szepsel Alperm" (i.e. Szepsel Szuster), who was a member of the PPR and a functionary of the UB, was killed by "an unknown fighting group of the reactionary underground" in Sokółka, the Province of Białystok, on December 3, 1945. On April 5, 1945, in Brzozów, Aron Szerc, who was described rather incongruously as "a PPR member" and "a merchant," also lost his life at the hands of "unknown perpetrators." On January 11, 1945, two members of the Communist Party, Szloma Goldwaser and Szloma Gruda were shot in Drohiczyn, the county of Siemiatycze, the Province of Białystok, allegedly by the AK-WiN unit under the command of Captain Władysław Łukasiuk ("Młot"). In the same month an NSZ unit allegedly killed Szloma Gruda's brother, Dawid, in nearby Smarklice. Some time afterwards, another NSZ unit allegedly killed the Communist Party veteran activist Jankiel Leski in Biała Rawska, the county of Rawa Mazowiecka. In April 1945 the NSZ allegedly assassinated Szmul Lew (Lewin?), who was the secretary of the City Committee of the PPR in Kałuszyn, the county of Mińsk Mazowiecki. On April 30, 1946, Communist army Captain Izrael Hoeningsfeld was killed by "the reactionary underground" near Wyszków. On December 17, 1947, in Świebodzice in the county of Świdnica, the underground "Wicherek" (NN) unit allegedly killed Szmul Sztaj, who was a secret policeman and a member of the Communist Party. We are left in the dark about the circumstances of these deeds, although the authors of the compilation admit that they relied on official documents to identify the perpetrators.[14]

In yet another instance, there seems to be enough evidence to blame the insurgents but it is still insufficient to determine exactly who the perpetrators were. Basing himself on a UB report, military historian Tadeusz Frączak claims that on February 17, 1945, "the NSZ" killed 6 Jews in Sokoły, the Province of Białystok. However, other scholars established beyond any doubt that the action was carried out by the "Huzar" unit of the AK.[15] Relying on a Communist secret police report, the regional historian Rafał Wnuk writes that on "June 31, 1945," near Strzyżów, the county of Hrubieszów, the Province of Lublin, "a Home Army soldier" killed Włodzimierz Jankiel Rajs for supporting the Communists. Without elaborating on the circumstances, Wnuk also mentions that on the same day Dawid Berger and his two children were killed. This historian was able to establish neither the identity of the killers nor the veracity of accusations about the alleged Communist sympathies of the slain Jewish man. Moreover, Wnuk failed to notice that the date of the report ("June 31, 1945") is clearly either a mistake or a falsification: the month of June has only 30 days. Secret police records alone do not suffice.[16]

Routine reports also fail to describe the circumstances of anti-Jewish violence. According to an official account, on June 9, 1945, in Lublin unknown perpetrators burst into a hospital run by Catholic nuns, singled out two Jewish patients, and shot them. Who were the perpetrators? Why did they kill Jews?[17]

A contemporary account in *The American Jewish Year Book* blamed the assassination at the hospital on the same "terrorists" who earlier had killed "two Jewish soldiers, Rozenblum of Lodz [Łódź] and Pachler [sic Tafler] of Rowno [Równe] after their ten Polish [Christian] colleagues had been released" near Łęczna.[18] However, the author of the account fails to mention any details. It appears that a detachment of Polish "people's" army troops was taken prisoner by the insurgents. Most were freed, while others shot. Were these "Jewish soldiers" victims of racial stereotyping? Or were they perhaps commissioned officers and Communist Party members put in charge of unwilling Polish draftees? Or did they simply continue to resist after their Gentile comrades had surrendered? Or was it perhaps yet another concoction of Communist propaganda?[19]

On the night of August 10, 1945, according to a Communist dispatch, "a Jewish tailor- and shoemaker cooperative [in Radom] was attacked and 4 Jews and one Red Army officer were murdered." Was this a political assassination of a Soviet officer? Was it a common robbery? Or was it an anti-Semitic attack? We have no answers.[20] Another document is equally unenlightening. According to an NKVD report,

> On 19 November [1945] in Kraków two men entered the apartment of ci[tizen] Hohberg, claiming to be employees of public security [i.e. the UB]. In the apartment, aside from the host, his mother, and two sisters, there were six men of Jewish nationality.
> The bandits told everyone present in the house to lift their hands and face the wall; and next they killed with their pistols three men, wounded one of the women, and disappeared.[21]

It is of course necessary to rely on Communist documents, but only with utmost caution. For instance, the Communists accused the AK-WiN unit "Zapora" of killing Abram and Cukier Zeltman in Janów Lubelski on April 30, 1945. However, an internal secret police report never mentioned the "Zapora" detachment but merely noted the death of these two Jewish men, one of whom was a soldier of the Polish Communist army. Moreover, neither the "Zapora" group nor any other partisan unit spent time in Janów on that day. In fact, on April 27, 1945, the insurgents had attacked Janów to free prisoners and capture supplies. Having accomplished their objectives, they fled swiftly to avoid a punitive expedition of the NKVD. We have no idea who killed the Zeltmans and why.[22]

It is often difficult to reconstruct the circumstances of anti-Jewish violence and contradictory accounts abound, as is the case of Lejb Feldhendler of Żółkiewka. According to the testimony of Harold Werner (Hersz Cymerman), "Leon Feldhendler" was killed in Lublin by "mobs of anti-Semitic Poles." However, Joseph Tenenbaum insisted that "Leon Feldhendler" was killed by the NSZ. Later, the historian Isaiah Trunk claimed that "Leibl Felhendler" was assassinated by "some partisans" of the AK, as did the *Encyclopedia of Jewish Communities* published by Yad Vashem. According to the scholar Martin Gilbert, on April 2, 1945, "Leon Feldhendler, one of the leaders of the Sobibor [Sobibór] death camp revolt in 1943, was murdered by the Poles." However, my own inquiry with the former Citizens Militia archives in Lublin failed to yield any confirmation of Feldhendler's death, let alone the identity of his killers. Furthermore, Feldhendler's name is missing from the official registry of victims of the independentist underground. Clearly, further research is needed.[23] Likewise, no satisfactory explanation has been published by any historian concerning the killing of five Jews in Skarżysko, although the court records pertaining to the case are extant.[24]

There are many accounts of violent deeds against Jews that lack independent confirmation. Jewish survivors blame "the AK," "boys from the forest," or "the Poles." Specific information, however, is lacking. Although he was not present in the area at the time, Noach Lasman believes that "after the shift of the Soviet and Polish armies to the west, the 'boys from the forest' became active and for a few hours on the night of March 11 [1945], seized control of three little towns, Mordy, Mokobody, and Łosice. In Mordy they killed eleven Jews and one militiaman, in Mokobody seven Jews, and in Łosice the Jews were warned and all went into hiding. There were women and children among the victims."[25] What was the reason for the attack? Who carried it out? What were the circumstances?

Lasman's suggestion notwithstanding, this was not a concerted attack on Jews in the area of Siedlce. Both the dates of assaults and the victim statistics are wrong. According to a Polish witness, during a night attack in March 1945 an unidentified insurgent unit killed "several Jews and Poles as well as an NKVD man" in Mordy.[26] According to Dobroszycki, "seven Jews [died] in the town of Mordy, in the district of Siedlce on the night of 26/27 March 1945."[27] A Jewish second-hand witness stated incorrectly that "in the neighboring town of Mordy, all its thirteen survivors were massacred in the sleep by a troop of AK men."[28] According to a contemporary Jewish document, the attack on Mokobody took place on March 8 and eight Jews died in it.[29] Another contemporary Jewish report states, however, that five Jews were killed in Mokobody.[30] The authors of an official Communist compilation of the victims of the underground fail to report these assaults but mention that Srul Szulmajster, "a member of the PPR" and "a functionary of the MO [Communist militia]" was killed on March 15, 1945, in Mężenin, the county of Łosice, allegedly by the AK-WiN unit of "Młot."[31] To confuse the issue even further, a Polish witness, A. Czajkowski, claims that a family of Polish millers in Mokobody had sheltered a Jewish man, Hirszek, for two years during the Nazi occupation. After the arrival of the Soviets, "Hirszek brought the UB to the mill, [and] accused the millers of membership in the AK as well as hostility to people's [Communist] Poland and Jews. For those 'crimes' eight persons were shot on the spot in the mill. Only one employee, Piotrowski, survived because he hid in a stove and he was not discovered."[32] Moreover, a Jewish source (Renee G.) recalled that a Polish farmer who had rescued her during the Nazi occupation was shot by the independentist underground allegedly for helping Jews near Łosice.[33] It is greatly baffling that the perplexing circumstances of the attacks on Mordy, Mokobody, and Łosice have largely escaped any serious scholarly scrutiny. It is likewise the case with the following information in a memorial book, "Very few Jews were left in Kosow [sic Kosów Lacki near Sokołów Podlaski] after the war. Eleven of those were killed by Polish armed bands after the war had ended."[34] What bands? Under what circumstances?

According to another source, in the spring 1945 in the environs of Radzyń Podlaski allegedly seven Jews were killed in Wohyń and a few others, including Hershel Pontshak, in Czemierniki. The "Polish murderers" allegedly responsible for their deaths belonged to "the reactionary Polish Underground Organization" and to "the partisan 'Armye Kryova' [sic]." The former is impossible to identify, if it existed at all. The AK had been dissolved by then and, therefore, if the killers were indeed insurgents they belonged to one of the successor organizations. But which one? And who were they?[35]

Equally confusing is the following account from the county of Bielsk Podlaski in the Białystok area:

> But even after liberation there was no peace for the survivors. Their lives were still imperilled by the 'A.K.' who

wanted to exterminate them, and many Jews were slain by their bullets. In Drogoczyn [Drohiczyn] the first Jewish victim after liberation was Arie Bluestein, and an 'A.K.' bomb killed Simche Warshawsky. In Semiatych [Siemiatycze] the miller Benye Lev was killed by Poles. They put a bomb under Grodzitski's house, and a Jewish girl was wounded in the explosion.

After liberation Hershl Shabbes and his [pro-Soviet partisan] group returned to Semiatych with their arms, which they surrendered to the [Soviet] commandant, and officially received new equipment [i.e. were armed to become militiamen].

For the fear of attacks by the 'A.K.' the surviving Semiatych Jews lived together in large groups. At night they stayed inside, fastening the shutters. But if Polish bands would try to attack Jewish homes, they were prepared to reply to fire with fire.

On April 6, 1945, there was a battle. A band of about 100 'A.K.' attacked the two-story house of Yudl Blumberg, which sheltered 28 Jews. The 'A.K.' burst into the first floor, where there were no Jews, and started to go up the stairs. But the Jews opened fire with their one machine-gun, operated by Yudl Blumberg, as well as with grenades, rifles and revolvers. The battle lasted all night. In the morning a signal from the nearby Soviet base frightened off the bandits, and they ran away.[36]

The above account presents a vivid depiction of a Jewish community under siege. Unfortunately, it lumps all Jewish victims together, *a priori* assuming anti-Semitism on the part of the insurgents as the reason for their killing. Further, it is cryptic about the Jewish involvement with Soviets and Polish Communists. Finally, the account also fails to provide a broader context for the events.

Thus, there are more than a few problems with the accuracy of the aforementioned Jewish tale of Drohiczyn and Siemiatycze. Chronologically the first Jewish victim (probably Arie Bluestein) after the entry of the Red Army in Drohiczyn was killed in December 1944 by the Soviets, who covered it up, so that the Jews were led to believe that the AK was the culprit and commenced revenge against the Poles.[37] Second, on January 1, 1945, Symcha Warszawski (Simche Warshawsky) fell victim to a granade attack by an unknown perpetrator, who also wounded two other persons. Third, on January 4, 1945, Beniamin Lew (Benye Lev) was killed not by the AK but by six common bandits, who also wounded his Polish worker Kalinowski and completely robbed his household. Fourth, on the night of January 13, a bomb was planted under the house of Kuperhan and not "Grodzitzky" as the memorial book would have it.[38] Fifth, the attack on Siemiatycze on April 6, 1945, between 6:00pm and 10:00pm, was staged by the National Armed Forces, and not the AK as the Jewish source claims. The objective was to intercept a Communist shipment of weapons, which was accomplished. Further, the NSZ struck at the militia post and the government offices in Siemiatycze, which they captured. They destroyed draft and tax registers and disarmed the militiamen and a few Red Army soldiers. Nonetheless, the partisans failed to seize the Soviet headquarters.[39] It seems that the Jewish stronghold in the house of Yudl Blumberg was attacked in conjunction with the assault on the militia station. After all, these Jews were armed and the insurgents considered them supporters of the Communist regime. Basing himself on an underground report, a Polish scholar claims that a Jewish woman perished in the attack and several persons were wounded – either Jews or Gentiles. The Jewish source quoted above indicates that the woman was only wounded.[40]

Finally, the Jewish account fails to note that after the arrival of the Soviets the NKVD arrested at least several hundred members of the Polish independentist underground in the area of Siemiatycze and Drohiczyn, including 200 in December 1944 alone. Some Polish insurgents were killed. Recent research has revealed that the local Belorussian Communist sympathizers were especially instrumental in denouncing the AK and NSZ to the NKVD. In reprisal, many Belorussian Communist collaborators were whipped; some Belorussian (and Polish) informers of the NKVD were assassinated, as was the head of the NKVD for the county of Bielsk Podlaski, Lieutenant Aleksandr Dokshin, who was shot in Jakubowo on January 5, 1945, along with a Polish Communist militia commander and two civilian sympathizers. However, the Jewish role still remains unclear. According to two Polish scholars, who based themselves on clandestine insurgent reports, "most Jews [of Drohiczyn, Siemiatycze, and other nearby towns] became involved actively on the side of the 'Lublin' authorities [i.e. the Communists]. They were disposed with hostility toward the underground independentist work and 'supplied the largest number of snitches [informers for the Soviets].' After the commencement by the AKO [the Citizen Home Army] of the action to liquidate confidence men in May 1945, they [the Jews] left the settlements and towns of the county and went to larger cities."[41] Such a comprehensive depiction of events is altogether lacking from the Jewish memorial book, which is excusable, and from most Western scholarly monographs, which is incomprehensible. Many other Jewish testimonies (and Western scholars) follow the same pattern.

After his liberation from the Theresienstadt concentration camp in Czechoslovakia, sixteen-year-old Jack Rubinfeld returned to Przemyśl in the Province of Rzeszów. "The members of the local Jewish Committee warned me not to go to Bircza or any other village. Survivors were getting killed by Ukrainian nationalists and Polish nationalists. I also learned that approximately forty men, who had escaped in 1944 from our camp in Rzeszów, had been killed by Polish nationalists. Obviously we had to get the hell out of there."[42]

Unfortunately, the scholar who quoted Rubinfeld with approval eschewed elaborating on this testimony. Were forty Jewish men killed during the Nazi occupation or after? Under what circumstances? Did it have anything to do with the fact that, according to an underground dispatch, some Jews were enrolled in the Communist militia of Przemyśl?[43]

Most likely in December 1944, Shmuel Koniuchowski and Yosef Dembiowski were killed during a visit to the former's home in Stężice near Dęblin, the Province of Lublin. According to a Jewish account, "the Polish antisemites and the notorious N.S.Z. killed the two heroic Jewish fighters, who fought so gallantly for the freedom of Poland."[44] The author of the account fails to provide the circumstances of the killing or to consider that perhaps Koniuchowski and Dembiowski's participation in the Communist security apparatus had anything to do with the assault.[45] Likewise, no reason other than the "anti-Semitic atmosphere in the country" was given for the death sentence allegedly passed by the Home Army on the former Communist partisan Lipman Sznajder of Rejowiec near Chełm.[45] When the Red Army officer Eliachu Lipszowicz was killed in Legnica in May 1945, it was also perfunctorily blamed on "an antisemitic Pole," thus automatically alleging racism rather than pondering other possible factors for this deed.[47] Likewise, after "a couple of hand grenades" had been tossed into the apartment of Lieutenant Barek Eisenstein, aka Bolesław Jurkowski, in Katowice, he considered it a sign that "the Poles were anti-Semitic," completely disregarding the possibility that his high rank in the local UB could have had something to do with the failed attempt to assassinate him.[48] Even more strangely, after an unsuccessful assassination attempt on a Soviet major in Łosice, in which the NKVD man was only wounded, at least one of the Jewish bystanders maintained that this was in fact an anti-Semitic attack on the Jews by the independentists.[49]

Inexplicably, purely racist reasons were ascribed to an attack that took place probably in Zabłudów near Białystok. Neither criminal nor political factors were considered. According to a Jewish source,

Pella Lafta had no luck after the war. He fell in love with a Christian girl. They decided to get married and move to an agricultural farm. A large celebration was organized for them. This news arrived to the anti-Semitic Polish organization AK (Army of the State [sic Home Army]). Members of the organization set the house on fire during the celebration. They killed the girl and wounded Pella and his friends. In the same attack, Moshe Flicker was killed. This is how the anti-Semitic organization avenged [itself on] the Jewish survivors. Their goal was to destroy any survivors.[50]

Sometime in May 1945, in Zaręby Kościelne, it is alleged that some "members of the Polish nationalist movement" killed eight Jews who returned home after the war. The Jewish witness repeating these second-hand allegations failed to provide any background to the tragedy.[51] On the night of June 16, 1945, in Działoszyce, the Province of Kielce, according to a memorial book, "the Poles had made up their minds that once the town was without Jews it must remain so. One day they murdered Samuel Piekarz, Ben-Zion Chernocha and Yorista. Those murders served as a warning to the others, who fled that selfsame night."[52] Again, no specific information on the perpetrators or circumstances is provided.[53] That is also the case with the testimony of Mina Deutsch, who, based on hearsay, alleges that after the war the Polish underground undertook a coordinated action to exterminate Jewish professionals:

We seemed to travel endlessly before stopping in Przemyśl. We never knew how long we would be at a station, but Leon [Deutsch] decided to take a chance and run to his parents' house not too far away. I stayed in the wagon with Eva and our belongings. Leon returned soon with bad news: two friends of his, a Jewish lawyer and doctor, had been shot to death by Poles. A man who was staying at his parents' house warned Leon to continue with the transport because it would be too dangerous to stay in chaotic Przemyśl...[and] we reached Katowice in Silesia.

It was impossible to earn a living as a doctor. We were afraid to even admit we were physicians since several Jewish doctors had been murdered in their Katowice offices by the Polish underground, the "A.K." It had happened at the same time one afternoon. A man went into each of their offices and told the receptionists that they had no appointments but were willing to wait until the other patients were seen. They then went in and shot the doctors.[53]

No available evidence supports Deutsch's contention about a concerted or any other assassination campaign against Jewish professionals by the independentists. In fact, all we know about the decentralized nature of the underground argues against such an interpretation.[54]

Attacks on Jewish passengers riding on trains in Poland have often been noted by witnesses and scholars. According to a rather typical testimony, in November 1945, "on that day-long ride to Poznan [Poznań] they saw four Jewish passengers thrown out of windows while the train lumbered on, victims of roving bands of ultranationalistic *Armia Krajowa*."[55] Often, the survivors of the attacks on the trains were utterly confused about the identity of the perpetrators. At least in one instance, a Jewish witness seems to have blamed the Communist police for an assault that took place sometime in 1946:

> We went to Woldenburg [sic Waldenburg, Wałbrzych], in the Russian zone. In Woldenburg everything was expensive, in Chelm [Chełm in the Province of Lublin] everything was cheap, so I would buy five kilos butter in Chelm [Chełm], then sell it in Woldenburg. I was on the train and this Polish organization took about thirty Jews off the train and killed them. A Polish policeman did not recognize I'm a Jew and asks me if maybe I saw Jews. I said I didn't know! He shot a Jewish woman, and her little girl, maybe seven years old, starts crying, "Mother! Mother!" So he shot the little girl, too.[56]

However, at least one Jewish recollection suggests that the attacks on trains had an anti-Soviet edge, alas lumping Jews with Communists. In May 1946, en route from Lublin to Chełm,

> the train was stopped at night by a gang of Polish soldiers that emerged from the forest; they were the "white" soldiers that opposed the current [proxy] regime. Floodlights lighted the train and the soldiers wearing uniforms of the Polish army before the war and armed with machine guns gave an order: "Jews! Soviets and policemen! Outside! Out of the cars!" I felt a trembling in my bones; a deep fear of death passed me. A few Holocaust survivors were shot [like this] nearby the cars! Fuchs tells me: "Pretend you are sleeping." Darkness in the cars. At the entrance of our cars stood two soldiers. They lit the car and repeat the same orders. A Christian woman answered: "there are none like

these here." Suddenly there was commotion. And again darkness. The gang leaves quickly without taking anybody from the train. A miracle happened. They noticed an approaching train and fled.[57]

The same source claims that near Małkinia "four [Zionist] pioneers were taken off a train and were killed when they traveled to Warsaw [from Białystok] to take care of the formal papers regarding their aliyah to Israel." Once again, however, the "Polish gangs" responsible for the attack remain anonymous.[58] On June 29, 1945, two Jewish men, escorting relief gifts from Lublin to Biała Podlaska, were attacked on the train near Sieniawa. One was shot and killed, while the other seriously wounded. The perpetrators also "slashed the throat of a 22 year old" Jewish woman who was traveling on the same train. The two perpetrators responsible for the horrible deed were never identified but they were almost certainly common bandits.[59] Finally, at the end of June 1946, a "gang of marauders" stopped a train to the west of Rawa Ruska. According to a Jewish witness, "from a list made out when we boarded the train, they called out three Jewish names. Asking only one question, 'Zyd [Żyd – Jew]?' They ordered the men to leave the car. Scrutinizing the people in the car, they asked, 'Any more Jews here?'" The attackers kidnapped a number of people, including "two rabbis and their families. During the entire night we heard shooting and shrill screams, as the Jews were murdered in the forest."[60] Again, this is a good point of departure for further research but the testimony alone tells us too little to identify the attackers. The same applies to many other individual testimonies and reports. It is clear that Jews were killed. The questions should be: by whom? and why? Without such evidence scholars should be very careful before speculating about the motives and identity of the attackers. To uncover evidence about these events presents a serious challenge for historians.

It simply will not do anymore to blame any specific organization when practically no research has been done to investigate any of the particular attacks. Therefore, the claims of Cała and Śpiewak-Datner to the contrary, it is premature to maintain that "these murders [on the trains] were perpetrated by these armed units, who saw [in the Jews] the allies of Communism, or, as in the case of the National Armed Forces, not only identified them with the system imposed [by the Soviets] but also with all that is evil."[61]

It is also unscholarly to see these assaults as a coordinated action against the Jews. There is no evidence to suggest that the "train action" was ordered from above. If anything, we may just as well claim that it was a local, decentralized initiative often perpetrated by common bandits rather than underground fighters, as Jan Tomasz Gross seems to be suggesting. Moreover, according to Józef Adelson of the Jewish Historical Institute in Warsaw, it was the Central Committee of the Polish Jews itself which first began calling the phenomenon of the attacks on Jewish passengers "the train operation" (akcja pociągowa), thus alleging that it was organized from above by the underground leadership. Basing himself on a single oral testimony given about 40 years after the events, Adelson estimated that 200 Jews were killed in such manner. Joanna Michlic-Coren automatically embraced this guess as credible.[62] However, no available evidence from the insurgent side warrants such assertions. Much more research is required before we can arrive at any solid conclusions.[63]

In addition to assassinations and individual attacks, the Polish insurgents have also been accused of instigating pogroms and mob violence against the Jews. So far research has yielded no direct link between the independentist leadership and the pogroms. Moreover, the current state of the scholarship allows us to reject this thesis outright.

A number of pogroms broke out following false rumors that "Jews" had kidnapped and killed Polish children for ritual purposes. Anti-Jewish violence took place in Rzeszów (June 11, 1945), Kraków (March 20 and August 11, 1945), Tarnów (April 27, 1946), Kalisz (July 22 and 23, 1946), Lublin (August 19, 1946), Kolbuszowa (September 24, 1946), and Mielec (October 25, 1946). The most serious pogrom occurred in Kielce on July 4, 1946, where a mob of militiamen, soldiers, and civilians murdered forty-two Jews. Tellingly, the Communist security forces took part in each of these anti-Jewish attacks, including forty militiamen in Kraków who were subsequently arrested, according to an NKVD report.[64] In Chełm, the mob was led by a Red Army NCO. Bernard Weinryb claims that in Rzeszów the local head of the Communist secret police organized the expulsion of Jewish survivors from that city and killed a Jewish girl in the process. Incidentally, the same security man was assigned to the UB in Kielce right before the pogrom there. Felix Zandman recalls that in Gdańsk the Polish Communist militia refused to disperse a mob readying for a pogrom, while the Red Army promptly came to the rescue. In Kielce, according to a testimony of a Jewish witness which was published by Alina Cała and Helena Datner-Śpiewak, the Soviet commander of the local military garrison publicly rejoiced over the lot of the Jews, while the slaughter was in progress.

True, a few members of the underground, or people with links to the insurgents, also participated in the violence. However, there is absolutely no evidence that the insurgents instigated the pogroms, while, as historian

Joseph Rothschild stresses, there have been plausible allegations of anti-Jewish provocations by the secret police. For instance, the prominent Zionist activist Yitzhak Zuckerman argues that the security forces were involved in staging the pogrom in Kielce because a day before they had disarmed the Jews and later ignored their pleas for help. Further, at least one underground newspaper claimed that the pogroms were police provocations that got out of hand because of the spontaneous response of the Polish crowd. However, the investigative reporter Krzysztof Kąkolewski discovered that at least in Kielce much of the civilian mob was, in fact, composed of the Communist militia auxiliaries (ORMO). Anti-Jewish prejudice among some Communist militiamen and soldiers should not be overlooked.[65]

It is undeniable that the spontaneous participation of anti-Jewish mobs did escalate the violence. However, we can dismiss the allegations about pogroms as carefully planned operations of the Polish underground. Currently available materials have neither confirmed nor denied the possibility that the pogroms were instigated by the secret police.[66] They do prove however that anti-Jewish violence was subsequently exploited by Communist propaganda against the democratic opposition, the Catholic Church, and the insurgents.[67]

Threats of violence against Jews were most likely much more widespread than violence itself. These threats expressed themselves in rude remarks to survivors and in anti-Jewish posters and leaflets. Some posters called on Jews to leave their domicile on pain of death. For example, on July 29, 1945, a bill was posted giving the Jews an ultimatum to move out of Jedlińsk near Radom. The author stated that "It has been established that the jews [sic] generally work in the intelligence [i.e. security police] for the benefit of the current regime, which has been brutally imposed upon us, thus working to the detriment of Polish Society [sic]... I am warning [the Jews] that exceeding the deadline [of the ultimatum to depart Jedlińsk and Radom] or requesting of the current [Communist] authorities to intervene will be punished ruthlessly."[68]

Similar posters appeared in Zakopane, Kraśnik, Tarnów, Miechów, Opatów, Częstochowa, Klementynów, and other localities. To lend gravity and authority to such threats, they were often signed allegedly by the underground. However, most names provided were usually of non-existent groups. For instance, in Piaski near Lublin anti-Jewish leaflets were signed by the chimeric "Polish Military Organization" (*Polska Organizacja Wojskowa*). This probably means that the leaflets were either products of a local underground group that did not want to be identified or groups of unaffiliated individuals who strove to hide their anti-Jewish sentiments behind an imaginary clandestine structure, thus making themselves institutionally "patriotic." To complicate things further, the Communists clandestinely put up similar anti-Semitic posters at least once, for example in Jasło in the fall of 1945, and presumably blamed it on the underground. There are still too many variables and unanswered questions concerning this matter. Thus, the circumstances under which the threats of violence were allegedly issued by the underground should be scrutinized as closely as the instances of violence themselves.[69]

The acts of violence against the Jews occurred mostly throughout central Poland, in particular in the provinces east of the Vistula River, where the insurgency was very strong. This does not mean that the insurgents were automatically the responsible party. Most likely common bandits were the most frequent perpetrators. Simply, the independentists prevented the Communists from building their state institutions and vice versa. Hence, lawlessness ruled.[70]

In some cases of unexplored killings, it is quite possible that the independentists were involved. In particular, if Jewish secret policemen or Jewish Communists died under mysterious circumstances, it is almost certain that the insurgents were responsible. In other cases where unaffiliated Jews died, it is anybody's guess who the perpetrators were. Common bandits are likely candidates, although we should remember that a number of rank-and-file insurgents turned rogue and resorted to banditry and that, on occasion, politically unaffiliated individuals impersonated insurgents or bandits to carry out deeds against Jews, and others, to enrich themselves. Moreover, Poland was full of marauders and deserters of various armies, the Soviet forces in particular, who looted, raped, and killed without any mercy. Finally, it is entirely possible that some Jewish avengers dealt summarily with a few erstwhile Jewish ghetto policemen and members of Jewish councils who had collaborated with the Nazis. That must certainly have been the least likely factor but it cannot be excluded from our consideration of anti-Jewish violence.

According to the sources analyzed in this chapter, a minimum of 271 and a maximum of 474 Jews died in unclear circumstances. Of the Jewish victims, a minimum of 157 and a maximum of 330 died in 42 localities and further, a minimum of 114 and a maximum of 144 perished in unknown locations.

Table 6
Jewish victims of violence by locality:
A sample estimate of confirmed and unconfirmed cases

	minimum	maximum
Biała Rawska	1	1
Białystok	1	1
Brzozów	1	1
Chełm Lubelski	4	32
Czemierniki	1	5
Drohiczyn	2	4
Działoszyce	3	4
Janów Lubelski	2	14
Kałuszyn	1	1
Kańczuga	5	10
Kawęczyn	4	4
Katowice	1	5
Kielce	42	60
Klimontów	5	25
Kosów Lacki	5	11
Kraków	3	5
Kraśnik	2	2
Legnica	1	1
Lublin	3	3
Łęczna	2	2
Małkinia	4	4
Mężenin	1	1
Mokobody	5	11
Mordy	7	13
Połaniec	5	5
Poznań	4	4
Przemyśl	2	42
Radom	4	4
Rawa Ruska	11	20
Rzeszów	1	1
Siemiatycze	1	1
Sieniawa	2	3
Smarklice	1	1
Sokółka	1	1
Stężice	2	2
Strzyżów	4	4

Świebodzice	1	1
Wasiliszki	1	4
Wohyń	1	7
Wyszków	1	1
Zabłudów	1	1
Zaręby Kościelne	8	8
Total	157	330
Unknown locations[71]	114	144
Total	271	474

However, only 113 Jewish deaths can be confirmed as having indisputably occurred;[72] the remaining 361 instances oscillate between an unfounded rumor and an unverified possibility.

Table 7
Jewish deaths by unknown perpetrators:
A sample estimate

confirmed	unconfirmed
113	361

Most instances of killing of Jews by unknown perpetrators involved individual victims. The single largest case of murder involved the well-known mob violence in Kielce, where most of the direct perpetrators remain unknown because of the anonymity of the crowd and the unwillingness of the Communist authorities to investigate the case thoroughly. Unfortunately, until the trailblazing study by David Engel, historians were equally averse to assessing and verifying Jewish losses in post-war Poland and they were as unwilling to ponder the reasons behind anti-Jewish violence, rarely abandoning the unidimentional cliche of Polish "anti-Semitism" as the sole explanation for what occurred between the Poles and the Jews in the aftermath of the Second World War.

Notes

1 Izaak Goldberg, *The Miracles Versus Tyranny* (New York: Philosophical Library, 1979), 504 [afterward *Miracles*].

2 Sack, *An Eye for an Eye*, 184-89.

3 See Raport sytuacyjny i wyw[iadowczo]-poli[tyczny] nr 9 za m[iesiąc] październik 1944 r., Sarna, 5 November 1944, *Dokumenty*, 2 (April 1994): 48, 55 [afterward Raport nr 9].

4 I researched this topic extensively for the purpose of my doctorate. See Nuchim Rozenel, AŻIH, file 301/2221; Góra and Jakubowski, *Z dziejów organów*, 111; Engel, "Patterns of Anti-Jewish Violence," 45-46; Stanisław Łokuciewski, "Przygotowania do akcji 'Burza,'" 17 January 1966, Biblioteka im. Hieronima Łopacińskiego in Lublin, the collection of Ireneusz Caban and Zygmunt Mańkowski [afterward BHŁ, CCM], file 2079, 927-41; Relacje ustne Stanisława Łokuciewskiego ps. "Mały" złożone mgr Ireneuszowi Cabanowi i dr Zygmuntowi Mańkowskiemu w Michałówce k/Puław, 17 August and 17 November 1965, BHŁ, CCM, file 2079, 907-25; Caban, *8 Pułk*, 111, 117-20.

5 Sprawozdanie za okres sprawozdawczy od dnia 14 do dnia 21 b.m. włącznie, 21 October 1944, APLOK, SPK, Sprawozdania sytuacyjne i doraźne, 1944, file 137.

6 Engel, "Patterns of Anti-Jewish Violence," 74.

7 Dobroszycki, "Restoring Jewish Life," 66.

8 Another Jewish author also limits himself to recounting the events in Połaniec and likewise fails to elaborate on them. See Hillel, *Le Massacre des survivants*, 238.

9 Warhaftig, *Refugee and Survivor*, 298. This probably took place at the beginning of March 1946. See Memoriał Centralnego Komitetu Żydów Polskich do Prezesa Rady Ministrów Ob. Osóbki-Morawskiego, 15 March 1946, AURM, PRM, BP, file 5/133, 34.

10 According to a list at the Jewish Historical Institute in Warsaw, the local Poles were allegedly responsible for killing 39 Jews in and out of Klimontów between 1943 and 1945. See Radosław Januszewski, "Szkoła tysiąclecia," *Rzeczpospolita*, 27 October 2001; Eugeniusz Niebelski, *W dobrach Ossolińskich: Klimontów i okolice* (Klimontów: Urząd Gminy, 1999).

11 According to Etel Kravitz, three Jews, Zalman Mednitzky, Siomke Boyarsky, and Yankel Kushner "fell after the liberation at the hands of Poles (A.K.) in Vasilishok." Elsewhere Binyamin Statsky explains more specifically that following the return of the Red Army in July 1944 Yankel Kushner "feel [sic fell] from a Soviet bullet," Zalman Mednitsky was "murdered by the local Christians," and Siomkeh Boyarsky was "murdered by the White Poles," that is the AK insurgents. However, Poland's foremost scholarly authority on the area, Kazimierz Krajewski, claims that the only person of Jewish origin killed by the post-AK insurgent self-defense force was a Jewish member of the NKVD (or its auxiliary militia) called "Filinowicz" or "Filmanowicz" (a pseudonym), who was assassinated probably in January 1946. See Etel Kravitz, "Vasilishok Partisans," and Binyamin Statsky, "After the Liberation," in *Sefer zikaron le-kehilot Szczuczyn Wasiliszki Ostryna Nowy-Dwor Rozanka (Memorial book of the communities Szczuczyn, Wasiliszki, Ostryna, Nowy-Dwor, Rozanka)*, ed. by L. Losh (Tel Aviv: Former Residents of Szczuczyn Wasiliszki, 1966), 262 (348) and 270 (356), posted at http://www.jewishgen.org/yizkor/szczuczyn-belarus/szczuczyn.html; Kazimierz Krajewski to Richard Tyndorf, 19 February 2002 (a copy in my collection).

12 See Stanisław Janicki, "Działalność i likwidacja Rzeszowskiego Okręgu 'Narodowej Organizacji Wojskowej' w latach 1944-1947," in Turlejska, *W walce*, 240. One source

mentions Kańczuga as a place where "murders and hostile attacks transpired" but also fails to elaborate. See Cała and Datner-Śpiewak, *Dzieje Żydów*, 17-18.

13 See Anatol Leszczyński, "Zagłada Żydów w Choroszczy," *BŻIH*, 3 (July-September 1971): 67 n. 92, which is based on the testimony of Izaak Sznajder, AŻIH, file 1976.

14 Brzeziński, Chrzanowski, and Halaba, *Polegli w walce*, 75, 158, 166, 251, 256, 398, 401, 491. So far no evidence concerning any of the Jewish victims has been found, with the possible exception of the brothers Szloma and Dawid Gruda, who may have been involved in a particularly brutal robbery and murder of the Maksymiuk family in Miłkowice Maćki and of the Jarocki family of Kłyzówka near Siemiatycze on the night of December 5, 1944. A local historian mentions "the Grudas" as the leaders of the perpetrators. Thus, it seems that they were probably killed in reprisal. See Andrzej Olędzki, "Hersz Szebes — morderstwa w Czartajewie – marzec 1944, oraz podobne w Miłkowicach Maćkach i Kłyzówce," *Głos Siemiatycz* on line, posted at <http://box.zetobi.com.pl/glos_siemiatycz/histor_zydzi_1944.htm>. For a description of the wartime exploits of Shloyme Gruda see Tash (Tur-Shalom), *The Community of Semiatych*, xii–xiii.

15 See Tadeusz Frączak, "Fromacje zbrojne obozu narodowego na Białostocczyźnie w latach 1939-1956," (Ph.D. thesis, Warsaw, Wojskowy Instytut Historyczny, 1996), 254 [afterward "Formacje zbrojne obozu narodowego"]; Krajewski and Łabuszewski, *Białostocki*, 240-41.

16 See Wnuk, *Konspiracja*, 139.

17 The first victim, Kanowicz, died immediately; the other, Milsztaj, was mortally wounded and expired later. According to Kopcikowski, this was a "murder of a typical, anti-Semitic kind." According to Gilbert, the two Jewish men had been earlier wounded in an ambush on a bus. The execution in the hospital seems to have been a follow-up of the earlier action, thus strongly suggesting that the two targets were not any random Jews but, rather, supporters of the regime. On the other hand, they could have been inconvenient witnesses of a common crime and, therefore, to eliminate them, the perpetrators pursued them with such stubborness. See Gilbert, *Holocaust*, 817; Sprawozdanie Referatu za czerwiec 1945, AURM, PR M, file 5/137, 11-14 in Aleksiun-Mądrzak, "Nielegalna emigracja Żydów, cz. 1," 81; Adam Kopcikowski, "Problemy bezpieczeństwa," posted at <http://kft.umcs.lublin.pl/stona/lublin_po_1944_bezpeczenstwo.html>.

18 Mahler, "Eastern," in Schneiderman and Maller, *American*, 47: 405.

19 According to Kopcikowski, there is no mention of the incident in the documents of the civilian Communist authorities. However, Kopcikowski admits that the source of information for the deaths of Rozenblum and Tafler (and not Pachler) was the Communist paper *Sztandar Ludu*. See Adam Kopcikowski, "Problemy bezpieczeństwa," posted at <http://kft.umcs.lublin.pl/stona/lublin_po_1944_bezpeczenstwo.html>.

20 Rzeczpospolita Polska, Ministerstwo Pracy i Opieki Społecznej, Referat dla Spraw Pomocy Ludności Żydowskiej, Czternaste sprawozdanie z działalności (za miesiąc sierpień roku 1945), 31 August 1945, AURM, PRM, BP, file 5/133, 68. See also Cała and Datner-Śpiewak, *Dzieje Żydów*, 31. Jewish documents mention only that four Jews were killed in the assault. See Okólnik nr 40, Centralny Komitet Żydów Polskich, 17 August 1945, Archiwum Państwowe w Radomiu, Okręgowy Komitet Żydowski [afterward APR, OKŻ], vol. 1, 24; and the letter of Okręgowy Komitet Żydowski, Radom, to Miejski Urząd Bezpieczeństwa Publicznego, 31 August 1945, APR, OKŻ,

vol. 20, 13. Both documents are published in Adam Penkalla, "Stosunki polsko-żydowskie w Radomiu (kwiecień 1945-luty 1946)," *BŻIH*, 175-176 (July 1995-June 1996): 63-64 [afterward "Stosunki polsko-żydowskie"].

21 Cariewskaja, *Teczka specjalna*, 425.

22 The assault on Janów was not carried out by "Zapora" but by the ROAK units of Lieutenant Tadeusz Kuncewicz ("Podkowa"), Second Lieutenant Tadeusz Borkowski ("Mat"), and Second Lieutenant Antoni Sanetra ("Mściciel"). At that time "Zapora" was fighting in the Province of Rzeszów to the south of Janów. See Henryk Pająk, ed., *Akcje oddziałów "Zapory" w tajnych raportach UB-MO* (Lublin: Wydawnictwo Retro, 1996), 8 [afterward *Akcje*]; Wnuk, *Konspiracja*, 65; Elżbieta Misiak, "Nie byłoby zbrojnego podziemia, gdyby w sierpniu 1944 nie aresztowano ujawniających się żołnierzy AK," *Ład* [Warszawa], 25 June 1989, 9; Bolesław Stolarz, "Moja działalność w Armii Krajowej," TMsS, Warszawa, 1992, 142-52 (in my collection).

23 See Werner, *Fighting Back*, 233; Tenenbaum, *In Search of a Lost People*, 286; Gilbert, *Holocaust*, 789; Isaiah Trunk, *Judenrat: The Jewish Councils in Eastern Europe under Nazi Occupation* (Lincoln: University of Nebraska Press, 1996), 474 [afterward *Judenrat*]; Marek Jan Chodakiewicz, "Wina imputowana," *Rzeczpospolita*, 22-23 August 1998, 17; "Żółkiewka," in *Pinkas Hakehillot Polin: Encyclopedia of Jewish Communities: Poland*, vol. 7 (Jerusalem: Yad Vashem, 1977), 196-98 posted online at <http://www.jewishgen.org/yizkor/pinkas_poland/pol7_00196.html>. According to Kopcikowski, Feldhendler was shot by mistake during the successful assassination attempt on a Communist secret police agent, Hersz Blanke, in Lublin on November 4, 1944. However, Kopcikowski admits that the police and court records mention no second victim of the assassination. Instead, he bases himself on a second-hand testimony of a neighbor, Tuwie Blatt, who lived in the same apartment building on 4 Kowalska Street. Nonetheless, according to Kister, Zofia Rosen née Burstein, who resided in the same apartment as Blanke and witnessed the assassination, did not mention a second victim. See Kister, "Koniec," 7; Blatt, *Sobibor*, 109; Adam Kopcikowski, "Sprawa zabójstwa Feldhendlera," TMs, Lublin, 7 July 1997 (a copy in my collection); Adam Kopcikowski, "Problemy bezpieczeństwa," at <http://kft.umcs.lublin.pl/stona/lublin_po_1944_bezpeczenstwo.html>. Feldhendler had been the chairman of the Judenrat in the town of Żółkiewka, and together with the Jewish police was responsible for providing the Germans with forced labor.

24 Hillel, *Le Massacre des survivants*, 134.

25 Lasman, *Wspomnienia*, 51.

26 See Alfons Nurski quoted in Marek Jerzman, "Po drugiej stronie rzeki," *Gazeta Polska*, 13 June 2001.

27 See Dobroszycki, "Restoring Jewish Life," 67.

28 See Oscar Pinkus, *The House of Ashes* (Schenectady, NY: Union College Press, 1990), 237.

29 See Cała and Datner-Śpiewak, *Dzieje Żydów*, 23.

30 See Danuta Blus-Węgrowska, "Atmosfera pogromowa," *Karta*, 18 (1996): 88 [afterward "Atmosfera"].

31 See Brzeziński, Chrzanowski, and Halaba, *Polegli w walce*, 402.

32 See Bednarczyk, *Życie codzienne*, 309.

180 AFTER THE HOLOCAUST

33 See *Voices from the Holocaust*, ed. by Joshua M. Greene and Shiva Kumar (New York: The Free Press, 2000), 65 [afterward *Voices*].

34 Oscar Berland, "A Word from the Translator," *Kosow Lacki* (San Francisco: Holocaust Center of Northern California, 1992), 39.

35 The Holocaust Survivors from Radzyn: On the Road to their Homeland in Israel and to Other Countries (According to Material Provided by Tzvi Liberzon)," *Sefer Radzyn (Radzyn Memorial Book)*, ed. by Y. Avi-Ara et al. (Tel Aviv: Published by the Radzyn (Podlaski) Immigrants Association, 1957), posted at http://www.jewishgen.org/yizkor/radzyn/rad312.html.

36 Tash (Tur-Shalom), *The Community of Semiatych*, xiii.

37 See Raport nr 11, 5 January 1945, in *Dokumenty* 2 (April 1994): 80.

38 Kuperhan's house was located on Grodziska Street. See Zastępca Starosty Powiatowego w Bielsku ppor. A. Petolec do Pana Wojewody w Białymstoku, 17 January 1945, APB, UWB, file 297, 1.

39 See Zarząd Miejski w Siemiatyczach, Burmistrz St. Bujalski do Pana Starosty Powiatowego w Bielsku Podlaskim, 9 April 1945, APB, UWB, file 297, 9; Krajewski and Łabuszewski, *Białostocki*, 168-209; Ks. Grzegorz Sosna, ed., *Sprawy narodowościowe i wyznaniowe na Białostocczyźnie (1944-1948) w ocenie władz Rzeczpospolitej Polskiej: Wybór dokumentów: Sytuacyjne sprawozdania wojewody białostockiego w Białymstoku oraz powiatowych starostów białostockiego, bielskopodlaskiego i sokólskiego w latach 1944-1948* (Ryboły: No publisher, 1996), 67.

40 See "Sprawozdanie kierownika informacji Komendy Powiatu XIII/1 NSZ [Okręg Białystok, Powiat Bielsk Podlaski] za kwiecień 1945," in Frączak, "Formacje zbrojne obozu narodowego," 257; Tash (Tur-Shalom), *The Community of Semiatych*, xiii.

41 See Krajewski and Łabuszewski, *Białostocki*, 184.

42 Jack Rubinfeld quoted in Gilbert, *The Boys*, 273.

43 Gryciuk and Matusak, *Represje NKWD*, 1: 138.

44 "The Partisan Officer Shmuel Koniuchowski," in *Anthology on Armed Jewish Resistance, 1939-1945*, vol. 3, ed. by Isaac Kowalski (Brooklyn, NY: Jewish Combatants Publishers House, 1986), 3: 191 [afterward "The Partisan Officer" in *Anthology*].

45 Koniuchowski was a veteran Communist revolutionary who fought in Spain (1936-1939). Afterwards, he was brought to the Soviet Union where, eventually, as a commissioned officer, he was assigned to the security detail of the Polish Communist military. In the spring of 1944, as a member of the so-called Polish Independent Special Battalion (*Polski Samodzielny Batalion Specjalny*), or Special Storm Battalion (*Specjalny Batalion Szturmowy*), which operated under control of the NKVD, Koniuchowski was parachuted into Nazi-occupied Poland, where he fought as a commando until the arrival of the Red Army in the summer of that year. His subsequent career path is unclear but the storm battalion personnel was assigned *en bloc* to train internal security troops (KBW) under the guidance of the NKVD. Koniuchowski's colleague, Yosef Dembiowski, most likely came from a similar background. See "The Partisan Officer," in Kowalski, *Anthology*, 3: 190; Bordiugow, *Polska-ZSRR*, 38-46; Jaworski, *Korpus*, 12, 23-27; *Z archiwów sowieckich*, vol. 3: *Konflikty polsko-sowieckie*, ed. by Wojciech Roszkowski and Wojciech Materski (Warszawa: ISP PAN, 1993), 117-33, 137, 155-59; Marek Jan Chodakiewicz, *Zagrabiona pamięć: Wojna w Hiszpanii, 1936-1939* (Warszawa: Fronda, 1997), 96.

46   The alleged sentence was never carried out. See Lipman Sznajder, *Wladek war ein falscher Name: Die wahre Geschichte eines dreizehnjährige Jungen* (München: Sznajder Lipman Verlag, 1991), 349.

47   Thus, the Oxford historian Martin Gilbert ajudged this killing to have been motivated by anti-Semitism. Alas, he failed to substantiate this charge by a thorough discussion of the incident. This historian apparently dismisses the possibility that any Soviet officer, as a member of the occupation force, was a fair target for the insurgents. Gilbert follows this mode of scholarship in regards to other incidents of anti-Jewish violence as well, relying mostly on unverified Jewish testimonies. Even when he consults British diplomatic dispatches, he fails to compare them with any non-Communist sources. After all, British diplomats usually got their accounts from official government sources, which were heavily tainted by propaganda. See Gilbert, *Holocaust*, 816-19.

48   The assault occurred most likely in the fall of 1945. See Sack, *An Eye for an Eye*, 139-40; John Sack, interview by Marek Jan Chodakiewicz, 8 August 1999; John Sack to Marek Jan Chodakiewicz, 16 August 1999.

49   In a bizarre twist, although the AK seems to have been responsible for the assault, which occurred in the spring of 1945, the NKVD allegedly blamed the Jews. See Pinkus, *A Choice of Masks*, 14-21.

50   Phinia Korovski, "Our Dear City of Birth and its Convulsive and Terrible Demise," in Shmueli-Schmusch, *Zabludow*, Internet.

51   It is also alleged that, after the war, probably the same perpetrators murdered a Polish (Christian) woman who had harbored a Jewish child during the Nazi occupation, after she refused to pay money to the assailants or to surrender the girl to them. This suggests that common bandits were involved rather than insurgents. See Aharon Manor (Mankuta) in *Inherited Memories: Israeli Children of Holocaust Survivors*, ed. by Tamar Fox (London and New York: Cassell, 1999), 81. In a similar case, it was falsely alleged that on June 23, 1946, the NZW killed a teacher, Eugenia Majcherska, for having sheltered a Jewish girl in Kołaki near Rogienice Wielkie, the county of Łomża. However, according to a Communist secret policeman, Majcherska was assassinated because she was an active sympathizer of the proxy regime and volunteered to oversee a faudulent referendum which the underground opposed. See Tadeusz Sadowski, *Jeszcze raz Jedwabne: Dojść prawdy* (Ciechanów: By the author, 2001), 6-7.

52   *Yizkor Book of the Jewish Community in Działoszyce and Surroundings* (Tel Aviv: "Hamenora" Publishing House, 1973), 44 [afterward *Yizkor Działoszyce*]. A scholar affiliated with the Jewish Historical Institute in Warsaw, basing herself on an official account, established that "when the inhabitants refused to open the door, a grenade was tossed into their house, killing four Jews. The chairman of the local [Jewish] committee died as well. Entire families were beaten — altogether over 50 persons, and Jewish households were looted." However, even in this case no perpetrators were named specifically, although a similarity to the events in Parczew was noted. See Sprawozdanie Referatu za czerwiec 1945, AURM, PRM, file 5/137, 11-14 in Aleksiun-Mądrzak, "Nielegalna emigracja cz. 1," 82. According to an Oxford historian, "four of the twenty-five Jews who had returned were murdered by Polish anti-Semites" in Działoszyce at the time. See Gilbert, *Holocaust*, 812. A survivor of the Działoszyce assault recalled the events briefly mentioning 5 killed and one wounded. See Chaim Wolf Szlamowitz in Elinor J. Brecher, *Schindler's Legacy: True Stories of the List Survivors* (New York: Penguin Group, 1994), 352 [afterward *Schindler's Legacy*].

53 Mina Deutsch, *Mina's Story: A Doctor's Memoir of the Holocaust* (Toronto: ECW Press, 1994), 100, 104.

54 Characteristically, another Jewish witness wrote about "the prominent physician, Dr. Mehrer of Lwów, who was [allegedly] murdered by the NSZ" in Katowice in September 1946. To be sure, the author of the memoir was in Wrocław at the time, so he must have been repeating Communist propaganda which usually blamed such assaults on the NSZ. In fact, we have no idea who the perpetrators were. See Steinhaus, *Wspomnienia*, 354. Equally confusing is the account by Stanley Bors, who conflates the activities of the independentists and the Communist secret police: "We went back to Sosnowiec, where I had friends and relatives, and I almost immediately found a job in the Agricultural Department. They [i.e. the Communists] gave me an apartment and a car. The new Polish administration needed people and all the specialists they could find in order to get started. I was sent to Katowice in Silesia and we were living peacefully again until the Polish Underground, former resistance fighters, began killing Jews. In 1945 they began murdering the liberated Jews, the handful who survived the Holocaust. They [i.e. the secret police] also began to investigate people and arrest them without provocation. In the [government] office where I worked someone was arrested, nobody knew why. People began to be afraid to talk to each other. A friend of mine who was a doctor was killed in his office. They just came and killed him." Were "they" the secret police, the bandits, or the independentists? See Stanley Bors in Rothchild, *Voices*, 226.

55 Mark Wyman, *DP: Europe's Displaced Persons, 1945-1951* (Philadelphia, London, and Toronto: The Balch Institute and Associated University Presses, 1989), 141.

56 See the testimony of Allen Mastbaum in *Witnesses to the Holocaust: An Oral History*, ed. by Rhoda G. Lewin (Boston: Twayne Publishers, 1990), 158.

57 David Zabludovsky, "Horrors, Death and Destruction (Experiences of a Holocaust Survivor)," in Shmueli-Schmusch, *Zabludow*, Internet.

58 ibid.

59 Rzeczpospolita Polska, Ministerstwo Pracy i Opieki Społecznej, Referat dla Spraw Pomocy Ludności Żydowskiej, Trzynaste sprawozdanie z działalności (za miesiąc lipiec b.r.), 31 July 1945, AURM, PRM, BP, file 5/137, 22.

60 Joachim Schoenfeld, *Holocaust Memoirs: Jews in the Lwów Ghetto, the Janowski Concentration Camp, and as Deportees in Siberia* (Hoboken, NJ: Ktav Publishing House, Inc., 1985), 165-66 [afterward *Holocaust Memoirs*].

61 Cała and Datner-Śpiewak, *Z dziejów Żydów*, 15.

62 Adelson, "W Polsce," in Tomaszewski, *Najnowsze*, 393; Michlic-Coren, "Anti-Jewish Violence in Poland," 39; Jan Tomasz Gross, "A Tangled Web: Confronting Stereotypes Concerning Relations between Poles, Germans, Jews, and Communists," in Deák, Gross, and Judt, *The Politics of Retribution*, 127.

63 It should not be construed that all assaults targeted Jews only. Two insurgents recalled separate attacks on trains by NSZ units but Jews were not their target. See Mikołajczuk, "Przyczynek," in Bechta and Żebrowski, *NSZ na Podlasiu*, 2: 230; Kurek, *Zaporczycy*, 213. Similarly, no Jewish victims are mentioned in the detailed reports of the attacks on trains by the Wilno Brigade. See Łabuszewski and Krajewski, *Od "Łupaszki"*, 163-68. Nonetheless, a Polish witness described an attack on her train by common hooligans, who chanted anti-Jewish slogans and threw stones, but stresses that Polish passengers protected their Jewish friends. There were no casualties. See Julia Hubert Budzyńska, *Syberyjska dziatwa: Wojenne losy kresowiaków* (Lublin: Norbertinum,

1993), 80-81. Another witness recalled the general hostility of Polish peasants, who reportedly greeted a train full of Jewish returnees with stones and angry shouts "Go back to Siberia, you dirty Jews." See Esther Hautzic, *The Endless Steppe: Growing up in Siberia* (New York: Thomas Y. Crowell Company, 1968), 241. For other examples of assaults on trains see Poufne, Sprawozdanie sytuacyjne Wydziału Społeczno-Politycznego za miesiąc styczeń 1946, APB, UWB, file 95, 1, 9; Cała and Datner-Śpiewak, *Dzieje Żydów*, 45-47, 49-50, 73; Munro, *Białystok to Birkenau*, 224; Shapiro, "Poland," in Schneiderman and Fine, *American*, 49: 386; Weinryb, "Poland," in Meyer et al., *The Jews in the Soviet Satellites*, 251; Gross, *Upiorna dekada*, 96-98; Gilbert, *Holocaust*, 816-17; Genie Golembiowski, *In Search for Survival* (Miami, FL: n.p., [1985]), 154; Kazimierz Zybert, "Nie dobity," in *Losy żydowskie: Świadectwo żywych*, vol. 2, ed. by Marian Turski (Warszawa: Stowarzyszenie Żydów Kombatantów i Poszkodowanych w II Wojnie Światowej, 1999), 400-401; Danuta Blus-Węgrowska, "Atmosfera pogromowa," *Karta*, 18 (1996): 89-91; Ewa Koźmińska-Frejlak, "Nieudana odbudowa," *Midrasz* [Warszawa] 7-8 (July-August 1998): 8-9 [afterward "Nieudana"].

64 See Cariewskaja, *Teczka specjalna*, 363. Rather characteristically, a Jewish witness (Martin S.) recalled that upon his return to Kraków after the war he survived an attack on a refugee shelter for Jews because the Russians protected the inmates from a group of Polish assailants with rifles and guns. Most likely the witness was referring to the anti-Jewish tumult that the Communist militiamen took part in. See Greene and Kumar, *Voices*, 216-17. See also Julian Kwiek, "Wydarzenia antyżydowskie 11 sierpnia 1945 r. w Krakowie: Dokumenty," *BŻIH*, no. 1 (March 2001): 77-89; *Pogrom Żydów w Krakowie 11 sierpnia 1945: Wstęp do badań*, ed. by Anna Cichopek (Warszawa: Żydowski Instytut Historyczny, 2000).

65 See Odpis, *Informator*, 3-4 (November-December 1945): 1-2 in AAN, KC PPR, file 295/VII-192, 54-55; Raport WiN [after August 1945], "Polityka narodowościowa PPR," AAN, KC PPR, file 295/VII-255, 1-3; Minister St. Radkiewicz, Rozkaz nr. 46 o tępieniu wystąpień antysemickich, 13 August 1945, Archiwum Urzędu Ochrony Państwa w Lublinie [afterward AUOP Lublin], Wojewódzki Urząd Bezpieczeństwa Publicznego Lublin [afterward WUBP Lublin], file 24/36, 127; Minister BP Stanisław Radkiewicz, Okólnik, "Wszystkim szefom Wojewodzkich [sic] i Powiatowych Urzędow [sic] Bezpieczenstwa [sic] Publicznego, komendantom Milicji Obywatelskiej i dowodcom [sic] K.B.W.," 5 July 1946, AUOP Lublin, WUBP Lublin, file 24/37, 118; Rzeczpospolita Polska, Ministerstwo Pracy i Opieki Społecznej, Referat dla Spraw Pomocy Ludności Żydowskiej, Czternaste sprawozdanie z działalności (za miesiąc sierpień roku 1945), 31 August 1945, AURM, PRM, BP, file 5/133, 68; Zrzeszenie WiN w dokumentach, 1: 441; Cariewskaja, *Teczka specjalna*, 362-64, 378-79, 421; Cała and Datner-Śpiewak, *Dzieje Żydów*, 17 n. 20, 34, 45-57, 70; Chudzik, Marzak, and Olkuśnik, *Biuletyny 1946*, 18, 25-26, 55; Wald, *Rzeszów Jews*, 116; Zandman, *Never the Last Journey*, 163-64; Tenenbaum, *In Search of A Lost People*, 208-10, 215-16; Tenenbaum, *Underground*, 498-502; Weinryb, "Poland," in Meyer et al., *The Jews in the Soviet Satellites*, 251; Zuckerman, *A Surplus of Memory*, 661; Hillel, *Le Massacre des survivants*, 125-27, 194-200, 239, 250-302, 305-306; Kwiek, *Żydzi, Łemkowie, Słowacy*, 31-43; Checinski, *Poland Communism*, 17-18, 21-34; Rothschild, *Return to Diversity*, 229; Piotrowski, *Poland's Holocaust*, 133-41; Pogonowski, *Jews in Poland*, 403-20; *Kielce*, 5-126; David Zabludovsky, "Horrors, Death and Destruction (Experiences of a Holocaust Survivor)," in Shmueli-Schmusch, *Zabludow*, Internet; Stanisław Meducki, "The Pogrom in Kielce on 4 July 1946," *Polin: Studies in Polish*

Jewry 9 (1996): 158-69; Bożena Szaynok, "The Jewish Pogrom in Kielce, July 1946: New Evidence," *Intermarium* (Online Journal, Institute on East Central Europe, Columbia University, New York), vol 1. no. 3; Bożena Szaynok, *Pogrom Żydów w Kielcach, 4 lipca 1946* (Warszawa: Wydawnictwo Bellona, 1992) [afterward *Pogrom*]; Krystyna Kersten, *Pogrom Żydów w Kielcach 4 lipca 1946 r.* (Warszawa: PISM, 1996); Jerzy Daniel, *Żyd w zielonym kapeluszu: Rzecz o kieleckim pogromie 4 lipca 1946* (Kielce: "Scriptum," 1996); Krzysztof Kąkolewski, *Umarły cmętarz: Wstęp do studiów nad wyjaśnienieniem przyczyn i przebiegu morderstwa na Żydach w Kielcach dnia 4 lipca 1946 roku* (Warszawa: Wydawnictwo von Borowiecky, 1996), 96 [afterward *Umarły cmentarz*]; Jan Śledzianowski, *Pytania nad pogromem kieleckim* (Kielce: "Jedność," 1998); Anna Grażyna Kister, "Antyżydowskie prowokacje komunistów," *Gazeta Polska*, 6 May 1998, 17; Leszek Żebrowski, "Pretekst kielecki," *Gazeta Polska*, 29 February 1996, 10-11.

66 Basing himself on a report of November 1945 by General Nikolai Silvanovskii, who headed the NKVD mission with the Ministry of Public Security in Poland, the Russian journalist Yevgenii Zirnov (*Kommersant Vlast*, 28 March 2000, 50-53), alleged that the anti-Jewish riots in Cracow and Kielce were provoked by the Soviet secret police to create for the benefit of the English and Americans an impression of instability in Poland that necessitated the presence of Red Army there. See T.T.S., "Raport o pogromach w Kielcach i Krakowie," *Rzeczpospolita*, 1 April 2000.

67 A typical piece of Communist propaganda reads: "The plans of the Staff of Anders concerning the Jews! Paris. French Zionist press published an article by a French journalist who, as an Englishman, was allowed access to one of the aces of Anders' "Sixth" [department] (i.e. diversion and intelligence), one Capt. "Janek." Captain "Janek" informed his English friend that "the Staff of General Anders had prepared a plan to murder all the Jews in Poland." Capt. "Janek" confessed that the Kielce pogrom was perpetrated by the Andersites [soldiers of General Anders]. He stressed that one of the first persons to be murdered in Kielce had been Dr. Kahane, the chairman of the local Jewish Committee, which was in congruence with the instructions of the Staff of Anders that planned to murder Jewish activists first and only then other Jews." See *Kurier Szczeciński*, 13-14 October 1946, quoted in Urbankowski, *Czerwona msza*, 2nd ed., 2: 189. Similar calumnies heaped daily on Poland's other "reactionaries" proved durable beyond the wildest dream of the Communist propaganda machine, entering mainstream Western scholarship practically without any challenge. For instance, the respected Yehuda Bauer wrote that in Kielce "a pogrom incited by a blood-libel took place – a pogrom, one must add, in which the local government militia, *members of the clergy*, and even a socialist factory director and his workers took part [emphasis added]." See Yehuda Bauer, *The Jewish Emergence from Powerlessness* (Toronto and Buffalo: University of Toronto Press, 1979), 65. The author of a recent in-depth analysis based on internal Communist and church documents has shown that the local clergymen attempted to intervene to halt the pogrom but were physically prevented from doing so by the security forces. See Ryszard Gryz, *Państwo a Kościół w Polsce, 1945-1956: Na przykładzie województwa kieleckiego* (Kraków: Zakład Wydawniczy "Nomos," 1999), 146-53. See also, Śledzianowski, *Ksiądz Czesław Kaczmarek*, 102-116; Paul, "Catholic," in *Kielce*, 102-116.

68 Pismo D.O.W.S, 29 July 1945, APR, OKŻ, vol. 5, 11 in Penkalla, "Stosunki," 63. See also Chojnacki, *Bibliografia*, 138.

69 Odpis, *Informator* 3-4 (November-December 1945): 2, in AAN, KC PPR, file 295/VII-192, 55; Rzeczpospolita Polska, Ministerstwo Pracy i Opieki Społecznej, Referat dla

Spraw Pomocy Ludności Żydowskiej, Czternaste sprawozdanie z działalności (za miesiąc sierpień roku 1945), 31 August 1945, AURM, PRM, BP, file 5/133, 69; Cariewskaja, *Teczka specjalna*, 364, 420; Maciej Pisarski, "Emigracja Żydów z Polski," in Tomaszewski, *Studia*, 30 n. 44 [afterward "Emigracja"]; Cała and Datner-Śpiewak, *Dzieje Żydów*, 31, 35-37, 106; Weinryb, "Poland," in Meyer et al., *The Jews in the Soviet Satellites*, 252.

70   A single Communist government report lists six attacks on the Jews between June 10 and 29. Only one of those attacks was staged clearly by the insurgents and resulted in no casualties (the victims were released). The remaining cases involved robber attacks, four of which ended in the murder of six Jews (in Biała Podlaska, Sianiawa near Lublin, and Żarnów in the county of Opoczyn). See Rzeczpospolita Polska, Ministerstwo Pracy i Opieki Społecznej, Referat dla Spraw Pomocy Ludności Żydowskiej, Trzynaste sprawozdanie z działalności (za miesiąc lipiec b.r.), 31 July 1945, AURM, PRM, BP, file 5/137, 22. And see also similar reports on anti-Jewish deeds of banditry in Protokoły, 20 and 23 August 1945, 13 and 19 September 1945, 7 February 1946, AURM, PRM, BP, file 5/133, 13, 17-19, 64, 74.

71   The victims for the rubric "unknown locations" were estimated as follows. In this chapter there are approximately 246 unconfirmed Jewish victims who were killed in unknown localities. That number includes 46 mentioned by Werhaftig as having been killed somewhere in the Province of Białystok and about 200 allegedly killed during the assaults on trains. However, we have been able to establish the locations of at least three assaults on trains where an unconfirmed minimum of 16 and a maximum of 58 victims perished, leaving us with a minimum of 144 and a maximum of 184 Jews dead during railway attacks. Further, that estimate is reduced by 30 (by subtracting from Werhaftig's 46 victims killed somewhere from the Province of Białystok about 30 Jews whose circumstances and location of death we have been able to reconstruct in that province). Therefore between 114 and 144 Jews discussed in this chapter are alleged to have been killed in unknown locations throughout Poland.

72   Admittedly, we have applied a rigorous yardstick to verify death statistics: at least two primary sources (such as a testimony or a report) generated by at least two separate entities (a Jewish witness, an insurgent commander, a secret policeman, or a government official).

IX

PERSONAL RELATIONS AND JEWISH ASSISTANCE

Like most other matters concerning Polish-Jewish relations between 1944 and 1947, the topic of the interaction between Jews and Poles is understudied and mostly skewed toward conflict. Casual contacts of a neutral nature between representatives of both groups are largely overlooked.[1] Cooperation is simply ignored. Nonetheless, a few preliminary corrective observations can be made. Surprisingly, personal relations between some Jewish survivors and some Poles were rather cordial. A Jewish witness recalls that during the first few weeks after the arrival of the Soviet army in Lublin the Poles were "friendly" toward the Jews. In Strzyżów, the Poles welcomed at least one Jewish family "with politeness."[2] In Potoczno near Łysobyki and Kock Michał Leib Rudawski was welcomed back cordially by his neighbors. Despite the fact that the locality was staunchly independentist and Rudawski was an officer of the Communist army, the peasants fed him, returned his belongings to him, and protected him lest an outside insurgent unit decide to assassinate him by mistake since Rudawski was parading around in his uniform.[3] In Kielce, initially, according to Moishe Sokolowski, who returned home from Auschwitz, "the Poles were very nice, very well behaved. They said: 'You alive? How did you survive?' They couldn't believe there were going to be any more Jews."[4]

At this point it is impossible to determine whether such positive occurrences were exceptional. Evidence culled from a number of Jewish memoirs suggests that on the personal level friendliness persisted beyond the initial period. It ranged from sustained contacts based on mutual affinities or professional dealings to single acts of charity. For example, after July 1944, a Polish acquaintance helped a Jewish man to regain his apartment in Lublin and to procure a job for him. Another Polish acquaintance found him a new apartment when the Jewish man moved to Gdańsk in January 1946.[5] In Wałbrzych, a Polish woman and her pre-war Jewish friend, Hesiu Krochmal-Sznajder, established a business

187

partnership, which thrived for a while despite Communist harassment.[6] In yet another case, a Polish peasant couple took care of a Jewish boy by feeding him and transporting him from the countryside to Chełm.[7] In Warsaw, after he returned home in July 1945, Morris Wyszogrod met a few of his pre-war Polish friends and acquaintances who welcomed and hosted him with cordiality.[8] As late as 1949 in Łomazy "some Christian workers" helped four local Jews in exhuming victims of the Holocaust. For the burial ceremony, "though it was raining all the day [sic], many local [Polish] inhabitants came, including children with their teachers."[9] An assimilated person of Jewish origin left the following account from post-war Wrocław, which sheds some light on the important question of personal self-identification and of the changing perception of reality under various conditions:

> Until then [the author's departure from Poland in 1956] I would have adamantly told anyone asking about it that I had experienced no anti-Semitism in Communist Poland. Nearly all my friends were Catholic. So were nearly all of the girls I went to bed with. My Jewishness had never been an issue or an obstacle. I spoke like a Pole, acted like a Pole, thought like a Pole. All the time I lived in Poland, I had felt that I was at home. It took Israel to make me realize that home had been a hotel.[10]

Although the topic of Jewish intercourse with the Polish civilian population remains outside of the scope of this work, the existence of a certain amount of positive rapport between the two groups challenges the uniformly hostile vision of Polish-Jewish relations after the war. It also allows us to understand better the nature of personal affairs between some Jews and Polish independentists. In fact, they were better than is generally assumed. Most of the time such positive relationships between the two groups were directly related to the sympathy of individual Poles toward the Jewish tragedy under the Nazi occupation. Some Jews felt that under the Soviet occupation it was their turn to help their erstwhile Polish benefactors. To put it plainly, in certain cases Jewish survivors repaid a debt of gratitude to their saviors by aiding them against the Communist regime. However, there were also Jews who showed kindness without any prior obligation. Their assistance mainly consisted of protecting Poles from the secret police in a variety of ways.

After the entry of the Red Army in June 1944, the Soviet security police discovered a secret arms depot and arrested the Home Army soldiers Jan Hawryliszyn and Śliwa in Kolonia Hetmańska near Kopyczyńce, the

Province of Tarnopol. However, several Jewish survivors, led by Halpern, interceded on behalf of the AK men with the NKVD. After the Jewish witnesses claimed falsely that the weapons had been used by them for self-protection, the Home Army soldiers were released.[11]

The sisters Jasia and Krysia Necman, aka Bychawski, survived the Nazi occupation in Izbica, the county of Krasnystaw, thanks to the assistance of several soldiers of the National Armed Forces (NSZ). After July 1944, they reciprocated the kindness. For instance, in the fall of 1944 the Necman sisters provided their apartment in Lublin for secret meetings of the insurgents.[12]

In February 1945 the famous Jewish partisan Abram Braun ("Adam," "Adolf") saved his friends, Stanisław Saganowski ("Dąb") and his son Jerzy ("Brzoza") of Aleksandrówka, the county of Kraśnik, from the NKVD and the UB. Both men had assisted Braun during the Nazi occupation. They were active members of the NSZ, however, and thus had to go into hiding after the arrival of the Red Army. Braun arranged for immunity for the Saganowskis from the local secret police and protected them afterward. Braun helped them move to his house in Kraśnik. Subsequently, Saganowski senior went into a black market business with his Jewish friend. Saganowski junior enrolled at a high school in Kraśnik. Both maintained personal contacts with their NSZ colleagues but remained passive in the anti-Communist struggle. The authorities did not molest them.[13]

In March 1945 the secret police in Częstochowa arrested Colonel Zygmunt Reliszko ("Kołodziejski") of the NSZ, a senior Polish commander during the anti-German Warsaw Uprising of August-October 1944. Colonel Reliszko was released partly because several Jews, who had fought under his command in the Uprising, intervened with the Communists on his behalf.[14]

In the late spring of 1945 in Kraków, Shlomo Wolkowicz successfully intervened with the UB on behalf of a Pole, Mr. Kominowski, who had helped his father during the Nazi occupation but was later accused by the Communists of having collaborated with the Germans, a common device to implicate independentists. Fortunately, the Pole was released within two weeks because Wolkowicz became friendly with the security officer responsible for the case, who happened to be Jewish.[15]

In 1945, in Warsaw, Aleksander Skotnicki-Zajdman saved from the Communist secret service Paweł Gołąbek (Gołombek?), a Polish policeman who was secretly in the Underground, by whom he had been ushered out of the ghetto during the Nazi occupation. Aleksander's sister, Renata Skotnicka-Zajdman, found her war-time benefactors, the

Czerniakowski family, hiding from the NKVD. They were threatened with arrest both as AK soldiers and nobles. This Jewish woman provided Mr. Czerniakowski with an affidavit, endorsed by the Jewish community, about their rescue activities during the war. "This saved him from immediate arrest, perhaps even execution. However, when the Stalinist regime was firmly entrenched, Count Czerniakowski was sent to prison for five years; his wife, Dr. Czerniakowska, was sentenced to three years and [their daughter] Leszka was barred from further medical studies." Alas, Renata and Aleksander Skotnicki-Zajdman had emigrated from Poland previously and could no longer help their friends.[16]

Felicja Raszkin-Nowak survived the Holocaust hidden by a Polish family in Ponikła near Białystok. After the arrival of the Red Army, she went to study in Moscow. When she learned, in 1945, that her benefactors, including Józef Zalewski ("Pan Piotr"), were arrested for "collaboration with the AK," Raszkin-Nowak

> immediately began a flourish [sic flurry] of activity at the Polish embassy. I explained, wrote declarations, made requests. I beat a path to a Polish [Communist] agency seeking their intervention in the matter. I have no way of knowing how effective my actions were or how significant. Most important was that after spending half a year in prison, they were finally released.[17]

In 1947, Charlota Frank-Oltramare beseeched the Communist president of Poland, Bolesław Bierut, to pardon Maria Nachtman, a soldier of the NSZ. During the Nazi occupation Nachtman had assisted several Jews, including Dr. Zacharjasz Frank, Dr. Bronisława Warmanowa, and Dr. Leon Szafrin. This NSZ soldier arranged their escape from the ghetto and provided for them afterwards. As Charlota Frank-Oltramare put it, Nachtman "showed her deep understanding especially during the times when the help rendered to the Jewish population was subject to terrible repressions."[18] Similarly, the famous poet Julian Tuwim interceded with Bierut and the secret police to save the life of five NSZ partisans, including Lieutenant Jerzy Kozarzewski ("Konrad"), who had assisted the poet's mother during the Nazi occupation.[19]

Reportedly, some Polish independentists used false Jewish documents to escape from Poland. Many failed, however, because of the vigilance of the secret police.[20] For instance, in the fall of 1946, Jewish assistance was enlisted to spirit Wiesław Chrzanowski, a National Democratic activist and a soldier of the Home Army, out of Poland. According to his account, a friend established one more contact to cross the border illegally. This time it was in Szczecin and so I had to go to Szczecin. There was an entire Jewish quarter in Szczecin. The Szczecin kehilot [Jewish council] undertook smuggling Jews out of Poland and Russia to the West. The UB [secret police] tolerated it. I was to go [to the West] through this venue as well. Unfortunately, when I arrived there, the situation changed a bit. One of the buses with [Jewish] refugees had been fired upon [by the secret police]. Therefore the Jews were scared and refused to take me with them because, if [the bus] were stopped, they would be in serious trouble. So it did not work out.[21]

Subsequent attempts to leave Poland failed likewise and Chrzanowski was arrested by the UB. He found himself incarcerated with the Zionist-Revisionist leader Dawid Draznin, who became his friend.[22]

Some Jews also took advantage of their official posts to assist the independentists. In 1944 the Zionist activist Emil Sommerstein was released from the Gulag after he had agreed to join the proxy regime of the Communists as minister representing the Jewish community. He was also appointed the head of the Central Committee of Polish Jews. Nonetheless, in the fall of 1944, Sommerstein met secretly with Witold Bieńkowski ("Kalski"), who was the head of the Jewish Bureau of the Office of the Government Delegate of the Polish Underground State. Sommerstein was part of a plot to send two secret couriers of the Polish insurgents via Russia to London disguised as Jews. Alas, Bieńkowski was arrested by the NKVD and the plan fell through.[23]

In December 1944, Noah N. Shneidman of Wilno, who avoided serving the NKVD and, instead, enlisted with the regular Red Army, was posted in the environs of Warsaw. Shneidman interceded on behalf of local Poles, very likely including independentists, who fell victim to Soviet plunder, abuse, and rapine. In the process, the Jewish man endangered himself. According to his account,

> By the end of the war, close to half of the Soviet rank and file consisted of members of national minorities, mainly from Central Asia and the Caucasus. They were unfamiliar with European traditions and way of life, nor did they speak Russian well. Some of them could hardly make a distinction between Germans and Poles and treated both equally, as enemies. Some of them plundered the local population, abused women, and offended those who resisted their advances. The Poles did not

submit easily. They were just recently liberated from Nazi occupation and were already familiar with the brute force of invaders. They sought out Soviet commanders, complained of maltreatment, and demanded justice. Since I was the only one in our detachment able to speak Polish, many Poles came to me and asked for assistance. The political officer of our battalion became suspicious. He suspected that I could be in collusion with the enemy. I was soon summoned to the counter intelligence department at the corps headquarters for interrogation. I provided the officer in charge with information about my background, and submitted my partisan credentials. The colonel in charge said that the reliability of my testimony would be checked and that I would be informed of the results as soon as they would become available. I returned to my battalion, but I was aware that I was watched, and that my movements were restricted.[24]

In the spring of 1945, during a secret police sweep of Urzędów, the county of Kraśnik, UB functionaries caught two teenagers, Staś (Stanisław) Gajewski and Józio (Józef) Wyrostek. The two boys had connections to the AK-WiN unit of "Zapora." While policemen were searching one of the farmsteads, the teenagers fled thanks to the assistance of a friendly Jewish police trooper. According to a Polish source, "they ran across the yard and were about to approach the road when their path was blocked by a soldier with a rifle. Staś recognized the son of Sulim [Shmuel], a local Jew. 'Dawid!' he yelled softly. The young [son of] Sulim halted, lowered his rifle, and allowed them to escape."[25]

In August 1945, a Home Army liaison who had survived the Gestapo and NKVD jails in Wilno fled the Eastern Borderlands to central Poland. She eventually reestablished contacts with her underground commanders but worked at a cosmetics factory under an assumed identity. When in 1946 the secret police came to arrest her at the factory, her Jewish manager, Mr. Lewin, misled the security men claiming that their quarry was not at work. She fled Bydgoszcz immediately. This Jewish rescuer had no obligations whatsoever toward the Polish woman but nonetheless saved her out of pity and distaste for the Communist regime. Mr. Lewin himself fled to Palestine soon after.[26]

After it was revealed that he had been a cadet officer of the NSZ, the secret police wanted to arrest Bohdan Szucki ("Artur"), who worked as a junior scientist in Lublin after the war. However, his supervisor, Dr. Józef Parnas, felt sorry for the young man and mistakenly considered the accusations false. A former Soviet partisan of Jewish origin, Parnas intervened with the UB on the behalf of Szucki. Subsequently, the authorities left the NSZ fighter alone.[27]

Sometime after the Soviet takeover of Poland a leading activist of the National Party (SN) of Szczebrzeszyn, Dr. Zygmunt Klukowski, was arrested twice for his connections to the underground. During his second incarceration he was tortured nearly to death by the security men, who abandoned him to die in his cell in the Mokotów jail in Warsaw. However, the prison physicians, who were Jewish, intervened. Klukowski was transferred to the prison hospital, where he recuperated under the watchful eye of the Jewish doctors. Here again the help was a function of human kindness rather than of any personal debt.[28]

In many cases, however, the connection between rescuing of Jews during the Nazi occupation and the subsequent Jewish assistance to the victims of Communism is obvious. Perhaps in one of the most high-profile cases, the conservative Catholic writer Zofia Kossak-Szczucka was a prime target for Communist persecution. In the early fall of 1945, this Catholic activist, who was a founding member of the clandestine Council for Aid to Jews during the Nazi occupation, received assistance from unexpected quarters. The second most important man in the proxy regime, Jakub Berman, who supervised the secret police and cultural policy on behalf of the ruling Politburo of the Central Committee of the PPR, helped Kossak-Szczucka flee to the West. Berman explained his actions as follows: "I owe your family a debt which I want to repay. You rescued my brother's children from the ghetto... I can assure your departure from the country. I recommend you go."[29]

Anti-Communist underground Second Lieutenant Władysław Bartoszewski was first seized by the secret police in July 1945. He was released immediately after the intercession of Zofia Rudnicka, a high-up official with the Communist Ministry of Justice. During the Nazi occupation Rudnicka had cooperated with Bartoszewski in the Council for Aid to Jews. When in 1948 the UB re-arrested Bartoszewski, who meanwhile became an opposition journalist, his release was arranged by the brother of the secret police boss himself, Adolf Berman, who had been a beneficiary of Bartoszewski's war-time charity. Nonetheless, soon after Adolf Berman left Poland for Israel, Bartoszewski was seized yet again and spent seven years in jail.[30]

In February 1946, the Home Army liaison Irena Gut ("Mała") was arrested by the NKVD in Katowice. She was tortured but managed to escape from prison and hide with the Jewish Haller family, whose lives Gut had saved during the Nazi occupation in Tarnopol. Eventually, with the assistance of a local rabbi and a Soviet soldier, who was a brother-in-law of

Ida and Lazar Haller, Irena Gut was spirited out of Katowice and placed in a Jewish household in Kraków. Moishe Lifsitz and his wife nursed her back to health. In April 1946 a local Jewish organization supplied her with false documents. As "Sonia Sofierstein," a Jewess, Gut left Poland with a transport of Jewish refugees and successfully reached the West.[31]

Most likely in 1946 Jewish lawyers connected to the CKŻP's branch in Kraków intervened successfully on behalf of the son of Dr. Antoni Ptaszek. The young man was a WiN liaison apprehended by the police while crossing the border illegally. Dr. Ptaszek had helped Jews during the Nazi occupation. Now the representatives of the Jewish community reciprocated in kind.[32]

In 1949 the secret police arrested Irena Sendler ("Joanna"), a Home Army member and a progressive socialist. She was denounced for sheltering former AK soldiers. Consequently, although pregnant, Sendler was brutally manhandled during the interrogation, which resulted in a miscarriage. Eventually, the UB released Sendler but placed her under surveillance and planned to rearrest her. However, her Jewish friend Irena Majewska successfully begged her husband, Colonel Zbigniew Paszkowski, who headed the secret police in Warsaw, to spare Sendler. The Polish woman remained free. As a leading activist of the Council for Aid to Jews, Irena Sendler is credited with saving about 2,500 Jewish children from the Warsaw ghetto. She also rescued many Jewish adults and Irena Majewska was one of them. As Majewska put it later to Sendler, "I have paid off my debt I owed to you."[33]

A relatively frequent form of Jewish assistance to the independentists was providing favorable testimony in court proceedings. In December 1945, the UB arrested Edward Kemnitz, a prominent activist of the National Radical Camp, and an officer of the AK and NSZ, who remained underground after the Soviet entry into Poland in 1944. The court refrained from handing him a death penalty and sentenced him to fifteen years. The judges were swayed by several affidavits written on his behalf by Jewish survivors. According to one of them, "the Central Jewish Historical Commission would like to verify in congruence with the testimony of citizen Leon Hercberg in the archives of the CKŻH, that citizens Wojciech [Edward's father] and Edward Kemnitz of Warsaw provided him and his family with far-reaching help during the [Nazi] occupation, often endangering their lives."[34] The list of Jewish beneficiaries of Kemnitz is longer. As a "Righteous Gentile," he has a tree in Yad Vashem.[35]

Another future Yad Vashem award recipient, the NSZ Lieutenant Sławomir Modzelewski ("Lanc"), also had his death penalty commuted to fifteen years' imprisonment very likely after the intervention of Jews he and his mother had rescued in Warsaw during the Nazi occupation.[36]

Under similar circumstances, a Jewish witness testified on behalf of his war-time rescuer, Wacław Nowiński, who had served in the Polish police under the Nazis and almost certainly in the independentist underground. Nowiński was exonerated and, later, honored by Yad Vashem.[37]

In 1946 a Communist court tried Captain Mirosław Ostromęcki ("Orski"), a national radical activist and an officer of the NSZ. He received a death sentence but it was commuted because of the intercession of Aniela Steinsbergowa, a prominent Jewish lawyer whose niece Ostromęcki had saved during the Nazi occupation.[38]

At the time, a Jewish witness testified in favor of Jerzy Regulski, an adjutant of the last Commander-in-Chief of the NSZ. Significantly, the assistance Regulski had rendered to Jews during the Nazi occupation was haphazard (his mother was much more involved) but the witness simply felt sorry for him.[39]

In October 1946 in Rzeszów, a Home Army liaison was sentenced to three years in jail. Apolinary Kozubski credits "the leniency of the sentence" to a Polish court employee and to a secret policeman "of Jewish origin" who had been his acquaintance and neighbor before the war.[40]

Father Szczepan Sobalkowski ("Andrzej Bobola"), chief chaplain of the Kielce Region of the NSZ, was arrested by the secret police in 1948 and interrogated for several years. Finally, when his case came to trial in 1954, Father Sobalkowski drew a relatively lenient sentence of seven years because the court apparently accepted as extenuating evidence the fact that, during the Nazi occupation, the priest had sheltered and saved the Jewish Walter family from Wieluń.[41]

Father Marian Pirożyński, a chaplain of the AK in Kraków-Podgórze, was arrested by the Communists for publishing and disseminating underground literature. During the Nazi occupation this Redemptorist priest had sheltered many Jewish children, some of whom came forth to testify on his behalf during his second trial.[42]

With likewise positive results, Lejbko Goldman and Izaak Halber testified as friendly witnesses at the trial of the officers of the Podlasie District of the NSZ, including Lieutenant Władysław Wyczółkowski ("Sęp"), Captain Jerzy Wojciechowski ("Drzazga"), and Rev. (Major) Stanisław Jurczak ("Brzoza"). According to Goldman and Halber, "the NSZ men" in general, and Lt. Wyczółkowski in particular, "hid Jews and preserved [Jewish] property." The officers were spared and survived incarceration.[43] In another instance, a Communist court refrained from imposing a death penalty on several NSZ officers in Częstochowa after Jewish witnesses intervened on their behalf. In particular, they praised Stefan Karpiński, "a member of the NSZ command [who] in some instances assisted Jews quite selflessly."[44]

Dr. Juliusz Kamiński ("Migoń") had fought as a partisan in the ranks of the AK and NSZ in the Kielce region. In particular, he served as the head surgeon in the NSZ unit of Captain Władysław Kołaciński ("Żbik"), who saved his life. After the war, Dr. Kamiński routinely appeared in court to testify as a friendly witness at numerous trials of soldiers of the NSZ. He assisted even the fighters he did not know personally. For example, after an impassioned plea by Dr. Kamiński in defense of Lieutenant Bogusław Denkiewicz ("Bolesław"), the Communist court showed mercy and changed its verdict from the death penalty to life in prison.[45] Frequent rescue missions by Dr. Kamiński coupled with his open defiance of the local Communist authorities in his native Przedbórz instilled in the local population a great admiration for the physician. As a Catholic priest put it, "although they know he is a Jew, he enjoys the respect of the population... He is a noble man."[46]

In November 1948, a military court in Warsaw sentenced to death Captain Władysław Siła-Nowicki, a prominent Christian democrat and an officer of the AK and WiN. His sentence was commuted to life imprisonment partly because of the intercession of a Jewish woman from Białystok. According to her affidavit,

I, *Barbara Łaczyńska, the daughter of Lejzor Ludwik Nowak and Sabina née Warenholc* hereby state, and I am ready to confirm this with an oath if the Authorities [sic] or Courts [sic] so demand, that between June 27, 1943, and the end of October 1944, I was hiding from the persecution of the Jewish population by the germans [sic] at the apartment of citizen Władysław Nowicki in Warsaw. I was employed by him as a nanny for his two small children. I had escaped from a transport of jews [sic] being deported to an unknown destination and *citizen Nowicki took me in upon my request and he knew very well about my Jewish origin.* However, he hid me at his place and arranged [false] documents for me under a Polish name. After the capitulation of Warsaw [following the Uprising of 1944], I remained with him and his family until December 1947. Throughout my stay in the household of citizen Nowicki, he always protected me and hid my Jewish origin from the germans [sic] and the administration of the building as well as from strangers. Both he and his family always treated me in the best and most cordial manner [emphasis in the original].[47]

Of course, Jewish assistance did not always bear positive fruit. Monsignor Paweł Dziubiński of Lublin was arrested by the Communists as an alleged "Nazi collaborator." Immediately, Krystyna Modrzewska, a daughter of a converted Jewish woman whom the priest had saved during the Nazi period, intervened on his behalf with his captors. However, because Modrzewska was a Home Army soldier who retained her independentist allegiances and anti-Communist views, her pleas fell on deaf ears.[48]

Certain Jews showed gratitude to their rescuers in other ways. In Warsaw Adam Glück, aka Głuchowski, arranged for the employment of his wartime benefactor, Zoja Nakoniecznikow, a blacklisted widow of Colonel Stanisław Nakoniecznikow ("Kmicic"), the erstwhile Commander-in-Chief of the NSZ. Julian Gojcherman, aka Dobrowolski, another Jewish man saved by the Nakoniecznikows, openly kept in touch with the family throughout the darkest times of Stalinist terror.[49] In a more prosaic manner, Shmercio Halpern, who became a manager of the distillery in Trembowla, Province of Tarnopol, "made a point of giving vodka to those Gentiles who had saved Jews," both Communists and anti-Communists.[50]

At times, pragmatism informed Jewish assistance to the independentists. For instance, the head of the Communist radio network in Poland, Wilhelm Billig, helped underground fighters although it is unclear whether any of his beneficiaries ever participated in rescuing Jews during the Nazi occupation. Nonetheless, Billig occasionally hired ex-Home Army soldiers (for instance Edmund Rudnicki) to take advantage of their expertise in broadcasting (since Communist experts were lacking), to help them legalize themselves under the proxy regime, and, at the same time, to undercut the strength of the anti-Soviet insurgency by luring them away from their underground existence.[51]

Finally, there were Jews who helped the independentists for financial reasons. At least once, altruism mixed with the desire for material gain. At his trial, Second Lieutenant Jerzy Karwowski ("Newada") of the NZW (National Military Union) received five consecutive death sentences. However, the defense lawyer Gross, who happened to be Jewish, filed an appeal. Meanwhile, after much travail, the sentenced man's sister, Alicja Karwowska-Sokołowska, located a Jewish woman who survived the war thanks to the Karwowskis and who immediately agreed to help her erstwhile saviors. During the final hearing, Neoma Żołądź, aka Anna Krawcewicz, testified that Karwowski and his family had selflessly rescued more than a dozen Jews during the Nazi occupation, including herself and her two brothers. The judges became visibly less stringent toward the accused. Meanwhile, the parents of Karwowski sold most of their possessions and turned the funds over to Gross to save their son. The lawyer kept some of the money for himself but gave most of it as a bribe to the presiding military judge Oswald Sznepf, who also happened to be Jewish. Karwowski's death sentence was commuted to life imprisonment.[52]

At other times, the material factor behind the assistance was much more straightforward. In January 1945, in Zakrzów near Lipno, the Province of Kielce, an NKVD unit disarmed and imprisoned a group of Home Army soldiers. However, following an interrogation, a Jewish major of the NKVD released his captives for a handsome bribe. According to Jerzy Lech Rolski ("Babinicz"), "this allowed us to avoid getting deported to the USSR."[53]

In Łódź, after a cruel interrogation and a mock trial, two soldiers of the NSZ received death sentences and several of their co-conspirators lengthy jail sentences. Their appeals for clemency were torpedoed by the leading secret policeman Nikolai Demko, aka Mieczysław Moczar, who was of Ruthenian background, and by the Director of the Legal Office of the Civilian Chancellery of the President of Poland, Izaak Klajnerman, who was of Jewish origin. "However, other Jews helped us, albeit taking a great deal of money for it," according to one of the imprisoned underground fighters. In particular, the Jewish lawyer Kneppel "managed to convince Major Leo Hochberg, who was the judge of the Supreme Military Court, and Major Rubin Szwajg, who was the deputy prosecutor with the Supreme Office of the Military Prosecutor, to lessen the sentences (including two death penalties [which were thus commuted])."[54]

It is impossible to determine at this stage whether the material factor behind Jewish assistance to the independentists was more frequent than the altruistic one. However, it is important to remember that in those times testifying before a Communist judge or interceding with the secret police on behalf of insurgents required an enormous amount of bravery. Casual contact with "fascists" and "reactionaries" exposed an ordinary citizen to Communist persecution and even a party apparatchik risked a great deal by showing kindness to the persecuted.[55] Although no evidence has been found yet that any Jew suffered because of his assistance to the Poles, the lethal specter of the Stalinist terror sufficed to make the danger palpable enough. The potential for punishment of the kind always existed. Despite the risk, some Jews assisted the independentists.[56] In fact, the independentists actively courted Jewish aid because they were convinced, with some justification, that Jewish Communists who handled their case in the secret police, judiciary, and civilian administration, where the appeals for clemency were reviewed, would lend their ears more willingly to the friendly Jewish witnesses than to the non-Communist Polish ones. It was desirable, if not outright life-saving, to be able to procure friendly Jewish witnesses at one's trial, or at least a second-hand testimony about one's saving Jews during Nazi times.[57]

The full extent and effectiveness of Jewish assistance are still unknown. In most cases the assistance rendered during the Soviet occupation followed a past rescue operation on the part of an independentist during the Nazi period. The number of such rescue operations carried out by NSZ members is noteworthy as it challenges the prevailing steretype. However, there also were a few instances of Jewish kindness without any previous obligation toward the Poles. Future research should concentrate on the question whether the assistance rendered is indicative of the existence of high level contacts and influence on the part of the Jews which the independentist Poles did not enjoy. Were the Jews successful in aiding the independentists because their contacts in the secret police and judiciary were Jews? Or is the effectiveness of Jewish assistance indicative of the state of mind of the Communist secret police and judiciary which viewed the anti-Communist transgressors as somehow less guilty if they could establish their pro-Jewish credentials? The available evidence seems to suggest that a combination of both factors allowed some Jews to assist a number of independentists successfully at a time of extreme peril.[58]

Notes

1   For a Jewish testimony where post-war relations with the Poles are described as rather neutral see Abraham Morgenstern, *Chortkov Remembered: The Annihilation of a Jewish Community* (Dumont, NJ: By the author, 1990) posted at <http://www. jewishgen.org/yizkor/Chortkova/Chortkov.html>. Likewise, although they expressed general concerns about hostility and violence in Poland, most Jewish returnees to Cracow, quoted by a scholar, do not report personal incidents of abuse by Poles. Instead, the reports of kindness mix with the accounts of indifference and hostility. See Brecher, *Schindler's Legacy*, 45, 93-94, 116-17, 136, 152, 172, 187. For data from Brwinów and Konin see Roma Elster, *28, rue Nowolipki (Varsovie 1939-1945)* (Aix-en-Provence: Alinea, 1993), 118-19; Issy Hahn, *A Life Sentence of Memories: Konin, Auschwitz, London* (London and Portland, OR: Valentine Mitchell, 2001), 141-54.

2   Later in Lublin, according to the memoir, the Poles turned hostile toward the Jews. See Gruber, *I Chose Life*, 155. However, the witness from Strzyżów does not report any hostility, even though he visited that town as late as July or August 1946: "We were received in town with politeness. The offices which we had visited to arrange the return of our home, did everything to alleviate the formalities as quickly as possible." The Jewish man and his niece slept at a house of a Christian friend, Dr. Adam Patryn, a member of the pre-war elite, who assisted Jews during the Nazi occupation and whose family even before the war opposed the anti-Jewish economic boycott. See Itzhok Berglass, "After the War and the Holocaust," in *Sefer Strizhuv*, Internet.

3   Nonetheless, the witness recalls rumors about other Jews being assassinated in the area. See Rudawski, *Mój obcy kraj?*, 145-63.

4   Sokolowski claims that after the initial period of friendliness, "over the next months, things changed. By the summer of 1946, Jewish people were afraid to go out in the evening. The [Polish] people were not being friendly. I wouldn't say all of them, but most weren't too nice to the Jewish people." See Moishe Sokolowski as told to David Nudelman and quoted in Bill Taylor, "Gentle Holocaust survivor finally tells story to family," *The Toronto Star*, 23 April 1995, A6.

5   See Bronowski, *They Were Few*, 42-43.

6   See Janina Ziemiańska, "Z Kresów do Nowego Jorku: Wspomnienia. Część 9," *Nasz Głos* [Brooklyn], 15 October 1999, 4.

7   See Michał Głowiński, *Czarne sezony* (Warszawa: Open, 1998), 134-35.

8   Morris Wyszogrod, *A Brush With Death: An Artist in the Death Camps* (Albany, NY: State University of New York Press, 1999), 217-23.

9   Alperovitz, *The Lomaz Book*, 62.

10   Frister, *The Cap or the Price of a Life*, 302.

11   During the war, Halpern and other Jews had been hiding in a bunker built by Stanisław Grocholski on his farmstead in Kolonia Hetmańska. Grocholski was a pre-war regimental colleague of Halpern and an underling of the local AK commander Hawryliszyn. See Jerzy Julian Szewczyński, *Nasze Kopyczyńce* (Malbork: Wydawnictwo Heldruk, 1995), 98.

12   Marian Bobolewski, interview by the author, Wrocław, 28 November 1994.

13   Shmuel Krakowski, *The War of the Doomed: Jewish Armed Resistance in Poland, 1942-1944* (New York and London: Holmes & Meier Publishers, Inc., 1984), 91-92 [afterward

The War of the Doomed]; Biuletyn informacyjny z działalności za lata 1990-1991 (Lublin: Związek Żołnierzy Narodowych Sił Zbrojnych Okręg Lublin, 1992), 21 [afterward *Biuletyn*]; Jerzy Saganowski, interview by the author, Kraśnik, 12 August 1993.

14 Siemaszko, *Narodowe*, 206; Leszek Żebrowski, interview by the author, 12 July 2000. Other Jews who fought with the NSZ during the Warsaw Uprising include Calel Perechodnik, who served in the "Neda"-"Kosa" company of the NSZ-AK "Chrobry II" unit, Feliks Pisarewski-Parry, who served in Major Mieczysław Osmólski's ("Kozłowski") NSZ unit after being freed by them from Pawiak prison, and Dr. Roman Born-Borstein, who headed the medical services for "Chrobry II". See Born-Bornstein, *Powstanie Warszawskie*, 77-78; Feliks Pisarewski-Parry, *Orły i reszki* (Warszawa: Iskra, 1984), 61-65.

15 Shlomo Wolkowicz, *Das Grab bei Zloczow: Geschichte meines Überlebens, Galizien 1939-1945* (Berlin: Wichern-Verlag, 1996), 134-35.

16 Irene Tomaszewski and Tecia Werbowski, *Żegota: The Rescue of Jews in Wartime Poland* (Montreal: Price-Patterson Ltd., 1994), 114 [afterward *Żegota*]. Second revised edition of this work was published as *Żegota: The Council for Aid to Jews in Occupied Poland, 1942-1945* (Montreal: Price-Patterson Ltd., 1999), 107-108.

17 Felicja Nowak, *My Star: Memoirs of a Holocaust Survivor* (Toronto: Polish Canadian Publishing Fund, 1996), 155.

18 Charlota Frank-Oltramare to Bolesław Bierut, no date [1947] (a copy in my collection).

19 Jerzy Kozarzewski, "W imię pojednania," *Gazeta Wyborcza*, 26 March 1993, 13; Fijałkowska, *Borejsza i Różański*, 190; Urbankowski, *Czerwona msza*, 364; ibid., idem, 2nd ed., 2: 296-97. A leftist pundit incorrectly claimed that, to save the NSZ man, the poet had lied to the secret police about the assistance rendered to his mother, Adela Tuwim. The pundit must have confused Kozarzewski with Mirosław Ostromęcki, who indeed was helped by Tuwim without any pior obligations. See Ryszard Marek Groński, "Piętro wyżej," *Polityka*, 9 October 1999, 85; and see below.

20 Herzog, *And Heaven*, 305.

21 Wiesław Chrzanowski, *Pół wieku polityki, czyli rzecz o obronie czynnej* (Warszawa: Inicjatywa Wydawnicza "Ad Astra," 1997), 158 [afterward *Pół wieku*].

22 The *spiritus movens* behind the operation to save Chrzanowski was Celina Broniewska, a close relative of the erstwhile Commander-in-Chief of the NSZ, General Zygmunt Broniewski ("Bogucki"). She was also friendly with top leaders of the pre-war populist movement (having sheltered Stefan Korboński, the last civilian head the Polish Underground State) and, apparently, with Jewish politicians, most likely because she assisted Jews during the Nazi occupation. See Chrzanowski, *Pół wieku*, 84, 140, 215-16; Stefan Korboński, *Fighting Warsaw: The Story of the Polish Underground State, 1939-1945* ([New York:] Minerva Press, 1968), 63.

23 The Soviets arrested Sommerstein in November 1939 in Lwów because he had been a deputy in Poland's parliament (Sejm) before the war. According to a Soviet dispatch of December 1944, the NKVD suspected Sommerstein of being a "British agent." During the Nazi occupation Bieńkowski was also active in the AK's Council for Aid to Jews (*Żegota*). See Don Levin, *The Lesser of Two Evils: East European Jewry under Soviet Rule, 1939-1941* (Philadelphia and Jerusalem: The Jewish Publication Society, 1995), 260; Cariewskaja, *Teczka specjalna*, 147-49; Raport Kalskiego — 510/W [Witolda Bieńkowskiego ("Kalski")], 28 June 1945, in *Dokumenty* 1 (January 1993): 81 [afterward "Raport"].

24 N.N. Shneidman, *Jerusalem of Lithuania: The Rise and Fall of Jewish Vilnius. A Personal Perspective* (Oakville, ON and Buffalo, NY: Mosaic Press, 1998), 138.

25 Kurek, *Zaporczycy*, 246.

26 See Schemat polskiego podziemia (Delegatura Rządu) sporządzony przez NKGB Litewskiej SSR, 6 August 1945, in Wołkonowski, *Okręg Wileński*, a photostatic copy at the end of the book, no page number; Marek Chodakiewicz, "Chodakiewiczowa Irena (1912-1979), pseud. 'Irena,'" *Wileńskie Rozmaitości: Towarzystwo Miłośników Wilna i Ziemi Wileńskiej-Oddział w Bydgoszczy*, no. 6 (32) (November-December 1995): 50-51.

27 The incident occurred in 1952 in connection with a trial of several NSZ soldiers during which Szucki testified as a friendly witness. Currently, Dr. Szucki is the chairman of the Union of the Soldiers of the NSZ. He is still very grateful to Parnas, who only recently has learned the truth. See Bohdan Szucki, interview by the author, 15 June 1993, Lublin.

28 Dr. Klukowski was arrested first in 1948 and then in 1953. He was released in 1956 but died in 1959. The UB shot his adopted son, Tadeusz Klukowski, in 1952. Tadeusz was a member of the WiN and, later, "Kraj." Surrounded by the UB, he perished in a firefight together with his superior Zenon Tomasz Sobota ("Tomaszewski"). See Zygmunt Klukowski, *Dziennik 1944-1945* (Lublin: Oficyna Wydawnicza Fundacji Solidarności Regionu Środkowowschodniego, 1990), 15 [afterward *Dziennik*], which was translated as *Red Shadow: A Physician's Memoir of the Soviet Occupation of Eastern Poland, 1944-1956* (Jefferson, NC: McFarland & Company, 1997); Urbankowski, *Czerwona msza*, 2nd ed., 2: 489; Jerzy Szwede, interview by the author, Palo Alto, CA, 21 April 1998. For a description of Dr. Klukowski by a Jewish witness see Devora Fleischer, "On the Personality of Dr. [Zygmunt] Klukowski," in *Book of Memory to the Jewish Community of Shebreshin* [Sefer Zikaron le-kebilat Shebreshin], ed. by Don Shuval (Haifa: Association of Former Inhabitants of Shebreshin [Szczebrzeszyn] in Israel and the Diaspora, 1984).

29 Piotrowski, *Poland's Holocaust*, 342 n. 326; Tomaszewski and Werbowski, *Żegota*, 104; ibid., idem, 2nd ed., 98.

30 During the Nazi occupation, Bartoszewski was involved with a conservative Catholic underground group, Front for the Rebirth of Poland (Front Odrodzenia Polski – FOP) led by Zofia Kossak-Szczucka. In addition to saving Jews, he cooperated closely with several clandestine right-wing youth organizations, including a few connected to the NSZ. He survived Auschwitz; joined the Home Army; fought in the Warsaw Uprising of 1944; volunteered for the secret anti-Communist group NIE (Independence); and, subsequently, became active in the populist PSL. Having emerged from jail in 1956, Bartoszewski involved himself with liberal Catholic dissidents and was recognized as Righteous Gentile by Yad Vashem. In the early 1990s he served as Poland's Foreign Minister. See Jerzy Morawski, "Życie prawdziwe, życie ponumerowane," *Rzeczpospolita*, 16-17 February 2002; Witold Bereś and Jerzy Skoczylas, "Władysław Bartoszewski – świadek epoki," *Gazeta Wyborcza*, 15 February 2002; Marek Jan Chodakiewicz, "Hitler nie pobłogosławił: 55. Rocznica powstania Narodowych Sił Zbrojnych," *Rzeczpospolita*, 20-21 September 1997.

31 Irena Gut lives in the US and is recognized by Yad Vashem as a Righteous Gentile. See Irene Gut Opdyke, *Into the Flames: The Life Story of A Righteous Gentile* (San Bernardino, CA: The Borgo Press, 1992), 139-63; Michael Posner, "A Saviour's Story," *The Globe and Mail* [Toronto], 11 December 1999, D6; Irena Gut, interview by the author, 15 April 2000.

32 Cała, "Mniejszość żydowska," in Madajczyk, *Mniejszości narodowe w Polsce*, 261.

33 Magdalena Grochowska, "Lista Sendlerowej," *Gazeta Wyborcza*, 8 June 2001. Sendler also miraculously survived her imprisonment by the Gestapo. See Irena Sendlerowa ("Jolanta"), "Ci, którzy pomagali Żydom: Wspomnienia z czasów okupacji hitlerowskiej," *BŻIH*, no. 45-46 (January-June 1963): 234-47; Tomaszewski and Werbowski, *Żegota*, 61-65; ibid., idem, 2nd ed., 59-63.

34 Zaświadczenie z 6.VII.1946, L.dz.675/46 S.G., AŻIH.

35 After serving time in a Communist jail, Kemnitz settled in Canada after 1956. See Edward Kemnitz to Vera Prausnitz, 25 September 1981, YVA, Departament of Righteous Gentiles, file 3211 (a copy in the collection of Professor Szymon Rudnicki, Warsaw); Edward Marcin Kemnitz in *Out of the Inferno: Poles Remember the Holocaust*, ed. by Richard C. Lukas (Lexington, KY: The University of Kentucky Press, 1989), 87-89; Tomaszewski and Werbowski, *Żegota*, 125-27; ibid., idem, 2nd ed., 116-18; Jan Żaryn, "O rzetelny rachunek prawdy," *Słowo: Dziennik katolicki*, 19 July 1993, 10; Żebrowski, *NSZ dokumenty*, 3: 70-71, 90-91, 140-42, 198.

36 The sentencing occurred on August 6, 1946. Modzelewski was released in 1956. He and his mother Zofia were recognized as "Righteous Gentiles" on November 26, 1991. See Sebastian Bojemski, "Pisane krwią bohaterów," *Nasz Dziennik*, 22 August 2000, 12; Leszek Żebrowski to the author, 28 March 1999.

37 In January 1985 Nowiński, his wife Janina, and their children, Danuta and Wacław, received their awards in Jerusalem. The Nowiński's "hid in their apartment the Jewish family Rapaport, Dr. Berlowicz, and Janina Penska. None of this was for material gain; they were motivated solely by their conscience and their humane attitude to their fellow men." They also assisted Alexander Bronowski, who, before a Communist commission, "attested to his patriotic [i.e. Nowiński's] and humane attitude to the persecuted Jews." See Bronowski, *They Were Few*, 33; and Adam Hempel, *Pogrobowcy klęski: Rzecz o policji "granatowej" w Generalnym Gubernatorstwie, 1939-1945* (Warszawa: Państwowe Wydawnictwo Naukowe, 1990), 268.

38 The poet Julian Tuwim and Adam Cardinal Sapieha appealed to the Communists on behalf of the NSZ man as well. See Akta sprawy Mirosława Ostromęckiego i towarzyszy, Wojskowy Sąd Rejonowy, Archiwum Historyczne Miasta Stołecznego Warszawy, file Sr 78/47 [afterward WSR, AHMSW]; "Pamięci Mirosława Ostromęckiego," *Szczerbiec* [Lublin], no. 10 (January 2000): 74-90.

39 Akta sprawy Antoniego Symonowicza i towarzyszy, WSR, AHMSW, file 23/46; and Sebastian Bojemski, interview by the author, Santa Barbara, 12 July 2000.

40 See the testimony of Apolinary Kozubski of Białozórka in *Śladami ludobójstwa na Wołyniu*, vol. 2: *Okrutna przestroga*, ed. by Leon Karłowicz and Leon Popek (Lublin: Polihymnia, 1998), 2: 182.

41 Sobalkowski Szczepan. Akta w sprawie Szczepana Sobalkowskiego, 1948-1956, AAN, Prokuratura Generalna, file 17/332.

42 Father Pirożyński had to flee Warsaw in May 1942 because he was sought by the Gestapo, who had learned about his involvement with the independentists. After the Soviet entry, the priest returned underground in October 1948. He was arrested in September 1953 and sentenced to a year in jail. He was rearrested in May 1958 and remained incarcerated for two years. See *Słownik polskich teologów katolickich, 1918-1981*, vol. 6, ed. by Ludwik Grzebień (Warszawa: Akademia Teologii Katolickiej, 1983), 6: 685.

43 Leszek Żebrowski, "'Odpowiedź' prof. Krzysztofa Dunin-Wąsowicza, czyli o potrzebie dekomunizacji nauki," *Zeszyty Historyczne WiN-u* [Kraków] 9 (December 1996): 284-85. Lt. Wyczółkowski was the adjutant of the district commander Lieutenant Colonel Stanisław Miodoński ("Sokół"). See the letter of Mariusz Bechta to MJCh, 28 February 2001.

44 Odpis, Wyrok z dnia 16 stycznia 1956 r., Sąd Wojewódzki w Stalinogrodzie w Wydziale IV Karnym, sygn. akt IV K 130/55 (a copy in my collection); Leszek Żebrowski, interview by the author, 4 May 1998.

45 See Odpis, Julian Kamiński do Pana Prezydenta Rzeczpospolitej w Warszawie, Przedbórz, 10 May 1947 (a copy in my collection); Kołaciński, *Między młotem*, 234-36; Siemaszko, *Narodowe*, 156-57; Bohun-Dąbrowski, *Byłem dowódcą Brygady*, 147-48; Leszek Żebrowski, interview by the author, 5 April 1998.

46 The letter of Father Zygmunt Maj, Ubly, Michigan, to Władysław Kołaciński, Chicago, Illinois, 12 September 1962, a copy in CLŻ.

47 Pająk, *Zaporowcy*, 239. It was also helpful that Nowicki was a nephew of the wife of Ignacy Dzierżyński, the brother of the founder of the Soviet secret police, Feliks Dzierżyński (Dzerzhinsky). Ibid., 239-40.

48 Modrzewska, *Trzy razy Lublin*, 93-94.

49 Henryk Nakoniecznikow, interview by Leszek Żebrowski, 21 July 1996, CLŻ.

50 Halpern, *Darkness and Hope*, 144.

51 Zawadzka-Wetz, *Refleksje*, 39, 53; Kisielewski, *Dzienniki*, 48.

52 Jerzy Karwowski was eventually amnestied and died in 2000. During the Nazi occupation he was a cadet officer of the NSZ, fighting part time in a partisan unit in the county of Łomża. The Karwowskis hid Żołądź and her brothers after their successful escape from a transport either to Treblinka or Majdanek. Without any remuneration, the Karwowskis also fed a group of Jews hiding in a bunker near their farmstead. Following the entry of the Soviet Army into Poland, Karwowski commanded the Emergency Special Action of the National Military Union (NZW) in the Olsztyn region. See Notaryzowane zeznanie Naomy Żołądź (Anny Krawcewicz), Wyrok w sprawie Jerzego Karwowskiego, Wojskowy Sąd Rejonowy w Olsztynie, 20 June 1949, file SR 165/49 (a copy in my collection); Wąsowski and Żebrowski, *Żołnierze*, 174; Bohdan Łukaszewicz, *Wojskowy Sąd Rejonowy w Olsztynie 1946-1955: Szkice do monografii* (Olsztyn: Ośrodek Badań Naukowych im. W. Kętrzyńskiego, 2000); Leszek Żebrowski to MJCh, 8 and 9 January 2001; Tomasz Grotowicz, "Oswald Sznepf," *Nasza Polska*, 4 December 2001.

53 Jerzy Lech Rolski ps. "Babinicz," "Relacja," *Tropem zbrodni stalinowskich: Materiały Ogólnopolskiego Sympozjum "Zbrodnie stalinowskie wobec Polski," Chańcza 5-7 października 1990*, ed. by Maciej Andrzej Zarębski (Staszów: Staszowskie Towarzystwo Kulturalne, 1992), 159-61. Afterward, following a denunciation by a Polish Communist, in April 1945, Rolski was arrested by the UB but managed to escape from a town jail in Jędrzejów. He was captured in January 1947 in Jelenia Góra, where his adversaries included three Communists allegedly of Jewish origin: a prosecutor, the county UB chief Nowak, and his deputy Baumgarten. However, although Jewish Communists were among his chief tormentors, Rolski befriended a Jewish prisoner who was also a victim of the Communists.

54 Lech Maria Wojciechowski, "Jak Moczar chciał zrobić ze mnie agenta," *Myśl Polska*, 24 August 1997, 10.

55 For example, during the Nazi occupation, Father Jerzy Mirewicz was involved with the AK and Żegota. He saved numerous Jews, including 17 Jewish prisoners from the infamous Lipowa sub-camp of the Majdanek concentration camp. Only one of them dared to visit the priest to express his gratitude. "In 1944, when at least three of them returned to Lublin with the liberation forces of the Russians, Mirewicz was disappointed to learn that two of those whom he had rescued wanted nothing to do with him lest they be exiled to Siberia by the Lublin Government on the suspicion of having collaborated with a sympathizer of the exiled Polish Government." See Vincent A. Lapomarda, *The Jesuits and the Third Reich* (Lewiston/Queenston and Lampeter: The Edwin Mellen Press, 1989), 129-31.

56 Jewish rescuers also helped persons politically unaffiliated who were tried by the Stalinists. For example, in 1947, Ruchla Chęcińska testified favorably on behalf of a peasant who had been coerced to participate in a "Jew-hunt" by his neighbors in 1943. His sentence was subsequently quite lenient. See Kałowska, *Uciekać, aby żyć*, 247-49.

57 This continued well beyond 1947. One of the last insurgents, Andrzej Kiszka ("Dąb") of the NOW-AK and NZW, was captured by the Communist police in his bunker in the Janów Forest in the Province of Lublin on January 31, 1961. At his trial in 1962 a lawyer for the defense attempted to secure a lenient sentence for the insurgent by reminding the court that "according to the witness Franciszek Bednarz... Kiszka had hidden the jew [sic] Nochema without the knowledge and consent of his parents. This fact is attested to by the accused Pawęzka, who had been informed about it by a jew [sic] named Hela." Kiszka received 15 years. See Pismo mecenasa Leszka Hofmana do SN Izby Karnej, no date [1962], in Protokół rozprawy, Wyrok w sprawie karnej Andrzeja Kiszki, 25 July 1962, Sąd Wojewódzki IV Wydziału Karnego w Lublinie, file IV, K. 80/62, p. 230 (a copy in my collection); Dionizy Garbacz, "Leśniczy," *Sztafeta* [Stalowa Wola], 11 August 1994, 4; Bogusław Kopacz, "Ostatni oddział, ostatnia walka," *Tygodnik Nadwiślański*, 12 August 1994.

58 Of course, the examples cited above cannot be taken to constitute the rule. They can be countered with many cases where individuals of Jewish origin serving the regime carried out their duties rigorously to the detriment of Polish patriots. For example, as Norman Davies points out, on the basis of evidence supplied by Jewish participants, in 1945 every single commander but one and three-quarters of the local commissioned officers of the Communist Security Office in Upper Silesia were of Jewish origin; that ex-Nazi camps and prisons were refilled with totally innocent people, among them Polish and German civilians as well as members of the Home Army; and that torture, starvation, sadistic beatings, and murder were routine. See Norman Davies, *Europe: A History* (Oxford and New York: Oxford University Press, 1996), 1022-23. Bishop Czesław Kaczmarek of Kielce was arrested by the UB Colonel Józef Światło, who was Jewish. Tortured cruelly, the bishop confessed to being an American spy, a Nazi collaborator, and an instigator of the Kielce pogrom (in reality, he was neither of these and he was also absent from Kielce during the pogrom). During the bishop's trial, following the traditional Stalinist pattern of "defense," his lawyer, Mieczysław Maślanko, who was Jewish, worked very closely with the prosecutor and the UB, trying to coerce Kaczmarek to confess his "crimes." The bishop received a lengthy jail sentence but was fully rehabilitated after the Stalinists fell from power in 1956. See Paul, "Church," in *Kielce*, 108-109. Another high profile case with heavy involvement of Communists of Jewish origin concerned General August Emil Fieldorf ("Nil") of the Home Army, who masterminded the assassination of SS-General Franz Kutschera, the head of the Nazi police in Warsaw. Fieldorf's gallantry during and after the war was

exemplary. He was seized by the UB in 1950. The warrant for his arrest was issued *in blanco* after the fact by the ever-obedient Colonel Fajga Mindla Danielak, aka Helena Wolińska-Brus, of the State Prosecutor's Office. In 1952, prosecutor Beniamin Wajsblech falsely accused Fieldorf of "murdering Communists" during the war and collaborating with the Gestapo. The judge Maria Zand, aka Gurowska, sentenced the general to death. The judges Emil Mertz, Gustaw Auscaler (who later emigrated to Israel), and Igor Andrejew heard the appeal and, in harmony with the arguments of prosecutor Paulina Kernowa, upheld the death penalty. Fieldorf was executed by shooting. After 1956 he was fully exonerated. There is still no satisfactory monograph of the Fieldorf case. See "Investigation against Ms. Helena Wolińska-Brus," posted at <http://www.ipn.gov.pl/index_eng.html>; Maria Fieldorf and Leszek Zachuta, *Generał "Nil": August Fieldorf* (Warsaw: PAX, 1993); Tadeusz A. Płużański, "Prześladowczyni 'Nila' żyje w Anglii," *Życie Warszawy*, 8 October 1998; Tadeusz A. Płużański, "Czy dojdzie do ekstradycji Heleny Wolińskiej?" *Tygodnik Solidarność*, 15 June 2001; and for an extreme interpretation see Henryk Pająk and Stanisław Żochowski, *Rządy zbirów 1940–1990* (Lublin: Retro, 1996), 212–15. Also the independentist rank-and-file often faced Communist adversaries of Jewish origin. An erstwhile cadet officer of the AK, and later a naval officer, who was falsely imprisoned in 1952, as an "English spy" in Polish merchant marine, Tadeusz Jędrzejkiewicz was sentenced to death after a mock trial in 1953. Jędrzejkiewicz claims that three of his judges were Communists of Jewish origin and the fourth one was a Soviet officer: "Adamski and Bogucki, who later escaped to Israel; Stefan Michnik, who left for Sweden in 1968 and changed his name to Karol Szwedowicz, and one more, who later escaped to the Soviet Union." See Marek Domagalski, "Świadkowie umierają, protokoły zostają," *Rzeczpospolita*, 9 November 2001. There were also cases of blatant ingratitude. During the Nazi occupation, at the request of her university friend, Stefan Kurowski, who was Jewish, Romana Gokieli rescued his nephew Marcin Król, who hid at her apartment. Kurowski and another Jewish man, Batawia, visited Gokieli frequently for food. After the war, Kurowski joined the Communists and became the Chief Prosecutor of Poland. Meanwhile, the rescuer's brother, Witold Gokieli ("Ryszard"), a high-ranking AK officer, was arrested by the secret police and held without any charges for five years. Throughout his incarceration, Gokieli's family begged Kurowski and his Jewish Communist subordinates who were in charge of the investigation to release the AK officer. The request was denied for a long time. Finally, "the case was dropped after five years and [my] grandfather died a year and a half after his release. He was only 51 years old and before his incarceration he was very healthy." See Dariusz Witold Kulczyński, "Zakończenie dyskusji," *Nowy Kurier: Polish-Canadian Independent Courier*, 15-30 April 2001, 1, 4. On August 5, 1944, a Home Army unit liberated 348 Jews from a concentration camp "Gęsiówka" in Warsaw. Many of the liberated joined the unit, where they fought together with the Poles against the Nazis during the Warsaw Uprising. After the Uprising, one of the Jewish soldiers allegedly joined the Communist secret police and unsuccessfully searched for his erstwhile commanding officers, including Lieutenant Bolesław Stańczyk ("Xen"), to arrest them. See "348 Żydów i jeden order: Z ostatnim dowódcą harcerskiego batalionu 'Zośka,' por. Bolesławem Stańczykiem pd. 'Xen,' rozmawia Ryszard Krzyżanowski," *Dziennik Związkowy* [Chicago], 7-9 September 2001.

X

THE PROBLEM OF STATISTICS

The sources analyzed in this study yielded a minimum of 253 and a maximum of 615 Jews who were killed in Poland between 1944 and 1947. Nonetheless, if other sources are taken under consideration, it can be estimated that the number of Jewish victims was as high as 700.[1] This estimate is much lower than the current scholarly consensus would allow.

Communist propaganda, individual testimonies, the failure to understand Jewish-insurgent relations in their proper context as well as a virtual lack of any in-depth research adversely influenced the study of statistics of the Jewish victims. Basing themselves on the extant sources even some respectable scholars believe that as many as 2,500 Jews perished in Poland after 1944. How reliable are the official figures? According to a contemporary account in *The American Jewish Year Book*,

> On April 16, 1945, the Polish [i.e. Communist] embassy in Moscow accused the Polish Home Guard [i.e. AK] of having killed within the past four weeks about 150 Jews. The murders occurred in Lublin, Siedlice [sic Siedlce], Sokolow [Sokołów], Jaroslaw [Jarosław] and several towns in the Warsaw and Lublin districts. This charge was substantiated by a public protest of Dr. [Emil] Sommerstein, and similar accusations of collaboration with the Nazis were corroborated by the Association of Jewish Partisans in Poland in a Yiddish broadcast from Lublin.[2]

However, on May 11, 1945, the leader of the Jewish community in Poland Emil Sommerstein stated in fact that "during the last quarter [*kwartał*]," that is in January, February, and March 1945, "100 [Jewish] persons perished."[3] Thus, the Communist propaganda exaggerated Jewish losses several-fold just for the period between March 15 and April 15, 1945.

Unfortunately, this misinformation quickly found its way into respectable scholarship. For instance, in 1953 Bernard Weinryb asserted that "in March 1945 alone, 150 Jews were killed." However, Weinryb failed to stress that the data originated with the Communists, crediting only *The American Jewish Year Book* and the Jewish Telegraphic Agency as his sources. Nonetheless, Weinryb also drew on the data of the Central Committee of Polish Jews. According to these figures, "during 1945, 350 Jews were killed; by April 1946 it was estimated that over 800 Jews had been killed."[4] In other words, Weinryb claimed that 450 Jews lost their lives to violence between January and April 1946. However, *The American Jewish Year Book* noted that "about 400 Jews had been murdered in Poland in 1945, while in the first three months of 1946, the toll of anti-Semitic assaults reached *fifty* [emphasis added]." This contention is based on an April 12, 1946, radio address from Poland by the far-left Zionist leader Adolf Berman, who was the brother of Jakub Berman, the head of the Communist secret police.[5] In its next edition, *The American Jewish Year Book* clarified that "according to reliable data, between January 1 and May 4, 1946, 54 Jews were killed by Polish bandits."[6]

Even without this definite clarification, it should have been difficult to believe that fewer Jews (350) were killed during the period of the most intensive insurgent offensive of 1945 than in the spring of 1946, when the fighting was much less intense (450). My own research suggests a correlation between Jewish losses and the intensity of the anti-Soviet rising. This does not necessarily mean that the insurgents were responsible for most of the killings but, rather, that the fighting between the Communists and the independentists wreaked so much havoc that it resulted in the breakdown of law and order, thus creating conditions propitious to abusing and killing anyone, including Jews. The anarchic conditions of rampant lawlessness, where anyone could be targeted, were not synonymous with any sort of an anti-Semitic killing campaign directed either from above or springing from below.

At any rate, the number of victims, including the Jewish ones, of the period between 1944 and 1947 proved quite difficult to present with any accuracy. Until recently most scholars settled comfortably on approximations culled from the unreliable sources mentioned above. Martin Gilbert estimated that between January and December 1945, 350 Jews were killed in Poland. Lucy Dawidowicz believed that between March 1945 and June 1946 about 800 Jews lost their lives. Both scholars based themselves on *The American Jewish Yearbook* and Weinryb.[7] Citing a Communist government memorandum, Yisrael Gutman and Shmuel Krakowski estimated that between July 1944 and July 1947 "as many as 1,000 Jews" died violently, including "351 Jews [who] were murdered between November 1944 and December 1945."[8] Thus, the Israeli scholars improbably suggest that the bulk of the Jewish casualties was sustained when the Polish insurrection was on the wane, and, thus, the situation in the country more stable, that is between January 1946 and July 1947.

The military intelligence expert Michael Checinski (Michał Chęciński), who left Poland after the anti-Semitic purge in the Communist Party in 1968, claims that "at least in 115 localities 1,500 Jews lost their lives in Poland between the time of liberation [i.e. the Soviet entry in the summer of 1944] and the summer of 1947."[9] Checinski relied on the estimates presented by another refugee from Communist anti-Semitism, Lucjan Dobroszycki. This historian also based himself on both Communist propaganda and imprecise Jewish estimates. His figures have been embraced by such disparate authorities as the sociologist Jan Tomasz Gross, political scientist Jaff Schatz, journalist Mark Kurlansky, historian Norman Davies, researcher Joanna Michlic-Coren and others.[10] Michael Steinlauf averred that "from 1944 to 1947 between fifteen hundred and two thousand Jews were murdered, the great majority specifically because they were Jews."[11] However, according to a study published recently under the auspices of the Mordechaj Anielewicz Center for the Research and Teaching of the History and Culture of the Jews in Poland at the Institute of History of the University of Warsaw, "it is estimated that from 1944 to 1947 between 1,500 and 2,000 Jews were killed. *That number includes the victims of attacks on the members of the PPR [i.e. the Communist Party] of Jewish nationality carried out for political reasons*" (emphasis added).[12] Finally, while embracing the approximation of 1,500 victims, Jan Tomasz Gross concludes that "given the general level of disorder at the time and the fact that many victims were not killed as Jews but as targets of political violence or armed robbery, only a fraction of their deaths can be attributed to anti-Semitism."[13]

While not disputing the presence of Communists among the Jewish victims of violence in Poland, David Engel flatly rejected the approximations of Dobroszycki (1,500) and Gutman (1,000), stating that "both estimates seem high."[14] Engel compiled detailed tables of "Jewish deaths by violence" based on Communist and Jewish documents. According to him, between September 1944 and September 1946, 327 Jews met with violent death, including 189 who were killed between March and August 1945. These are not complete records, though.[15] As Engel put it, at present "it does not seem possible to determine with any reasonable degree of certainty the total number of Jews killed by Poles in the years following the liberation."[16]

Nevertheless, Engel attempted to compare the incidence of Jewish deaths with the incidence of deaths of Polish supporters of the proxy regime. Relying on a dated Communist compilation, he claims that between September 1944 and December 1947, 6,475 ethnic Poles were killed by the insurgents. Moreover, Engel discovered that "to be sure, the high point of Polish-Polish violence, in the Spring of 1945, coincided roughly with the period of greatest Jewish exposure, and the moderate swell in deaths of government supporters during the spring of 1946 was matched to some extent by a similar rise in the number of Jewish casualties."[17] Yet he questions his own findings because in certain months, for instance in March 1945, more Jews died than Polish supporters of the regime. Therefore "it appears highly unlikely that the relative peak in Jewish deaths noted in this month can be taken as reflecting simply a knee-jerk association of Jews with Communists."[18] This may be a valid observation to the extent that, at this time, common banditry was rampant and a number of Jews as well as many Poles were indeed killed in the course of robberies in the spring of 1945.

Nonetheless, there are some problems with the data used by Engel. First, it is unclear whether Engel calculated the losses only among persons who identified themselves explicitly and openly as members of the Jewish community. Were Communists of Jewish origin excluded from the tally? If not, including them should not increase the number of victims significantly. On the one hand, many Communists of Jewish origin, in the terror apparatus in particular, were higher-ups whose jobs kept them out of direct combat. On the other hand, as the liberal scholar Andrzej Paczkowski has suggested, the overall Communist combat losses are probably overblown. This concerns the security forces in particular. For instance, the secret police in the Province of Silesia counted drunk driving accidents among its personnel as deaths in battle.[19] If in reality fewer policemen died at the hands of the insurgents than it was officially reported, and if the overall statistics for death are correct, that means that the civilian victims of the insurgents probably constitute a higher proportion of all deaths than is generally accepted. Simply, perhaps as during the Nazi occupation, the underground killed those who were the closest to the guerrillas, thus constituting the greatest threat, real or imagined, and the one that could be attacked with the least danger. This, of course, also affected Jews.

The total number of civilian victims currently ascribed to the insurgents, however, ought to be revised downward because the victims of common banditry have not been sufficiently taken into consideration. For instance, the data for the period between July 1, 1945 and February 1,

1946, for the Province of Kielce shows that in the course of 840 bandit attacks 135 people were killed, including 5 Jews. There were also 24 secret policemen (UB) and 17 regular militiamen (MO) among the casualties.[20] However, no distinction is made between political assassinations and common murders and the ethnic background of the assassinated security personnel is not provided. Still, because mostly lower ranks were involved in combat, it is doubtful that policemen of Jewish origin constituted the majority killed. After all, NKVD documents and other sources quoted earlier in this work indicate that, after the initial period, Jewish Communists occupied mostly leadership ranks and, therefore, very likely eschewed direct combat. Thus, all these factors suggest that it is premature to talk about the overrepresentation of Jewish victims of the insurgents (and maybe even of common bandits).

Moreover, Engel wrongly assumes that, aside from Jews, the insurgents killed only Poles. In fact, at least initially, perhaps the single highest category of people who died at the hands of the insurgents were Soviets. According to General Sergei S. Shatilov, the head of the Military Mission of the USSR in Poland, between July and December 1944, more than 300 Soviet commissioned officers alone died in the fight against the insurgents in just three provinces of "People's Poland" (Lublin, Rzeszów, and Białystok).[21] Although no precise statistics for Soviet losses are available for the spring of 1945, the NKVD reported that in operations in the same area, between March 21 and April 16, 1945, "more than 900 bandits were killed and 1,300 captured."[22] Presumably, the insurgents fought back and killed at least 100 Soviets, in addition to 27 Polish Communists listed by Engel for March and April.[23] This alone places the Jewish losses of 49 for that period in the more congruous light of "knee-jerk anti-Communism." Of course, further research is needed because there indeed are some discrepancies.

Engel's data for November 1945 show no Jewish deaths. However, an NKVD report mentions that on November 19, 1945, unknown perpetrators shot three Jews execution-style in Kraków. Another Soviet document for the period between November 10 and November 30, 1945, claims that the Communist side lost 156 men, among them Soviets, Polish security men, party members, and civilian supporters. The insurgent side had 113 killed and 1,573 arrested. It is unknown whether the aforementioned three Jewish men were counted among the pro-Communist casualties for November. However, it is clear that this period saw a relative lull in the fighting and the shift of the Jewish population to large cities and to western Poland. The data for the spring of 1946, when the Communists stepped up their anti-insurgent operations, again show a certain congruence between killing Communist supporters and Jews by the insurgents. Whereas Engel listed 71 Jews killed between January and April 1946, the NKVD reported overall Communist losses at 836 killed, mostly civilian, ethnically Polish supporters of the proxy regime. At the time, the insurgents suffered 596 killed and 10,950 arrested.[24]

Nonetheless, some data presented by Engel was confirmed in this work, some revised, but much remains unverified. Our own cumulative estimate based on the material presented follows.

Table 8
Jewish victims of violence:
A cumulative estimate by chapter[25]

	minimum	maximum
Introduction	4	5
Chapter Five	1	1
Chapter Six	3	3
Chapter Seven	132	132
Chapter Eight	113	474
Total	253	615

The minimum of 253 concerns all fully confirmed Jewish deaths. The maximum of 615 includes 253 victims who have been fully verified and 358 whose fate requires more research. Some of them likely perished; others were just rumored to have been killed, usually by inflating the number of victims in any one case. Using our own and Engel's data, we can estimate that perhaps roughly between 350 and 500 Jewish civilians were killed in Poland from July 1944 to January 1947. The perpetrators were bandits, insurgents, and Soviet and Polish soldiers and policemen, including Communists. It is unclear if these statistics concern just the self-identified members of the Jewish community. However, it is obvious that the circumstances of their deaths have not been examined sufficiently. Therefore it is impossible to determine how many actual Communist sympathizers, free-lance informers, and police agents were among them. As far as secret police officers, militiamen, party activists, and government employees of Jewish origin are concerned, their losses can only be guessed at this point. It is not even known whether they were included by the Jewish community in its official statistics of deaths or whether they were counted separately by the Communists. Nonetheless, their numbers could not have been very high, perhaps between 50 and 100. After all, it seems that the Communists of Jewish extraction were prominent in the leadership posts on central and province levels. Therefore they were generally unaffected by violence in the countryside. However, because of the tricky issue of national consciousness and ethno-religious self-identification among Communists and secret policemen, the share of persons of Jewish origin killed within that group may be even larger.[26] *In sum, probably a minimum of 400 and a maximum of 700 Jews and persons of Jewish origin perished in Poland from July 1944 to January 1947.*

If only the minuscule size of the Jewish community in Poland is taken under the consideration, then perhaps it is true that Jews were somewhat overrepresented among victims of violence after 1944, but so too were they overrepresented, initially, in auxiliary positions in the Communist terror apparatus (Jewish self-defense, militia, and security) and, gradually, in the leadership positions of the proxy regime. Moreover, if each incidence of violence is judged individually, the size of Jewish casualties may take on a different significance. To anchor this in the context of the anti-Communist insurgency, it is not enough to calculate the losses on the side of the supporters of the proxy regime. To evaluate the "knee-jerk anti-Communism" of the insurgents, it is also necessary to consider the "frenzy and ferocity" of the Communist terror, as John Micgiel put it.[27]

Within the context of the Communist terror some persons of Jewish origin in self-defense or in revenge, acting independently or in concert with the Stalinists, denounced, abused, and despoiled at least 7,000 Poles, even killing some of them. Only a very rough estimate can be attempted without access to secret police records and without more openness from the perpetrators, the witnesses, and the victims.

Table 9
Jewish involvement against Poles: An estimate[28]

Poles	minimum	maximum
denounced	3,128	6,238
arrested	2,408	6,625
killed directly	63	125
caused to be killed	195	455

To stress, the above estimate is based only on the sources analyzed in this work and not on any groundless speculation about the alleged "Jewish responsibility" for all the actions of the security forces in Poland. The argument about the alleged collective "Jewish responsibility" is usually based on the fact that the chief supervisor of the secret police in Poland, Jakub Berman, along with many leaders of the terror apparatus, were of Jewish origin and that an active minority of Jews was involved with the proxy regime. Such a syllogism is plainly unfair, unscholarly, and patently anti-Semitic, because it would lay blame for Communism and its crimes collectively on "the Jews." This line of reasoning must be rejected because it was one's individual choices and deeds that ultimately mattered and not the person's ethno-religious background. Nonetheless, when assessing the larger topic of Polish-Jewish relations, we must remember that the violent actions of the active minority of the Jewish community, including prominent secret police leaders, were real enough. The guilty should not be absolved of any and all accountability and their actions cannot be ignored when assessing the conflict that pitted some Poles against some Jews, and vice versa. According to Władysław Bartoszewski (Junior),

> Most Poles particularly resent the application of this double standard to those Jewish individuals who were active in, and high ranking members of, the Communist Party, and especially of the security police. These are sometimes excused on the grounds that Communist ideology offered them hope of achieving equal status with the Gentile population and of living in a country free of anti-semitism where social justice and liberal ideals would prevail. It is also often suggested that the Jews, being more vulnerable because of their ethnic background, had no choice but to participate in the construction of the new order. This view is offensive both to the majority of the Jews who did not want to live under Communism and left Poland, and because it implies that different moral standards can be applied to judge Jewish and Gentile moral behaviour. It is also important to make a distinction here between those who supported and joined the Communist Party and even became its propagandists and activists for whatever misguided reason, and those who were directly involved in the security apparatus. The latter involved active participation in arrests and interrogations, and thus torture, deportations, and, in some instances, killing of the civilian population. One can treat the former cases with some sympathy and understanding, but it is not possible to excuse the latter. Whatever the conditions existing in Poland between 1945 and 1956, no one — Gentile or Jewish — can claim that

he or (very often) she *had* to be a member of the Stalinist political police or the judiciary and, for one reason or another, had no choice but to torture and kill their innocent political opponents. After all, no one looks for extenuating circumstances for ex-members of the Gestapo.[29] [emphasis in the original]

One of the most prominent leaders of the Jewish community in Poland, Stanisław Krajewski, explains that

The archetype of the Jews during the first ten years of the Polish People's Republic was generally perceived as an agent of the secret political police. It is true that under [Bolesław] Bierut and [Władysław] Gomułka (prior to 1948) the key positions in the Ministry of State Security were held by Jews or persons of Jewish background. It is a fact which cannot be overlooked, little known in the West and seldom mentioned by the Jews in Poland. Both prefer to talk about Stalin's anti-Semitism (the "doctors" plot, etc.). The machine of communist terror functioned in Poland in a manner similar to that used in other communist ruled countries in Europe and elsewhere.[30]

Krajewski also holds that

I disagree that the Jewish role in the 'communist past' was 'quite marginal'. The number and influence of Jewish communists in post-war Poland was so important that their role was far more than marginal. The challenge for Jews is to accept the fact that in the middle of this century Jews in Central and Eastern Europe were not only among the victims but also among the victimizers. In my view, the number and the quasi-religious character of some Jewish communists, for whom Stalin was the messiah, generate a Jewish share of moral responsibility.[31]

Still, violence by some Jews directed at Poles was just the tip of the iceberg. As mentioned earlier, from July 1944 to August 1945, at the initial stage of the Soviet occupation of the State of Poland, including the "Recovered Territories" acquired from Germany, between 20,000 and 50,000 people died. The victims included probably between 5,000 and 8,000 ethnic Poles who were real or alleged Communist supporters, mainly civilians, and between 2,000 and 5,000 Soviets. The rest of the victims were independentists, their supporters, and innocent bystanders.[32]

It is important to stress once again that, according to the Polish legal scholar Maria Stanowska, the Communists carried out 3,000 court-mandated death sentences. An estimated 10,000 people were summarily executed or tortured to death during interrogation. Between 1944 and 1956, there were 150,000 political prisoners in Poland. Additionally, 518,000 peasants were imprisoned for resisting collectivization or failing to deliver their food quota. However, Stanowska failed to calculate significant numbers of people periodically arrested and held temporarily under interrogation without warrants. Also, the precise number of inmates of Poland's 300 forced labor camps remains unknown, although Tadeusz Wolsza estimates that at least 250,000 persons experienced this form of punishment. There are still no statistics of mortality among the 100,000 people deported from Poland to the Gulag after 1944. Neither have scholars established the level of repression, terror, and violent deaths among the Poles in the Eastern Borderlands after the return of the Red Army in 1944. The available data for the two former Polish Provinces of Wilno and Nowogródek shows that within three years the NKVD arrested 13,000 Home Army soldiers, killed up to 3,000 Polish insurgents, and deported more than 20,000 people to the Gulag.[33]

These statistics demonstrate that Polish insurgents were themselves under siege no less than the Jews and why they felt the need to defend themselves from the Soviet occupation and its proxy regime. Of course, none of this justifies the killing of innocent victims, whether Jews or Poles.

Notes

1   See below.

2   Mahler, "Eastern," in Schneiderman and Maller, *American*, 47: 405.

3   Cała and Datner-Śpiewak, *Dzieje Żydów*, 106.

4   Weinryb, "Poland," in Meyer et al., *The Jews in the Soviet Satellites*, 252, 320 n. 19.

5   Schneiderman, "Eastern," in Schneiderman and Maller, *American*, 48: 337. See also Hillel, *Le Massacre des survivants*, 233-34.

6   Shapiro, "Poland," in Schneiderman and Fine, *American*, 49: 383.

7   Gilbert, *Holocaust*, 816; Lucy S. Dawidowicz, *The Holocaust and the Historians* (Cambridge, MA, and London: Harvard University Press, 1981), 95 [afterward *Holocaust*].

8   Gutman and Krakowski, *Unequal Victims*, 370. According to "very incomplete data" of the NKVD, between January 1 and September 15, 1945, 291 "persons of Jewish nationality" were killed in Poland. See Cariewskaja, *Teczka specjalna*, 421.

9   Checinski, *Poland Communism*, 17.

10 Dobroszycki, "Restoring Jewish Life," 66; Gross, *Upiorna dekada*, 96; Schatz, *Generation*, 207; Steinlauf, *Bondage to the Dead*, 51-52; Kurlansky, *A Chosen Few*, 73; Chesnoff, *Pack of Thieves*, 179; Michlic-Coren, "Anti-Jewish Violence in Poland," 39; Norman Davies, "Poles and Jews: An Exchange," *The New York Review of Books*, 9 April 1987, 41-44.

11 Steinlauf, "Poland," in Wyman and Rosenzveig, *The World Reacts*, 112.

12 Pisarski, "Emigracja," in Tomaszewski, *Studia*, 30 and n. 45 on p. 30.

13 Gross, "A Tangled Web," in Deák, *The Politics of Retribution*, 107.

14 Engel, "Patterns of Anti-Jewish Violence," 60.

15 ibid., 50, 52.

16 ibid., 60.

17 ibid., 65.

18 ibid., 66.

19 Andrzej Paczkowski, "Aparat bezpieczeństwa wobec podziemia niepodległościowego w latach 1944-1948," in Ajnenkiel, *Wojna domowa*, 83-103.

20 Danuta Blus-Węgrowska, "Atmosfera pogromowa," *Karta*, 18 (1996): 99.

21 Kochański, *Protokoły BP*, 80.

22 Cariewskaja, *Teczka specjalna*, 248. This number included Ukrainian guerrillas.

23 My estimate of roughly 100 Soviets killed between March 21 and April 15, 1945, comes from the combat losses of the Red Army and the NKVD for the period from May 10 to May 20, 1945. According to an NKVD report of May 29, 1945, in the Province of Białystok alone the insurgents killed 12 Soviets and kidnapped 26, who were presumed dead. In addition, they shot to death 3 members of the UB and 9 of the PPR. The insurgents lost 65 killed, 67 taken prisoner in battle, and 75 arrested. "In sum from May 10 to 20, according to incomplete data [from the entire territory of post-war Poland], the bandits [i.e. the insurgents] carried out 130 attacks against the organs of public security [i.e. secret police], militia, prisons, chekists [i.e. NKVD men], border guards, and groups of Soviet soldiers. The bandits freed 583 prisoners and killed 153 persons, including 49 soldiers of the Red Army, 46 employees of public security and

militia, 44 members of the PPR and local activists, [and] 14 Polish soldiers." In addition, the NKVD lost 12 men killed and 27 wounded. The insurgents had "330 killed, 17 wounded, and 702 captured" in battle. Moreover, "within ten days 892 members of the AK, 36 members of the NSZ, 21 members of the OUN [Organization of Ukrainian Nationalists], [and] 90 collaborators of the bandits" were arrested. See Cariewskaja, *Teczka specjalna*, 281-83.

24   Cariewskaja, *Teczka specjalna*, 425, 427-28, 499, 501.

25   No case was counted twice. See Introduction, Chapter 5, and Tables 4 through 7 in Chapters 7 and 8.

26   Hurwic-Nowakowska, *Żydzi polscy*, 52-80.

27   John S. Micgiel, "'Frenzy and Ferocity': The Stalinist Judicial System in Poland, 1944-1947, and the Search for Redress," *The Carl Beck Papers in Russian & East European Studies* [Pittsburgh], no. 1101 (February 1994): 1-48 [afterward "Frenzy"].

28   The rubric "Poles denounced" concerns specific denunciations and general complaints to the Communist authorities. The rubric "Poles arrested" includes direct and indirect actions of the Jewish security men in the Communist employ. The rubric "Poles killed directly" concerns Jewish perpetrators acting alone. The rubric "Poles caused to be killed" includes the victims of Jewish denunciations or other actions that resulted in Polish deaths, including the activities of Jewish security men acting in concert with their Polish and Soviet counterparts. See Tables 1 through 3 in Chapters 5 and 6, and see Chapter 7.

29   Władysław T. Bartoszewski, *The Convent at Auschwitz* (London: Bowerdean Press, 1990), 29.

30   Stefan Korbonski, *The Jews and Poles in World War II* (New York: Hippocrene Books, 1989), 78-79; *From the Polish Underground: Selections from Krytyka, 1978-1993*, ed. by Michael Bernhard and Henryk Szlajfer (The Pennsylvania State University Press, 1995), 381.

31   Stanisław Krajewski, "Reflexions of a Polish Polish Jew," *East European Jewish Affairs* 27, no. 1 (1997): 64-65.

32   These are my estimates for the period from 1944 to 1956 culled from Paczkowski, *Powrót żołnierzy AK*, 11; Jakubowski, *Milicja*, 432; Caban and Machocki, *Za władzę*, 17; Pająk, *Straceni*, 7-8; Maria Turlejska (aka Łukasz Socha), *Te pokolenia żałobami czarne: Skazani na śmierć i ich sędziowie, 1944-1954* (London: Aneks, 1989), 52, 71, 74-75.

33   Maria Stanowska, "Sprawy polityczne z lat 1944-56 w świetle orzeczeń rehabilitacyjnych Sądu Najwyższego w latach 1988-91," *Studia Juridica* [Warszawa], 27 (1995): 67; Henryk Piskunowicz, "Zwalczanie polskiego podziemia przez NKWD i NKGB na kresach północno-wschodnich II Rzeczypospolitej," in Ajnenkiel, *Wojna domowa*, 70. For information about concentration camps and forced labor in Poland after 1944 see Jarosław Butkiewicz, "Pamiątka służby wojskowej," *Nowy Świat*, 18 March 1992, 3; Piotr Jakucki, "Karne bataliony LWP," *Nowy Świat*, 10 March 1992, 2; Mateusz Wyrwich, "Łagier Jaworzno," *Gazeta Polska*, 30 March 1995, 12-13; Mateusz Wyrwich, "Komunistyczna sprawiedliwość," *Nowe Państwo*, 28 June 1996, 10; Mateusz Wyrwich, "Makarenko po polsku," *Rzeczpospolita: Plus-Minus*, 21-22 December 1996, 18; Mateusz Wyrwich, "Czarni Baronowie polskiego Gułagu," *Nowe Państwo*, 22 November 1996, 8; Krzysztof Sidorkiewicz, "Lekarstwem był tylko pistolet," *Gazeta Polska*, 17 March 1997, 17; "Kilof dla krwiopijcy [Rozkaz Nr.

008/MON, Ministra ON i Marszałka Polski Konstantego Rokossowskiego]," *Gazeta Polska*, 11 March 1998, 16; Tadeusz Wolsza, "Obozy na ziemiach polskich w latach 1945-1956 (ze szczególnym uwzględnieniem obozów pracy przymusowej," in Szarota, *Komunizm*, 80-98; Mateusz Wyrwich, *Łagier Jaworzno: Z dziejów czerwonego terroru* (Warszawa : Editions Spotkania, 1995).

XI

CONCLUSION

After the summer of 1944, between 400 and 700 persons of Jewish origin were killed in Poland by various perpetrators: Polish insurgents, Ukrainian partisans, local mobs, bandits, Polish Communists, and Soviets. Jews were killed for various reasons. Some perished because of anti-Semitism; others because of their Communist affiliation; still others died in robberies and property disputes, and sometimes even in accidents.[1] Jewish victims constituted but a tiny fraction of the human losses occasioned by the imposition of Soviet power on Poland, representing a minimum of one percent and a maximum of two percent of the total number of victims estimated at between 25,000 to 50,000. Although Jews constitued about one percent of the country's population at their peak, they were especially vulnerable because of their overrepresentation in the proxy regime and its organs.

It is impossible to ascertain at this point how many Jews precisely died at the hands of the insurgents. Even the circumstances of those deaths remain unstudied for the most part. Therefore, it is unwarranted to attribute Jewish deaths *a priori* to anti-Semitism. It is logically fallacious and historically inaccurate to attribute automatically any violent death of a Jewish person occurring after the Holocaust to Polish anti-Semitism. It is also incorrect to postulate a continuum between the Holocaust and the events in Poland after the entry of the Red Army in the summer of 1944.

Instead, we have discerned another set of causes altogether for anti-Jewish violence. A convergence of only partly related but simultaneous actions by Jewish Communists to support Stalin and to strike at the Polish independentists, by Jewish avengers to punish real and alleged perpetrators of crimes against Jews during the Nazi occupation, and by the majority of the Jewish community to reclaim their property, caused a variety of adverse Polish reactions. Some of them resulted in violence against Jews. The Jewish side tended to regard these Polish reactions as uniformly stemming from anti-Semitism. The Poles considered Jewish actions as proof of Jewish collusion with the Communists.

This partly explains why Polish insurgents continued to use anti-Jewish rhetoric in their propaganda, lumping Jews and Communism together in the hateful abstraction *żydokomuna*. The rank-and-file insurgents, along with the Christian population at large, employed the concept of the Judaeo-Commune to describe the proxy regime installed by Stalin in Poland. However, in and of itself, theoretical anti-Semitism and the animosity inherent in the abstract *żydokomuna* did not automatically trigger anti-Jewish violence by the underground. Rather, violence against Jews, and others, stemmed mostly from anti-Communism as determined by perceived threats to the underground in particular local conditions.

Most of the time, the insurgents simply reacted to real and imagined threats from the Communist security forces. Alas, the conditions of partisan war and its attendant siege mentality caused the insurgents to react violently to any such presumed threats and perhaps to regard most Jews as guilty of collaboration with the Communists. Thus, the criminal deeds of the Jewish secret policemen and Jewish collaborators were projected onto the Jewish population at large. Whether such assumed collective guilt led to collective retribution against the Jews depended on the level of control by the central or provincial command of the underground over the field units, on the level of severity of secret police terror against the insurgents, and on the perceived visibility of Jewish collaboration in a given locality.

It is a scholarly duty to study the circumstances of Jewish deaths to determine whether the roots lie in anti-Semitism, banditry, or anti-Communism. It is morally wrong to equate the racist murder of an innocent Jewish civilian with the political assassination of a Communist secret policeman who happened to be Jewish. Failure to differentiate between such deeds defiles the memory of the victims of anti-Semitism in general and the Holocaust in particular. Furthermore, in order to assess comprehensively the situation in Poland after 1944, historians must study the predicament of all of her people, minorities included, under the Soviet occupation. In the context of anti-Jewish violence, it is crucial to determine the precise role of Jews in the Stalinist terror that engulfed Poland. After all, it appears that the Soviet occupation regime victimized ethnic Poles primarily, while they and national minorities were caught up in the turmoil resulting from the Communist reordering and repression. Finally, we must explore whether there were any links between anti-Jewish violence in Poland and elsewhere in Europe, the Soviet Bloc in particular.[2]

Similarly a rigorous litmus test must be applied to the question of anti-Polish violence perpetrated by some Jews. We have estimated that perhaps between 3,128 and 6,625 Poles were victimized by Jewish perpetrators. We must scrutinize each event carefully to distinguish between justified Jewsh self-defense, extrajudicial search for justice, and plain murder perpetrated in the service or at the behest of the Communists. We should also keep in mind that anti-Polish violence perpetrated by some Jews was a relatively minor phenomenon in the context of ubiquitous Soviet terror. Moreover, revenge in postwar Poland, whether directed at presumed Polish or Jewish wrongdoers, should be viewed through the lense of the acts of mass retribution that engulfed Europe at the time. As the war was drawing to a close, across Europe people settled scores with real and alleged Nazi collaborators. In France between 8,000 and 9,000 people were lynched in the course of the *épuration*. At least as many were killed extrajudicially in spontaneous or organized acts of retribution in Italy. Tito's Communist partisans killed tens of thousands of people in Yugoslavia, while the victims of "savage purging" reached as many as 40,000 in Bulgaria. Courts and tribunals were also overburdened. In France, 350,000 persons were investigated, 45,000 convicted, and 1,500 executed. In Holland up to 150,000 citizens were arrested and tens of thousands fired from their jobs. In Belgium, more than 400,000 individuals were investigated and almost 60,000 tried in court. Life sentences were proclaimed in 2,340 cases, while 2,940 were sentenced to die (only 242 sentences were carried out).[3] Thus, in a way, post-1944 retribution in Poland fits into a general European pattern of violence, though it hardly touched Soviet collaborators. However, in Poland its savagery was multiplied manifold because of the Soviet factor and the pervasive instability of the proxy regime. Moreover, retribution against Communist collaborators, although unofficial, cannot be divorced from this broader phenomenon of settling accounts.

All of the above conclusions are not firm because Soviet and Polish Communist secret police archives have not been consulted as they are alas still off limits to independent scholars. Further research may or may not alter these tentative conclusions. However, there is no returning to the simplistic stereotypes concerning Jewish-Polish relations that haunted academia for the past fifty years.

To judge relations between two groups fairly, it is necessary to study all factors influencing the predicament of each group separately, then to compare their experiences and, finally, to isolate those ingredients influencing contacts between the groups without neglecting any of them. So far, however, aside from the present work, no such synthesis has been attempted.

In summary, rather than try to make new archival discoveries compatible with a historical consensus that was created during the Cold War era, we need to abandon the consensus and set to work on restoring history based on what actually transpired. To this end, regional studies are sorely needed before we can begin to generalize again.

Notes

1   This includes also car accidents. For instance, in the fall of 1945 near Mysłowice two Jews died when the truck they were traveling on collided head on with a Soviet military vehicle. See Kornbluth, *Sentenced to Remember*, 154. The question of the breakdown of law and order during and after the Second World War in Poland has not yet been addressed adequately. Nonetheless, evidence from various parts of Poland suggests it was a universal phenomenon involving enormous material losses and many human casulties. See Raporty starościnskie, 1944-45, APLOK, Starostwo Powiatowe w Kraśniku, files 135, 137-140, 147; Piotr Niwiński, "Problem bandycenia się członków konspiracji na przykładzie wybranych struktur Okręgu AK Wilno, 1944-1948," in *Polska — Walka, Opozycja, Niepodległość: Studia z dziejów II RP, Polskiego Państwa Podziemnego i PRL*, ed. by Adam F. Baran (Sandomierz: Wydawnictwo Diecezjalne, 2000), 143-52; Hieronim Wysocki, *Jasienica Rosielna: Zarys historii i wspomnień* (Kraków and Jasienica Rosielna: Zarząd Gminy w Jasiennicy Rosielnej, 2000), 140-41.

2   There is still insufficient data concerning not only the events in Poland but also the anti-Jewish pogroms in May 1945 in Kiev (Soviet Ukraine); in May 1945 in Kosice, and in September 1945 in Vel'ké Topočany (Slovakia); and in May 1946 in Kunmadaras, Mezőkövesd, and Hajdúhadháza and in June 1946 in Diósgyör (Hungary). Were they examples of popular anti-Semitism or were they organized from the above? See Zuckerman, *A Surplus of Memory*, 582; Meyer et al., *The Jews in the Soviet Satellites*, 105-109, 419-31; Jerzy Robert Nowak, *Spory o historię i współczesność* (Warszawa: Wydawnictwo von borowiecky, 2000) 267-68.

3   László Karsai, "Crime and Punishment: People's Courts, Revolutionary Legality, and the Hungarian Holocaust," *Intermarium: The First Online Journal of East Central European Postwar History and Politics*, vol. 4, no. 1, posted on the Internet at <http://www.columbia.edu/cu/sipa/REGIONAL/ECE/intermar.html>. See also Norman Davies, *Europe: A History* (Oxford and New York: Oxford University Press, 1996), 1060.

BIBLIOGRAPHY

1. Archives

Archiwum Akt Nowych (AAN)

Archiwum Historyczne Miasta Stołecznego Warszawy (AHMSW)

Archiwum Państwowe w Białymstoku (APB)

Archiwum Państwowe w Białymstoku Oddział w Łomży (APBOŁ)

Archiwum Państwowe w Lublinie (APL)

Archiwum Państwowe w Lublinie Oddział w Kraśniku (APLOK)

Archiwum Państwowe w Radomiu (APR)

Archiwum Państwowe w Rzeszowie (APRz)

Archiwum Państwowe w Szczecinie (APSz)

Archiwum Urzędu Ochrony Państwa w Lublinie (AUOP)

Archiwum Urzędu Rady Ministrów w Warszawie (AURM)

Archiwum Zakładu Historii Ruchu Ludowego (AZHRL)

Archiwum Żydowskiego Instytutu Historycznego (AŻIH)

Centralne Archiwum Wojskowe (CAW)

Yad Vashem Archive (YVA)

Zbiory Instytutu Historii Polskiej Akademii Nauk (ZIHPAN)

Zbiory Prywatne (Private Collections)

2. Published Documents

Bombicki, Maciej Roman, ed., *Księża przed sądami specjalnymi, 1944-1954*. Poznań: Polski Dom Wydawniczy Ławica, 1993.

Boradyn, Zygmunt, Andrzej Chmielarz and Henryk Piskunowicz, eds. *Armia Krajowa na Nowogródczyźnie i Wileńszczyźnie (1942-1945) w świetle dokumentów sowieckich*. Warszawa: Instytut Studiów Politycznych PAN, 1997.

Bordiugow, Giennadij A. et al., eds. *Polska-ZSRR Struktury Podległości: Dokumenty WKP(b), 1944-1949*. Warszawa: ISP PAN and Stowarzyszenie Współpracy Polska-Wschód, 1995.

Cała, Alina and Helena Datner-Śpiewak, eds. *Dzieje Żydów w Polsce, 1944-1968: Teksty źródłowe*. Warszawa: Żydowski Instytut Historyczny, 1997.

Cariewskaja, Tatiana et al., eds. *Teczka specjalna J.W. Stalina: Raporty NKWD z Polski, 1944-1946*. Warszawa: ISP PAN, IH UW, Rytm i APFR, 1998.

Cichopek, Anna, ed., *Pogrom Żydów w Krakowie 11 sierpnia 1945: Wstęp do badań*. Warszawa: Żydowski Instytut Historyczny, 2000.

Chodakiewicz, Marek Jan, Piotr Gontarczyk, and Leszek Żebrowski, eds. *Tajne Oblicze: Dokumenty GL-AL i PPR, 3 Volumes*. Warszawa: Burchard Edition, 1997-1999.

Chojnacki, Władysław, ed. *Bibliografia polskich publikacji podziemnych wydanych pod rządami komunistycznymi w latach 1939-1941 i 1944-1953: Czasopisma, druki zwarte, druki ulotne*. Warszawa: Literackie Towarzystwo Wydawnicze, 1996.

Chudzik, Wanda, Irena Marczak and Marek Olkuśnik, eds. *Biuletyny Informacyjne Ministerstwa Bezpieczeństwa Publicznego, 1946*. Warszawa: Ministerstwo Spraw Wewnętrznych, 1996.

Dokumenty i materiały Archiwum Polski Podziemnej, 1939-1956 [Warszawa] 1-2 (January 1993-April 1994).

Drozd, Roman, ed. *Ukraińska Powstańcza Armia: Dokumenty-struktury*. Warszawa: Burchard Edition, 1998.

Dudek, Antoni and Andrzej Paczkowski, eds. *Aparat bezpieczeństwa w Polsce w latach 1950-1952: Taktyka, strategia, metody*. Warszawa: Dom Wydawniczy Bellona, 2000.

Garlicki, Andrzej, ed. *Z tajnych archiwów*. Warszawa: Polska Oficyna Wydawnicza "BGW," 1993.

Gomułka, Władysław. *W walce o demokrację ludową (Artykuły i przemówienia), 2 Volumes*. Warszawa: Książka, 1947.

Gryciuk, Franciszek and Piotr Matusak, eds. *Represje NKWD wobec żołnierzy podziemnego Państwa Polskiego w latach 1944-1945, 2 Volumes: Wybór źródeł*. Siedlce: WSRP, 1995.

Informator o nielegalnych antypaństwowych organizacjach i bandach zbrojnych działających w Polsce Ludowej w latach 1944-1956. Warszawa: Ministerstwo Spraw Wewnętrznych, Biuro "C", 1964, Reprint. Lublin: Wydawnictwo Retro, 1993.

Kochanowski, Jerzy, ed. *Protokoły posiedzeń Prezydium Krajowej Rady*

Narodowej, 1944-1947. Warszawa: Wydawnictwo Sejmowe, 1995.

Kochański, Aleksander et al., eds. *Polska w dokumentach z archiwów rosyjskich, 1939-1953*. Warszawa: IS PAN, 2000.

Kochański, Aleksander, ed. *Protokoły posiedzeń Biura Politycznego KC PPR, 1944-1945*. Warszawa: ISP PAN, 1992.

Kochański, Aleksander, ed. *Protokół obrad KC PPR w maju 1945*. Warszawa: ISP PAN, 1992.

Korespondencja Stalin — Roosevelt, Truman. Warszawa: Wydawnictwo M.O.N., 1960.

Krawczyk, Andrzej, ed. *Pierwsza próba indoktrynacji: Działalność Ministerstwa Informacji i Propagandy w latach 1944-1947*. Warszawa: Instytut Studiów Politycznych PAN, 1994.

Kułak, Jan, ed. *Białostocczyzna 1944-1945 w dokumentach podziemia i oficjalnych władz*. Warszawa: Instytut Studiów Politycznych Polskiej Akademii Nauk, 1998.

Łabuszewski, Tomasz and Kazimierz Krajewski, eds. *Od "Łupaszki" do "Młota," 1944-1949: Materiały źródłowe do dziejów V i VI Brygady Wileńskiej*. Warszawa: Oficyna Wydawnicza Volumen, 1994.

Lenczewski, Tomasz, ed. "Zaginiony list kpt. NSZ Władysława Kołacińskiego – 'Żbika' do władz bezpieczeństwa z lipca 1945 r.," *Mars* 2 (1994): 323-326.

Marat, Stanisław and Jacek Snopkiewicz. *Ludzie bezpieki: Dokumentacja czasu bezprawia*. Warszawa: Wydawnictwo Alfa, 1990.

Misiło, Eugeniusz. *Akcja Wisła: Dokumenty*. Warszawa: Wydawnictwo Łódzkie DWN, 1993.

Noskova, A.F. et al., eds. *NKVD i polskoe podpole, 1944-1945 (Po "Osobym papkam" I.V. Stalina)*. Moskva: Institut slavianovedeniia i balkanistiki RAN, 1994.

Paczkowski, Andrzej, ed. *Aparat Bezpieczeństwa w latach 1944-1956: Taktyka, Strategia, Metody, Część I: Lata 1945-1947*. Warszawa: ISP PAN, 1994.

Paczkowski, Andrzej, ed. *Referendum z 30 czerwca 1946: Przebieg i wyniki*. Warszawa: ISP PAN, 1993.

Paczkowski, Andrzej and Wojciech Materski, eds. *Z Archiwów Sowieckich, Volume V: Powrót Żołnierzy AK z Sowieckich Łagrów*. Warszawa: ISP PAN, 1995.

Pająk, Henryk, ed. *Akcje oddziałów "Zapory" w tajnych raportach UB-MO*. Lublin: Wydawnictwo Retro, 1996.

Pająk, Henryk, ed. *"Zaporowcy" przed sądem UB.* Lublin: Wydawnictwo Retro, 1997.

Pająk, Henryk, ed. *Zbrodnie UB-NKWD.* Lublin: No publisher [Retro], 1991.

Pająk, Sławomir, ed. *Straceni w polskich więzieniach, 1944-1956.* Lublin: Retro, 1994.

Penkalla, Adam, ed. "Stosunki polsko-żydowskie w Radomiu (kwiecień 1945-luty 1946)." *Biuletyn Żydowskiego Instytutu Historycznego,* 175-176 (July 1995-June 1996): 57-66.

Persak, Krzysztof, ed. *Komuniści wobec harcerstwa, 1944-1950.* Warszawa: ISP PAN, 1998.

Pogranichnye voiska v gody velikoi otechestvennoi voiny, 1941-1945: Sbornik dokumentov. Moskva: Izdatel'stvo "Nauka," 1968.

Pogranichnye voiska SSSR, mai 1945-1950: Sbornik dokumentov i materialov. Moskva: Izdatel'stvo "Nauka," 1975.

Poksiński, Jerzy, ed. *"My, sędziowie, nie od Boga...": Z dziejów Sądownictwa Wojskowego PRL, 1944-1956, Materiały i dokumenty.* Warszawa: Gryf, 1996.

Polonsky, Antony and Bolesław Drukier, eds. *The Beginnings of Communist Rule in Poland.* London, Boston and Henley: Routledge & Kegan Paul, 1980.

Reale, Eugenio. *Raporty: Polska, 1945-1946.* Warszawa: Państwowy Instytut Wydawniczy, 1991.

Sawicki, Jerzy. *Przed polskim prokuratorem: Dokumenty i komentarze* Warszawa: Iskry, 1958.

Służba Bezpieczeństwa Polskiej Rzeczypospolitej Ludowej w latach 1944-1978. [Warszawa:] Ministerstwo Spraw Wewnętrznych, Biuro "C" [1978?].

Sosna, Grzegorz ks. ed. *Sprawy narodowościowe i wyznaniowe na Białostocczyźnie (1944-1948) w ocenie władz Rzeczpospolitej Polskiej: Wybór dokumentów: Sytuacyjne sprawozdania wojewody białostockiego w Białymstoku oraz powiatowych starostów białostockiego, bielskopodlaskiego i sokólskiego w latach 1944-1948.* Ryboły: No publisher, 1996.

Soviet-Polish Relations: A Collection of Official Documents and Press Extracts, 1944-1946. London: "Soviet News," 1946.

Strzałkowski, Waldemar ed. *Proces Szesnastu: Dokumenty NKWD.* Warszawa: Rytm, 1995.

Strzembosz, Tomasz, ed. *NKWD o polskim podziemiu 1944-1948: Konspiracja polska na Nowogródczyźnie i Grodzieńszczyźnie.* Warszawa: ISP PAN, 1997.

Szwagrzyk, Krzysztof, ed. *Golgota wrocławska, 1945-1956*. Wrocław: Wydawnictwo "Klio," 1996.

Turlejska, Maria (aka Łukasz Socha). *Te pokolenia żałobami czarne...: Skazani na śmierć i ich sędziowie, 1944-1954*. London: Aneks, 1989.

"Z gminy Ejszyskiej: Przyczynek do dziejów AK na Wileńszczyźnie po lipcu 1944 r." *Kurier Wileński*, 11, 14, 15, 16, 17, 18, 21, 22, 23, 24, 25, 28, 29, 30 and 31 July and 4, 5, 7, 8, 11, 12, 13, 14, 15, 18, 19, 20, 21, 22, 25, 26, 27 and 28 August 1992.

Zrzeszenie "Wolność i Niezawisłość" w dokumentach, 3 Volumes. Wrocław: Zarząd Główny WiN, 1997.

Żebrowski, Leszek, ed. *Narodowe Siły Zbrojne: Dokumenty, struktury, personalia, 3 Volumes*. Warszawa: Burchard Edition, 1994-1996.

3. Memoirs and Recollections

Alperovitz, Yitzhak, ed. *The Lomaz Book: A Memorial to the Jewish Community of Lomaz*. Tel Aviv: Published by the Lomaz Society in Israel with the Participation of the Lomaz Society in the United States of America, 1994.

Alufi, Peretz and Shaul Kaleko (Barkeli), eds. *"Aishishuk" — Its History and Its Destruction: Documentaries, Memories and Illustrations*. Translated by Shoshanna Gavish. [Jerusalem?]: No Publisher, 1980.

Alufi, Peretz and Shaul Kaleko (Barkeli), eds. *Eishishok, koroteha ve-hurbanah: pirke zikhoronot ve-eduyot (be-tseruf temunot)/liket*. Jerusalem: ha-Va'ad le-nitsole Eishishok bi-medinat Yisra'el, [1950].

Andruszkiewicz, Witold. "Holocaust w Ejszyszkach." *Zeszyty Historyczne* [Paris] 120 (1997): 83-96.

Bartnik, Czesław Stanisław. *Mistyka wsi: Z autobiografii młodości, 1929-1956*. Źrebce: No publisher, 1999.

Berling, Zygmunt. *Wspomnienia: Przeciw 17 Republice*. Warszawa: Polski Dom Wydawniczy Sp. z o.o., 1991.

Bialer, Seweryn. "I Chose Truth: A Former Leading Polish Communist's Story." *News From Behind the Iron Curtain* vol. 5, no. 10 (October 1956): 3-15.

Biderman, Abraham H. *The World of My Past*. Sydney: Random House, 1995.

Bodek, Helena. *Jak tropione zwierzęta: Wspomnienia*. Kraków: Wydawnictwo Literackie, 1993.

Bohun-Dąbrowski [Szacki-Skarbek], Antoni. *Byłem dowódcą Brygady Świętokrzyskiej Narodowych Sił Zbrojnych: Pamiętnik dowódcy, świadectwa żołnierzy, dokumenty.* London: Veritas Foundation Publication Centre, 1984.

Born-Bornstein, Roman. *Powstanie Warszawskie: Wspomnienia.* London: Poets' and Painters' Press, 1988.

Bronowski, Alexander. *They Were Few.* New York: Peter Lang, 1991.

Chrzanowski, Wiesław. *Pół wieku polityki, czyli rzecz o obronie czynnej.* Warszawa: Inicjatywa Wydawnicza "Ad Astra," 1997.

Davies, Raymond Arthur. *Odyssey Through Hell.* New York: L.B. Fischer, 1946.

Dąbrowska, Maria. *Dzienniki powojenne, 1945-1965, Volume 1.* Warszawa: Czytelnik, 1996.

Deutsch, Mina. *Mina's Story: A Doctor's Memoir of the Holocaust.* Toronto: ECW Press, 1994.

Drix, Samuel. *Witness to Annihilation: Surviving the Holocaust, A Memoir.* Washington, D.C., and London: Brassey's, 1994.

Egit, Jacob. *Grand Illusion.* Toronto: Lugus, 1991.

Fass, Michael Walter, ed. *Nowy-Targ and Vicinity: Zakopane, Charni Dunaietz, Rabka, Yordanov, Shchavnitza, Kroshchenko, Yablonka, Makov Podhalanski.* Tel-Aviv: Townspeople Association of Nowy-Targ and Vicinity, 1979.

Fisher, Josey G., ed. *The Persistence of Youth: Oral Testimonies of The Holocaust.* Westport, CT: Greenwood Press, 1991.

Fox, Tamar, ed. *Inherited Memories: Israeli Children of Holocaust Survivors.* London and New York: Cassell, 1999.

Friedman, Henry. *I'm No Hero: Journeys of A Holocaust Survivor.* Seattle and London: University of Washington Press, 1999.

Frister, Roman. *The Cap or the Price of a Life.* London: Weidenfeld & Nicolson, 1999.

Frydland, Rachmiel. *When Being Jewish Was A Crime.* Nashville and New York: Thomas Nelson Inc., Publishers, 1978.

Garbuny Vogel, Carole, ed. *We Shall Not Forget! Memories of the Holocaust.* Second Edition. Lexington, Mass.: Temple Isaiah, 1995.

[Gefen, Aba]. *Hope in Darkness: The Aba Gefen Diaries.* New York: Holocaust Library, 1989.

Geier, Arnold, ed. *Heroes of the Holocaust.* Miami, FL: Londonbooks, 1993.

Głowiński, Michał. *Czarne sezony.* Warszawa: Open, 1998.

Goldberg, Izaak. *The Miracles Versus Tyranny*. New York: Philosophical Library, 1979.

Golembiowski, Genie. *In Search for Survival*. Miami, FL: No publisher, [1985].

Gotfryd, Bernard. *Anton the Dove Fancier and Other Tales of the Holocaust*. Baltimore and London: The Johns Hopkins University Press, 2000.

Gray, Martin [aka, Mieczysław Grajewski, aka, Mieczysław Zamojski]. *For Those I Loved*. Boston and Toronto: Little, Brown, and Company, 1972.

Greene, Joshua M. and Shiva Kumar, eds. *Voices from the Holocaust*. New York: The Free Press, 2000.

Gronczewski, Edward. "Trudne dni: Wspomnienia z lat 1945-1946." *Wojskowy Przegląd Historyczny* 4 (October-December 1976): 131-54.

Gruber, Samuel. *I Chose Life*. New York: Shengold Publishers, Inc., 1978.

Grupińska, Anka. *Po kole: Rozmowy z żydowskimi żołnierzami*. Warszawa: Wydawnictwo Alfa, 1991.

Grynberg, Henryk. *Dziedzictwo*. London: Aneks, 1993.

Grynberg, Henryk. *The Victory*. Evanston, Illinois: Northwestern University Press, 1993.

Halpern, Sam. *Darkness and Hope*. New York: Shengold Publishers, Inc., 1996.

Hass, Aaron. *The Aftermath: Living With the Holocaust*. New York: Cambridge University Press, 1995.

Hautzic, Esther. *The Endless Steppe: Growing up in Siberia*. New York: Thomas Y. Crowell Company, 1968.

Herzog, Henry Armin. *And Heaven Shed No Tears*. New York: Shengold Publishers, 1995.

Horowitz, Irene and Carl. *Of Human Agony*. New York: Shengold Publishers, Inc., 1992.

Hubert Budzyńska, Julia. *Syberyjska dziatwa: Wojenne losy kresowiaków*. Lublin: Norbertinum, 1993.

Kagan, Berl, ed. *Memorial Book Szydłowiec*. New York: Published by Shidlowtzer Benevolent Association of New York, 1989.

Kahn, Leon. *No Time to Mourn: A True Story of a Jewish Partisan Fighter*. Vancouver: Laurelton Press, 1978.

Kałowska, Sabina Rachela. *Uciekać, aby żyć*. Lublin: Norbertinum, 2000.

Kariv, Yosef, ed. *Horchiv Memorial Book*. Tel Aviv: Horchiv Committee in Israel, 1966.

Karłowicz, Leon and Leon Popek, eds. *Śladami ludobójstwa na Wołyniu,* *2 Volumes.* Lublin: Polihymnia, 1998.

Kazimirski, Ann. *Witness to Horror.* Montreal: Devonshire Press, 1993.

Kisielewski, Stefan. *Dzienniki.* Warszawa: Iskry, 1996.

Klukowski, Zygmunt. *Dziennik 1944-1945.* Lublin: Oficyna Wydawnicza Fundacji Solidarności Regionu Środkowowschodniego, 1990.

Klukowski, Zygmunt. *Red Shadow: A Physician's Memoir of the Soviet Occupation of Eastern Poland, 1944-1956.* Jefferson, NC: McFarland & Company, 1997.

Kołaciński, Władysław. *Między młotem a swastyką.* Warszawa: Wydawnictwo "Słowo Narodowe," 1991.

Korboński, Stefan. *Fighting Warsaw: The Story of the Polish Underground State, 1939-1945* [New York:] Minerva Press, 1968.

Korenblit, Michael and Kathleen Janger. *Until We Meet Again: A True Story of Love and War, Separation and Reunion.* New York: G.P. Putnam's Sons, 1983.

Kornbluth, William. *Sentenced to Remember: My Legacy of Life in Pre-1939 Poland and Sixty-Eight Months of Nazi Occupation.* Bethlehem, London and Toronto: Lehigh University Press and Associated University Press, 1994.

Kosow Lacki. San Francisco: Holocaust Center of Northern California, 1992.

Kowalski, Isaac, ed. *Anthology on Armed Jewish Resistance, 1939-1945, Volume III.* Brooklyn, NY: Jewish Combatants Publishers House, 1986.

_____. *A Secret Press in Nazi Europe.* New York: Central Guide Publishers, Inc., 1969.

Kownacki, Andrzej. *Czy było warto? Wspomnienia.* Lublin: Towarzystwo Naukowe Katolickiego Uniwersytetu Lubelskiego, 2000.

Kozarzewski, Jerzy. "W imię pojednania." *Gazeta Wyborcza,* 26 March 1993, 13.

Kugelmass, Jack and Jonathan Boyarin, eds. *From a Ruined Garden: The Memorial Books of Polish Jewry.* Second, Enlarged Edition. Washington, D.C., Bloomington and Indianopolis: United States Holocaust Memorial Museum and Indiana University Press, 1998.

Kuper, Jack [Jankiel Kuperblum]. *After the Smoke Cleared.* Toronto: Stoddart, 1994.

Küchler-Silberman, Lena. *My Hundred Children.* New York: Laurel-Leaf/Dell, 1987.

Lasman, Noach. *Wspomnienia z Polski.* Warszawa: Żydowski Instytut Historyczny, 1997.

Lazar, Chaim. *Destruction and Resistance.* New York: Shengold Publishers, Inc., and The Museum of Combatants and Partisans in Israel, 1985.

Lewin, Rhoda G., ed. *Witnesses to the Holocaust: An Oral History.* Boston: Twayne Publishers, 1990.

Lisowska, Wanda. "Wspomnienia 'Grażyny.'" *Zeszyty Historyczne* [Paris] 36 (1976): 27-35.

Luboml: The Memorial Book of a Vanished Shtetl. Hoboken, New Jersey: Ktav Publishing House, Inc., 1997.

Lukas, Richard C., ed. *Out of the Inferno: Poles Remember the Holocaust.* Lexington, KY: The University of Kentucky Press, 1989.

Mandelkern, Benjamin. *Escape from the Nazis.* Toronto: James Lorimer & Company, Publishers, 1988.

Modrzewska, Krystyna. *Trzy razy Lublin.* Lublin: Wydawnictwo Panta, 1991.

Munro, John. *Białystok to Birkenau: The Holocaust Journey of Michel Mielnicki.* Vancouver: Ronsdale Press and Vancouver Holocaust Education Centre, 2000.

Niewyk, Donald L. ed. *Fresh Wounds: Early Narratives of Holocaust Survival.* Chapel Hill, NC, and London: The University of North Carolina Press, 1998.

Nowak, Felicja. *My Star: Memoirs of a Holocaust Survivor.* Toronto: Polish Canadian Publishing Fund, 1996.

Nowicki, Wacław. *Żywe Echa.* Komorów: Wydawnictwo "Antyk", 1993.

Oliner, Samuel P. *Narrow Escapes: A Boy's Holocaust Memories and Their Legacy.* St. Paul, Minnesota: Paragon House, 2000.

Oliner, Samuel P. *Restless Memories: Recollections of the Holocaust Years.* Berkeley, Ca.: Judah L. Magnes Museum, 1988.

Opdyke, Irene Gut. *Into the Flames: The Life Story of A Righteous Gentile.* San Bernardino, CA: The Borgo Press, 1992.

Pinkus, Oscar. *A Choice of Masks.* Englewood Cliffs, N.J.: Prentice-Hall, Inc., 1969.

Pinkus, Oscar. *The House of Ashes.* Schenectady, NY: Union College Press, 1990.

Piotrowski, Tadeusz, ed. *Genocide and Rescue in Wołyń: Recollections of the Ukrainian Nationalist Ethnic Cleansing Campaign Against the Poles During World War II.* Jefferson, NC: McFarland & Company, 2000.

236   AFTER THE HOLOCAUST

Pragier, Ruta. *Żydzi czy Polacy*. Warszawa: Oficyna Wydawnicza Rytm, 1992.

Prywes, Moshe as told to Haim Chertok. *Prisoner of Hope*. Hanover and London: Brandeis University Press and University Press of New England, 1996.

Puchalski, Stanisław. *Partyzanci "Ojca Jana"*. Stalowa Wola: Światowy Związek Żołnierzy AK — Koło w Stalowej Woli, 1996.

Reich-Ranicki, Marcel. *Mein Leben*. Stuttgart: Deutsche Verlags-Anstalt, 1999.

Riwash, Joseph. *Resistance and Revenge, 1939-1949*. Montreal: No Publisher, 1981.

Rosen, Sara. *My Lost World: A Survivor's Tale*. London: Vallentine Mitchell, 1993.

Rothchild, Sylvia, ed. *Voices from the Holocaust*. New York and Scarborough, ON: Nal Books, 1981.

Rudawski, Michał. *Mój obcy kraj?* Warszawa: Agencja Wydawnicza Tu, 1996.

Salsitz, Norman [Naftali Saleschutz] and Amalie Petranker Salsitz. *Against All Odds: A Tale of Two Survivors*. New York: Holocaust Library, 1990.

Schneiderman, S.E. *Between Fear and Hope*. New York: Arco Publishing Company, 1947.

Schoenfeld, Joachim. *Holocaust Memoirs: Jews in the Lwów Ghetto, the Janowski Concentration Camp, and as Deportees in Siberia* Hoboken, NJ: Ktav Publishing House, Inc., 1985.

Silberberg, Gershon ed. *Ostrowiec: A Monument On The Ruins of An Anihilated Jewish Community* [Tel Aviv:] The Society of Ostrovtser Jews in Israel, no date [1970s?].

Shainberg, Maurice [aka Mieczysław Prużański]. *Breaking from the KGB: Warsaw Ghetto Fighter, Intelligence Officer, Defector to the West*. New York, Jerusalem, and Tel Aviv: Shapolsky Publishing of North America, Inc., 1986.

Shapiro, Chaim. *Go, My Son*. Jerusalem and New York: Feldheim Publishers, 1989.

Shmueli-Schmusch, Nechama, ed. *Zabludow: dapim mi-tokh yisker-bukh*. [Tel Aviv:] Former Residents of Zabludow in Israel, 1987; on-line at www.jewishgen.org/yizokr/zabludow.

Shneidman, N.N. *Jerusalem of Lithuania: The Rise and Fall of Jewish Vilnius. A Personal Perspective*. Oakville, ON and Buffalo, NY: Mosaic Press, 1998.

Skakun, Michael. *On Burning Ground: A Son's Memoir*. New York: St. Martin's Press, 1999.

Stanisławczyk, Barbara. *Czterdzieści twardych*. Warszawa: Wydawnictwo ABC, 1997.

Steinhaus, Hugo. *Wspomnienia i zapiski*. London: Aneks, 1992.

Sternberg, Yitzhak. *Under Assumed Identity*. [Tel Aviv?]: Hakibbutz Hameuchad Publishing House and Ghetto Fighters' House, 1986.

Strasz, Małgorzata, and Tomasz Gleb, eds. "Henryk Urbanowicz: Człowiek na krze." *Karta* 12 (1994): 3-32.

Szewczyński, Jerzy Julian. *Nasze Kopyczyńce*. Malbork: Wydawnictwo Heldruk, 1995.

Sznajder, Lipman. *Wladek war ein falscher Name: Die wahre Geschichte eines dreizehnjährige Jungen*. München: Sznajder Lipman Verlag, 1991.

Taranienko, Zbigniew, ed. *Nasze Termopile: Dokumenty terroru, 1944-1956*. Warszawa: Wydawnictwo Archidiecezji Warszawskiej, 1993.

Tatarkiewicz, Anna. "Prawda, tylko cała prawda." *Więź* (October 1999): 131-35.

Tec, Nechama. *Dry Tears: The Story of a Lost Childhood*. New York: Oxford University Press, 1984.

Torańska, Teresa. *Oni*. London: Aneks, 1985.

Torańska, Teresa. *"Them": Stalin's Polish Puppets*. New York: Harper and Row, 1987.

Tsoref, E., ed. *Gal-Ed: Memorial Book of the Community of Racionz, Selected Chapters*. Tel Aviv: Former Residents of Racionz, 1965.

Turski, Marian, ed. *Losy żydowskie: Świadectwo żywych, 2 Volumes*. Warszawa: Stowarzyszenie Żydów Kombatantów i Poszkodowanych w II Wojnie Światowej, 1996-1999.

Vachon, Ann, ed. *Poland, 1946: The Photographs and Letters of John Vachon*. Washington D.C. and London: Smithsonian Institution Press, 1995.

Verstandig, Mark. *I Rest My Case*. Melbourne: Saga Press, 1995.

Vogelfanger, Isaac J. *The Life of a Surgeon in the Gulag*. Montreal, Kingston, London, and Buffalo: McGill-Queen's University Press, 1996.

Wald, Moshe Yaari ed. *Rzeszów Jews Memorial Book, Part Three: English*. Tel Aviv: Rzeszower Societies in Israel and U.S.A., 1967.

Werner, Harold [Hersz Cymerman ("Heniek")]. *Fighting Back: A Memoir of Jewish Resistance in World War II*. New York: Columbia University Press, 1992.

Wojciechowski, Lech Maria. "Jak Moczar chciał zrobić ze mnie agenta." *Myśl Polska*, 24 August 1997, 10.

Wolkowicz, Shlomo. *Das Grab bei Zloczow: Geschichte meines Überlebens, Galizien 1939-1945.* Berlin: Wichern-Verlag, 1996.

Wolozhinski Rubin, Sulia. *Against the Tide: The Story of an Unknown Partisan.* Jerusalem: Posner & Sons, Ltd., 1980.

Wspomnienia Sybiraków: "Polsza budiet kakda woron zbieliejet". Volume 1, Warszawa: Wydawnictwo Pomost, 1989.

Wurman, Nachemia. *Nachemia: German and Jew in the Holocaust.* Far Hills, N.J.: New Horizon Press, 1988.

Wyszogrod, Morris. *A Brush With Death: An Artist in the Death Camps.* Albany, NY: State University of New York Press, 1999.

Yoran, Shalom. *The Defiant: A True Story.* New York: St. Martin's Press, 1996.

Zandman, Felix. *Never the Last Journey.* New York: Schocken Books, 1995.

Zarębski, Maciej Andrzej, ed. *Tropem zbrodni stalinowskich: Materiały Ogólnopolskiego Sympozjum "Zbrodnie stalinowskie wobec Polski," Chańcza 5-7 października 1990.* Staszów: Staszowskie Towarzystwo Kulturalne, 1992.

Zawadzka-Wetz, Alicja. *Refleksje pewnego życia.* Paris: Instytut Literacki, 1967.

Ziemiańska, Janina. "Z Kresów do Nowego Jorku: Wspomnienia. Część 9." *Nasz Głos* [Brooklyn], 15 October 1999, 4.

Zik, Gershon ed. *Rożyszcze: My Old Home.* Tel Aviv: The Rozhishcher Committee in Israel, 1976.

Zuckerman, Yitzhak ("Antek"). *A Surplus of Memory: Chronicle of the Warsaw Ghetto Uprising.* Berkeley, CA: University of California Press, 1993.

Yizkor Book of the Jewish Community in Działoszyce and Surroundings. Tel Aviv: "Hamenora" Publishing House, 1973.

4. Articles in Press and Periodicals

Achmatowicz, Aleksander. "Wilno w latach wojny i okupacji w pamięci i według badań źródłowych." *Kwartalnik Historyczny* 2 (1998): 108-21.

Aleksiun-Mądrzak, Natalia. "Nielegalna emigracja Żydów z Polski w latach 1945-1947." *Biuletyn Żydowskiego Instytutu Historycznego.* Part I: no. 3/95-2/96 (July 1995-June 1996): 67-90; Part II: no. 3/96 (July-September 1996): 33-49; Part III: no. 4/96 (October-December 1996): 35-48.

[Baniewicz, Anna]. "Oblicza prawdy: Z prof. Krystyną Kerstenową rozmawia Anna Baniewicz." *Rzeczpospolita: Plus Minus*. 8-9 May 1993, I.

Białostocki, Izrael. "Wojewódzki Komitet Żydów Polskich w Szczecinie (1946-1950)." *Biuletyn Żydowskiego Instytutu Historycznego* [Warszawa] 71-72 (July-December 1969): 83-105.

Blatman, Daniel. "Polish Anti-Semitism and 'Judeo-Communism': Historiography and Memory." *East European Jewish Affairs* 27, no. 1 (1997): 23-43.

Blus-Węgrowska, Danuta. "Atmosfera pogromowa." *Karta* 18 (1996): 87-106.

Bojemski, Sebastian. "Pisane krwią bohaterów." *Nasz Dziennik*, 22 August 2000, 12.

Butkiewicz, Jarosław. "Pamiątka służby wojskowej." *Nowy Świat*, 18 March 1992, 3.

"Celem akcji był radziecki kapitan: Rozmowa z dr. Jarosławem Wołkonowskim." *Gazeta Wyborcza*, 8 August 1996, 2.

Chadaj, Magdalena. "Na hańbę i potępienie oprawcom." *Nasza Polska*, 1 September 1999, 4.

Chodakiewicz, Marek. "Chodakiewiczowa Irena (1912-1979), pseud. 'Irena.'" *Wileńskie Rozmaitości: Towarzystwo Miłośników Wilna i Ziemi Wileńskiej — Oddział w Bydgoszczy*. Nr. 6 (32) (November-December 1995): 50-51.

Chodakiewicz, Marek Jan. "Akcja Specjalna NSZ na Lubelszczyźnie: Część I." *Wojskowy Przegląd Historyczny* 2 (1993): 53-87.

_____. "Nieznani czy nie ukarani sprawcy?" *Słowo: Dziennik katolicki*, 14-15 June 1995, 11.

_____. "W służbie Ojczyzny (Wspomnienie o 'cichociemnym,' Kawalerze Virtuti Militari, płk. Marianie Goełbiewskim ps. 'Irka,' 'Ster,' 'Korab')." *Dziennik Związkowy* [Chicago], 8-10 November 1996, 11, 26.

_____. "Wina imputowana." *Rzeczpospolita: Plus-Minus*, 22-23 August 1998, 17.

Chudy, Krzysztof. "Ucieczka, wypędzenie i wysiedlenie ludności niemieckiej z Ziemi Wschowskiej w latach 1945-1947." *Przegląd Zachodni*. Volume 55, no. 2 (April-June 1999): 205-18.

Davies, Norman. "Poles and Jews: An Exchange." *The New York Review of Books*, 9 April 1987, 41-44.

Dobroszycki, Lucjan. "Restoring Jewish Life in Post-War Poland." *Soviet Jewish Affairs*, 2 (1973): 58-72.

Eberstadt, Nick. "The Latest Myths About the Soviet Union." *Commentary* (May 1987): 17-27.

Engel, David. "Patterns of Anti-Jewish Violence in Poland, 1944-1946." *Yad Vashem Studies* [Jerusalem] 26 (1998): 43-85.

Friedrich, Klaus-Peter. "Wygnanie: Mit niemieckiej historii." *Więź* (July 1997): 153-64.

Fuks, Marian. "Prasa PPR i PZPR w języku żydowskim ('Fołks-Sztyme' 1946-1956)." *BŻIH* 3 (111) (July-September 1979): 21-35.

Gontarczyk, Piotr. "Dał rozkaz aby wymordować: Bojownicy AL, w tym późniejszy generał LWP [Grzegorz Korczyński] mają na sumieniu zabójstwa Żydów." *Życie*, 15-16 March 1997, 15.

Gringauz, Samuel. "Some Methodological Problems in the Study of the Ghetto." *Jewish Social Studies: A Quarterly Journal Devoted to the Historical Aspects of the Jewish Life* [New York] 12 (1950): 65-72.

Groński, Ryszard Marek. "Piętro wyżej." *Polityka*, 9 October 1999, 85.

Hoffman, Zygmunt. "Związek Partyzantów Żydów." *BŻIH* 2 (94) (April-June 1975): 49-55.

J.M. [Jerzy Morawski?]. "Imperium wiecznie żywe." *Życie*, 17 June 1997, 10-11.

Jakucki, Piotr. "Karne bataliony LWP." *Nowy Świat*, 10 March 1992, 2.

Karsai, Laszlo. "Crime and Punishment: People's Courts, Revolutionary Legality, and the Hungarian Holocaust." *Intermarium: The First Online Journal of East Central European Postwar History and Politics*. Vol. 4, No. 1 (posted on the Internet at <www.columbia.edu/cu/sipa/Regional/ece/intermar.html).Ä

Kister, Anna Grażyna. "Antyżydowskie prowokacje komunistów." *Gazeta Polska*, 6 May 1998, 17.

Kister, Anna Grażyna. "Koniec donosiciela." *Gazeta Polska*, 14 September 1995, 7.

Korkuć, Maciej. "Oddziały prowokacyjne UB i KBW w Małopolsce." *Zeszyty Historyczne WiN-u* 8 (1996): 97-108.

Korkuć, Maciej. "'Ogień' bez odwrotu." *Życie*, 22 and 23 February 1997, 16.

Koźmińska-Frejlak, Ewa. "Nieudana odbudowa." *Midrasz* [Warszawa] 7-8 (July-August 1998): 8-9.

Kułak, Jerzy. "Pacyfikacja wsi białoruskich w styczniu 1946 roku." *Biuletyn Instytutu Pamięci Narodowej* no. 8 (September 2001): 49-54.

Leszczyński, Anatol. "Zagłada Żydów w Choroszczy." *Biuletyn*

Żydowskiego Instytutu Historycznego, 3 (July-September 1971): 49-67.

Meducki, Stanisław. "The Pogrom in Kielce on 4 July 1946." *Polin: Studies in Polish Jewry* 9 (1996): 158-69.

Micgiel, John S. "'Frenzy and Ferocity': The Stalinist Judicial System in Poland, 1944-1947, and the Search for Redress." *The Carl Beck Papers in Russian & East European Studies* [Pittsburgh], no. 1101 (February 1994): 1-48.

Micgiel, John. "Kościół katolicki i pogrom kielecki." *Niepodległość* [New York] 25 (1992): 134-72.

Michalik, Marek. "Wizerunek Zrzeszenia 'Wolność i Niezawisłość' w wybranych tytułach prasy centralnej z lat 1945-1947: Część I." *Zeszyty Historyczne WiN-u* 12 (March 1999): 5-42.

Michlic-Coren, Joanna. "Anti-Jewish Violence in Poland, 1918-1939 and 1945-1947." *Polin*, Vol. 13 (2000): 34-61.

Minc, Hilary. "Concerning the basis of planning in the people's democracies." *For a Lasting Peace, For a People's Democracy!* 18 November 1949, 2-3.

Misiak, Elżbieta. "Nie byłoby zbrojnego podziemia, gdyby w sierpniu 1944 nie aresztowano ujawniających się żołnierzy AK." *Ład* [Warsaw] 25 June 1989, 9.

Musiał, Bogdan. "Stosunki polsko-żydowskie na Kresach Wschodnich R.P. pod okupacją sowiecką 1939-1941." *Biuletyn kwartalny Radomskiego Towarzystwa Naukowego* 34, no. 1 (1999): 103-26.

Noskowski, Wiktor. "Czy Yaffa Eliach przeprosi Polaków?" *Myśl Polska* [Warsaw] 20-27 July 1997, 1, 7-9.

Overmans, Rüdiger. "Personelle Verluste der destschen Bevölkerung durch flucht und Vertreibung." *Dzieje Najnowsze* Vol. 26, No. 2 (1994): 51-65.

Ostrovitianov, K. "Lenin i Stalin ob ekonomike i politike." *Voprosy ekonomiki* [Moscow] 2 (1949): 3-29.

Paczkowski, Andrzej. "Communist Poland, 1944-1989: Some Controversies and a Single Conclusion." *The Polish Review* 2 (1999): 217-25.

Podgórski, Maciej. "Zbrodnia UB w Hrubieszowie." *Rzeczpospolita*, 26 May 1998, 1, 14.

Radzilowski, John. "Yaffa Eliach's Big Book of Holocaust Revisionism." *Journal of Genocide Studies* 1, no. 2 (1999): 273-80.

Rok, Adam. "Kto, komu i co imputuje?" *Słowo Żydowskie, Dos Jidisze*

Wort: Dwutygodnik społeczno-kulturalny [Warsaw], 18 September 1998, 4, 6.

Sidorkiewicz, Krzysztof. "Lekarstwem był tylko pistolet." *Gazeta Polska*, 17 March 1997, 17.

Skurnowicz, Joan S. "Soviet Polonia, the Polish State, and the New Mythology of National Origins, 1943-1945." *Nationalities Papers* (Special Issue) Vol. XXII, Supplement No. 1 (Summer 1994): 93-110.

Smilovitsky, Leonid. "The Struggle of Belorussian Jews for the Restitution of Possessions and Housing in the First Postwar Decade." *East European Jewish Affairs* Vol. 30, No. 2 (2000): 53-70.

Stanowska, Maria. "Sprawy polityczne z lat 1944-1956 w świetle orzeczeń rehabilitacyjnych Sądu Najwyższego w latach 1988-91." *Studia Juridica* [Warsaw] 27 (1995): 65-92.

Szaynok, Bożena. "Początki osadnictwa żydowskiego na Dolnym Śląsku po II wojnie światowej (maj 1945-styczeń 1946)." *Biuletyn Żydowskiego Instytutu Historycznego*, no. 172-174 (October 1994-June 1995): 45-64.

Szczepański, Piotr [Zbigniew Romaniuk]. "Pogromy i pogromiki." *Kurier Poranny* [Białystok], 12 April 1996, 6.

Taylor, Bill. "Gentle Holocaust survivor finally tells story to family." *The Toronto Star*, 23 April 1995, A1, A6-A7.

Turski, Marian. "Pogrom kielecki w protokołach Centralnego Komitetu Żydów Polskich." *Almanach żydowski* [Warszawa] (1996-1997): 48-62.

Tuszyński, Marek. "Soviet War Crimes Against Poland During the Second World War and Its Aftermath." *The Polish Review*, 2 (1999): 183-216.

Varga, E. "Demokratiia novogo tipa." *Mirovoe khoziaistvo i mirovaia politika* [Moscow] (March 1947): 3-14.

Wnuk, Rafał. "Zorganizowany opór wobec państwa komunistycznego na przykładzie Okręgu Lublin AK-DSZ-WiN (1944-1945)." *Dzieje Najnowsze*, 4 (1999): 175-84.

Wojciechowski, Marian. "The Exodus of the Germans from the Odra and Lusatian Nysa Territories." *Polish Western Affairs* No. 1/2 (1990): 1-18.

Wołkonowski, Jarosław. "Ejszyszki — zniekształcony obraz przeszłości." *Kurier Wileński*, 6 September 1996, 3.

Wołłejko, Michał. "Opowieści chasydzkie." *Gazeta Polska*, 15 August 1995, 11.

Wyrwich, Mateusz. "Czarni baronowie polskiego Gułagu." *Nowe Państwo*, 22 November 1996, 8.

Wyrwich, Mateusz. "Komunistyczna sprawiedliwość." *Nowe Państwo*, 28 June 1996, 10.

Wyrwich, Mateusz. "Makarenko po polsku." *Rzeczpospolita: Dodatek Plus-Minus*, 21-22 December 1996, 18.

Zaborski, Marcin. "Zbrodnia nie popełniona przez NSZ." *Gazeta Polska*, 15 September 1994, 8-9.

Żaryn, Jan. "O rzetelny rachunek prawdy." *Słowo: Dziennik katolicki*, 19 July 1993, 10.

Żebrowski, Leszek. "'Odpowiedź' prof. Krzysztofa Dunin-Wąsowicza, czyli o potrzebie dekomunizacji nauki." *Zeszyty Historyczne WiN-u* [Kraków] 9 (December 1996): 280-92.

Żebrowski, Leszek. "Rozstrzelano siedemnastu." *Gazeta Polska*, 8 June 1995, 10.

Żebrowski, Leszek. "Sprawa Yaffy Eliach." *Gazeta Polska*, 22 August 1996, 12-13.

5. Monographs

Ajnenkiel, Andrzej, ed. *Wojna domowa czy nowa okupacja? Polska po roku 1944*. Wrocław, Warszawa, and Kraków: Wydawnictwo Zakładu Narodowego imienia Ossolińskich, 1998.

Armstrong, Diane. *Mosaic: A Chronicle of Five Generations*. Sydney: Random House, 1998.

Balbus, Tomasz. *Major Ludwik Marszałek "Zbroja" (1912-1948): Żołnierz polski podziemnej*. Wrocław: Gajt Wydawnictwo s.c., 1999.

Baran, Adam, ed. *Polska – Walka, Opozycja, Niepodległość: Studia z dziejów II RP, Polskiego Państwa Podziemnego i PRL*. Sandomierz: Wydawnictwo Diecezjalne, 2000.

Barnaszewski, Bogusław. *Polityka PPR wobec zalegalizowanych partii i stronnictw*. Warszawa: Wydawnictwo Naukowe Semper, 1996.

Bauer, Yehuda. *Flight and Rescue: Brichah*. New York: Random House, 1970.

_____. *The Jewish Emergence from Powerlessness*. Toronto and Buffalo: University of Toronto Press, 1979.

Bäcker, Roman et al. *Skryte oblicze systemu komunistycznego: U źródeł zła*. Warszawa: Towarzystwo im. Stanisława ze Skarbmierza i Wydawnictwo DiG, 1997.

Bartoszewski, Wladyslaw T. *The Convent at Auschwitz*. London: The Bowerdean Press, 1990.

Bechta, Mariusz. *Rewolucja, mit, bandytyzm: Komuniści na Podlasiu w latach 1939-1944*. Warszawa and Biała Podlaska: Rekonkwista-Rachocki i ska, 2000.

_____, and Leszek Żebrowski, eds. *Narodowe Siły Zbrojne na Podlasiu, Volume 1: Materiały posesyjne*. Siedlce: Związek Żołnierzy Narodowych Sił Zbrojnych, 1997.

_____, eds. *Narodowe Siły Zbrojne na Podlasiu, Volume 2: W walce z systemem komunistycznym w latach 1944-1952*. Siedlce: Związek Żołnierzy Narodowych Sił Zbrojnych, 1998.

Beckman, Morris. *The Jewish Brigade: An Army with Two Masters, 1944-1945*. Staplehurst: Spellmount, 1998.

Bednarczyk, Tadeusz. *Życie codzienne warszawskiego getta: Warszawskie getto i ludzie (1939-1945 i dalej)*. Warszawa: Wydawnictwo Ojczyzna, 1995.

Ewa Berberyusz, *Książę z Maisons-Laffitte*. Gdańsk: Wydawnictwo Marabut, 1995.

Berger, Ronald J. *Constructing a Collective Memory of the Holocaust: A Life History of Two Brothers' Survival*. Niwot, CO: University Press of Colorado, 1995.

Blum, Ignacy. *Z dziejów Wojska Polskiego w latach 1944-1948: Szkice i dokumenty*. Warszawa: Wydawnictwo Ministerstwa Obrony Narodowej, 1968.

Boćkowski, Daniel. *Czas nadziei: Obywatele Rzeczpospolitej Polskiej w ZSRR i opieka nad nimi placówek polskich w latach 1939-1943*. Warszawa: Noriton and Wydawnictwo IH PAN, 1999.

Brociek, Waldemar R., Adam Penkalla, and Regina Renz. *Żydzi ostrowieccy: Zarys dziejów*. Ostrowiec Świętokrzyski: Muzeum Historyczno-Archeologiczne, 1996.

Brzeziński, Bogdan, Leon Chrzanowski, and Ryszard Halaba, eds. *Polegli w walce o władzę ludową: Materiały i zestawienia statystyczne*. Warszawa: Książka i Wiedza, 1970.

Caban, Ireneusz. *8 Pułk Piechoty Legionów Armii Krajowej: Organizacja i działania bojowe*. Warszawa: Wydawnictwo Bellona, 1994.

Caban, Ireneusz and Edward Machocki. *Za władzę ludu*. Lublin: Wydawnictwo Lubelskie, 1975.

Carr, E.H. *The Comintern and the Spanish Civil War*. New York: Pantheon Books, 1984.

Ciesielski, Stanisław ed. *Przesiedlenie ludności polskiej z Kresów Wschodnich do Polski, 1944-1947*. Warszawa: Wydawnictwo Neriton and Instytut Historii PAN, 1999.

Ciesielski, Stanisław, Grzegorz Hryciuk, and Aleksander Srebrakowski. *Masowe deportacje radzieckie w okresie II Wojny Światowej.* Wrocław: Instytut Historyczny Uniwersytetu Wrocławskiego and Wrocławskie Towarzystwo Miłośników Historii, 1994.

Checinski, Michael. *Poland: Communism, Nationalism, Anti-Semitism.* New York: Karz-Cohl, 1982.

Chesnoff, Richard Z. *Pack of Thieves: How Hitler and Europe Plundered the Jews and Committed the Greatest Theft in History.* New York: Doubleday, 1999.

Chodakiewicz, Marek Jan. *Narodowe Siły Zbrojne: "Ząb" przeciw dwu wrogom.* Warszawa: WAMA, 1994.

_____. *Narodowe Siły Zbrojne: "Ząb" przeciw dwu wrogom.* 2nd, Expanded Edition. Warszawa: Fronda, 1999.

_____. *Polacy i Żydzi, 1918-1955: Współistnienie, Zagłada, Komunizm.* Warszawa: Fronda, 2001.

_____. *Zagrabiona pamięć: Wojna w Hiszpanii, 1936-1939.* Warszawa: Fronda, 1997.

Cimek, Henryk. *Komuniści, Polska, Stalin.* Białystok: Krajowa Agencja Wydawnicza, 1990.

Close, David H. *The Origins of the Greek Civil War.* London and New York: Longman, 1995.

Courtois, Stéphane et al. *The Black Book of Communism: Crimes, Terror, Repression.* Cambridge, Mass., and London: Harvard University Press, 1999.

Coutouvidis, John, and Jaime Reynolds. *Poland, 1939-1947.* New York: Holmes & Meier, 1986.

Czubiński, Antoni. *Polska i Polacy po II wojnie światowej.* Poznań: Wydawnictwo Naukowe Uniwersytetu im. Adama Mickiewicza w Poznaniu, 1998.

Ćwik, Władysław. *Dzieje Józefowa.* Rzeszów: Krajowa Agencja Wydawnicza, 1992.

D'Agostino, Anthony. *Soviet Succession Struggles: Kremlinology and the Russian Question from Lenin to Gorbachov.* Boston: Allen and Unwin, 1988.

Davies, Norman and Antony Polonsky, eds. *Jews in Eastern Poland and the USSR, 1939-1946.* London: Macmillan, 1991.

Dawidowicz, Lucy S. *The Holocaust and the Historians.* Cambridge, MA, and London: Harvard University Press, 1981.

Deák, István, Jan T. Gross, and Tony Judt, eds. *The Politics of Retribution in Europe: World War II and Its Aftermath*. Princeton, NJ: Princeton University Press, 2000.

Dereń, Bolesław. *Józef Kuraś "Ogień": Partyzant Podhala*. Kraków: Secesja, 1995.

Dinnerstein, Leonard. *America and the Survivors of the Holocaust*. New York: Columbia University Press, 1982.

Długoborski, Wacław, Bożena Klimczak, and Elżbieta Kaszuba, eds. *Gospodarcze i społeczne skutki wojny i okupacji dla Polski oraz drogi ich przezwyciężania: Materiały z konferencji naukowej zorganizowanej przez Katedrę Historii Gospodarczej Akademii Ekonomicznej we Wrocławiu, Karpacz, 4-6 grudnia 1985*. Wrocław: Wydawnictwo Uczelniane Akademii Ekonomicznej we Wrocławiu, 1989.

Dobroszycki, Lucjan. *Survivors of the Holocaust in Poland: A Portrait Based Jewish Community Records, 1944-1947*. Armonk, NY, and London: M.E. Sharpe, 1994.

Dominiczak, Henryk. *Organy bezpieczeństwa PRL, 1944-1990: Rozwój i działalność w świetle dokumentów MSW*. Warszawa: Dom Wydawniczy Bellona, 1997.

Eliach, Yaffa. *There Once Was A World: A Nine-Hundred-Year Chronicle of the Shtetl of Eishyshok*. Boston: Little, Brown and Company, 1998.

Epstein, Eric Joseph and Philip Rosen. *Dictionary of the Holocaust: Biography, Geography, and Terminology*. Westport, CT, and London: Greenwood Press, 1997.

Fijałkowska, Barbara. *Borejsza i Różański: Przyczynek do dziejów stalinizmu w Polsce*. Olsztyn: Wyższa Szkoła Pedagogiczna, 1995.

Frankel, Henryk. *Poland: The Struggle for Power*. London: Lindsay Drummond Ltd., 1946.

Friedman, Saul S. ed. *Holocaust Literature: A Handbook of Critical, Historical, and Literary Writings*. Westport, CT: Greenwood Press, 1993.

Garbacz, Dionizy. *Wołyniak: Legenda prawdziwa*. Stalowa Wola: Wydawnictwo "Sztafeta", 1996.

Garliński, Józef. *Poland in the Second World War*. London: Macmillan Press, 1985.

Gella, Aleksander. *Zagłada Drugiej Rzeczypospolitej, 1945-1947*. Warszawa: Agencja Wydawnicza CB, 1998.

Gilbert, Martin. *The Boys: Triumph over Adversity*. Vancouver and Toronto: Douglas & McIntyre, 1996.

_____. *The Holocaust: The Jewish Tragedy*. Glasgow: William Collins, 1986.

Gontarczyk, Piotr. "Powstawanie elit politycznych PRL: Przypadek Ajzenmana-Kaniewskiego." MA thesis, University of Warsaw, 1997.

Góra, Władysław and Janusz Gołębiowski, eds. *Z najnowszych dziejów Polski, 1939-1947*. Warszawa: Państwowe Zakłady Wydawnictw Szkolnych, 1963.

Góra, Władysław and Zenon Jakubowski. *Z dziejów organów bezpieczeństwa i porządku publicznego w województwie lubelskim, 1944-1948*. Lublin: Wydawnictwo Lubelskie, 1978.

Grabowski, Waldemar. *Delegatura Rządu Rzeczypospolitej Polskiej na Kraj, 1940-1945*. Warszawa: Instytut Wydawniczy Pax, 1995.

Gross, Jan Tomasz. *Polish Society Under German Occupation: The Generalgouvernement, 1939-1944*. Princeton, N.J.: Princeton University Press, 1979.

Gross, Jan T. *Revolution from Abroad: The Soviet Conquest of Poland's Western Ukraine and Western Belorussia*. Princeton, N.J.: Princeton University Press, 1988.

Gross, Jan Tomasz. *Upiorna dekada: Trzy eseje o stereotypach na temat Żydów, Polaków, Niemców i komunistów, 1939-1948*. Kraków: TAiWPN Universitas, 1998.

Gryz, Ryszard. *Państwo a Kościół w Polsce, 1945-1956: Na przykładzie województwa kieleckiego*. Kraków: Zakład Wydawniczy "Nomos," 1999.

Grzebień, Ludwik ed. *Słownik polskich teologów katolickich, 1918-1981*, Volume 6. Warszawa: Akademia Teologii Katolickiej, 1983.

Gunther, John. *Behind the Curtain*. New York: Harper and Brothers Publishers, 1949.

Gutman, Yisrael and Shmuel Krakowski. *Unequal Victims: Poles and Jews During World War Two*. New York: Holocaust Library, 1986.

Hempel, Adam. *Pogrobowcy klęski: Rzecz o policji "granatowej" w Generalnym Gubernatorstwie, 1939-1945*. Warszawa: Państwowe Wydawnictwo Naukowe, 1990.

Hillel, Marc. *Le Massacre des survivants: En Pologne aprés l'holocauste (1945-1947)*. Paris: Plon, 1985.

Hurwic-Nowakowska, Irena. *Żydzi polscy (1947-1950): Analiza więzi społecznej ludności żydowskiej*. Warszawa: Wydawnictwo Instytutu Filozofii i Socjologii Polskiej Akademii Nauk, 1996.

Iwaniec, Elżbieta and Stefan Zwolniński, eds. *Polskie Państwo Podziemne i Wojsko Polskie w latach 1944-1945*. Warszawa: Wojskowy Instytut Historyczny, 1991.

Jaczyński, Stanisław. *Zygmunt Berling*. Warszawa: Książka i Wiedza, 1993.

Jakubowski, Zenon. *Milicja Obywatelska, 1944-1948*. Warszawa: Państwowe Wydawnictwo Naukowe, 1988.

Jasiewicz, Krzysztof, ed. *Europa nieprowincjonalna: Przemiany na ziemiach wschodnich dawnej Rzeczypospoiltaje (Białoruś, Litwa, Łotwa, Ukraina, wschodnie pogranicze III Rzeczpospolitej Polskiej) w latach 1772-1999. Non-Provincial Europe: Changes on the Eastern Territories of the former Polish Republic (Belarus, Latvia, Lithuania, Ukraine, eastern borderlands of the III Republic) in 1772-1999.* Warszawa and London: ISP PAN, Rytm, and Polonia Aid Foundation Trust, 1999.

Jaworski, Mieczysław. *Korpus Bezpieczeństwa Wewnętrznego, 1945-1965*. Warszawa: Wydawnictwo Ministerstwa Obrony Narodowej, 1984.

Jelavich, Barbara. *History of the Balkans*, Volume 2: *Twentieth Century*. Cambridge: Cambridge University Press, 1983.

Judt, Tony, ed. *Resistance and Revolution in Mediterranean Europe, 1939-1948*. London and New York: Routledge, 1989.

Kamiński, Łukasz. *Polacy wobec nowej rzeczywistości, 1944-1948: Formy pozainstytucjonalnego, żywiołowego oporu społecznego*. Toruń: Wydawnictwo Adam Marszałek, 2000.

Kantyka, Jan. *Na tropie "Bartka", "Mściciela", i "Zemsty": Z dziejów walki o utrwalenia władzy ludowej*. Katowice: Śląski Instytut Naukowy, 1984.

Kaufman, Jonathan. *A Hole in the Heart of the World: Being Jewish in Eastern Europe*. New York: Viking, 1997.

Kawalec, Krzysztof. *Narodowa Demokracja wobec faszyzmu, 1922-1939: Ze studiów nad dziejami myśli politycznej Obozu Narodowego*. Warszawa: Państwowy Instytut Wydawniczy, 1989.

Kąkolewski, Krzysztof. *Umarły cmętarz: Wstęp do studiów nad wyjaśnienieniem przyczyn i przebiegu morderstwa na Żydach w Kielcach dnia 4 lipca 1946 roku*. Warszawa: Wydawnictwo von borowiecky, 1996.

Kenney, Padraic. *Rebuilding Poland: Workers and Communists, 1945-1950*. Ithaca and London: Cornell University Press, 1997.

Kersten, Krystyna. *The Establishment of Communist Rule in Poland, 1943-48*. Berkeley: University of California Press, 1991.

_____. *Między wyzwoleniem a zniewoleniem, 1944-1956*. London: Aneks, 1993.

_____. *Narodziny systemu władzy: Polska, 1943-1948* Warszawa: Wydawnictwo Krąg, 1985.

_____. *Polacy, Żydzi, komunizm: Anatomia półprawd 1939-1968*. Warszawa: Niezależna Oficyna Wydawnicza, 1992.

Kielce — July 4, 1946: Background, Context and Events. Toronto and Chicago: The Polish Educational Foundation in North America, 1996.

Kirschbaum, Stanislav J. *A History of Slovakia: The Struggle for Survival.* New York: St. Martin's Griffin, 1995.

Korboński, Stefan. *The Jews and Poles in World War II.* New York: Hippocrene Books, 1989.

Korboński, Stefan. *The Polish Underground State: A Guide to the Underground, 1939-1945.* Boulder, CO and New York: East European Quarterly and Columbia University Press, 1978.

Kovachi, Arieh J. *Post-Holocaust Politics: Britain, the United States, and Jewish Refugees,1945-1948.* University of North Carolina Press, 2001.

Krajewski, Kazimierz. *Na Ziemi Nowogródzkiej: "Nów" — Nowogródzki Okręg Armii Krajowej.* Warszawa: Instytut Wydawniczy PAX, 1997.

Krajewski, Kazimierz and Tomasz Łabuszewski. *Białostocki Okręg AK-AKO, VII 1944-VIII 1945.* Warszawa: Oficyna Wydawnicza Volumen i Dom Wydawniczy Bellona, 1997.

Kurek, Ewa. *Zaporczycy 1943-1949.* Lublin: Wydawnictwo Clio, 1995.

Kurlansky, Mark. *A Chosen Few: The Resurrection of European Jewry.* Reading, Mass.: Addison-Wesley Publishing Company, 1995.

Kwiek, Julian. *Żydzi, Łemkowie, Słowacy w województwie krakowskim w latach 1945-1949/50.* Kraków: Wydawnictwo Naukowe Księgarnia Akademicka, 1998.

Lapomarda, Vincent A. *The Jesuits and the Third Reich.* Lewiston/Queenston and Lampeter: The Edwin Mellen Press, 1989.

Latyński, Marek. *Nie paść na kolana: Szkice o opozycji lat czterdziestych.* London: Polonia Book Fund Ltd., 1985.

Leopold, Czesław and Krzysztof Lechicki. *Więźniowie polityczni w Polsce, 1945-56.* Paris: Editions Spotkania, 1983.

Levin, Don. *The Lesser of Two Evils: East European Jewry under Soviet Rule, 1939-1941.* Philadelphia and Jerusalem: The Jewish Publication Society, 1995.

Lewandowska, Stanisława. *Życie codzienne Wilna w latach II wojny światowej.* Warszawa: Wydawnictwo Neriton and Instytut Historii PAN, 1997.

Lewczuk, Elżbieta, ed. *Studia z dziejów Żydów w Polsce: Materiały edukacyjne dla szkół średnich i wyższych, 2 Volumes.* Warszawa: Żydowski Instytut Historyczny and Instytut Naukowo-Badawczy, 1995.

Locke, Hubert G. and Marcia Sachs Littell, eds. *Holocaust and Church Struggle: Religion, Power and the Politics of Resistance.* Lanham, New York, and London: University Press of America, 1996.

Lukas, Richard C. *The Forgotten Holocaust: The Poles Under German Occupation, 1939-1944.* Second, Revised Edition. New York: Hippocrene Books, 1997.

Łuczak, Czesław. *Polska i Polacy w drugiej wojnie światowej.* Poznań: Wydawnictwo Naukowe Uniwersytetu im. Adama Mickiewicza, 1993.

Madajczyk, Piotr, ed. *Mniejszości narodowe w Polsce: Państwo i społeczeństwo polskie a mniejszości narodowe w okresach przełomów politycznych (1944-1989).* Warszawa: Instytut Studiów Politycznych Polskiej Akademii Nauk, 1998.

Mantel, Feliks. *Stosunki polsko-żydowskie: Próba analizy.* Paris: Księgarnia Polska, 1986.

Mazur, Grzegorz, Wojciech Rojek, and Marian Zgórniak. *Wojna i okupacja na Podkarpaciu i Podhalu na obszarze Inspektoratu ZWZ-AK Nowy Sącz, 1939-1945.* Kraków: Wydawnictwo Naukowe Księgarnia Akademicka, 1998.

Meyer, Peter et al. *The Jews in the Soviet Satellites.* Syracuse, NY: Syracuse University Press, 1953.

Mich, Włodzimierz. *Obcy w polskim domu: Nacjonalistyczne koncepcje rozwiązania problemu mniejszości narodowych, 1918-1939.* Lublin: Wydawnictwo Uniwersytetu Marii Curie-Skłodowskiej, 1994.

Michalczyk, John J. ed. *Resisters, Rescuers, and Refugees: Historical and Ethical Issues.* Kansas City: Sheed & Ward, 1997.

Motyka, Grzegorz. *Tak było w Bieszczadach: Walki polsko-ukraińskie, 1943-1948.* Warszawa: Oficyna Wydawnicza "Volumen," 1999.

_____, and Rafał Wnuk. *Pany i rezuny: Współpraca AK-WiN i UPA, 1945-1947.* Warszawa: Oficyna Wydawnicza Volumen, 1997.

Muszyński, Wojciech Jerzy. *W walce o Wielką Polskę: Propaganda zaplecza politycznego Narodowych Sił Zbrojnych (1939-1945).* Warszawa and Biała Podlaska: Rekonkwista-Rachocki i ska, 2000.

Murzański, Stanisław. *PRL Zbrodnia niedoskonała: Rozważania o terrorze władzy i społecznym oporze.* Warszawa: Oficyna Wydawnicza Volumen i Wydawnictwo Alfa, 1996.

Naimark, Norman and Leonid Gibianskii, eds. *The Establishment of Communist Regimes in Eastern Europe, 1944-1949.* Boulder, CO.: Westview Press, 1997.

Nalepa, Edward Jan. *Oficerowie Armii Radzieckiej w Wojsku Polskim,*

1943-1968. Warszawa: Wydawnictwo Bellona, 1995.

Niezabitowska, Małgorzata. *Remnants: The Last Jews of Poland* (New York: Friendly Press, Inc., 1986.

Nowak, Jerzy Robert. *Spory o historię i współczesność*. Warszawa: Wydawnictwo von borowiecky, 2000.

_____. *Zagrożenia dla Polski i polskości*. Warszawa: Inicjatywa Wydawnicza "ad astra," 1998.

Orłowski, Hubert and Andrzej Sakson, eds. *Utracona Ojczyzna: Przymusowe deportacje i przesiedlenia jako wspólne doświadczenia*. Poznań: Instytut Zachodni, 1997.

Orlicki, Józef. *Szkice z dziejów stosunków polsko-żydowskich, 1918-1949*. Szczecin: Krajowa Agencja Wydawnicza, 1983.

Otwinowska, Barbara and Jan Żaryn, eds. *Polacy wobec przemocy, 1944-1956*. Warszawa: Editions Spotkania, 1996.

Paczkowski, Andrzej. *Stanisław Mikołajczyk: Klęska realisty (Zarys biografii politycznej)*. Warszawa: Agencja Omnipress, 1991.

Pająk, Henryk. *Konspiracja młodzieży szkolnej, 1945-1955*. Lublin: Wydawnictwo Retro, 1994.

Pająk, Henryk. *Oni się nigdy nie poddali*. Lublin: Wydawnictwo Retro, 1997.

Paldiel, Mordecai. *Saving the Jews: Amazing Stories of Men and Women Who defied the "Final Solution"*. Rockville, Maryland: Schreiber Publishing, 2000.

Paul, Mark. *Neighbors on the Eve of the Holocaust: Jewish-Polish Relations in Soviet-Occupied Eastern Poland, 1939-1941*. Toronto: PEFINA Press, 2002.

Piątkowska, Małgorzata, ed. *Żydzi szydłowieccy: Materiały sesji popularnonaukowej 22 lutego 1997 roku*. Szydłowiec: Muzeum Ludowych Instrumentów Muzycznych w Szydłowcu, 1997.

Pinchuk, Ben-Cion. *Shtetl Jews under Soviet Rule: Eastern Poland on the Eve of the Holocaust*. London: Basil Blackwell, 1990.

Piotrowski, Tadeusz. *Poland's Holocaust: Ethnic Strife, Collaboration with Occupying Forces and Genocide in the Second Republic, 1918-1947*. Jefferson, NC, and London: McFarland & Company, 1998.

Podolska, Aldona. *Służba Porządkowa w getcie warszawskim w latach 1940-1943*. Warszawa: Wydawnictwo Fundacji "Historia Pro Futuro," 1996.

Pogonowski, Iwo Cyprian. *Jews in Poland: A Documentary History.* Revised edition. New York: Hippocrene Books, Inc., 1998.

Polak, Jerzy and Janusz Spyra, eds. *Żydzi w Bielsku, Białej i okolicy: Materiały z sesji naukowej odbytej w dniu 19 stycznia 1996 r.* Bielsko-Biała: Muzeum Okręgowe i Urząd Miejski w Bielsku-Białej, 1996.

Poliszczuk, Wiktor. *Bitter Truth: The Criminality of the Organization of Ukrainian Nationalists and the Ukrainian Insurgent Army (The Testimony of a Ukrainian).* Toronto: No publisher, 1999.

Pulzer, Peter. *The Rise of Political Anti-Semitism in Germany and Austria.* Cambridge, MA: Harvard University Press, 1988.

Raina, Peter. *Mordercy uchodza bezkarnie: Sprawa Bohdana P.* Warszawa: Wydawnictwo von borowiecky, 2000.

Roszkowski, Wojciech. *Historia Polski, 1914-2000.* Warszawa: PWN, 2001.

Rothschild, Joseph. *Return to Diversity: A Political History of East Central Europe Since World War II.* New York and Oxford: Oxford University Press, 1989.

Rudnicki, Szymon. *Obóz Narodowo-Radykalny: Geneza i działalność.* Warszawa: Czytelnik, 1985.

Ryszka, Franciszek et al. *Polska Ludowa, 1944-1950: Przemiany społeczne.* Wrocław: Wydawnictwo Zakładu Narodowego im. Ossolińskich, 1974.

Sack, John. *An Eye for An Eye.* New York: Basic Books, 1993 (1995).

Schatz, Jaff. *The Generation: The Rise and Fall of the Jewish Communists of Poland.* Berkeley: University of California Press, 1991.

Schneiderman, Harry, ed. *The American Jewish Yearbook, 5705. Volume 46: September 18, 1944 to September 7, 1945.* Philadelphia: The Jewish Publication Society of America, 1944

Schneiderman, Harry and Julius B. Maller, eds. *The American Jewish Yearbook, 5706. Volume 47: 1945-46.* Philadelphia: The Jewish Publication Society of America, 1945.

Schneiderman, Harry and Julius B. Maller, eds. *The American Jewish Yearbook, 5707. Volume 48: 1946-47.* Philadelphia: The Jewish Publication Society of America, 1946.

Schneiderman, Harry and Morris Fine, eds. *The American Jewish Yearbook, 5708. Volume 49: 1947-48.* Philadelphia: The Jewish Publication Society of America, 1947.

Segev, Tom. *The Seventh Million: The Israelis and the Holocaust.* New York: Hill and Wang, 1993.

Seton-Watson, Hugh. *The East European Revolutions.* New York:

Frederic A. Praeger, 1951.

Siedlecka, Joanna. *Czarny ptasior*. Gdańsk and Warszawa: Wydawnictwo Marabut and Wydawnictwo Cis, 1994.

Siemaszko, Zbigniew S. *Narodowe Siły Zbrojne*. London: Odnowa, 1982.

Sloan, James Park. *Jerzy Kosiński: A Biography*. New York: Dutton-Penguin, 1996.

[Sowińska, Stanisława "Barbara"]. *Obóz reakcji polskiej w latach 1939-45*. Warszawa: Główny Zarząd Informacji W.P., 1948.

Steinlauf, Michael C. *Bondage to the Dead: Poland and the Memory of the Holocaust*. New York: Syracuse University Press, 1997.

Stola, Dariusz. *Nadzieja i Zagłada Ignacy Schwarzbart – żydowski przedstawiciel w Radzie Narodowej RP (1940-1945)*. Warszawa: Oficyna Naukowa, 1995.

Strzembosz, Tomasz, ed. *Studia z dziejów okupacji sowieckiej (1939-1941): Obywatele polscy na kresach północno-wschodnich II Rzeczypospolitej pod okupacją sowiecką w latach 1939-1941*. Warszawa: ISP PAN, 1997.

The Story of Two Shtetls, Brańsk and Ejszyszki: An Overview of Polish-Jewish Relations in Northeastern Poland During World War II (Two Parts). Toronto and Chicago: The Polish Educational Foundation in North America, 1998.

Sword, Keith, ed. *The Soviet Takeover of the Polish Eastern Provinces, 1939-41*. New York: St. Martin's Press, 1991.

Szarota, Tomasz ed. *Komunizm: Ideologia, System, Ludzie*. Warszawa: Wydawnictwo Neriton and Instytut Historii PAN, 2001.

Szaynok, Bożena. *Pogrom Żydów w Kielcach, 4 lipca 1946*. Warszawa: Wydawnictwo Bellona, 1992.

Szwagrzyk, Krzysztof. *Zbrodnie w majestacie prawa*. Warszawa: ABC, 2000.

Ślaski, Jerzy. *Żołnierze wyklęci*. Warszawa: Oficyna Wydawnicza Rytm, 1996.

Śledzianowski, Jan. *Ksiądz Czesław Kaczmarek biskup kielecki, 1895-1963*. Kielce: No Publisher, 1991.

Tenenbaum, Joseph. *In Search of a Lost People: The Old and the New Poland*. New York: The Beechhurst Press, 1948.

Tenenbaum, Joseph. *Underground: The Story of a People*. New York: Philosophical Library, 1952.

Terlecki, Ryszard. *Dyktatura zdrady: Polska w 1947 roku*. Kraków: Wydawnictwo Arka, 1991.

Tkaczew, Władysław. *Powstanie i działalność organów Informacji Wojska Polskiego w latach 1943-1948: Kontrwywiad wojskowy*. Warszawa: Wydawnictwo Bellona, 1994.

Tomaszewski, Irene and Tecia Werbowski. *Żegota: The Rescue of Jews in Wartime Poland*. Montreal: Price-Patterson Ltd., 1994.

_____. *Żegota: The Council for Aid to Jews in Occupied Poland, 1942-1945*. Montreal: Price-Patterson Ltd., 1999.

Tomaszewski, Jerzy, ed. *Najnowsze dzieje Żydów w Polsce w zarysie (do 1950 roku)*. Warszawa: Wydawnictwo Naukowe PWN, 1993.

_____, ed. *Studia z dziejów i kultury Żydów w Polsce po 1945 roku*. Warszawa: Wydawnictwo TRIO, 1997.

Trunk, Isaiah. *Judenrat: The Jewish Councils in Eastern Europe under Nazi Occupation*. Lincoln: University of Nebraska Press, 1996.

Turkowski, Romuald. *Polskie Stronnictwo Ludowe w obronie demokracji 1945-1949*. Warszawa: Wydawnictwo Sejmowe, 1992.

Turlejska, Maria, ed. *W walce ze zbrojnym podziemiem 1945-1947*. Warszawa: Wydawnictwo Ministerstwa Obrony Narodowej, 1972.

Urbankowski, Bohdan. *Czerwona msza albo uśmiech Stalina*. Warszawa: Wydawnictwo Alfa, 1995.

_____. *Czerwona msza czyli uśmiech Stalina, 2 Volumes*, Second, Expanded Edition. Warszawa: Wydawnictwo Alfa, 1998.

Urbański, Krzysztof. *Kieleccy Żydzi*. Kraków: Małopolska Oficyna Wydawnicza, no date [1993].

_____. *Zagłada ludności żydowskiej Kielc, 1939-1945*. Kielce: Kieleckie Towarzystwo Naukowe, 1994.

Wąsowski, Grzegorz and Leszek Żebrowski, eds. *Żołnierze wyklęci: Antykomunistyczne podziemie zbrojne po 1944 roku*. Warszawa: Oficyna Wydawnicza Volumen and Liga Republikańska, 1999.

Warhaftig, Zorach. *Refugee and Survivor: Rescue Efforts During the Holocaust*. Jerusalem: Yad Vashem and Torah Education, 1988.

Weydenthal, Jan B. de *The Communists of Poland: An Historical Outline*. Stanford, CA: Hoover Institution Press, 1986.

Wiącek, Tadeusz, ed. *Zabić Żyda: Kulisy i tajemnice pogromu kieleckiego, 1946*. Kraków: Oficyna Wydawnicza "Temax", 1992.

Wolpert, Stanley. *A New History of India*. New York and Oxford: Oxford University Press, 1982.

Wołkonowski, Jarosław. *Okręg Wileński Związku Walki Zbrojnej Armii Krajowej w latach 1939-1945*. Warszawa: Adiutor, 1996.

Woźniczka, Zygmunt. *Zrzeszenie "Wolność i Niezawisłość" 1945-1952*. Warszawa: Instytut Prasy i Wydawnictw "Novum" – "Semex," 1992.

Wójcik, Zbigniew K. *Rzeszów w latach drugiej wojny światowej: Okupacja i konspiracja, 1939-1944-1945*. Rzeszów and Kraków: Instytut Europejskich Studiów Społecznych w Rzeszowie and Towarzystwo Sympatyków Historii w Krakowie, 1998.

Wnuk, Rafał. *Konspiracja akowska i poakowska na Zamojszczyźnie od lipca 1945 do 1956 roku*. Zamość: Zakład Poligraficzny "Attyla," 1993.

Wyman, David S. and Charles H. Rosenzveig, eds. *The World Reacts to the Holocaust*. Baltimore and London: The Johns Hopkins University Press, 1996.

Wyman, Mark. *DP: Europe's Displaced Persons, 1945-1951*. Philadelphia, London, and Toronto: The Balch Institute and Associated University Presses, 1989.

Wyrwich, Mateusz. *Łagier Jaworzno: Z dziejów czerwonego terroru*. Warszawa: Editions Spotkania, 1995.

Wysocki, Hieronim. *Jasienica Rosielna: Zarys historii i wspomnień*. Kraków and Jasienica Rosielna: Zarząd Gminy w Jasiennicy Rosielnej, 2000.

de Zayas, Alfred-Maurice. *A Terrible Revenge: The Ethnic Cleansing of the East European Germans, 1944-1950*. New York: St. Martin's Press, 1994.

Z.Z.Z. *Syndykat zbrodni: Kartki z dziejów UB i SB w czterdziestoleciu PRL*. [Paris]: Editions Spotkania, 1986.

Zajączkowski, Wacław. *Martyrs of Charity, 2 Parts*. Washington, D.C.: St. Maximilian Kolbe Foundation, 1988.

Żaryn, Jan. *Kościół a władza w Polsce (1945-1950)*. Warszawa: Towarzystwo im. Stanisława ze Skarbimierza i Wydawnictwo DiG, 1997.

Żebrowski, Rafał and Zofia Borzymińska. *Po-lin: Kultura Żydów polskich w XX wieku (Zarys)*. Warszawa: Wydawnictwo Amarant, 1993.

Żenczykowski, Tadeusz. *Polska Lubelska 1944*. Paris: Editions Spotkania, 1987.

INDEX OF NAMES

Tauber, Abram, 135
Terlecki, Ryszard, 25
Tenenbaum, Joseph, 3, 164
Toruńczyk, Henryk, 40
Tracz, 108
Turski, 60
Tuwim, Julian, 190

Urbański, Krzysztof, 34, 74

Verstandig, Mark, 35, 73, 84, 92

Wajnryb, Adam, 36
Walter, 195
Warda, Marian, 134
Warenholc, 196
Warhaftig, Zorach, 119, 160
Warmanowa, Bronisława, 190
Warszawer, Zygmunt (Srul), 36
Warszawski, Symcha, 166
Wasersztejn, Szmul, 114
Wasilewski, 103
Wąsowski, Grzegorz, 108
Weinryb, Bernard, 38, 172, 207, 208
Weintraub, Teofila, 71
Wendrowski, Henryk, 108
Westreich, Maryla, 33
Wiesenfeld, 120
Wiesenthal, Simon, 78, 81
Wnuk, Rafał, 56, 140, 162
Wnuk, Stanisław, 135
Wojciechowski, Jerzy, 195
Wójcik, Stanisław, 135
Wolińska, Helena, 40
Wolkowicz, Shlomo, 189
Wołodkiewicz, Edmund, 135
Wolsza, Tadeusz, 216
Wunderboim, Abraham, 76, 92
Wurman, Nachemia, 119
Wyczółkowski, Władysław, 195
Wyrostek, Józio (Józef), 192
Wyszogrod, Morris, 188

Zadzierski, Józef, 137
Zaitzev, Gregory, 77

Zakrzewski, Lucjan, 134
Zakrzewski, Zdzisław, ii
Zalcberg, Wolf, 74
Zaleski, Tadeusz, 86
Zalewski, Józef, 190
Zambrowski, Roman, 40
Zamojski, Mieczysław, 85
Zandman, Felix, 172
Zarecki, Tadeusz, 74
Żebrowski, Leszek, 25, 108
Zeltman, Abram, 164
Zeltman, Cukier, 163
Złotnik, Abram, 161
Żołądź, Neoma, aka Anna
  Krawcewicz 197
Zuckerman, Yitzhak, 35, 69, 81, 173
Zylberberg, Beniamin, 40
Zysman, Abraham, 139

INDEX OF PLACES